CAMBRIDGE URBAN AND ARCHITECTURAL ST

General Editors

LESLIE MARTIN
Emeritus Professor of Architecture, University of Cambridge

LIONEL MARCH
Rector and Vice Provost, Royal College of Art, London

◇◇

6 BRUNO TAUT AND THE ARCHITECTURE OF ACTIVISM

VOLUMES IN THIS SERIES

TO DEBORAH

1 Bruno Taut in 1916.

Bruno Taut and the Architecture of Activism

IAIN BOYD WHYTE

CAMBRIDGE UNIVERSITY PRESS

CAMBRIDGE

LONDON   NEW YORK   NEW ROCHELLE

MELBOURNE   SYDNEY

CAMBRIDGE UNIVERSITY PRESS
Cambridge, New York, Melbourne, Madrid, Cape Town, Singapore,
São Paulo, Delhi, Dubai, Tokyo

Cambridge University Press
The Edinburgh Building, Cambridge CB2 8RU, UK

Published in the United States of America by Cambridge University Press, New York

www.cambridge.org
Information on this title: www.cambridge.org/9780521131834

First published 1982
This digitally printed version 2010

A catalogue record for this publication is available from the British Library

Library of Congress Catalogue Card Number: 81-12301

ISBN 978-0-521-23655-3 Hardback
ISBN 978-0-521-13183-4 Paperback

Contents

Illustrations

Preface

This book is based substantially on a doctoral dissertation of the same title, which was submitted to the University of Cambridge in 1978.

For their help and advice in the preparation of the dissertation I would like to thank Professor Tilmann Buddensieg (Bonn), Frank Whitford (Cambridge) and Nicholas Bullock (Cambridge). For granting me access to unpublished material I am most grateful to Marlene Poelzig (Hamburg), Elisabeth Taut (West Berlin), Bendix Klingeberg (Hamburg), Professor O. M. Ungers (Cologne) and Professor Heinrich Taut (Lehnitz). I was further aided by the archivists and staff at the Bauhaus-Archiv (West Berlin), and Werkbund-Archiv (West Berlin), the Akademie der Künste (West Berlin) and the Karl-Ernst-Osthaus-Archiv (Hagen).

In the task of re-writing the text for this publication I was generously helped by Edward Timms (Cambridge) and by Professor Buddensieg.

Financial support for my research was provided by the British Academy/Wolfson Foundation for the academic year 1976–7, and by the Alexander von Humboldt-Stiftung (Bonn) for the year 1979–80. I am deeply indebted to both institutions for their considerable support.

Finally, I would like to express my gratitude to Colin Rowe, who first implanted the idea for this research in my mind in the course of a lecture which I attended at Cornell University in 1971. In his recent book *Collage City*, Rowe has complained that 'the ecstatic component of modern architecture has received a completely insufficient attention'. This study is an attempt to rectify at least one part of this omission.

I. B. W.
West Berlin, 1980

Introduction

The first problem affecting the study of Bruno Taut and his circle during and after the great war is that of nomenclature. The writings of Taut and Adolf Behne during the war, and the architectural programmes and fantasies of Taut and his circle after the war, have invariably been dubbed Expressionist. Although Taut clearly drew on contemporary Expressionist writing and painting for many of his ideas, and although Behne actually coined the term 'Expressionistische Architektur',[1] it does not adequately describe Taut's movement. The reason for this is the subsequent use of the term Expressionist to describe anything and everything which falls outside the rationalist histories of architecture as originally defined by Pevsner and Giedion. Thus Wolfgang Pehnt, in his recent book *Die Architektur des Expressionismus*, has included in this category late Jugendstil, the Wagnerschule, Italian Futurism, North German brick vernacular, Michel de Klerk, Hugo Häring, and numerous other anti-rationalists and eccentrics.

By being stretched to cover such a wide and diverse range of architecture, the term Expressionist has been weakened semantically; for Taut and Höger, or Finsterlin and Hoetger, have very little in common.

As a result of this inexactitude it is almost impossible to state when and why Expressionist architecture began, and, perhaps more important, when and why it ended. The latter question is especially important in the case of Taut and his circle, for no satisfactory explanation has yet been given for their sudden change of direction which occurred during 1920, and led them to abandon their visionary stance in favour of a new programme of objectivity and *Sachlichkeit*.

It has not proved possible to explain this change of heart using Expressionism as a context. This can be seen in a sampling of subsequent historical judgements. Pehnt, for example, simply states that there was a change of direction, without offering any reasons for it. 'In architecture the progressives moved away from the idea of the artist receiving inspiration in a trance of creativity to the idea of architecture as a social service. They sought to hide irrational impulses behind pragmatic arguments. Cooling off, sobering down, even "quietening down" were the new key words.'[2] For Pehnt, the shift away from Expressionism was simply a shift from subjectivity to objectivity.

In the context of the Bauhaus, Marcel Franciscono considers the founding ideals to be Expressionist inspired. He does not, however, see any contradiction between this early Expressionism and the Functionalism of the mature Bauhaus. The tendency towards Functionalism first appeared, according to Franciscono, in 1921 and was merely 'a clarification of goals and methods'.[3] Indeed, he states that the basic concern of the book 'is with the Bauhaus at the period of its birth, with the initial synthesizing vision of the school and its very first years of creative ferment before its goals began to crystallize and to a certain extent become simplified'.[4] This approach, which favours a continuity from Expressionism to Functionalism and tends to understate the differences between the two, can also be found in Borsi and König's book *Architettura dell'Espressionismo*.

Borsi implies that the foundation of the Ring was the natural extension of the Arbeitsrat für Kunst. The only difference which he notes between the two groups is one of membership: the Arbeitsrat was open to artists and critics of all persuasions, while the Ring was composed entirely of architects. He does not differentiate between the programmes or intentions of the two groups, thus endorsing a questionable continuity. 'Ma accanto alle manifestazione culturali della Arbeitsrat für Kunst e alle richerche fatte di confidenzia epistolari della Gläserne Kette, esiste un'esigenza professionale. E, in nome di questa che un gruppo di architetti che appartiene all' Arbeitsrat forma spontaneamente, senza alcuna formalità il Ring...per iniziativa di Bruno Taut.'[5] Indeed, Borsi side-steps the whole problem of the crisis of 1920 by suggesting that the battle for Expressionism was not finally lost until the CIAM Conference in 1928, when the Ring joined the CIAM: 'L'Esprit Nouveau aveva vinto'.[6]

A more thoughtful analysis of the end of Expressionism appears in Norbert Huse's book *Neues Bauen 1918 bis 1933*. Huse approaches the problem from a stylistic viewpoint, and notes the obvious change in the formal vocabulary of the architects which took place in 1921 and 1922. For this change he suggests the positive influence of abstract painting. As a negative influence he offers the collapse of interest in Expressionism. Wisely, however, he does not insist on a connection between the two. He writes: 'Although the withdrawal from utopianism and Expressionism defined what was no longer wanted, it in no way defined what should stand in their place.'[7] As he correctly notes, the demise of Expressionism was a precondition but not a cause of the sweeping success of Functionalist design. Conversely, Functionalism was the successor to Expressionism, but was not the cause of its demise. The real link between the two, as Huse indicates, was a vacuum. 'Only the resulting vacuum led to a review of the alternatives and to a receptivity for phenomena which had previously received little or no attention.'[8] Thus it is incorrect to say that Taut and his group abandoned their Expressionist beliefs in favour of Functionalism. Rather, Functionalism filled the vacuum already created by the decline of Expressionism. The reasons for this decline, therefore, must be sought in the internal make-up and dynamics of Taut's group, rather than in the upsurge of Functionalism as an alternative ideology.

It is at this point that a new nomenclature is needed, for, as already noted, the conceptual framework of Expressionism in architecture is too ill-defined to throw any light on the specific workings and dynamics of the Taut group. A more specific frame of reference is needed.

This is offered by the concept of Activism. For Taut's vision of an ideal society, as expressed in his writings, letters and drawings between 1914 and 1921, links him intimately with the Activist movement in German literature. Taut's Activist phase in architecture was exactly contemporaneous to the Activist movement in literature, which flowered between 1914 and 1919 under the leadership of Kurt Hiller. Without exception, the presuppositions which informed Taut's architectural Activism were shared by his literary counterparts. Both movements appeared at the same moment in response to the same stimuli, and, equally, both collapsed at the same time and for the same reasons. In addition, there were direct personal links between Taut and the literary Activists.

This interpretation of Taut's movement as a parallel development to literary Activism is reinforced by the nature of Taut's work during the period in question. There is only one actual building – the Glashaus at Cologne,[9] virtually no plans, sites, contracts, owners or materials. Instead, we are offered articles and manifestos, sketches and drawings and a limited number of letters. The basis of Taut's movement, although concerned with architectural questions, was strictly literary. It is therefore appropriate to consider Taut's Activist movement as a literary phenomenon as well as an architectural one.

There is a final problem which should be mentioned here concerning the material available. The lack of exact information on Taut's activity during and immediately after the First World War is one result of the destruction of Taut's private and business papers in 1933. While Taut's published writings give a comprehensive picture of his thinking during this period, his day-to-day work and his relations with fellow architects and artists can only be glimpsed at through the letters which have survived in the collections of their addressees.

All material which has been translated here into English can be found in the original in the German edition of this book: *Bruno Taut – Baumeister einer neuen Welt: Architektur und Aktivismus 1914–1920*, Verlag Gerd Hatje, Stuttgart, 1981.

Part 1

The roots of Activism

1

❖◇❖

Reformism and Expressionism

The best definition of the Activist movement in literature has been given by Renato Poggioli: 'Kurt Hiller originally coined the term, to define a precise formal tendency within German Expressionism. He did so intending to reduce the individualistic and anarchistic impulses in Expressionism, to reform them in the direction of neo-enlightenment by elevating psychological revolt to the level of practical and social reform.'[1] Activism, thus defined, represented an attempt to bring together the two tendencies which had dominated radical intellectual life in Germany during the decade which preceded the outbreak of war in 1914.

The first of these two tendencies was Expressionism – which principally affected literature and painting. The second tendency can be dubbed the reform movement. This was a larger and more loosely defined movement than Expressionism, and encompassed a diverse range of groups which advocated specific reforms in such matters as land ownership, mutual aid, housing, education and the arts, clothing and diet. According to Poggioli's definition, it was the ambition of the literary Activists to unite these two currents into one potent *kulturpolitische* force. The same ambition, as we shall see, was shared by Bruno Taut in the context of architecture and the plastic arts.

It would be inappropriate in this context to attempt to offer a complete account of both Expressionism and the reform movement. Instead, we shall concentrate on these two tendencies specifically as they influenced Taut's own development and work, thus providing the intellectual background to architectural Activism.

Taut had a strong affinity for the fundamentalism and rural ideals of the reform movement. He was a member of the Choriner Kreis, a group of young writers, artists and architects which met at Chorin, to the north-east of Berlin.[2] The group walked together in the woods and indulged in the slightly self-conscious communion with nature which inspired the *Wandervogel* movement. The monastery at Chorin, which had been established in 1270, and the surrounding woods offered considerable aesthetic delights to the *Wandervogel*. Among Taut's walking companions were the painters Max Beckmann and Franz Mutzenbecher, and the art historian Adolf Behne, with whom Taut established a lasting and fruitful friendship.

The Choriner Kreis was merely one of several groups of intellectuals

2 The ruins of the
monastery at Chorin.

3 Adolf Behne.

and artists, who sought refuge in the woods and on the land from the
stress and the harshness of the industrial cities. This intellectual
aversion against the burgeoning cities found its most effective expression
in the Deutsche Gartenstadtgesellschaft, a group with which Taut was
later to have close connections.

The Gartenstadtgesellschaft was founded in 1902, on the model of
the Garden Cities Association in England.[3] Like the Choriner Kreis, it was

a product of the anarcho-socialist, literary and reformist milieu which flourished in and around Berlin at the turn of the century. The roots of the Gartenstadtgesellschaft were to be found in the group of poets who set up a colony at Friedrichshagen, near Berlin, in 1888 – the Friedrichshagener Dichterkreis. Among the residents of Friedrichshagen were the brothers Heinrich and Julius Hart, Wilhelm Bölsche and Bruno Wille. They were regularly joined by such eminent visitors as Gerhart Hauptmann, Richard Dehmel, Frank Wedekind, Otto Erich Hartleben, John Mackay and Gustav Landauer. In his memoirs, Bruno Wille recalled:

> The following combination of motives was peculiar to the Friedrichshagen group: rural solitude alongside a bustling metropolis; literary bohemianism with socialist, even anarchist ideas; a devil-may-care quest for a distinctive life-style, free from prejudice; cameraderie between thinkers and talented craftsmen, though not excluding enlightened members of the monied classes. A creative love of art joined forces with sociology, natural science, philosophy and religion.[4]

In this account of the aims and ideals of the Friedrichshagen group one can already note the emergence of motifs which were to become central themes in Taut's Activist ideology. These included the rejection of the materialist, city-based culture and a return to the land, anarcho-socialist politics, a desire to reunite the work of the hand and the brain, and the holistic creed that sociology, religion and the natural sciences could be brought into a fruitful symbiosis under the guidance and leadership of the arts.

The political complexion of the Friedrichshagen group was, as we have seen, anarcho-socialist. The two leading theoreticians within the group were John Henry Mackay and Gustav Landauer. Mackay was born in Scotland, but was taken to Germany when he was two years old. He was both poet and novelist, and used his prose works as vehicles for polemical discussion on political reform. In 1891 he published *Die Anarchisten*, in which he propagated the views of Max Stirner and Proudhon, and attacked the notions of state socialism and communism. Similar views were held by Landauer, who published his first novel *Der Todesprediger* in 1893. The novel concludes with a political essay describing how the hero, Starkblom, will create a society of universal happiness. This was followed, at the end of 1895, by the pamphlet *Ein Weg zur Befreiung der Arbeiterklasse*, which contained a more concrete proposal for a happy society – an anarchist settlement on the land. This settlement would be independent from normal, bourgeois society and its finances would be based on Proudhon's theories of mutualism. To these and similar tracts which emerged from the Friedrichshagen circle, one can trace the sources both of the Gartenstadtgesellschaft and of Taut's subsequent plans for resettlement on the land.

The Friedrichshagen writers were not exclusively concerned, however, with a return to the soil or with the polemics of decentralization. They also produced two very urbane offspring, the Freie Volksbühne and the Neue Freie Volksbühne.

In July 1890, Bruno Wille – one of the Friedrichshagen residents –

founded the Freie Volksbühne. It was modelled, as its name suggests, on Antione's 'Théâtre libre' in Paris. The ambition of the Volksbühne was to make contemporary drama accessible to the lower middle and working class public which would not normally go to the commercial theatre. The Volksbühne was an instant success with its chosen public. After two years, however, a split occurred in the leadership between the independent socialists and anarchists, led by Wille himself, and the social democrats, led by the treasurer Julius Türk. At two extraordinary general meetings held in October 1892 the majority decided against Wille, who resigned from the executive committee and established a new group, the Neue Freie Volksbühne. Almost all the literary founders of the old group followed Wille into the new one, which counted among its membership Hartleben, Maximilian Harden, Max Marschalk, Fritz Mauthner, Gustav Landauer, the brothers Hart and Kampffmeyer and the independent socialist Georg Ledebour.

The schism was very symptomatic of the mutual distrust with which the established socialist party (Sozialdemokratische Partei Deutschlands – SPD) and the anarcho-socialist literati viewed each other. The literary wing, although committed to the cause of idealist socialism, wished to have nothing to do with party politics, which, in their eyes, were ridden with compromise and hypocrisy. Through the Volksbühne, the writers sought contact not with the Marxist proletariat, but with an idealized *Volk*. This was made clear in Heinrich Hart's account of the very first meeting of the group: 'At the writers' table we listened in rapt attention as the *Volk* put its seal of approval on the new art: the true, elemental art, rooted – as we discovered – deep in the soul of the populace.'[5] The literati felt that a direct and spontaneous resonance existed between the theatre and the *Volk*: a resonance which had nothing to do with political parties or with mass movements in politics.

The antipathy which the literati in the Neue Freie Volksbühne felt towards the capitalist and materialist society of Wilhelmine Germany was given a physical expression with the foundation of yet another group, the Neue Gemeinschaft. The same names which have been noted at Friedrichshagen and in the Volksbühne reappear as the progenitors of the Neue Gemeinschaft: Julius and Heinrich Hart, Bernhard Kampff-meyer, Fidus (pseud. Hugo Höppener), Willy Pastor and Gustav Landauer. The group initially rented rooms in Uhlandstrasse, Charlotten-burg, which they used for meetings and literary evenings. A magazine was also published from this address. As the group's name suggests, it was always planned that the members should ultimately live together in a mutualist community on the land – such as that already described by Landauer. This ambition was realized in 1901, when the group bought a house with a large garden at Schlachtensee, to the west of Berlin. The critic Albert Soergel described the hopes held by the group as follows: They envisaged a fine, rich, noble, community life, such as one can only dream of in today's world...a monastery without the restrictions of the monastic life, an order which would not pursue any narrow aims, but which would mould life in its totality into a work of art.'[6] The dream of an ideal, socialist community foundered, however, on the day-to-day problems of running the kitchen, and the experiment lasted for less than a year.

Out of the wreck of the Neue Gemeinschaft came the Deutsche Gartenstadtgesellschaft, founded, almost inevitably, by the brothers Hart and Kampffmeyer, Bruno Wille and Wilhelm Bölsche. An interesting omission from the list of founders was Gustav Landauer. Differences in political ideology had arisen between Landauer and the other members of the group during the Schlachtensee experiment and, as a result, he did not follow them into the Gartenstadtgesellschaft.

The nature and aims of the Gartenstadtgesellschaft were defined as follows in the founding statutes:

The Deutsche Gartenstadtgesellschaft is a propaganda society. It sees the winning over of the public to the garden city cause as its principal aim. The ultimate aim of a progressive garden city movement is internal colonization, which will promote industrial decentralization and an even distribution of industrial life across the land through the planned development of garden cities.[7]

Similar plans for decentralization and a shift of population away from the burgeoning cities were not uncommon for the period, and were proposed just as vigorously by the anti-semitic right as by the *Bodenreform* movement on the far left. Within this spectrum, the Gartenstadtgesell-schaft was located to the left of centre, among the revisionist socialists.

Ebenezer Howard entitled his original garden city pamphlet *Tomorrow, a Peaceful Path to Real Reform*. The garden city was seen by Howard as the means of replacing the intolerable squalor and deprivation endured by the urban working classes by a vigorous and healthy life in close communion with the land and the countryside. The political pressures building up amongst the working classes would thus be dispelled and the threat of a political revolution averted. The revisionist tone of Howard's writings had a great appeal to the German movement. Both Bernhard and Hans Kampffmeyer adhered to the revisionist socialism of the Bernstein wing of the SPD, and influential revisionists such as August Bebel were cited with approval in the *Gartenstadt* journal.[8]

The revisionist inclination of the Gartenstadtgesellschaft was most visible in its ambivalent relationship to capitalism. The stated intention of the group was to use all the means and skills offered by capitalism in the crusade against the social evils to which nineteenth-century capitalism had led. In an article in *Gartenstadt* in which the similar views of the Co-operative Movement and the Gartenstadtgesellschaft were compared, we read:

Unlike certain reactions at the outset of the capitalist economy, they do not exist to preserve or even renew the economic conditions of the pre-capitalist age, but rather they stand on the shoulders of the capitalist economy. They wish to use the particular achievements of this century in order to advance beyond and thus overcome the problems brought about by capitalism.[9]

By a process of propaganda and education, the Gartenstadtgesellschaft intended to reveal the shortcomings of capitalism and, at the same time, planned to offer feasible alternatives within the same general economic system.

This process was didactic and deterministic. The idealist literati and intellectuals felt able not only to diagnose the faults of contemporary society, but also, through appropriate action, to provide the remedies. The deterministic and slightly paternalistic tone of the movement can be seen in the following description, by Hans Kampffmeyer, of how the garden city resident should furnish his house:

It is self-evident that it is not enough simply to build attractive houses for the residents of the garden city without cultivating, as vigorously as possible, their understanding of the appropriate interior decoration. Such an endeavour will enjoy better prospects of success here, in artistically conceived surroundings, than in the existing towns, in which one is confronted everywhere by bad taste. It will thus be relatively easy to convince the occupier that simple and straightforward things are more appropriate to his house than over-ornamented bazaar furniture.[10]

This was typical of the paternalistic idealism of the reform movement. The industrial worker would be saved from the Marxists and the demagogues of revolution by the benign guidance of the intellectual. Not only would he be saved, but he would be reformed in his habits and his modes to conform to a pattern of taste established for him by the intellectuals.

The reformist ideology, as propagated most successfully by the Gartenstadtgesellschaft, was one of the twin supports on which the subsequent evolution of Activist architecture was based. The second support was the general milieu of pre-war Expressionism and the specific example of the Sturm group.

While the reform movement viewed contemporary society with profound dismay, the Expressionist avant-garde confronted it in a state of psychological shock. Black despair was the leitmotiv of the movement, in all its manifestations. The Expressionist avant-garde felt itself to be alienated psychologically, socially, economically and stylistically from the affirmative, materialist culture of Wilhelmine Germany. Kurt

Pinthus described this total ethical alienation in the introduction to his anthology of Expressionist poetry, *Menschheitsdämmerung*: 'However, one perceived ever more clearly the impossibility of a civilization which had made itself totally dependent upon its own creations, upon its science, technology, statistics, business and industry, upon an ossified social order, on bourgeois and conventional customs.'[11] This sense of alienation provoked a fierce antagonism. The targets, predictably, were materialism, militarism and nationalism, social and sexual hypocrisy, the philistinism of the bourgeoisie, the soullessness of the cities. Similar techniques were used in both painting and literature to express this antagonism. Realism and naturalism were abandoned in favour of fragmentation and distortion. Lyricism was replaced by paroxysms of ecstasy or suicidal pathos. The tones of the palette and the writers' vocabulary were freed from their descriptive role and invested with an autonomous existence as vehicles for the Expressionist spirit.

The urge to release the act of writing or painting from its descriptive burden was the dominant concern of the Sturm group. Between 1912 and 1914 Herwarth Walden's Sturm gallery in Berlin was unequalled as a focus for progressive painting in Europe.[12] At the same time, the journal *Der Sturm* provided an important forum for experimental writing and poetry.

Both the painters and the poets sought to abolish the discursive and syntactic elements in their works, to unshackle the painting or the poem from empirical reality and thus reduce the work to its absolute essence. In the context of poetry, Walter Sokel has noted that the Sturm group resisted all attempts to give poetry a moral or political tone. Among the several Expressionist groups, writes Sokel, 'only the periodical *Der Sturm* and the circle associated with its editor Herwarth Walden consciously promoted a pure abstractionism, free of ethical and political or religious elements'.[13] The Sturm poets and painters were concerned with the pure essence of poetry and painting, free from complex structures, non-essential functions or descriptiveness. August Stramm, named by Sokel as the originator of the Sturm method, distilled whole lines down to single words, and dispensed with conventional syntactic structures.

> *Verzweifelt*
> Droben schmettert ein greller Stein
> Nacht graut Glas
> Die Zeiten stehn
> Ich
> Steine.
> Weit
> Glast
> Du![14]

In exactly the same manner, Kandinsky sought to elevate the inner content of painting above its external forms and means of expression. He wrote in 1912: 'The form is the external expression of the inner content. One should not, therefore, deify form: one should not struggle for the form beyond the point at which it can serve as the vehicle which expresses the inner resonance.'[15] With their insistence on purity and on the true essence of painting or writing, the Sturm group sought for a way out of the impasse into which they felt the positivism and naturalism of the late nineteenth century had led.

Although there is little formal similarity between the mode of painting or writing favoured by the reform movement and the various modes favoured by Expressionism, it is clear that both were united by their rejection of the moral and cultural standards of contemporary, Wilhelmine Germany. This vigorous rejection of the present age was directly linked to the equally vigorous conviction that a new age was dawning. This conviction provided a link between, and a driving force behind, both the reform movement and Expressionism.

The belief in the emergence of a new age can be clearly seen in Heinrich Hart's first published volume of poetry, which appeared in 1872 with the significant title *Weltpfingsten, Gedichte eines Idealisten*. A typical stanza from the collection shows Hart already beckoning to the new century:

> Throw the doors open:
> come hither century, welcomed, admired,
> shining like the sun, clear as the morning light.
> You wear no golden crown
> but a garland of sweetly fragrant roses
> adorns your hair.[16]

The same faith in the new age was shared by the Expressionist avant-garde. The collapse of the old order and the emergence of a new, ideal society was a theme which obsessed the Expressionist period. Kurt Heynicke's poem *Aufbruch* is typical of the genre:

> *Awakening*
> Full blooming world!
> Lo, soaring heart, awake!
> Light up the world,
> shatter the night,
> burst into light!
>
> Open up, oh heart, for love.
> With gentle eyes enlighten man to man.
> Hand in hand,
> with naked innocence ascend the peaks.
> Oh, my flowering people!
> From my hands gather all the sun.
> Light up the world,
> shatter the night.
> Burst into light!
> Oh mankind, into light![17]

In a similar vein, Kandinsky hailed the new spirit in painting as a manifestation of the coming age: 'We have before us an age of conscious creation, and this new spirit in painting is going hand in hand with thought towards an epoch of great spirituality.'[18]

From their vantage point at the beginning of the new century, the reformist idealists and the Expressionists viewed both the past and the future with an historicist gaze. This idolization of history allowed for ideal models for the future to be based on the most admired examples drawn from the past. At this idolized point in time, at the momentous turning point between the past and the future, stood the creative will of the artist or intellectual. Julius Hart gave poetic form to the conviction that the artist acted as a fulcrum to history:

> Everything is mine, I pervade everything!
> I comprehend all past ages,
> I gaze upon the present
> and form and fashion new eras.[19]

From his unique comprehension of the past, the artist or intellectual could prescribe the most appropriate course for the future.

In the historicist balance between past and future, some groups or individuals are more inclined towards the past than the future and vice versa. The difference, nevertheless, is only one of emphasis, not of character. Thus the reformers, although concerned for the future, heavily stressed the importance of past models. In contrast, the eyes of the Expressionist avant-garde were predominantly aimed at the future. But not exclusively so, for running throughout Expressionism was an attachment to the philosophy of *Dekadenz*, with its nostalgic primitivism and its craving for the *Urwelt*.

Not only did reformism and Expressionism share the historicist method, they also both offered holistic solutions. The architectural reformers aimed to change not only the course of architecture and design, but the course of the whole society. For example, Hermann Muthesius assured the Deutscher Werkbund in 1911: 'The re-establishment of an architectonic culture, therefore, is the fundamental prerequisite for all the arts, and the essential foundation for an eminently desirable process of regeneration in the arts.'[20] This reformist belief in the total regenerative power of architecture was given an even grander expression by Karl Scheffler, the conservatively inclined critic who was a member both of the Dürerbund and the Werkbund:

If there is a vigorous discussion nowadays about a new style of architecture which will be unique to us, then this means that our age is beginning to think of itself as a new era in world history, that a self-consciousness is reawakening which strives to be the equal of the great eras of the past. There is an awareness of centuries in this call, if not of millennia: it implies a completely new sensibility and a comprehensive re-shaping of life.[21]

The spirit of the new age giving birth to the total solution for the future: Scheffler's description is a paradigm of historicism. Similar paradigms were common to Expressionism. In his preface to *Menschheitsdämmerung*, Pinthus applauded the poets for waging battle against the alienating and isolating tendencies of capitalism: 'no longer the individual but all men together, not the divisive but the uniting, not reality but the spirit, not the battle of everyone against everyone, but rather brotherhood was extolled'.[22] Only the total solution satisfied the Expressionist vision of the future. Small-scale tinkering was not enough. The 'epoch of great spirituality' was an holistic construction.

In spite of the fundamental concordance of type, which existed between the reform movement and the Expressionist avant-garde, there were strong political and emotional antipathies. The main groups within the reform movement, groups like the Dürerbund, the Werkbund and the Gartenstadtgesellschaft, were centred politically somewhere between liberal conservatism and revisionist socialism. In contrast, the Expressionists clung, in general, to a heady mixture of lyrical socialism, libertarianism, and anarchism. Furthermore, the overt antagonism of the Expressionists did not endear them to the more sober members of the reform movement. For example, Ferdinand Avenarius, the editor of *Kunstwart*, dismissed the Expressionists, along with the Cubists and Futurists, as *Meschuggisten* – lunatics.[23] It was rare to find a spirit sympathetic to both camps, even rarer to find anyone actively involved in both.

Bruno Taut, however, was. From 1912 on he was advisory architect to the Deutsche Gartenstadtgesellschaft. At the same time, he was an intimate of Herwarth Walden's Sturm circle. Taut's first contact with Walden was made through the poet and fantasist Paul Scheerbart and led, in turn, to Walden's circle, which included Heinrich Mann, Döblin and Strindberg.

To return, once again, to Poggioli's definition, Activism arose out of a desire to reconcile the anarchic impulses of Expressionism with the need for social reform. In his unique position, with one foot in the Gartenstadtgesellschaft and the other in the Sturm group, Bruno Taut was particularly well qualified to achieve, or at least to attempt this reconciliation.

2

◇✧◇

Bruno Taut: 1900–1914

In March 1902, Bruno Taut left his home town, Königsberg in East Prussia, on his first visit to Berlin. He recorded his impressions of the burgeoning capital city in a long letter which he sent to his brother, Max. The letter closely conveys the excitement felt by the 21-year-old Taut, when confronted for the first time in his life by a metropolis. As he wrote to Max:

I always felt happiest on the great traffic arteries of Berlin, Leipziger Straße and Friedrichstraße, where the life of the city pulsed most vigorously. The throng is particularly odd when viewed from the bus, and I had the feeling that the people, electric railways, etc., were bustling around down below simply to give me this picture.[1]

Besides giving his general reactions to the bustle and vitality of the city, Taut also described in detail the buildings and the paintings which he studied during his visit. His observations were very catholic, ranging from the Royal Palace, the cathedral and the new department stores, to the overhead railway, the sculpture of Schlüter, and the paintings of Van Dyck and of the Neo-Impressionists. In this wide-ranging catalogue of the plastic arts in Berlin, two figures stand out: the architect Messel and the painter Böcklin.

Messel had designed the new Wertheim store on Leipziger Platz, which was built between 1895 and 1904. Of all the buildings he saw in Berlin, it was the Wertheim store which most impressed and excited Taut. He wrote to his brother:

When I hear the word Berlin, one impression in particular out of all my various impressions pops up involuntarily and with especial clarity: this is the Wertheim store – one could almost say *the* store. For what Alfred Messel has created here is more than a store – it is the archetype for all stores. For this we must acknowledge the architect as extraordinarily gifted. When I saw the store for the first time I was captivated by its clarity and dignity. I had never seen a building before which exposed itself, so to speak, so nakedly to the observer, which said so directly, simply and without pathos: 'I am the way I am and nothing else.' Should anyone want to revive his tired and bewildered spirits I would recommend him to look at this building: at least, that's how it worked for me.[2]

The store was built around a central well, which extended up to the third level. The iron frame and the ironwork of the stairs and galleries were exposed in the interior, and glass walls were used to subdivide the

5 Berlin – Friedrichstraße
around 1900.

6 Aldred Messel, Wertheim
store, Leipziger Straße,
Berlin, 1895–1904.

internal spaces. To complete the picture of modernity, the interior was lit by electricity. In his breathless account of the building, Taut described the clarity of the plan and the articulation of the three floors as 'brilliant'. Above all, he was impressed by the way in which Messel had assembled the several parts of such a complex building into a clear and coherent unity. Taut concluded: 'The same harmony and individuality prevails throughout the building – be it in the laundry, or the furniture department, or in the art gallery...I would say that even if people travelled to Berlin just to see the "store", the journey would be worthwhile.'[3] Berlin, however, had countless other treats in store for the young Taut.

Taut had admired Messel's design for the Wertheim store for its sense of organization, its harmony and its honesty. Quite different characteristics attracted him to the painting of Arnold Böcklin. When the Berliner Museum bought Böcklin's *Gefilde der Seligen* in 1878, it caused a minor scandal and questions were asked in the Reichstag about the propriety of the purchase. Taut was strongly drawn to the painting and attempted to explain the reasons for this attraction to his brother:

Böcklin has now bewitched me. His *Gefilde der Seligen*, *Böcklin und der Tod*, the *Peità*, *Meeresbrandung*, and *Frühlingstag* – these are just names. One can only say that his work has got something, but what? One must experience it. The poetry of the colours is indescribable. I'm searching so hard for words, but words fail. One can simply look and – keep silent.[4]

8 Arnold Böcklin, *Die Gefilde der Seligen*, 1872.

He went on to describe the mysterious, almost demonic, fascination in which Böcklin's work had held him, and said how difficult he had found it to tear himself away from the paintings.

From the account of his Berlin trip two aesthetic qualities or characteristics emerge as especially important to Taut. In Messel's Wertheim store he had marvelled at the clear disposition of the plan, the sense of unity which Messel had established between the parts and the whole, and the honesty with which the building proclaimed both its structure and its function. These qualities, Taut implied, offered an alternative to the plaster and stucco eclecticism which had become the dominant manner in urban architecture in Germany during the thirty years since the unification. The second aesthetic quality which triggered a sympathetic response in Taut was the 'colour poetry' of Böcklin, which, in its mystical fascination, defied verbal description.

These two qualities appealed to quite different senses. Messel's architecture appealed to Taut's objective and rational sense of order, reason, sequence and harmony. In contrast, the symbolism and 'colour poetry' of Böcklin, as Taut himself admitted, worked on his subjective and irrational senses, and on his love of colour. The duality between the rational process of solving problems of architectural design, and a highly subjective delight in abstract colour and form, was to be a recurring element in Taut's intellectual development in the pre-war years.

Taut himself was aware of this duality in his creative character. In a diary entry from March 1905, Taut debated whether he should pursue a career as an architect or as a painter:

Thoughts about painting now occupy me constantly. It seems to me that I can give my character its fullest expression in this medium – probably better than in architecture...The idea which I have already carried around with me for two years still occupies me – the combination of my talents with regard to colour with my architectural ability. Spatial composition with colour, coloured architecture – these are areas in which I shall perhaps say something special. For exactly this reason, because painting always brings me back to architecture and vice-versa, I don't have to worry about a cleavage between the two.[5]

His resolution – to fuse the social and rational skills of the architect with the fantasy and subjectivism of the painter – anticipated, by a decade,

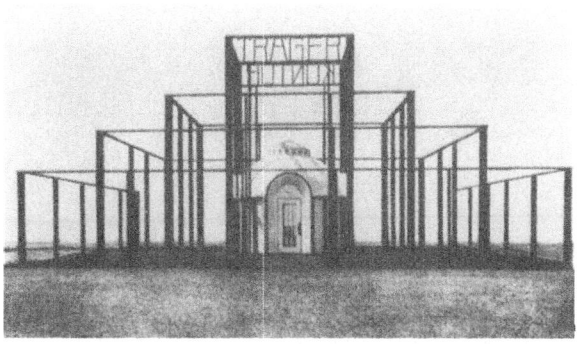

9 Bruno Taut, pavilion of the Träger-Verkaufskontor, Berlin, 1910.

10 Träger-Verkaufskontor pavilion, detail.

the founding precepts of the Activist movement. Taut's own work over this decade bore witness to his efforts to resolve the duality of architect and painter: to achieve a fusion of structural clarity and artistic fantasy.

In August 1909, Taut set up his own practice in Berlin and several designs from his drawing board were built over the following five years. In the majority of his designs from this period, Taut attempted to reconcile the conflicting attractions of architectural simplicity and painterly fantasy. As representative works from this period we shall consider three exhibition pavilions, three domestic buildings, a laundry and one garden suburb: all built between 1910 and 1914.

The earliest of the three exhibition pavilions was erected at a building exhibition held in Berlin in 1910. The pavilion was for the Berliner

11 Bruno Taut, Monument
des Eisens, Leipzig, 1913.

12 Monument des Eisens,
interior.

Verkaufskontor für Stahlträger and consisted of an open steel frame,
straddling a domed gazebo. Both frame and gazebo were free-standing
and were not linked to each other. This accentuated the contrast
between the geometric simplicity of the frame and the carefully detailed,
almost precious *tempietto* which was set inside it.

Taut pursued this contrast of the simple and the ornamented in the
pavilion which he designed for the 1913 Leipzig exhibition – the
Monument des Eisens. Following the model from the Berlin exhibition

and mindful of the need to advertise iron, Taut used a geometric iron frame, this time on an octagonal plan. On top of this frame, he set a golden ball – like a giant pearl in a claw-setting.

Taut's leading advocate in the pre-war years was Adolf Behne – his colleague from Chorin. In February 1914, Behne published two articles on Taut's current work. One was published in *Kunstgewerbeblatt*,[6] the other, significantly, in *Der Sturm*. In the *Sturm* article, Behne analysed both the functional and the fantasy elements in the Monument des Eisens and coined the term 'artistic realism' to describe the harmonious fusion of these two elements in Taut's design:

Nothing is further from Bruno Taut's nature than extravagance, silliness or bluff. He is distinguished by his rigorous realism – which, admittedly, is an artistic realism, not the realism of the 'functionalists' or the 'puritans'. In this artistic sense, the Monument des Eisens was entirely realistic. The gold sphere which sat on top of the octagonal pyramid, and which raised some doubts here and there, certainly had no practical or economic purpose. In artistic terms, however, it was entirely functional and could never have been dispensed with.[7]

In the same article, Behne bemoaned the fact that the public which had acclaimed Taut's Monument des Eisens was apparently unaware of his even greater achievements in the realm of house design.

In 1910 and 1911, Taut designed the façades for two large apartment houses on Kottbusser Damm, Berlin. The plans and the internal structure of the houses were the work of another architect, Arthur Vogdt, who also put up the capital. In both designs, Taut broke entirely with current practice and stripped the façades of the caryatids, neptunes, scrolls and swags which were the uniform of the Berlin tenement block. Instead, the articulation of the facade was entrusted to the natural openings – windows, balconies, doors – aided by restrained decorative patterns which were incorporated into the wall itself.

The obvious precedent for Taut's facades on Kottbusser Damm were the celebrated blocks built by Otto Wagner in 1898–9 in Linke Wienzeile, Vienna. Between 1906 and 1908, Taut had come under the influence of Hermann Billing, with whom his brother Max was then working. Billing was a vigorous supporter of the work of Wagner and the Wagnerschule, and his enthusiasm was shared at the time by Taut. Wagner's blocks at 38 and 40 Wienzeile were free of conventional stucco decoration. Only the sills of the windows were allowed to project from the flat facades. By removing the pediments from the windows and dispensing with horizontal ribbing or rustication, Wagner used the windows themselves as the principle punctuations on the facade, which was thus given a strong vertical thrust. The facades, although flat, were not bland. On no. 38, medallions, designed by Kolo Moser, were set between the upper row of windows and linked by arched fronds, which carefully arrested the vertical accents before they reached the roof-line. A similar technique was used on no. 40, which was festooned with a flat, floriate pattern set in coloured majolica into the façade itself. Once again, the vertical thrust was terminated under the roof-line – this time by lion's-head bosses.

The example of Wagner recurs in the façade which Taut designed in

13 Bruno Taut, Kottbusser
Damm 90, Berlin-Neukölin,
1910–11.

14 Otto Wagner, Linke
Wienzeile 38 and 40, Vienna
(both built 1898–9).

1911 for a house on Hardenbergstraße, Charlottenburg. As at Kottbusser
Damm, the plan was the work of Arthur Vogdt. Taut followed the
example of Wienzeile 38 very closely. The window openings and
mullions and the doorway were the main rhythmical elements around
which the façade was composed. For Kolo Moser's medallions, Taut
used a figurative relief by the sculptor Georg Kolbe. As at Linke

15 Linke Wienzeile 38, detail of façade.

16 Linke Wienzeile 40, detail of façade.

Wienzeile, the relief on the Hardenbergstraße house was used by Taut to tie the vertical bands of fenestration together and to terminate the vertical accents of the wall panels.

Behne was very enthusiastic about the Hardenbergstraße house. In his article in *Der Sturm* he proclaimed:

A new way of thinking, a new vitality lies behind this architecture. Everything superficial, all plaster trim, all 'decoration' has been swept away, as if by an iron brush. Taut exposes the wall, which, after all, is the meaning of the whole building, in its unfragmented totality – and beauty. He divests the windows of the accidental and struggling character which they display almost everywhere, re-establishes them as one of the two main motifs, and installs them in their own right.[8]

He also applauded Kolbe's relief: 'Under the roof, Kolbe has fashioned a row of floating female figures in almost full-relief. With their slight, flowing motion they add something lively and breathing to the house.'[9] The relief did not disturb Behne's appreciation of the simplicity of the façade, and he viewed the two elements, façade and decoration, as two autonomous entities, which worked together harmoniously but did not intermix. As he said: 'Here too, the dominant wish is to give something genuine instead of a mishmash.'[10] By differentiating the strictly functional elements on the façade from the strictly non-functional, Taut was faithful to his resolution that his work should express both architectural and painterly or sculptural values.

By banishing pediments, pilasters and stucco decoration from his façades, Taut concentrated attention onto the plane of the façade itself and onto the material with which it was built. At Kottbusser Damm 2–3 the lower two storeys were clad in dark clinker brick, as was the wall above the top row of windows. Between these two dark retaining bands, the wall and balconies were plastered white. The wall between the windows was treated with alternate bands of brick and plaster in an almost Siennese manner. To enliven this rhythm of dark and light, Taut

18 Bruno Taut, Kottbusser Damm 2–3, Berlin-Neukölln, 1910–11.

allowed the brick bands to project out slightly from the plaster. In a similar way he differentiated the plane of the four large brick arches from that of the flanking walls. The subtly projected brickwork thus took over the function of a relief.

Taut pursued this direction on the façade of the Reibedanz Laundry, which was built in 1914. The brickwork of this modest building, in an industrial suburb of Berlin, was treated with great assurance and virtuosity. As at Kottbusser Damm 2–3, contrasting colours were used as the basis of the composition. For the cornice, the bottom three rows of bricks, and for the vertical ribs which linked the two, Taut used very dark brown, almost black bricks. The contrasting bricks were yellow. The bricks making up the ribs were turned outwards, so that both faces met the plane of the façade at 135 degrees. The panels of yellow bricks above the windows were similarly treated and the panels themselves were set out from the plane of the windows, which themselves were moved back from the street-line. The end effect was one of movement and playfulness, which emphasized the structure and the materials used.

Taut's virtuosity was not limited, however, to the two-dimensional composition of the façade. Tilmann Buddensieg has suggested that Taut's pre-war work, and in particular Kottbusser Damm 2–3, reflected

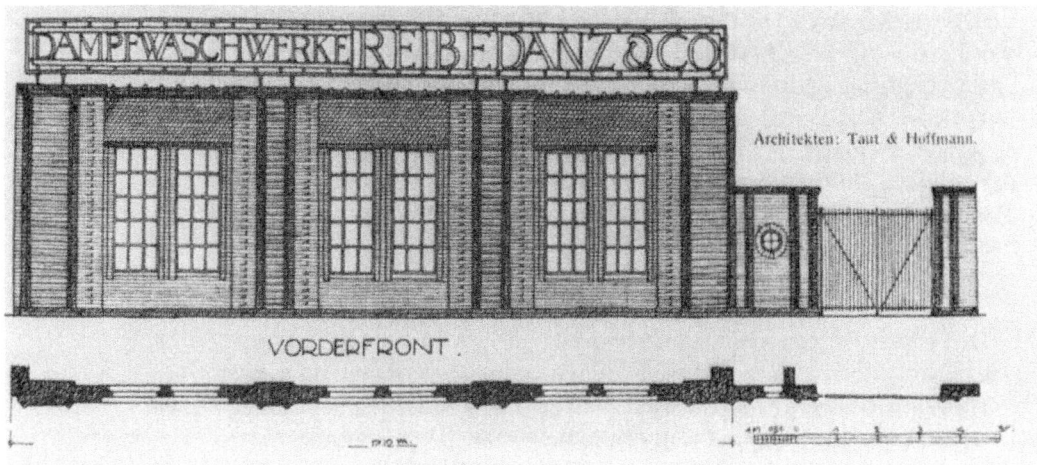

19 Bruno Taut, Reibedanz
Laundry, Berlin-Tempelhof,
1914.

20 Reibedanz Laundry,
elevation.

Taut's interest in contemporary painting. According to Buddensieg's very lucid argument, Taut's use of the arch motif at Kottbusser Damm was analogous to the contemporary experiments of the Cubists to portray three-dimensional form. Running along each of the horizontal bands of windows, Taut alternated, in groups of three, a balcony, a bay-window, and a flat window. The window opening thus appears as flat, concave and convex. As Buddensieg notes: 'The plane of the façade is curved, so to speak, three-dimensionally, the same element portrayed from three viewpoints, comparable to the procedure of the Cubists.'[11] Buddensieg supports his case by citing an article by Taut, which was published in *Der.Sturm* towards the end of 1913. In this article, entitled 'Eine Notwendigkeit', Taut held up the painting and sculpture of such contemporaries as Léger, Kandinsky, Archipenko, Marc, Delaunay and Campendonk as a model which the architects should follow: 'The architect must also recognize that architecture embraces from the outset the preconditions which the new painting has created: freedom from perspective and from the narrowness of a single viewpoint.'[12] The three-dimensional articulation of the façade at Kottbusser Damm 2–3 was a first step in Taut's campaign to free architecture from the restraints of academicism. From his article in *Der Sturm*, however, it is clear that Taut's dreams for a new architecture went far beyond the question of how a façade should be composed, and demanded nothing less than a total redefinition of the nature and function of architecture.

In attempting this reassessment and redefinition, Taut was clearly unresolved between the conflicting demands of function and simplicity on the one hand, and aesthetic delight and artistic fantasy on the other. In short, he was torn between the disparate ideologies of the Gartenstadtgesellschaft and the Sturm group. One standpoint represented concrete practical and social reform, the other, an extreme variant of artistic and intellectual freedom. The two main projects which occupied Taut in 1914, the Falkenberg estate and the Glashaus, perfectly reflected his antipodal interests and his relations with reformism and Expressionism.

In an article which was published in the *Sozialistische Monatshefte* in January 1914, Taut argued that the spirit of the age would be better expressed by the architecture of the garden cities than by monumental buildings. The monumental building in question was the proposed opera house for Berlin. Taut wrote:

Every epoch generates its typical building tasks, which correspond to the kernel questions of the age and which produce innovation in architecture. One must regard social engagement as the dominant concern of this age, as the concern with which everyone sympathizes. The new architecture will not be given to us by the Court Opera House, but by the Peoples' Theatres, the new garden cities, and by all the buildings which stem from social idealism.[13]

Two points are important in this quotation. One is the historicist belief in the particularity of the present; the other is the reformist insistence that the spirit of the age is best represented by social idealism.

Taut was commissioned to design the Falkenberg estate in 1912.

21 Bruno Taut, Akazienhof,
Gartenstadt Falkenberg,
1913–14.

22 Gartenstadt Falkenberg,
row-housing.

Building began in 1913 and continued into 1914.[14] The first phase, the Akazienhof, comprised one house by Tessenow and thirty-four dwellings by Taut, of which twenty-six were terrace houses and eight were flats in two-storey houses. In 1914 the second phase was built on Gartenstadtstraße, with ninety-three units, varying from one-room flats to five-room houses. All were in terraces. In his ground plans Taut used the simplest solution possible for each house-type. The various types were scattered throughout the estate, thus promoting a vigorous social mix between family houses and single-room flats. In an article written in 1919, Taut pointed to this social mix as one of the successes of the project. The harmonious co-existence of various social groups and classes was an important plank in both the reformist and the revisionist-socialist platforms. At Falkenberg Taut gave it a visible, architectural form: 'A lively neighbourliness exists, which cancels out differences and creates social values. Accordingly, the outward appearance offers a cheerful variation in house size and form, held together by the unity of roof-line and of materials. The picture is enlivened by an extremely vivacious and, at times, intensive application of colour.'[15] Taut saw his use of colour, and the play of colour-harmonies on the façades, as a means to achieving the desired harmony-in-diversity.[16] In the same article, Taut went on to describe the initial reaction of the public to the painted façades. 'The coloured appearance initially provoked a lot of surprise, for the earlier and ubiquitous tradition of coloured architecture had been totally lost. Especially the Berliners, coming from the grey tenement quarters, were beside themselves with genuine indignation and repeatedly declared that the architect deserved to be locked up.'[17] However, contemporary press comment was generally favourable, and it would be wrong to see Taut's use of colour at Falkenberg as a wild, avant-gardistic or antagonistic gesture. The colours used were comparatively muted – pink, olive-green, golden brown and a strong blue. In no way did they echo the palettes of the painters in the Sturm circle: indeed, the colour scheme at Falkenberg seems to have had more in common with Jugendstil than with Expressionism.

Furthermore, Taut's campaign against grey stucco was no new phenomenon, but had been current in reformist circles for some time. As early as 1900, Avenarius wrote a piece in *Kunstwart*, damning grey façades and asking:

Why do we not paint our houses with colour? There is no simpler or cheaper way to make a plain building more welcoming, delightful, and even truly beautiful than a well-chosen coat of paint. It is far better to colour the entire outside wall rather than decorate it with such things as coloured relief or strapwork, or with figurative decoration. So, to reiterate: let us have coloured stucco! We shall repeat the call for coloured houses until it is heard.[18]

The use of colour at Falkenberg was completely in accord with Avenarius's precepts. It was not a futuristic gesture but, rather, an example of the retrospective historicism which recurs throughout the reform movement. Taut actually alluded to this in the article quoted above, when he spoke of the lost tradition of coloured architecture. In an obituary notice for his teacher Theodor Goecke (whose close contact with Sitte is reflected in the site-planning at Falkenberg), Taut made this point even more clearly. 'And often enough, when the public protested against innovation (for example in the use of colour on houses), Goecke raised his voice and demonstrated, with all the force of his personality, that this novelty was actually not so new, but in reality very old, and therefore as fresh as old things can be.'[19]

23 Paul Scheerbart.

If the Falkenberg estate showed the reformist side of Taut in 1914, then the Glashaus at Cologne represented his Expressionist aspect. The sources for the Glashaus are to be found in the Sturm group in general, and in the influence of Paul Scheerbart in particular.

Herwarth Walden dubbed Scheerbart 'the first Expressionist'. In a series of fantasy novels, Scheerbart developed the theme of an earthly paradise which was founded on a new architecture of colour and glass. The theme first appeared in *Das Paradies. Die Heimat der Kunst* (1899). It was developed further in *Rakkox, der Billionär* (1900), and in the vision of a *Wunderpalast* in *Münchhausen und Clarissa* (1906). In *Das graue Tuch und zehn Prozent Weiß* (1914), Scheerbart gave his most detailed account of the new glass architecture. The typically episodic plot follows the progress of an architect named Krug, who flies around the world in an airship, supervising the construction of fabulous glass buildings. The sites for these glass palaces are suitably exotic: the Chicago lakeside, the Fiji Islands, the Antarctic, Japan, the Himalayan foothills, Ceylon, Arabia.[20]

Scheerbart's first contact with real architecture came about through the mediation of Walden. They had met in the early years of the century. Interestingly, Scheerbart often concluded his letters and cards to Walden with architectural greetings. A card sent on 28 April 1904 ended: 'Greetings from temple to temple'; one of 6 January 1909: 'Planetary greetings from cathedral to cathedral'; one of 29 April 1910: 'Hail! Hail! from cathedral to cathedral'; and one of 13 March 1914: 'With spring greetings from glass house to glass house.'[21] The temple, the cathedral, the Glashaus: clearly, Scheerbart and Walden were exchanging these ideas, one might say ideals, long before they became the common currency of the Activist avant-garde.

For a short while in 1909, Walden was editor of the theatre magazine *Der neue Weg* and Scheerbart was a contributor – as were Peter Behrens and Hermann Muthesius. A futher contributor was the poet Richard Dehmel, who had collaborated with Behrens at Darmstadt and who was to become a close friend of Scheerbart. Through these loose contacts, Scheerbart must have become aware of the architectural revival which was then under way in Germany. However, no direct results stemmed from these early contacts, and it was not until the Sturm group was

24 Bruno Taut, Glashaus, Cologne, 1914, exterior view.

established that Scheerbart was to find an architect who responded sympathetically to his vision of a glass architecture. This was Bruno Taut.

They appear to have met in the early days of *Der Sturm* and cultivated a close friendship. Both published architectural fantasies in *Der Sturm*. In 'Das Ozeansanatorium für Heukranke', Scheerbart described a floating glass island which would serve as a refuge for hay-fever sufferers. The island carried coloured glass pavilions with double walls, and was towed by tugs so that the same side was always kept facing towards the sun.[22]

A later edition of *Der Sturm* carried Taut's article 'Eine Notwendigkeit', in which Taut suggested that the time had come for the architects to follow the lead which had been given to them by the painters: 'Let us work together on a magnificent building! On a building which will not simply be architecture, but in which everything – painting, sculpture – will combine to create a great architecture, and in which architecture will once again fuse with the other arts. The architecture here will be simultaneously both frame and content.'[23] Scheerbart was so taken with this idea that he wrote to Taut, suggesting that they go ahead and buy

25 Glashaus, cascade.

26 Glashaus, staircase.

27 Glashaus, detail of dome.

some land on which to start building: 'I read with great plasure your tale about "Die Notwendigkeit". In my opinion land must be bought at the Schwielowsee. I shall be going there in the near future.'[24] Although nothing came of this idea, Taut and Scheerbart did collaborate on the Glashaus for the 1914 Werkbund exhibition at Cologne.

The Glashaus was set on a concrete plinth which carried a fourteen-sided drum made up of concrete beams. The sides were infilled with glass bricks. On top of the drum, Taut set a prismatic dome with a double skin of glass, which was supported by a lattice of concrete ribs. The lower floor housed a water cascade while the upper level depended for its effect on the 'Luxfer' prisms and coloured glass which made up the inner layer of the glazing. The natural effects of light on glass were heightened by the inclusion of a mechanical kaleidoscope, built in to the back of the pavilion.

The programmatic and didactic character of the pavilion provided a congenial framework for the fourteen aphorisms on glass which Taut had asked Scheerbart to compose for the pavilion, and which were incised around the top of the drum. In the accompanying letter which

he sent with the aphorisms in February 1914, Scheerbart remarked:
'Aphoristic poetry like this is no small matter. Many things easily sound
banal. I wanted to give the whole thing an improvised and unforced
character.' The fourteen aphorisms read:

1 Glück ohne Glas –
   Wie dumm ist das!
2 Backstein vergeht
   Glasfarbe besteht.
3 Das bunte Glas
   Zerstört den Haß.
4 Farbenglück nur
   in der Glaskultur,
5 Ohne einen Glaspalast
   Ist das Leben eine Last.
6 Im Glashaus brennt es nemmermehr;
   Man braucht da keine Feuerwehr.
7 Das Ungeziefer ist nicht fein
   Ins Glashaus kommt es niemals rein.
8 Brennbare Materialia
   Sind wirkliche Skandalia.
9 Größer als der Diamant
   Ist die doppelte Glashauswand.
10 Das Licht will durch das ganze All
   Und ist lebendig im Kristall.
11 Das Prisma ist doch groß
   Drum ist das Glas famos.
12 Wer die Farbe flieht
   nichts vom Weltall sieht.
13 Das Glas bringt alles Helle,
   Verbau es auf der Stelle.
14 Das Glas bringt uns die neue Zeit;
   Backsteinkultur tut uns nur leid.[25]

Appropriately, or rather, ironically for the summer of 1914, the third
aphorism was chosen to go above the entrance to the pavilion.

Taut's invitation to Scheerbart to write these aphorisms appears to
have stimulated the writing of *Glasarchitektur*. In a letter to Walden
written in April 1914, Scheerbart gave a progress report on the
Glashaus and asked if the Sturm press would be interested in publishing
Glasarchitektur, which he described as a 'programme for the new glass
architecture'.[26] Walden liked the book and it appeared the same year
under the Sturm-Verlag imprint.

Although the Glashaus was primarily inspired by Scheerbart's writings,
another source can also be cited: a project for a swimming pool by Franz
Roith, a pupil of Otto Wagner. The entrance pavilion to Roith's pool had
an octagonal plan. The walls were filled in with glass bricks and
supported a prismatic dome. Both Roith's pavilion and Taut's Monument
des Eisens at Leipzig shared the same plan. Similarly, the glass bricks
and the prismatic dome were common to both Roith's pavilion and
Taut's Glashaus at Cologne. As Roith's scheme was published in
Germany in 1910,[27] it seems highly likely that both of Taut's exhibition

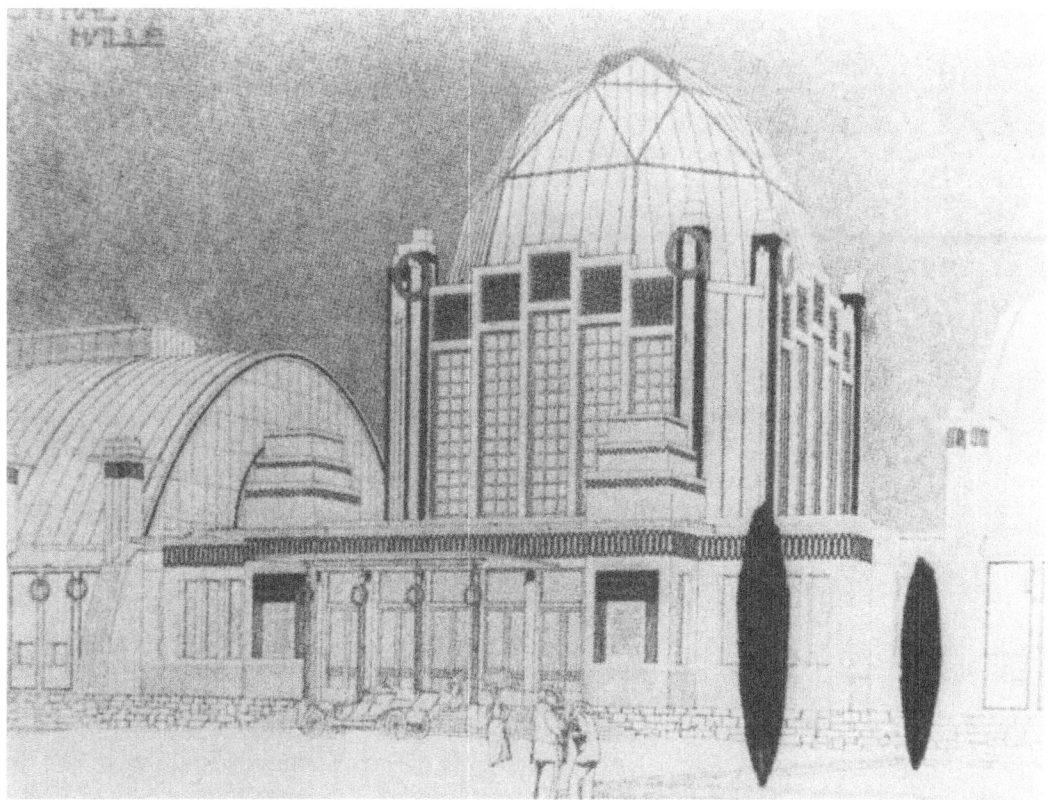

pavilions from 1913 and 1914 were directly influenced by this Viennese precedent.

Roith's scheme remained on paper, however, wheras Taut's was built. It created an immediate stir. In reviewing it for the *Sozialistische Monatshefte*, Felix Linke hailed it as the first step in an 'offensive along the entire front'. It was antagonistic not so much in its use of materials – concrete and glass, even coloured glass, were not so new in 1914[28] – but in its attitude to function and to the role and purpose of architecture in the age of the spirit, in the post-materialist age. For the Glashaus was both a refutation of materialism and a model for a new, non-materialistic architecture.

Taut had already proclaimed the new age in 'Eine Notwendigkeit'. The article began with the assertion: 'It is a joy to live in our age: if anyone does not feel that, then he is beyond help.'[29] The new age, according to the dogmas of historicism, naturally demanded new forms and types. We have already seen that Taut, in his exactly contemporaneous article in the *Sozialistische Monatshefte*, suggested that the new age would be best represented by the garden city, by an architecture which was informed by 'social idealism'. This was the reformist version, the retrospective historicist version. Now, with the Glashaus Taut offered the version which was firmly orientated towards the future.

As we have already seen, the Sturm group insisted that the sole purpose of any given art form was the exposition of its own expressive essence, unfettered by descriptive or empirical reality. According to the Sturm philosophy, literature was unnecessarily afflicted by its relation to facts or to objective truths. Similarly, architecture was afflicted by the demands put upon it by function and utility. In an essay which he wrote in 1914, Scheerbart suggested that a concern for function and practicality was outdated. In this piece, a father chides his son for being too practical: 'Your inclinations, my son, are directed too much at the practical. For that reason, you want to be an engineer. Forget that: it is no longer relevant. The present age now cries out for a great architect, who will at last make our lives worth living.'[30] Taut had made the same point in 'Eine Notwendigkeit', in the context of his proposed building project: 'This building does not need to have any purely practical function. Architecture, too, can free itself from utilitarian demands.'[31] His programme for the Glashaus put the thesis of functionlessness even more baldly. The opening sentence read: 'The Glashaus has no function other than to be beautiful.'[32] This was the Sturm aesthetic applied to architecture. In his painting Kandinsky sought to penetrate behind the external forms of mimesis in order to reveal the internal resonances of colour and line. Stramm, by a similar process of reduction, attempted to define the intimate laws of poetry. In the same way, Taut attempted, in his Glashaus, to show how a new and pure architecture of colour and light could serve not only the physical needs, but also satisfy the emotional and moral needs of man. His programme to the Glashaus concluded: 'Indeed, the prospect of glass architecture harbours a well-founded expectation that the eyes and sensibilities of the people will be won for more subtle stimuli. In today's architecture we desperately need to be freed from the saddening omnipresence of stereotyped monumentality. This alone can bring flowing forms and effortlessness.'[33] In accordance with the Sturm philosophy, moral and aesthetic imperatives took precedence over mundane functionality.

The purity and aestheticism of the Sturm group versus the pragmatic reformism of the Gartenstadtgesellschaft: Taut's work in 1914 was polarized between these two extremes. The two poles were linked only by a mutual historicist idealism. In every other respect they were diametrically opposed.

Writing about the Falkenberg estate, Taut stressed the need for and virtue of simplicity. 'With the economic and social context in mind, one must consider the most extreme simplicity. In this way one arrives at buildings which dispense with all decoration.'[34] This insistence on function and simplicity found a total contrast in the wilful, Sturm-inspired aestheticism which Taut proposed in 'Eine Notwendigkeit' and partly realized in the Glashaus.

The building should contain rooms in which the most characteristic developments of the new art are represented: the light compositions of Delaunay in large glass windows, cubistic rhythms, and paintings by Franz Marc and Kandinsky on the walls. The external and internal columns should await the constructional sculptures of Archipenko, the ornamentation will be the work of Campendonk.[35]

The Falkenberg project demanded that the architect should satisfy the physical and social needs of the residents as simply and as effectively as possible. In doing so, Taut offered a functional and feasible alternative to the tenement blocks of the city. In complete opposition to this socially informed architecture, Taut, in his conception of the temple to the arts, insisted that: 'Every thought of social purpose should be avoided.'[36] The temple of glass and concrete should, said Taut, spurn both mechanical and social function: it should exist simply as an object of aesthetic contemplation, a delight to the higher senses.

Although totally disparate as architectural ideologies, the Gartenstadt ideal and the Sturm ideal were united, in Taut's view, by their appropriateness to the age. As we have already seen, both were introduced in Taut's writings as suitable expressions of the new *Zeitgeist*. The former was inspired by the retrospective aspect of historicism, the latter by the futuristic aspect. The former was reformist, politically committed, and practical; the latter antagonistic, avant-gardistic, and intentionally non-practical. The attempt to fuse these two apparently irreconcilable ideologies into one programme led Taut to Activism.

Part 2

1914–1918: the foundations of
Activist architecture

3

❖◇❖

Pacifism

The outbreak of war in 1914 was received with widespread enthusiasm by the German public. The Kaiser's celebrated Burgfrieden speech of 4 August 1914, and the unanimous war credits vote in the Reichstag were both symptoms of an idealistic desire for national unity. The subsequent rush to the recruitment offices reflected not only patriotism, but also an irrational anticipation that somehow the war would make a final break with the old order. By joining the colours, the youth of Germany believed that they were supporting the spirit of progress and culture in the battle against the materialist civilization.

This enthusiasm for the war extended to a large segment of the intelligentsia, who also regarded it as a momentous turning point for German culture and society. Thomas Mann, for example, wrote in December 1914, in a letter to Richard Dehmel: 'One wonders how it will all turn out. The anxiety and curiosity are tremendous. But it is a joyful curiosity, isn't it? It's a feeling that everything will have to be *new* after this profound, mighty visitation, and that the German soul will emerge from it stronger, prouder, freer, happier. May it be so.'[1] Almost a year later, Karl Ernst Osthaus wrote to Gropius: 'How I rejoice, that you are so conscious of the greatness of the moment', and spoke of 'the spirit of the new Germany, which will be born in the front line'.[2] In a similar vein, Adolf Behne identified the German war effort as a new, revolutionary force in Europe. In an article published in July 1915, he dismissed the condemnation of Germany by the neutral powers as a conservative reaction against this new, radical force. 'Wherever a new and irresistable sense of pride develops, be it in politics, in science, or in art, it attracts the "hate of the neutrals".'[3] In the case of Bruno Taut, it is more difficult to establish what he thought or, indeed, did during the war years. Only the barest facts are known of his work and movements during this period. He worked initially as a conscripted worker in a munitions firm in Brandenburg and later worked in the office of the Stellawerk stove factory in Bergisch-Gladbach.

Something of Taut's feelings in the autumn of 1914 can be deduced, however, from a letter which he wrote in October 1914. It was a letter of condolence to his sister-in-law, Charlotte Wollgast, on the death of her fiancé. Taut was clearly influenced by the current mood of elation, and shared in the general expectation that everything would be changed by the war. He assured his sister-in-law that: 'The great current which sweeps us along will also take you. You have made a heavy sacrifice for the benefit of the whole enterprise, and I believe that your loved-one, were it possible, would say: "For this, my sacrifice was not too great. I made it willingly."[4] Continuing in this jingoistic tone, which may have owed more to the nature of the letter than to his true feelings at the time, Taut wrote of the need to break the power of the English and the Russians. 'The might of the English *must* be broken, and that of the Russians too. One's feelings almost demand the complete destruction of the Cossacks. These brutes must be exterminated like beasts of prey.'[5] Such passages, however, might be taken as the necessary recitation of empty clichés, as throughout the letter, Taut rejected the idea of fighting, especially of fighting merely for political advantage. 'What is the point of fighting over the political map, where woods and rivers still remain only woods and rivers?'[6] As far as he was personally involved, Taut saw before him a specific mission to be fulfilled, and this did not involve war. 'I often ask myself: for what do we actually live and die? For art and for beauty, for every fragment of a more beautiful existence which we can realize in this miserable world of ours.'[7] The main themes of Taut's Activism can already be perceived in this letter. The artist was accorded a different status to his fellow men on account of his special abilities and insights. It was the duty of the artist to put these abilities to their optimum use, in order to offer to the society at large alternatives to the terrible realities of the European war.

Following from this schema, Taut was especially disturbed at the thought that other specially gifted men, men like himself, were being killed on the battlefield. His laments for the dead were particularly aimed at the most gifted and most talented. 'The French are said to have already suffered 300,000 dead and injured, doubtless with many fine intellects amongst them. Similarly there must be many wonderful lives to mourn among the Russians.'[8] The duty of the artist or intellectual was to stay alive and to educate society away from war and killing. In his letter, Taut admitted an attraction to the artillery, as he was interested in the techniques of shooting, but he added: 'If only that wasn't desertion from the tasks which, even during the war, still lie ahead of me in my work.'[9] Taut felt that his profession as architect was directly opposed to that of warrior. Almost apologizing for the already quoted outburst against the Cossacks, Taut commented: 'You see, I am practising hate, even though my profession guides me along quite different paths.' The architect's job, also in time of war, was to build, not to destroy.

As the war went on, Taut's resistance to it developed into a bitter antipathy. He resorted to starving himself in order to avoid conscription. In March 1915, he wrote to his brother Max: 'The Territorial Reserve is being expanded further. Behne has already been called up, and I am also due for enlistment soon. I'm almost ill at the prospect. What's the use...'[10] By October 1917, writing to Max from Bergisch-Gladbach, Taut made it clear that he would prefer death at his own hands to death on the battlefield. His hint of suicide was thinly veiled:

We must all have the greatest patience and accept everything that comes. The destroying angel also haunts here. I must therefore prepare myself for the bitterest possibility. Whether or not I shall survive is very questionable; I will remain uncompromising and will not give up my right to my own person. I don't know what would then become of Hedwig [Taut's wife].[11]

In March 1916, Taut had already asked his brother Max to look after his family, should anything happen to him.[12]

In several of his war-time letters, Taut contrasted the gruesome reality of the war with the ideal world which existed in his mind. He perceived an element of his own alternative world, for example, in his son's paintings, and wrote to Max: 'I now see the bright side – and one with a delightful lustre – in a direction in which I had never expected to find it, with Heinrich. He paints and draws quite wonderfully. We are all delighted...One now hangs twice as much to anything which has sparkle: the realities are so hard, so terribly sober – ugh!'[13] The formulation of this *Glanzwelt*, of a glittering alternative world preoccupied Taut between 1914 and 1918. He offered it as a pacifist antithesis to the war and to the Wilhelmine society which had undertaken it.

The first public statement of this alternative world was made by Taut at the 1916 Werkbund conference at Bamberg, and took the form of an open letter – entitled 'Darlegungen'.[14] Although no copy of the letter survives, it is possible to piece together its contents from other letters, subsequently written by Taut's fellow members in the Werkbund who attended the Bamberg conference. Taut suggested a reform of architectural and design education which would be based on a more intense study of materials. In a letter to Gropius, Osthaus praised Taut's plan in the following terms:

What I particularly like about the statement is the demand for a collection of materials, which corresponds to some of my own long-cherished wishes. I had hoped to achieve this at the Deutsches Museum, but was hindered by the lack of a building. I am therefore doubly pleased that this call is now coming loudly from expert circles. I would supplement it by saying that the schools as well, and in particular the schools of arts and crafts, should pay more attention to the understanding and treatment of materials than simply to design. One can understand art when one releases it from the concept of formal training and provides, instead, the understanding of the instruments on which art can draw out a tune. Here is the point at which we can put the axe to the whole Muthesian teaching system.[15]

In his reply to Osthaus, Gropius was equally enthusiastic. 'I have written to Taut. His plans are excellent.'[16] Indeed, the 'Protokoll der gemeinsamen Sitzung des Vorstandes mit dem Ausschuss in Bamberg am 13. 6. 1916.' recorded that Gropius actually cited parts of Taut's letter during this meeting, in the context of elections to the *Vorstand* of the Werkbund. Taut stressed the need to ensure a continuity of artistic values within the Werkbund.[17]

Taut's 'Darlegungen' attacked the war, contemporary architectural education, and the enfeebled, democratic structure of the Werkbund. The letter, however, was not entirely antagonistic, as Taut also painted

29 Bruno Taut with his son,
Heinrich, 1914.

an ideal picture of the architecture of the future. Once again, we have no firm documentary evidence of what Taut suggested, but it would be fair to suppose that it corresponded to the *Kristallhaus* in *Die Stadtkrone*, which he was already working on in 1916. Osthaus saw Taut's suggested building as a direct descendant to the great pilgrimage church, Vierzehnheiligen, which is in the neighbourhood of Bamberg. Describing Balthasar Neumann's design, Osthaus wrote to Gropius:

The church is perhaps the most inspired design in all German architecture, in any case the most magnificent religious space that the Baroque era created. There could be no better example than this for the Werkbund, if it were properly understood. For this non-organic yet ingenious confusion of stucco and wood, representing stone, marble and wood, makes a mockery of all the rules of the materialists. To have the Werkbund adopt this example would be the fulfilment of all our efforts and achievements in the struggle for artistic freedom.

He added: 'For I believe that it will be our fault alone, if, from the basis established at Bamberg, no building results such as Taut has prophetically described in his letter. I find his statements truly excellent.'[18] Taut's ideas, sadly, did not find a wider audience. It was suggested to him, probably by Osthaus, that the 'Darlegungen' should be published in the *Kunstgewerbeblatt*. Fritz Hellwag was at this time both editor of the *Kunstgewerbeblatt* and also the secretary of the Werkbund. Publication was hampered, however, by the overtly pacifist nature of Taut's programme, and its contravention of the Burgfrieden pact. Hellwag canvassed the members of the *Vorstand* for their opinions and found no support for printing Taut's letter. Even Hans Poelzig, who was enthusiastic about Taut's ideas, feared the consequences of printing them. He wrote, in a confidential letter to Hellwag,

If you, as a member of the committee, are asking me whether or not the article should be published, then I would reply that this is something which only the whole committee can ultimately decide. Speaking personally, I have nothing to say against Taut's warm-hearted yet moderate essay: on the contrary, I find it splendid.

30 Balthasar Neumann,
Vierzehnheiligen, interior,
1743–72.

He went on to advise Hellwag: 'Tell Taut that I advise him to wait for
a while, so that those members who are of a different opinion will not
be given the chance to complain about the Burgfrieden pact.'[19] Taut
waited, in fact, until 1919, when an expanded version of his 'Darlegungen' was published as *Die Stadtkrone*.

When viewed together, *Die Stadtkrone* and Taut's other writings from
the war years offer an insight into Taut's thinking at this time. Several
dominant themes appear, which, as we shall subsequently see, link Taut
closely to the contemporary Activist movement in literature.

Taut's pacifism was the first presupposition of his war-time writings.
The dedication of *Die Stadtkrone* – 'to men of peace' – makes this clear.
Later in *Die Stadtkrone* he referred to the war as 'mass genocide',[20] a
sentiment which he had already expressed in an article published in *Die
Werkstatt der Kunst* at the beginning of 1917. The article was concerned
with the burial of the dead and with monuments appropriate to the dead.
It was entitled 'Die Vererdung' and began: 'The problem of the burial
cult pushes ever more into the foreground these days, when there are
very few Europeans remaining who have not lost a relative or friend
in the mass genocide.'[21] Later in the same article, Taut remarked sadly:
'The war phenomenon, with its immense fields of dead, gives us a new
measure of the transience of the human body.'[22] This pacifism, however,
was more than a simple 'O Mensch' reaction against the slaughter on
the battlefields. It sought both for prime causes and for plausible
antidotes.

The cause of, or the blame for the war was placed by Taut firmly at
the feet of the state, especially the concept of the German state as it had
evolved since 1870. In 'Architektur', Taut's own contribution to *Die
Stadtkrone*, he quoted a critique of the German view of the state which
had been made by Alexander von Gleichen-Rußwurm in February
1916. The critique ran: 'Increasingly in recent times, the ideal of the

German citizen consisted of allowing the state to think for him.'[23] Having relinquished all control and authority to a centralized, militaristic government, the public at large should not be surprised, said Taut, if war was the result. Thus in order to end the war, and to establish a lasting framework for peace, it was necessary to reorder the state, and to seize back the initiative from the generals and the politicians. Taut quoted Nietzsche as his authority: 'All states are badly organized in which other people in addition to statesmen must concern themselves with politics. Such states deserve to go to ruin as a result of these interventions.'[24] In order to reconstruct society along pacifist lines, it was essential to challenge the authority of the existing state. It was the duty of the cultural and spiritual élite to point out the shortcomings of the old society, and the disastrous results to which these shortcomings had led. At the same time, it was the duty of this élite to suggest suitable alternatives. In an article published in June 1915, entitled 'Krieger-Ehrung', Taut emphasized the importance of the architect for the necessary regeneration of German society after the war.

The sensibility of a whole nation is not to be measured by the same subtle standards as that of the individual. A broader context is necessary. The implanting of the great experiences of a nation into later generations, and the creation and renewal of this tradition play an important role here. What the living can no longer relate at first hand should be told to their descendants through poetry and art. Architecture must play a leading part in this, for no other artistic phenomenon is so firmly grounded on society in its totality. Of all the arts, architecture is most able to draw out the latent wishes and feelings of the people and to recast them in new forms.[25]

The artist or intellectual should not withdraw in horror from the war, said Taut, but should exert all his abilities and genius to produce viable alternatives. This was the first tenet of Taut's architectural Activism. No longer could the intelligentsia sit back, as it had done in 1914, and be swept along by the tide of militarism and nationalism. A positive lead was now called for, so that the lessons of the war could be comprehended by future generations and the mistakes of the past avoided.

4

Regeneration

How could the architect actively inspire social reform? Taut turned to the current problem of the war-dead in his efforts to show how architecture could work as a catalyst for social and even moral reform. He could achieve this not by theorizing or philosophizing, said Taut, but by building. 'Every artist should work within his own sphere, and the architect should *build*.'[1] In two articles 'Krieger-Ehrung' (1915) and 'Die Vererdung' (1917), Taut offered radical suggestions for the burial of the dead and for memorials to the fallen. In place of conventional burial in coffins or of cremation, Taut proposed in 'Die Vererdung' that the bodies should be allowed to decompose in the earth, and that this humus-enriched soil should then be used for special gardens. These gardens would have no headstones, plaques, monuments, or any other traces of *Grabesindividualismus*.[2] but, instead, would be devoted to exotic blooms, graceful glass architecture, fountains and waterfalls.

The humus plus top soil will be spread on a circular plot, which will be surrounded by pavilions. The architecture of these pavilions should be extremely light and graceful in character – it could be glass architecture. Since it results from the conquest of matter, the architecture must give a feeling of liberation, redemption, of something removed from material existence. Only glass can achieve this – the one building material which is rigid and solid and yet, in its transparent, shimmering, reflecting essence, is more than an ordinary material.[3]

For Taut, the dematerialization or decomposition of the bodies into humus, and the use of this humus in beautiful and exotic gardens was symbolic of the process of regeneration. 'I will gladly give the precious remains of my child to the earth, to be absorbed and re-used in the creation of new life.'[4] The humus from the corpses of the old age of war and materialism should provide the soil and the seedbed for the new age of the spirit.

If the war-dead were to be given a regenerative function as humus, what were Taut's plans for the wounded and injured? In 'Krieger-Ehrung', Taut proposed that homes for the wounded should be set up in pleasant surroundings, and with direct connections with the public. The homes should provide both domestic and workshop facilities. More exactly, Taut suggested:

homes for war-veterans, with quiet dormitory wings and quadrangles, attractive reading-rooms, libraries and common-rooms, halls, baths, playing-fields etc. The whole complex, which would be situated in a city park, would be open to the

31 Bruno Taut, Gartenstadt Falkenberg, projected home for the disabled, 1915.

public. Museums, theatres and suchlike could be added on, so that out of the initial impulse, something evolves which belongs to everybody.[5]

Not only would the homes provide for the wounded and the crippled, they would also act as memorials to the dead and as an inspiration for the future. 'The fallen should not be forgotten, their memory can be handed down to posterity on plaques in these buildings. The survivors, however, can best honour the dead by striving in thought and deed to create something new out of the legacy to which they have succeeded.'[6] As a practical example of his plans, Taut, together with the Deutsche Gartenstadtgesellschaft, drew up plans for a home for the disabled to be built onto the existing Falkenberg *Siedlung*. The whole complex consisted of a workshop, restaurant and kitchen, together with twenty-two flats for single men, twenty-four terrace-houses for married couples, plus a larger block with accommodation for fourteen couples. The home and its inhabitants were to be entirely integrated into the life of the *Siedlung*: 'Without living on top of each other, they could here be absorbed into a larger community, among people of similar standing and interests. Such a communal existence would promote the greatest possible understanding for the needs of the invalids.'[7] Taut included a communal kitchen and restaurant in the home. He also suggested that the workshops could provide work for the wives at Falkenberg. Instead of working at home for the miserly wages paid to outworkers, the women could get together, buy proper machines, and market their work directly to retailers, rather than through an entrepreneur. To free the women for such work, Taut recognized the need for communal crèches and kindergartens.[8]

To Taut, the invalid homes were more than homes for the wounded. They were blueprints, in microcosm, for a new social order in which mutual aid and co-operation in natural surroundings would replace the grasping individualism, isolation, and materialism of the industrial cities. In his description of the Falkenberg project, Taut commented:

Compared with the normal practice in the city, the costs of the dwellings at Falkenberg show that even the most minimal housing needs can be satisfied in an incomparably better and cheaper way. Even in Greater Berlin, therefore, the misery of the tenement block is not an unalterable economic necessity. Its place can be taken by spacious garden suburbs, which would be accessible not only to the well-to-do, but also to the middle classes and to those of moderate means, who at the moment are consigned to cheerless piles of masonry.[9]

The wider consequences of such a programme of invalid homes were elaborated by Taut in 'Krieger-Ehrung'. He felt that the microcosmic example of the homes could act as a catalyst for much greater social reforms.

Through such buildings, a new cult of remembrance will be created, a cult which will transcend the constraints of mere function and profitability, and which will symbolize the bridge between war and peace. In this way, the community would honour itself in the best manner possible...A fresh culture would also be created if one understands this much-used word to mean the style of life, rather than civilization or humanity.[10]

Out of the 'Darlegungen' which had been suppressed in 1916, and the small-scale model represented by the invalid home, Taut developed a larger plan for social reform involving a whole town. This was ultimately published as *Die Stadtkrone*. In this book Taut expounded his philosophy of architecture and illustrated it with his plan for an ideal city. Also included were two of Scheerbart's fantasy pieces and essays by Adolf Behne and Erich Baron.

5

◇◇

Chiliastic expectations – the *Gemeinschaft*

The tone of *Die Stadtkrone* was markedly, and perhaps predictably chiliastic. After 1916, the military impasse and the domestic privations caused by the war created near ideal conditions in Germany for an upsurge of chiliastic expectations. As Norman Cohn has commented: 'again and again, in situations of mass disorientation and anxiety, traditional beliefs about a future golden age or messianic kingdom come to serve as vehicles for social aspirations and animosities'.[1] Just as the traditional chiliastic eschatology predicted an end to the age of tyranny and hailed the Kingdom of the Saints, so the chiliastic impulse in war-time Germany demanded that the capitalist, Wilhelmine society be torn down and replaced by a new, egalitarian community.

Taut emphasized the chiliastic nature of his programme by including in *Die Stadtkrone* a short-story by Paul Scheerbart – 'Das neue Leben', subtitled 'Architektonische Apokalypse'. Scheerbart conjured up a brilliant picture of a new life which arose out of a dark and frozen planet. 'A shudder of longing murmers across the broad snowfields; a new life struggles into existence through the gnawing melancholy of the cold planet – the eternal life! The dead rise up...Yes! Yes! Who would not happily begin a new life!'[2] In accordance with the chiliastic tradition, Scheerbart's new society was divisionless and classless. 'The beggars consort with the kings, the priests with the warriors, the craftsmen with the scholars.'[3] In a similar vein, Taut's ideal new society was founded on his faith in the *Gemeinschaft*, seen as a just, equitable and harmonious community. He wrote in *Die Stadtkrone*: 'There must be something in everyone's breast which elevates him above temporal interests and allows him to sympathize with his contemporaries, with all humanity and the entire world.'[4] Taut's version of the *Gemeinschaft* was a mixture of an Hegelian view of progress and the Judeo-Christian belief in the immanence of God in man. As Taut insisted, 'Without religion there is no true culture, no art.'[5] The fusion of Christianity and socialism was called 'social commitment' by Taut: 'There is a phrase which pursues both rich and poor, which echoes everywhere and which, as it were, promises Christianity in a new form: social commitment.'[6] This he described, in perhaps the most-quoted passage in *Die Stadtkrone*, as follows:

A feeling exists, or at least slumbers in all of us, that somehow we should help to improve the lot of mankind, that somehow one should struggle to achieve spiritual salvation for oneself and thus for others, that one should feel a sense

52

of solidarity with all men. Socialism in the non-political, supra-political sense is the simple, straightforward relationship between men, far removed from any form of domination. It straddles the divide between warring classes and nations and binds mankind together.[7]

There was a particularly clear source for Taut's view of the *Gemeinschaft* as apolitical socialism. This was Gustav Landauer's *Aufruf zum Sozialismus*.

It is highly probable that Taut knew Landauer personally in the immediate pre-war years; it is certain that he knew of Landauer's writings. Taut's colleagues in the Deutsche Gartenstadtgesellschaft knew Landauer from the Neue Gemeinschaft experiment and, through them, Taut would have met Landauer. In addition, both Taut and Landauer had close connections with the literary community in Berlin, Landauer through his wife, the poetess Hedwig Lachmann.

As we have already seen, Landauer's pamphlet *Ein Weg zur Befreiung der Arbeiterklasse* (1895) was a direct source for the Schlachtensee experiment of the Neue Gemeinschaft group. Landauer followed this pamphlet with another on the same theme, *Durch Absonderung zur Gemeinschaft*, which was published by the Neue Gemeinschaft group in

1900. After the collapse of the Schlachtensee community, Landauer went to England with his wife. They lived from September 1901 until June 1902 in Bromley, Kent, as close neighbours to Peter Kropotkin. The direct results of this contact were translations by Landauer of two of Kropotkin's books.[8] The influence of Kropotkin on Landauer can be seen in a series of essays which Landauer wrote on his return to Berlin.[9] In 1908, he founded the Sozialistischer Bund, as a vehicle for propagating his views on decentralization and mutualism. The founding tenet of the Bund read: 'The fundamental structure of socialist society is a union of economically autonomous communities which trade together on mutualist principles.'[10] Like the Gartenstadtgesellschaft, the Sozialistischer Bund hoped to establish decentralist communities on the land: the two groups, therefore, had many practical aims in common. They differed, however, politically. Whereas the Gartenstadtgesellschaft accepted the capitalist economy as the basis on which it must work, the plans of the Sozialistischer Bund presupposed a mutualist system, which would, as far as possible, be independent of the money economy of capitalism. Landauer outlined the plans of the Bund in three essays: 'Was will der sozialistischer Bund?' (October 1908), 'Was ist zunächst zu tun?' (January 1909) and 'Die Siedlung' (May 1910). These three essays were brought together and published as *Aufruf zum Sozialismus* in 1911. The ideal society delineated by Taut in *Die Stadtkrone* derived directly from Landauer's *Aufruf*, and it would be fair to describe Taut's essay 'Architektur' in *Die Stadtkrone* as an attempt to give physical and architectural form to Landauer's abstract model.

As Taut was to do later, Landauer attacked the centralized state as the root of all contemporary evils: he saw the state as a tyrannical and repressive substitute for the natural relationships on which the *Gemeinschaft* should be based. The way forward to *Gemeinschaft* was via an intensification of *Geist*, but this way was blocked by the state, which represented the antithesis of *Geist*. 'Where there is no *Geist* and no inner compulsion, there is external power, legal compulsion, and the state. Where there is *Geist* there is community. Where *Geist* is absent one finds the state. The state is the surrogate for *Geist*.'[11] As we have already seen, Taut's view of the state, as expressed in *Die Stadtkrone* in the quotation from Alexander von Gleichen-Rußwurm, was exactly that held by Landauer. In Landauer's opposition of state and *Geist* it is comparatively easy to define the state, but much more difficult to define *Geist*. Yet his entire theory of socialism was founded on *Geist*. To understand the writings of Landauer and to understand his influence on Taut and on the contemporary Activists, it is first necessary to comprehend the concept of *Geist*.

6

Geist and *Volk*

Geist, according to Landauer, was the bond which linked mankind to the eternal. It was the vehicle through which the aspirations and strivings of mortal man might approach the creations of the Godhead. It is clear that *Geist* was firmly rooted in the Judeo-Christian tradition, and in the belief in the progressive movement or development of God through history. Landauer's close friend Martin Buber, whose Chasidic Judaism had a strong influence on Landauer's thought, offered the following definition of *Geist* in his novel *Daniel*:

In order to create something, a person must commit himself entirely. The worth of what is created is determined by his effort. There will therefore be a demand not for the man who merely reproduces, but for the creative producer. This leads to an absolutely new and undreamt of penetration of the world by the human spirit. This most original human quality can be called *Geist*.[1]

Thus the creative individual, motivated and guided by *Geist*, forges a link between humanity and the universe.

Geist, however, is not only connected to higher, more godly states of being, but is also related, reciprocally, to the mass of humanity, the *Volk*. *Geist* thus acts as an intermediary between the collective will of the *Volk* and an immanent Godhead, both of which are articulated and given form by the intercession of *Geist*.

Landauer felt that in a world fashioned by *Geist*, men would live in natural relationships, in peace and harmony, without the need for such artificial constructs as the state. '*Geist* is communal spirit, *Geist* is union and yet freedom, *Geist* is human federation. Soon we shall see it even more clearly: mankind will be seized by *Geist*, and wherever there is *Geist*, there is *Volk*.'[2] The latent goodness and wisdom of the *Volk* is released through the working of *Geist*, and the mundane world moves closer to an ideal, divine model.

The evolution of the twin concepts *Geist* and *Volk* was placed in an historicist context by Landauer. He identified the early middle ages, the Gothic period, as a high-point of *Geist*, as an age in which society was homogeneous, as an age in which the will of the *Volk* found a perfect expression in the constructions of the *geistig* leaders – the theologians and the master builders. The Christian middle ages, said Landauer, were models of the ideal of *Gemeinschaft*. 'At that time, the national character was not represented by the personalities of gifted individuals, it was

33 Strasbourg, from *Die Stadtkrone*.

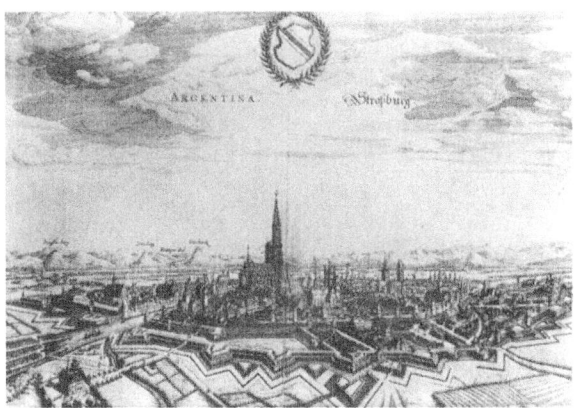

determined by simple groups. It was a primitive, communitarian existence.'³ The vision of primitive communism is a precondition for chiliastic socialism. It represents the first, golden age of natural innocence, when man existed in the primal, egalitarian state of nature. According to the revolutionary eschatology, the first age is followed by a period of fear and servitude, which increases and increases until the revolutionary moment arrives, when the chosen people, who have previously suffered under the oppression, will rise up against the power of evil and establish a new, perfect reign on earth. The new age, the millennium, will know no end.

Landauer identified the beginning of the second age with the post-Renaissance development of individualism, and with the subsequent spread of individualism via capitalism and the profit motive. 'That is why we call this epoch a period of decline, for the essential quality of culture, the *Geist* which joins men together, has declined.'⁴ The influence of this analysis on Taut can be clearly seen in Taut's essay 'Architektur' in *Die Stadtkrone*. The perfect unity between *Geist* and *Volk* was reflected, wrote Taut, in the relationship between the Gothic cathedral and the simple houses surrounding it. 'It was the same devotion in the Gothic age, which piled up the dazzling audacity of the cathedrals, yet at the same time produced a thorough penetration of practical and constructional demands in simple buildings.'⁵ Taut saw a similarly harmonious relationship between the sacred and the profane in the cultures of the Orient. The Gothic cathedral was related to its surroundings in the same way as the pagoda or temple in Asia was related to the simple huts surrounding them. Behne amplified this point in his essay 'Wiedergeburt der Baukunst', which Taut included in *Die Stadtkrone*. 'But isn't India even greater than the Gothic? At no time has Europe so nearly approached the Orient as during the Gothic age...Seen as a whole, however, the example of India stands high above all others as the purest oriental culture.'⁶ In the culture of India, Behne discerned an ideal relationship between the sacred and the profane:

The Indian temple penetrates deep into the surrounding countryside. The simple huts belong to it, for they derive from the same sensibility. The boats on the

rivers, the book illustrations, the carvings on their jewellery, the dances of the girls, and the patterns of their materials – all these things exist in a resonant relationship to the temple.[7]

Behne's description of this perfect unity as resonant was, as we shall see, an important component of the sacred–profane, *Geist–Volk* argument.

In *Die Stadtkrone*, Taut included photographs of the great oriental temples – Tschillambaram, Bangkok, Streevelliputtur, Rangoon, Angkor Vat, Madura. He returned to the theme enthusiastically in an article published at the beginning of 1919, 'Ex Oriente Lux'. In this article, even the high-points of European *Geist* suffered in Taut's comparison to their oriental counterparts.

Immersed in this magical world, sated with its honey – where is Europe now? Florence is meagre by comparison...the Baroque unbalanced, St Gereon is a box of building bricks, and even the Gothic is only contrived transcendentalism. How little remains! Strasbourg, Gothic stained glass, the Zwinger at Dresden – but better than their Indian counterparts? Bow down in humility, you Europeans![8]

The sources for Taut's infatuation with the Orient would not have included Landauer, who restricted his examples of an ideal *Gemeinschaft* to medieval Europe. Landauer's close friend Buber, however, did suggest in print that only oriental philosophies possessed the solutions in the quest for an integrated community life.[9] Furthermore, the belief in the superiority of the Gothic age over the post-Renaissance period, and in the superiority of the oriental cultures over the Gothic, was almost a commonplace at the time.

For example, a change in tone can be detected in German literature around 1910. The avant-garde moved away from the antagonistic immoralism of Edschmid, Klabund, Marinetti or Blaise Cendrars, and turned towards the transcendental Christianity of the middle ages or to similarly transcendental oriental religions – Hinduism, Taoism, Buddhism. Landauer's edition of the mystical writings of Meister Eckhart (1903)[10] was a forerunner of this change in direction.[11]

The most influential study of transcendental art was Wilhelm Worringer's *Formprobleme der Gotik*, first published in 1912. Seen from the viewpoint of 1916, Worringer's thesis brought together two powerful elements: chiliastic expectation and the interest in medieval and oriental transcendentalism. Worringer identified three basic types of mankind – primitive, classical and oriental.[12] He included Gothic man in the first category. Whereas primitive man found nature incomprehensible and had therefore feared it, and classical man had accepted and enjoyed it, oriental man had seen through nature to the mystical realms beyond.[13] The parallel between Worringer's sequence of primitive–classical–oriental and the chiliastic eschatology is very striking. Both systems have an age of innocence followed by an age of accomplishment which is, in truth, merely tyranny, and both systems resolve themselves after an appropriate struggle into an ideal third state. Especially important in both constructs is the kindred spirit which is seen to exist between the first and the last stages of development, a spirit to which the second stage is entirely inimical. In *Formprobleme* Worringer was at pains to note the similarities between primitive man and oriental man – especially their mutual reliance on instinct rather than knowledge. At the same time, he emphasized the essential difference: primitive man stood before cognition, oriental man beyond it.

Worringer's many followers and imitators tended to ignore this fundamental point. This was partly due to Worringer's own text, which, in its later stages, abandoned the three-sided argument in favour of a straight comparison between classical and Gothic architecture, a comparison which heavily favoured the Gothic. The appealing simplicity of a dialogue between good Gothic and bad classical led Worringer's followers to create an all-embracing ethos which combined Gothic, oriental, Egyptian and baroque architecture on the side of virtue and spirituality, and classicism on the side of superficiality and materialism. The most striking example of this tendency, and the most influential, was Karl Scheffler's *Der Geist der Gotik*, which appeared in 1917 and sold 20,000 copies in two years. The combination of *Geist* – seen simply as anti-materialism – and a passionate aversion to post-Renaissance Europe became a recurring theme during the war years. Thus Behne, as early as 1914, wrote: 'The builders, the sculptors, the painters and draughtsmen of the Gothic age were Expressionists.'[14] *Geist* meant unity and harmony. As Scheffler noted: 'The Gothic spirit is uncompromising: it chooses its forms simply on the principle of whether or not they stem from the same intuitive roots, whether they are of the same character, whether they express a distinct, unfragmented will. Uniformity and clarity mean everything to the Gothic spirit.'[15] In the Gothic cathedrals, seen as *Gesamtkunstwerke*, Worringer, Behne and Scheffler perceived a unity parallel to the social unity which Landauer and Taut saw in the medieval *Gemeinschaft*. Similarly, the unity of the cathedrals, like the unity of Landauer's *Gemeinschaft*, stemmed from *Geist*. 'Spirit [*Geist*] is the opposite of matter. To dematerialize stone is to spiritualize it. And by this statement we have made clear that the tendency of Greek architecture towards sensuousness is in direct contrast to the tendency of Gothic architecture towards spiritualization.'[16] The golden age of spirituality, *Geist* and harmony was destroyed, claimed the apologists, by the sweeping success of the Renaissance and by the spread of classical models which had been revived in Renaissance Italy. This catastrophic decline into the morass of sensuality and materialism was the artistic parallel to the triumph of tyranny in the second age of the millenarian eschatology. Paul Fechter made this parallel explicit in his pioneering book on Expressionism, first published in 1914. The book begins with the assertion that in all spheres of human activity, the nineteenth century witnessed an accelerating process of materialism and de-spiritualization. As a result, he said: 'The successes of the natural sciences led to the loss of the expressive instinct as a metaphysical necessity.'[17] Tracing this upsurge of materialism back to its source, Fechter alighted at the watershed between the Gothic and Renaissance ages. 'To cite Wilhelm Worringer, the last style foundered with the Gothic: the domination of naturalism – using the word in its widest sense – then began.'[18] Two of the prerequisites for the revolutionary eschatology were thus firmly established during the war years. The Gothic age in Europe and the diverse cultures of the Orient, corresponding to Worringer's primitive and oriental states of man, were adopted as models for the first and the third ages of society. The first was the golden age of innocence; the third, the new, fondly awaited age of peace and harmony. Separting these two ideal states was the second age, Worringer's classical state of man, which was seen as an age of individualism, calculation and tyranny. According to the theories current in 1914, this age began with the decline of the Gothic and the upsurge of the Renaissance spirit. It had developed via materialism and industrialism to reach a climax with the outbreak of war in 1914. The belief that the war represented a climax of the second age, the age of tyranny, naturally led to the third precondition of the revolutionary eschatology, which is the belief that the new dawn is imminent, that the end of the tyranny is nigh.

Even in the very early days of the war, when the intellectuals in large numbers were in favour of the conflict, it was felt that nothing could ever be quite the same again. Georg Simmel's famous essay 'Deutschlands innere Wandlung', written in the autumn of 1914, celebrated the new spirit of community which he sensed after the declaration of war:

This transformation initially drew upon a newly felt connection between the individual and the entire nation...The certainty of common ground must firstly be shaken by violent blows, so that you know that when the ground is torn up and moulded into new forms, it will not merely alter a limited aspect of your life. Instead, you will have a life in which the most individual and the most general aspects will fuse together at every point into a cohesive existence.[19]

This initial welcoming reaction to the war as a spiritual turning-point was shared, as we have seen, by Behne, Osthaus and Thomas Mann, and also by writers near the Activist camp like Buber and Max Brod. But as the war developed into a sanguinary stalemate, the initial enthusiasm turned into pacifism. Nevertheless, the belief in the war as the watershed, the Armageddon, the end of the old age lingered on. Indeed, it was reinforced in direct relation to the ever-mounting atrocities on the battlefields and the deprivations at home.

Taut had already insisted in his articles on the question of burial and on the invalid homes that the tragedy of the war offered a chance to rebuild afresh. This conviction was the driving force behind *Die Stadtkrone*: it was given powerful expression in the essay 'Aufbau', which Erich Baron had written for Taut in the spring of 1917. Baron's plea for a new *Gemeinschaft* concluded:

Our empire, our power begins beyond the war and without weapons. Just as our intoxication needs no wine, so our strength and defence need no metal, our victory can be achieved without battle honours. We shall not coerce the spirit with the methods of the barbarian hordes. It will arise out of the putrefaction of war, out of the Golgotha of crime, out of the defeat of the warriors. Humanity will lift its head again, the crushing hatred will be dismembered and over the graveyard of raw violence will vault the bridge to a new prosperity and fortune, to the emancipation of the world.[20]

Once again, the future good-fortune of the *Volk* was seen to be directly dependent on the workings of *Geist*.

The profoundly historicist sentiment that the revolutionary moment was imminent completed the pattern of chiliastic expectation. The evil had been identified, alternative models had been found, the moment for revolutionary change, for the beginning of the new era had arrived.

7

◇◇

The role of the Activist

The question now was not when – but how? Who was to guide the revolution? How was it to be controlled? Who was to take over the cultural and moral leadership from the discredited politicians and generals?

Taut's answer was: the architects. For the architect, alone amongst creative artists, must base his creations on the will of the people. Although the greatest architecture was indubitably a creation of the *Geist*, it was successful only in so far as it responded to the beliefs and convictions of the *Volk*.

> Although it is true that an individual is the *geistig* creator, the genesis of a building still demands many hands and many material resources. In order to set these in motion, the architect himself must possess an awareness and knowledge of all the deeper feelings and opinions which prevail among the populace for which he will build. This does not simply mean the ephemera which are dubbed the *Zeitgeist*, but much more the still slumbering, latent forces in the soul of the *Volk*; which, disguised as faith, hope and longing, struggle towards the light and seek, in the noblest sense, to 'build'.[1]

As Taut explained at some length, this beneficial dominion of architecture over the other arts was a characteristic of the cultures of the Orient and had last flourished in Europe in the Gothic age. Adolf Behne made the point very bluntly in his contribution to *Die Stadtkrone*. He began:

> I wish to indicate the downward path which art has followed since the Gothic age – the age in which art last flourished in Europe. I shall then attempt to throw some light on the potential models which, after we have passed through the absolute nadir, might serve as forerunners of a new creativity. I base my account on the verity, that architecture is the basis of all the plastic arts.[2]

In the expanded version of this essay, written in 1918 and published in 1919 as *Die Wiederkehr der Kunst*. Behne reiterated this theme. The mission of architecture, he wrote, should be to unite all the arts in order to create an ultimate statement of unity: unity of man with man, of man with nature, of man with the cosmos.

> One thing must be freely admitted: the highest and ultimate aim of today's architecture is beyond the reach of the architects of today. What is this ultimate aim? It is a building of great wondrousness, transcending all human limitations. Humanity will grow to match it in its scale and magnificance. Mankind's desire for universal love will be embodied in this work.[3]

This, encapsulated, was an ecstatic version of Taut's own argument in *Die Stadtkrone*.

Yet, as Behne admitted, the architects were not yet adequate to the task. There were signs of 'architectonic' stirrings in the work of painters such as Léger, Delaunay, Chagall, Klee, Feininger and Kandinsky, and in the sculpture of Archipenko. These creative spirits, however, lacked the unifying medium of a true architecture. 'True' architecture was defined by Behne as the architecture of fantasy, not that of the 'educated bourgeois, subscriber to *Kunstwart*, member of the Werkbund'.[4] 'Fantasy inhabits a higher stratum of human consciousness. All higher truths, therefore, are fantastic: that is to say, they spurn the human scale.'[5] And the prophet of this new architecture, proclaimed Behne, was Paul Scheerbart. 'For this reason, Scheerbart holds an important position for us. His first book, *Paradies*, appeared in 1889, in the annus mirabilis of Naturalism. Right from this earliest work, he has offered in his writings the first, purest, clearest, the most universal and, until now, the most coherent explanation of our intentions.'[6] By a process of apostolic succession, Scheerbart's position had been taken over by Bruno Taut. 'He alone, with a purity of feeling inspired by his love of Scheerbart's poetry, has repeatedly pushed back the limits. Again and again he has shown that behind the stupendous exists something even more stupendous. Again and again he has appealed: "Build! Build with the Creator's love of the world!"'[7] Behne thus cast Taut in the role of the saviour of architecture, and, by implication, the saviour of all the arts, and, indeed, of the moral aspirations of society. In doing this, he was merely echoing Taut's own estimation of the moral power of architecture.

Taut's belief that architecture could act as a regenerative force in society at large was very close to the views of Kurt Hiller and the literary Activists, who made exactly the same claims for literature and for the *Literat*. At this point, it would be appropriate to compare Taut's version of the role of the architect with the literary counterpart, as put forward by Hiller and his circle.

The Activist movement in literature was formally launched in 1915: the term was coined by Hiller together with Rudolf Kayser and Alfred Wolfenstein. Before 1918, there is no documentary evidence of a direct connection between Taut and the literary Activists. It is highly probable, however, that Taut, through his literary connections in Berlin, would have known their writings and sympathized with their views. Pacifism, in particular, would have provided a mutual link. The first demand in Hiller's first Activist manifesto was for the abolition of war.[8] A mutual contact between Taut and the literary Activists may have been Erich Baron. Baron had a lasting political influence on Taut right through until the 1930s.[9] In *Die Stadtkrone*, Taut included Baron's essay 'Aufbau', in which Baron referred directly to the Activist group by name, calling them 'die jungstürmenden Verkünder des "tätigen Geistes"'.[10] This was a reference to the Activist yearbook, *Das Ziel*, which was published intermittently between 1916 and 1924. The first was subtitled *Aufrüfe zu tätigem Geist.*[11]

35 Kurt Hiller.

Although there is no conclusive evidence of a direct link between Taut and the Activists before 1918, Taut's war-time writings are exactly in accord with the published work of the literary Activists. Futhermore, he shared with them a common mentor – Gustav Landauer. We have already seen how closely Taut's views on pacifism, *Geist* and the state were modelled on Landauer's *Aufruf zum Sozialismus*. Exactly the same can be said of the literary Activists. Indeed, in his conclusion to the first Activist yearbook, Hiller wrote: 'Our readers are further referred to the pamphlet *Aufruf zum Sozialismus* by the distinguished writer Gustav Landauer, whose non-participation on this book is deeply regretted by the editor.'[12] Landauer's hostility towards the centralized state and the established political parties and politicians, against materialism, positivism and Marxism, was adopted in its entirety by the literary Activists. Similarly, they planned for a socialist society based on Landauer's concepts of *Geist* and *Gemeinschaft*.

From the shared starting point of Landauer, Taut's essay 'Architektur' and Hiller's 'Philosophie des Ziels',[13] his first Activist manifesto, have much in common. Just as Taut's architectural vision was markedly chiliastic, so Hiller proclaimed: 'Having explained our beliefs, our aim must now be finally disclosed. Let it be stated quite clearly: we desire, while still alive, to reach paradise.'[14] Paradise was defined by Hiller as the point at which *Geist* transcends itself. 'Paradise...is that state of existence at which humanity has no further need for *Geist*. An incredible expenditure of *Geist* is necessary in order to achieve this state. We must infinitely intensify *Geist* until, at the extremity of an infinitely distant moment, it consumes itself.'[15] *Geist*, to Hiller and the Activists, was not the introspective *Geist* of Kandinsky or the Expressionists, which they denounced as 'merely reflective aestheticism',[16] but a new aggressive, and politically motivated *Geist*. Whereas the Expressionist poets, according to Hiller, 'degraded their genius to the role of reporter on the inner life',[17] the Activists would harness their theoretical premises to a programme of political action.

Geist thus became an all-embracing term for the chiliastic expectations of the new age. This is entirely consistent with the holistic nature of chiliastic faith. As Hiller wrote: *Geist* is an holistic power. It does not smugly disdain the temporal and incomplete, but with a fervent, piercing eye cuts through them in order to comprehend the whole.'[18] This total and unifying *Geist* was a close parallel to the *Geist* perceived by Taut and Behne, Worringer and Scheffler in the Gothic cathedral or the Indian temple. In its power to reconcile diverse and opposing tendencies into a unity, Hiller's *Geist* worked in exactly the same way as Taut's 'Socialism in the non-political, supra-political sense, which straddles the divide between warring classes and nations and binds mankind together'.[19]

Who was to implement these holistic, *Geist*-inspired solutions? According to Landauer's *Aurfruf zum Sozialismus*, it was to be the socialist. The socialist, said Landauer, possessed a comprehensive understanding of society, and, especially interesting as further evidence of the historicist and chiliastic nature of *Geist*, the socialist was also aware of the historical context and antecedents for the anticipated revolution.

The socialist comprehends the whole of society and its history. He understands, both through knowledge and instinct, where we have come from and, with this knowledge, determines where we are going...This is the mark of the socialist in contrast to the politician the socialist concerns himself with the totality. Hence, in thought, feeling and desire, he must be a visualizer of things in context, a collector and unifier of the multifarious.

In the same passage, Landauer also defined socialism as 'a cultural movement...a fight for beauty, greatness, for the fulfilment of the people'.[20] It follows, therefore, that the leaders of the *geistig* revolution should be the artists and creative spirits. As Landauer expressed it, in an article written in 1916: 'The consequence of poetry is revolution.'[21]

This was the dominant conviction of the literary Activists. They took up the idea not only from the Landauer, but also from Heinrich Mann, whose essay 'Geist und Tat', originally published in 1910, was republished by Hiller as the first contribution to the first *Ziel* yearbook. Mann was thus a founding father of literary Activism in the immediate pre-war years, the years when he and Bruno Taut were moving in the same circles in literary Berlin. In 'Geist und Tat', Heinrich Mann said that the time had come for the intellectuals to stir themselves out of their apathy and timidity. The time had come to lead an uprising against the authoritarian and militaristic state. 'The times cry out, and honour demands, that intellectuals at long, long last ensure that the dictates of *Geist* are met in this country too. They must become agitators, joining the *Volk* against the powers that be and lending the full weight of the pen to its struggle – which is no less the struggle of *Geist*.'[22] Once again, in this proto-Activist essay, Mann related *Geist* and *Volk*, saying that to fight for one was to fight for the other.

To the literary Activists, the new man was defined not as 'socialist', but as '*Literat*'. The *Literat* was a fusion of polemical writer and politician – politician not in the sense of party politics, but in the all-embracing sense described by Landauer. Ludwig Rubiner offered this ecstatic description of the *Literat* in 1916:

> The voice lives! The voice for others!
> The word lives, as bright as a clarion call!
> The round, opened mouth lives, calling loudly!
> The leader lives!
> The *Literat* lives [23]

Kurt Hiller urged the Activists to strive for concrete results, not to be content with bland theorizing or dogmatizing. He frequently used architectural imagery to emphasize the need for tangible action and tangible results.

> The strong-willed man of *geistig* blood, in other words the Activist, strives after the deed, which is the construction of an earthly paradise...The Activist calls to the intellectuals, philosophers, artists and literati: 'Do not simply list and describe ethical demands, don't leave them for ever as tissues of thought, doctrine, works of art or literature – as things peripheral to real life, as culture, opinion, mind or form. Translate them into spatial reality!' [24]

The *Literat*, according to Hiller's definition, had a prophetic, messianic function. In 1915, he wrote of the *Literat*: 'his entire intellect will lead him to action. He is the summoner, the realizer, the prophet, the leader.' [25] By virtue of his innate and superior abilities, the Activist leader would mediate between the subjective world of the *Volk* and the objective world of *Geist*.

This fundamental concept of Activism was adopted by Hiller from Simmel, under whom Hiller had studied in Berlin. Simmel had argued that the creative power of the individual could synthesize the objective and subjective elements of culture into a higher reality. [26] The function of the Activist was to guide the *Volk* away from materialism and naturalism towards a higher objective entity – *Geist*. Gustav Wyneken, one of the leading theoreticians of Activism, saw this process as the only true development open to man. 'This process of objectification marks the individual's true development as a man. For the essence of man does not consist in his standing on two feet, but rather in the fact that his subjective will is held in balance by an objective and, by nature of its origins, social world.' [27] It was, said Hiller, this ability to unite subject and object, *Volk* and *Geist*, political reality and messianic idealism, which distinguished the Activists from the passive and introspective Expressionists.

The parallel between Hiller's portrait of the prophetic *Literat* and Taut's portrayal of the architect is very striking. Who was better equipped, asked Taut, than the architect, to give concrete form to the will of the *Volk*, to transform subjective desires into objective truths.

> The architect must ponder his noble, priestly, magnificent, divine calling, and seek to raise the treasure which lies in the depths of man's soul. With total abandon he should immerse himself in the soul of the *Volk* and discover both himself and his noble calling by striving to give material expression to that which slumbers in every soul. [28]

In its very essence, architecture embodied the Activist ideal of a fusion of *Geist* and *Praxis*. In *Philosophie des Ziels*, Hiller wrote: '*Geist* and *Praxis* were formerly antithetical. Today these words signify a correlative interdependence. *Geist* defines the aims, *Praxis* translates them into reality.'[29] Taut, making the same correlation, described architecture as the physical realization of *Geist*. 'The word architecture [Bau-"Kunst"] seems almost too slight for something which means the world of ideas given material form.'[30] The combination, however, of *Geist* and *Praxis* was not, to Taut, a balanced or mutual symbiosis. Whereas he granted an autonomous existence to the 'higher' ideals of architecture, he constantly emphasized that practicality alone was worthless.

Die Stadtkrone is littered with polemics against mere functionalism. The will of the true architect, said Taut, should extend far beyond the simplistic parameters of function.

So it appears that the will of the architect is determined by factors quite other than the restraints of function. It is thus self-explanatory that this will is located above and beyond the essentially practical. The highest ideal for which the architect's will strives is to be found in buildings in which practical purpose is of little or no importance.[31]

This follows on from the programme to the Glashaus at Cologne, which denied that the pavilion had any function beyond being beautiful. As expressed in 1914, this sentiment could be read as a rejection of the current Werkbund orthodoxies of practicality and *Typisierung*. By 1916, however, the message carried wider implications, for it represented the rejection not only of function as an end in itself, but also the rejection of rationalism in the positivist sense.

8

◇◇

The rationalism of intuition

Taut's rejection of rationalism, functionalism and the warring materialist civilization of Europe found its most vigorous expression not in *Die Stadtkrone* but in *Alpine Architektur*. Taut began work on this folio of drawings in 1917. It was conceived as a homage to Scheerbart, whose death in the autumn of 1915 had affected Taut deeply. He wrote at the time to his brother Max:

My dear Max, nothing here is new – except for something very sad: our dear 'Glaspapa' Paul Scheerbart died on 14 October. He had a sudden stroke, fought for twenty-four hours without regaining consciousness, and then passed away. We were at the burial, which was very nasty. It was organised by the Poets' Union [Schutzverband der Dichter] and there were ghastly speeches. It was dreadfully upsetting.

The letter broke off, and then continued, six days later: 'That's now long past. For this reason it's so difficult to tell Mutz and yourself about it. That we no longer have him here makes one weep with grief. Even today I still feel orphaned. But Paul Scheerbart lives – not simply in his works, but in his full humanity.'[1] Taut made manifest his debt to Scheerbart by including a long quotation from *Münchhausen und Clarissa* in his description of the *Kristallhaus*. In keeping with its Scheerbartian origins, the predominant tone of *Alpine Architektur* was that of the Sturm group and the aestheticism of the pre-war years.[2] Lurking behind the immediate source of Scheerbart was the ghost of Nietzsche.

By following Zarathustra's path to the mountains, Taut dissociated his temples of *Geist* from the materialist rationalism of the world below. In his notes to the drawings he repeatedly damned technology and functionalism. The glass buildings were to be non-functional except in the most ethereal sense. 'Function of the cathedral? – none – if devotion to beauty is not enough.'[3] Technology was scorned as leading to conflict and war: 'Yes, non-practical and useless. But has utility made us any happier? Always utility and utility: comfort, ease, good food, education, knife, fork, railways, water closets... and also cannons, bombs, machines of war.'[4] Both technology and the concept of function were reduced to subservient roles, to serve the higher needs of *Geist* – 'Die Technik ist immer nur Dienerin'[5] The mechanics of the buildings should therefore be concealed, lest they distract from the higher contemplative and *geistig* task: 'The utilitarian functions should simply function and be as unobtrusive as possible.'[6] Such a rejection of materialism was not, as

we have seen, a particularly fresh idea at that time. What is interesting, however, are the means suggested by Taut to break away from the tyranny of nineteenth-century rationalism.

Instead of proposing a retrospective utopia, as the *Bodenreform* and *Heimatkunst* movements had done, Taut summonsed up a futurist utopia. Instead of damning technology as incompatible with *Geist*, Taut invoked a super-technology, which was to be the discreet servant of *Geist*. This super-technology, when allied to *Geist*, would transcend and thus make obsolete the discredited rationalism and materialism which had led, said Taut, to the war. The glass and steel architecture, the searchlights, airships and aeroplanes which were depicted in *Alpine Architektur* were seen by him as the means to break away from

SCHNEE
GLETSCHER
GLAS

materialism, not as materialist artefacts in themselves. Taut's irrational faith in the ability of super-technology to transcend the limitations of materialism was one aspect of the Activist challenge to rationalism.

Taut was not alone, in 1916–17, in his rejection of materialist or positivist rationalism. It was a widespread reaction to the war. The birth of Dada was the most conspicuous symptom of this anti-positivist tendency. As Allan Greenberg has commented: 'The Dadaists, along with many other artist-intellectuals, considered the irrationalism of war as the culmination of the rationalism of the nineteenth century: adherence to logic and morality exclusively in the sphere of the ideal led to illogic and immorality in the sphere of the real.'[7] However, the Activists, in contrast to the Dadaists, did not reject the concept of rationalism. Rather, they sought to transcend its limitations. Their ambition was to found a new rationalism based on creative rather than analytical thought. The *Literat* and the creative *Geist* would take over from the politician, the economist or the technologist. The Activist variant of rationalism had a distinctly messianic and mystical flavour.

In his essay 'Aktivismus und Rationalismus', Max Brod defined Activist rationalism as a search for the Godhead. 'True rationalism is nothing more than the clearest indication possible of the mystery of the world. Considered practically, in rationalist Activism, it seeks to promote the fullest possible concentration on the eternal, divine, and *geistig* among the greatest possible number of people.'[8] The super-rationalism of the Activists was conceived as the vehicle for the immanent God in man.[9] The way to the 'eternal, divine, and *geistig*' was not to be found via the calculating rationalism of the positivists, but, rather, via irrationalism. And, as Max Brod indicated, 'This true rationalism can not only tolerate a synthesis with genuine irrationalism, it virtually demands it.'[10] Also in contrast to their Dadaist contemporaries, the Activists did not regard irrationalism nihilistically, as an end in itself. Instead, they saw it as a necessary step on the way to a higher, transcendental rationalism. 'True rationalism strives, with a rational selection of rational and super-rational means, to achieve super-rationality.'[11] This higher rationalism can be seen as a striving for ultimate truths: to the Activists it was a search for objective truths – truths grounded not on the subjective emotions

of the individual, but on a higher *geistig* authority. Paulsen noted this tendency: 'The will of Activism means nothing except the desire to be both realistic and pure. Realistic, that means rational, and pure – true.'[12] This is very important both to the understanding of Activism and to the understanding of the movements which followed it. The reaction against the excessive subjectivity of Expressionism, which is generally associated with the Neue Sachlichkeit movement, can actually be traced back to Activism. Certainly, the Activists themselves thought that they were constructing a true alternative to indulgent Expressionist subjectivity. Thus the divide between Activism and Neue Sachlichkeit was much narrower than that between Expressionism and Neue Sachlichkeit. Both Activism and Neue Sachlichkeit were founded on the search for an anonymous, absolute, and 'pure' rationalism.[13]

How was this to be achieved in practice? Through mystical intuition, said Hiller.

The source of all rationality lies not in knowledge but in experience. Its deepest essence, therefore, is not be comprehended quasi-mathematically, but mystically...The impulse towards the benevolent, messianic reform of the world remains dark and inaccessible to all justification. An intellectualism which lusts

for proof – both pure and poor philosophy – fails here. For here rule the ardour
and the assurance of more sacred, more profound powers.[14]

This description of a quasi-mystical power to comprehend a given
phenomenon without 'understanding' it in the positivist sense clearly
derived from current intuitionist philosophies. In the visual arts, the
most potent variant of intuitionism was empathy theory, which would
have reached Taut via Worringer and Kandinsky.[15]

The core of empathy theory was the experience of a mutual resonance
which exists between the intellect, as a medium of perception, and a
physical object – for example, a painting, sculpture or building.
Kandinsky offered the following explanation:

So long as the mind remains united with the body it can, as a rule, only perceive
vibrations through the medium of sensation. Hence sensation is the bridge from
the non-material to the material (the artist), and from the material to the
non-material (the onlooker). Emotion – sensation – work – sensation – emotion ...The inward element created by the vibrations of the mind forms the
content of a work.[16]

Kandinsky's sequence was proto-typically Expressionist, in that it placed
the emotions at the beginning and end of the cycle. Empathy, to
Kandinsky, was a means of uncovering subjective truths. The Activists,
however, gave empathy a more vigorous reforming role, a role with a
social purpose.

Taut's goal, and that of the literary Activists, was, as we have seen,
an ideal *Gemeinschaft*. Taut's models, representing respectively the first
and third ages of the revolutionary eschatology, were the Gothic and
the Orient. The historicist belief in a new age represents the idolization
of both the past and the future. The vehicle for Taut's idolatry was
intuition, or empathy.

As an Activist, Taut assumed two roles simultaneously: the first as
historian and philosopher, the second as man of action. In his first role,
Taut's understanding of his Gothic and oriental models was based on
intuitive understanding – *Verstehen*. This historical method, developed
by Johann Droysen, Wilhelm Dilthey and Max Weber, was credited with
the ability of transporting the historical observer into the very core of
values and standards which allegedly gave meaning and pattern to
bygone societies. Thus the external historical records – in Taut's case the
cathedrals and temples – were projected into the observer's inner
experience, where they released intellectual and emotional processes
analogous to those experienced by historical characters.[17]

Thus via empathy, or *Verstehen*, Taut claimed he could see beyond
the merely technical or functional aspects of a medieval city like Speyer,
or an oriental temple group, and perceive through the architecture the
resonant tones of a united, organic society, of a *Gemeinschaft*. Not only
did Taut study these models intuitively rather than factually, but he also
perceived in them internal resonances and harmonies. As already noted,
Taut saw a unity between *Geist* and *Volk*, between sacred and profane

in Gothic and oriental societies. This unity, however, was not a fusion of similar elements, but a resonance between different, but complementary elements. Thus the architectural expressions of *Geist* and *Volk* provided mutual inspiration and a mutually beneficial context and scale, the one for the other.

The cathedral over the old city, the pagoda over the huts of the Indians, the incredible temple quarter in the rectangle of the Chinese city and the Acropolis rising above the simple housing of the antique city – they all show that the pinnacle, the highest point, the crystallized religious intuition, is both the ultimate goal and the starting point for all architecture. This central focus radiates its light over every building, right down to the simplest hut, and graces the solution of the simplest practical necessities with the shimmer of its brilliance.[18]

In this sequence, *Geist*, or the 'crystallized religious intuition', is taken as the beginning and end of the empathy chain. The profane architecture of the *Volk*, said Taut, is illuminated by the glory of *Geist*, and the society is thus harmoniously united. The sequence, however, can also flow in the other direction, due to the mutual nature of the *Geist–Volk* resonance. Then the great architecture of *Geist* draws its strength and context from the *Volkswille*. 'Not only great edifices are dependent on a profound and powerful philosophy of life. This passionate comprehension first produces beauty in small buildings.'[19] From these humble, profane beginnings, the *Gemeinschaft* takes its inspiration and also its scale from the great sacred enterprises. 'Only this philosophy of life achieves the correct evaluation of scale, which is part of the architects's task, and prevents the blurring of the borders between great and small, sacred and profane, from which our age suffers.'[20] Empathy and *Verstehen*, as historical resonance, were used by Taut to transcend the merely external evidence of earlier cultures, and to construct a highly idealized account of their harmonious inner workings. This was Taut in his first Activist role, as idolizer of the past.

In his second Activist role, as a man of practical action, Taut was also dependent on intuition and empathy. The first ambition of architectural Activism was to revive the intuitive, as against the scientific understanding of architecture. In an article on the Roland at Brandenburg, written while Taut was working there in 1916, he complained that the Roland was 'the victim of so-called art history...He was catalogued on account of his scale, but his quite unique beauty was never appreciated.'[21] Later in the same article, Taut made the general point: 'A living feeling for architecture is rare, very rare today. All feelings are stifled by principles and theories.'[22] The application of a positivistic *Kunstwissenschaft* to the study of architecture had led to an overriding concern for technical and functional details at the expense of an intuitive understanding of the true purpose of architecture.

This true purpose, said Taut, was to link man with nature. 'In all the arts, the notion of "nature" has never had any other meaning, except that the artist and his work are themselves part of nature.'[23] In this

40 Brandenburg, Roland,
1474.

empathetic chain, the architect and his work acted as intermediaries between the *Volk* and nature. Nature, in this sense, meant the higher ideals of life, an organic, harmonious society, a *Gemeinschaft*.

In 'Architektur', Taut returned to this image of the architect as the resonant medium through with the *Volk* could make contact with higher nature, with *Geist*. 'Our concern here is not with mere necessity, but to create a resonance between the building and a higher function.'[24] And just as Theodor Lipps, the most influential early advocate of empathy, had defined aesthetic enjoyment as objectified self-enjoyment: 'The perception of aesthetic worth is always the perception of a profound value which exists both in the object and in myself. In appreciating the abstract value I also enjoy its presence in myself.'[25] – so Taut defined architecture as being simultaneously the means of expression and also as the physical statement of the deepest longings of man: 'Architecture is an art and should be the highest of all arts. It derives only from strong emotions and speaks only to the senses. The head can, at best, work as a regulating influence. For the true essence of architecture can only spring from the heart: the heart alone must be allowed to speak.'[26] Such an architectural process, which 'entsteht nur aus einem starken Gefühl und spricht auch nur zum Gefühl', is clearly related to Kandinsky's empathetic chain: 'Emotion – Gefühl – Werk – Gefühl – Emotion.' Yet as we have already noted, Kandinsky's chain was typically Expressionist in that it limited itself to a deeper understanding of the emotions. Taut, as an Activist, saw his chain as a tool for social action.

Taut's ideal, as we have seen, derived principally from Landauer's version of a socialist *Gemeinschaft*, which could be derived through an intensification of *Geist*. The tendency of this scheme is centripetal. As society or the *Volk*, through the leadership of the architect/Activist,

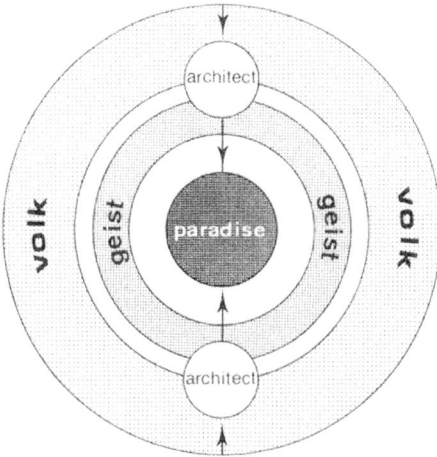

becomes more and more *geistig*, so the society as a whole moves closer and closer towards paradise. At its final resolution, society will become paradise and *Geist* will become superfluous – a means to an end, but not an end in itself. To quote Hiller's definition of paradise once again, 'Paradise...is that state of existence at which humanity has no further need for *Geist*.'[27] Until this ultimate stage of development is reached, however, the job of the Activist, said Hiller, was to articulate the resonances between *Geist* and *Volk* and to direct them, via the Activist's own work and leadership, towards the final goal – paradise. To Taut, paradise could be reached through architecture, and would be reached when the architect was able, once again, to bring into harmony the resonances which once existed between *Geist* and *Volk*, but which had become dissonant after the decline of the Gothic and the upsurge of individualism and materialism.

9

◇◇◇

The new city and the resonance of *Geist* and *Volk*

Taut's city plan in *Die Stadtkrone* was an attempt to re-tune *Geist* and *Volk*, according to the models of the Gothic and the Orient. As in most humanist utopias, from Thomas More on, Taut's layout was concentric. The circle was conceived as *axis mundi*, as a microcosm of the earth itself. The plan consisted of a central public core – the *Stadtkrone*, surrounded by a zoned town, broken down into housing, business, industrial and recreational zones according to the precepts of Taut's former teacher, Theodor Goecke. The distinction between the *Stadtkrone* and the surrounding zones corresponded to *Geist* and *Volk*, to sacred and profane.

The model for the housing – corresponding to the huts in the Orient and the humble housing of medieval Europe, was the row-housing which Taut had developed for the Deutsche Gartenstadtgesellschaft. Taut included illustrations of the Falkenberg estate as examples on which the housing in the new city could be based. He described the residential areas as follows: 'The housing is conceived on the garden city model, with low terrace-housing, and a long garden for every house...the residential area itself will function as a green zone and make allotment gardens unnecessary.'[1] The housing, low in profile, squatted around the physical and *geistig* focus of the city, the *Stadtkrone*.

Taut's sacred centre was built upon communal buildings. On these buildings depended the city's intellectual and cultural life. 'A grouping of all those buildings, which are the focus for the already mentioned social tendencies, and which a city of this size needs for its cultural and entertainment needs.'[2] These included an opera house, theatre, library, museum, aquarium, plant-house and assembly rooms. Elevated above these buildings on a reinforced concrete frame was to be a *Kristallhaus* – the ultimate glory of the *Stadtkrone* and a physical representation of *Geist*.

As we have already seen, Worringer, in *Formprobleme der Gotik*, identified the Gothic urge for dematerialization as an urge for *Vergeistigung*.[3] The distinction between the Gothic and classical spirit, between *Vergeistigung* and *Versinnlichung*, was adopted by Taut and applied to his own period as the contrast between the rationalism and materialism of the nineteenth century (*Versinnlichung*) and the contemporary desire for a new age of the spirit (*Vergeistigung*). Just as Worringer set the Gothic vault against the Greek column und lintel, so Taut set his new architecture of glass and iron against the stone and

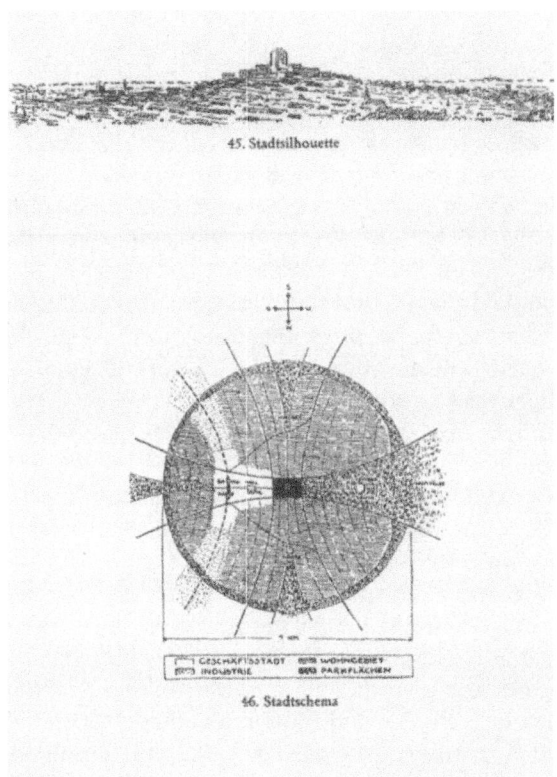

45. Stadtsilhouette

46. Stadtschema

41 Bruno Taut, *Die Stadtkrone*, silhouette and plan.

42 *Die Stadtkrone*, central area.

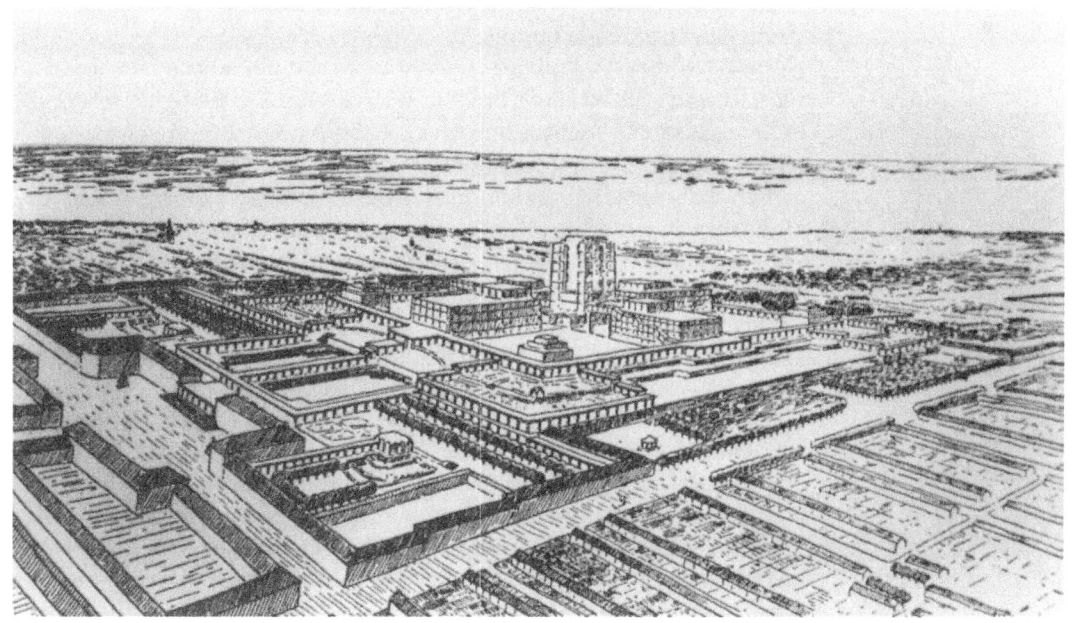

bricks of the nineteenth century. Through its power to dematerialize, glass lifted architecture above materialism to a higher, *geistig* level.

The *Kristallhaus* had no practical function, beyond simply being. 'The *Kristallhaus* contains nothing apart from an incredibly beautiful room, reached by steps and walkways to the right and left of the theatre and the small *Volkshaus*. But how can one hope to describe something that can only be built?'[4] And just as the Gothic cathedral, according to Taut's *Verstehen*, had radiated its beneficial glow over the entire town, so the *Kristallhaus*, with its shimmering and reflecting planes of coloured glass, would shine, as Taut said, 'over everything, like a sparkling diamond'.[5]

The silhouette of the city, rising from squat, profane housing to the sacred central crown, echoes the drawings of medieval cities which illustrated Taut's essay. A more immediate source was also Constantinople. In an article written in 1916, describing his visit to Turkey in connection with the 'Haus der Freundschaft' contest, Taut noted the harmonious union of sacred and profane architecture in Constantinople. 'Certainly, the great buildings are distinct from profane life, but they do not reject it: on the contrary, they attract it, with the result that everything – the mosques and the multi-coloured turmoil – form a total unity.'[6] There is a clear source for the silhouette of Taut's new city in his description of the skyline of Constantinople. He wrote: 'The great mosques crown the hills and the multifarious jumble of houses which, however chaotic and thrown together as one might describe them, still work harmoniously together.'[7] As in his description of the Roland, Taut once again leant heavily on intuition, on perceived resonances and harmonies in his account of Constantinople.

In spite of the manifesto-like nature of *Die Stadtkrone*, there was very little in the individual architectural elements which was new. Indeed, Taut urged that: 'Naturally, the architectural forms in this project are to be taken only as summaries.'[8] No suggestions were given as to the form the industrial buildings should take, and the housing, as we have seen, was based on Taut's pre-war work for the Gartenstadtgesellschaft. The very simple nature, however, of these pre-war designs was even more appropriate to the conditions of 1917 than to those of 1913–14, when they were first drawn up. For the crippling effects of the war and the 'turnip winter' of 1916–17[9] lead to a reassessment of the luxury and profligacy of the *Gründerzeit*. In an article on 'Bauluxus', written in 1917, the critic Paul Westheim attacked the architectural extravagance of the pre-war decades – singling out the enormous and lavishly appointed town halls for his particular scorn. In contrast, said Westheim, the post-war prospects for architecture were bleak. 'Everything will be lacking: cheap money, cheap labour, cheap materials, and, above all, the purchasing power and taxability of the population.'[10] Forecasting a slump in construction immediately after the war, Westheim added that the criteria for any new building would be the maximum of efficiency coupled with the minimum of the simplest materials – a formula on which Taut's housing could not be faulted. Westheim's thesis was shared by Cürlis and Stephany in their book *Die Künstlerischen und*

Wirtschaftlichen Irrwege unserer Baukunst, which Taut cited approvingly in *Die Stadtkrone*.[11]

Two other appeals for simplicity were also written in 1917 – one by Behne, one by Heinrich Tessenow. In his attack on the Werkbund, published in *Die Tat*, Behne dismissed the Werkbund premise that art and industry could be brought together. It was an abuse of art, he said, to attempt to package biscuits in artistic or tasteful wrappers or to 'create' artistic spoons. The only criteria for such things should be function and practicality – not 'taste'.

A spoon is good when it is made from suitable materials, is practical and honest – with the proviso that the best guarantee for the design of such a spoon would be to entrust it to a sensitive modern artist. Of course it would be better! The spoon would be even better still if one no longer bothered about the art in the life of the spoon. The same holds true for art and biscuit wrappers, matchboxes...and garden furniture.[12]

This proposition refuted the whole conception of the Werkbund as a meeting ground where artists, designers and industrialists could come together and, by their joint efforts, elevate the standards of industrial and commercial design. The much vaunted partnership between Behrens and the AEG was, according to Behne, a sham: for art had nothing to do with biscuit packets or garden furniture, or, for that matter, with light fittings or electric kettles.

To emphasize his scorn for 'good taste', Behne went even further, and claimed that the trashy furniture and kitschy knick-knacks which were anathema to the Werkbund were, in fact, preferable to the ghastly good taste of the *Kunstpuritaner*. At least, he said, they were interesting and amusing. 'If I were given the choice between a room designed "artistically" by Bruno Paul and the average, kitsch-filled room, then I would choose the latter: at least it is amusing and holds its surprises. I would choose it not out of contrariness, but by following my true feelings.'[13] As alternatives to the precious artiness of Bruno Paul, Behne advocated ultra-functionalism in the case of the spoon, and an indulgence in kitsch in the case of interior design. Both positions were vigorously anti-intellectual, the former replacing any value judgements by simple criteria of performance, the latter wallowing delightedly in whatever came along.

Behne felt that true art could only appear when all the would-be art and pseudo-artiness had been stamped out. The way forward to the new art was to be found, he said, via the primitive. 'Simply develop a feeling for the primitive in life, and art will appear over the horizon.'[14] Taking up Taut's opposition of the sacred and profane, Behne placed these opposing, yet complementary poles in a reciprocal relationship: the more simple, straightforward and honest the daily life, the more splendid and dazzling the art. 'Isn't that a splendid ambition: to enjoy a plain, simple and practical life, untroubled and without pretensions, finding pleasure in self-sufficiency – and in a magnificently proud, passionate, and illuminating art.'[15] The polemical style of this article and Behne's description of a 'splendid ambition', to be achieved through simplicity and practicality, suggest that, like Taut, he had been influenced by Hiller's writings. Certainly, Behne's appeal to primitivism and creativity echoed a passage in Hiller's proto-Activist tract *Die Weisheit der Langenweile*, in which he suggested that modern man should strive for 'a new naivety, like nature's children in the sphere of culture'.[16]

Behne's call for a return to the simple and the primitive was endorsed in Tessenow's *Handwerk und Kleinstadt*, begun in 1917, completed by Whitsun 1918, and published in 1919. Tessenow's plea for small-towns, *Handwerk*, mutualism and economic autonomy was based on the theories of Kropotkin and Landauer and was, as we shall see, to influence Taut's own work in 1919.

It is clear that Taut's housing scheme for the new town conformed exactly to current thinking on primitivism and austerity. Similarly, his plans for a symbolic city crown or temple can be related to contemporary projects. Obvious antecedents are the Festspielhaus in Bayreuth – opened in 1875, the Mathildenhöhe at Darmstadt (1900–14), Jaques-Dalcroze's music school at Hellerau (designed 1911 by Tessenow), and Steiner's first Goetheanum (1913–20). On a theoretical, unrealized or unrealizable level, Taut's principal source must have been Paul Scheerbart. He would also have known of Theodor Fritsch's scheme for *Die Stadt der Zukunft* (1896), which was also based on a circular, zoned plan,[17] centred around a monumental group comprising public buildings, museums, an opera house, library and 'the cathedral of German Christianity'.[18] Taut was also acquainted with Fidus's plans for theosophical temples, with their vivid use of water, glass and coloured light,[19] and of the fantastic architectural fantasies published by Otto Kohtz in 1909 as *Gedanken über Architecktur*.[20] Kohtz probably shared in Scheerbart a mutual source with Taut. A less obvious, but very interesting source may have been the scheme suggested by the brothers Horneffer for 'Das heilige Haus'. In an article of this name, published in 1912, August Horneffer advocated a return to practical Christianity. One way of achieving this, he said, would be to build new centres and focuses for Christian faith – 'heilige Häuser'. 'Only religion can bring together the divergent cultural components into a unity and create sacred houses with a compelling power of attraction.'[21] As a prototype for the sacred houses, Horneffer suggested the lodges of the medieval masons, which he saw as: 'a model for this close union of devotion, instruction, sociability, festivity, and pleasure in art.'[22] Ernst Horneffer returned to this theme in a long article on freemasonry which appeared in *Die Tat* in two parts in October and November 1912.[23] As a precursor to the subsequent views of Taut and Behne, Horneffer's vision of a new religiosity gained through architecture is extremely striking. 'To comprehend the world through the image of building, to summarize the entire idealism of man in the image of symbolic construction – this idea is so simple and therefore so convincing, that I credit it with an inexhaustible vitality.'[24] As Taut was later to do, he asked: 'Doesn't the symbol of building offer the most profound interpretation of nature which can be imagined? It is a form of worship which reveals the most intimate essence of nature.'[25] Taut himself had contributed to *Die Tat*, and it is likely that he knew of these articles by the journal's former editor.

If similar schemes were suggested by a radical conservative like Fritsch, a mystic and theosophist like Fidus and by Christian freemasons like the Horneffers, then why is Taut's *Stadtkrone* scheme particularly interesting, and in what way is it an Activist plan?

To return to Poggioli's definition of Activism, it was an attempt to redirect the individualistic impulses of Expressionism towards a more practical or tangible goal of social reform. In Taut's case, we have defined his Activism as an attempt to bring together his pre-war, Sturm- and Scheerbart-inspired Expressionist inclinations with his reformist spirit. The plan for the new city clearly did this. The reformist tendencies of the Gartenstadtgesellschaft were represented by the housing; the subjective, Expressionist tendencies by the *Kristallhaus*. The new city, however, was more than an enforced marriage between these two disparate elements.

At a superficial glance, the ideology of primitivism, as expressed in the row-housing, was the very antithesis of the ideology of fantasy – the exotic and doubtlessly very expensive *Kristallhaus*. Taut, however, conceived the two as being intimately related, the former as an expression of *Volk* and of the virtues of the *Volk*, the latter as a physical approximation of *Geist*. This relationship, as already noted, was to be perceived empathetically, as a mutual resonance. Although the resonance was mutual, however, the direction of Taut's social engineering ran from *Volk* to *Geist*, and from there to paradise. As society improved itself through an intensification of *Geist*, so the *Volkswille* would move through *Geist* to paradise.

The two mutually resonant components, *Volk* and *Geist* were, according to Taut, linked through the personality of the architect and through his work. Taut also suggested that this resonance could be given a physical and plastic form through the harmony of colour: 'The glowing light of purity and transcendence shimmers over the carnival of unrefracted, radiant colours. The city spreads out like a sea of colour, as proof of the happiness in the new life.'[26] He offered no details of his proposed colour harmonies, and, as the text was accompanied only by line drawings, there is no way of knowing what he intended. At Falkenberg he had used earth colours – browns, greens, yellows – but it was probably his intention to use stronger tones in the new city, in order to match the intensity of the coloured glass in the *Kristallhaus*. At this time Taut was particularly attracted to the painting of Chagall, and one might guess that Taut would have adopted Chagall's colour range, with dark resonant reds and blues, for his city harmonies. Another possible source was Wilhelm Ostwald's *Farbatlas*, a quasi-scientific theory of colour harmony, which Ostwald described at the 1916 Werkbund conference at Bamberg.[27]

That Taut should have seen no discrepancy between his primitivist and fantastic architecture, between the secular and the sacred, was quite in accord with contemporary Activist thinking. In his collection of aphorisms, written between 1913 and 1922, Kurt Hiller insisted that ecstasy was a precondition for rationalism. 'Rationalism does not exclude ecstasy: no, it needs it. Ecstasy is the motor which sets the machinery of practical reason in motion and keeps it going – its heart.'[28] As Hiller described ecstasy as the motor which sets rationalism in motion, so Taut's *geistig* focus, the *Kristallhaus*, was intended to inspire the *Volk* and the *Volkswille*, and thus move the *Volk* nearer to paradise.

The Activist paradise, furthermore, was not the rural idyll of the *Bodenreformer* or of Tessenow, but was conceived as a well-functioning city. It was an eminently reachable paradise. Hiller made this quite clear in the first of his self-consciously Activistic essays, 'Philosophie des Ziels'. 'Paradise is no Garden of Eden: rather, it looks like a beautiful, broad city...Paradise is not arcadian (although the lover will find the arcadian in it): much more, it displays the most fabulous civilization, with industry, technology, finance, schools, communications – everything.'[29] Hiller's 'attainable paradise' could almost be a description of Taut's new city, and typified the Activists' intention to contain the Expressionist ecstasy and to relate it to practical ends.

10

◇◇◇

The politics of Activism

In his plan for the new city, Taut saw the resonant relationship between *Volk* and *Geist* as an egalitarian relationship. He wrote: 'The architecture becomes a crystalline expression of human stratification. Everything is accessible to everybody. Each person will find a niche according to his desires. There will be no conflict, for people of similar opinions will find each other.'[1] The architecture of the *Stadtkrone* itself reflected, said Taut, the mutualist ideals of the new society, the ideals of the *Gemeinschaft*. Thus the theatre, the opera house and the two *Volkshäuser* were intended to express the social freedom and the natural social intercourse of the *Gemeinschaft*. 'The crowning climax is formed by the massive complex made up of the four large buildings which, in their cruciform plan, can be seen as a symbolic expression of fulfilment. On this plane, the socially orientated aspirations of the *Volk* find their realization.'[2] All four buildings are in harmony both with each other, and with the ideals of the *Volk*. 'The *Volkshäuser* strike a similar note – the full, harmonious tone of human brotherhood.'[3] The *Kristallhaus* – as the architectural embodiment of pure *Geist* was supported, both physically and symbolically by the *Volkshäuser*.

The dream of an harmonious *Menschengemeinschaft* was, as we have seen, the basis of Landauer's romantic socialism. Socialism to Landauer, was synonymous with *Gemeinschaft*, which, itself, was synonymous with the fruitful symbiosis of *Geist* and *Volk*. The gospel of romantic socialism was given expression in *Die Stadtkrone* in the essay 'Aufbau', by Erich Baron, who was Taut's political mentor during the war years.[4] Just as Landauer had claimed that 'The socialist comprehends the whole of society',[5] so Baron, in 'Aufbau', wrote: 'He who loves all forms of existence has become the conscious creator of communal life – he is a socialist. The idealistic aim of romantic, visionary socialism is to succeed in translating the abundance of the heart into an all-penetrating *Geist*.'[6] Taut was very enthusiastic about Baron's contribution, which clearly echoed Taut's own faith in lyrical, romantic socialism – in 'socialism in the non-political, supra-political sense', which he appealed to in his own essay.[7] The degree of Taut's enthusiasm for Baron's visionary essay can be judged from a letter which he wrote to his brother Max in October 1917: 'I've just had a great delight: Baron has given me his manuscript for *Die Stadtkrone*, so everything is now ready. Perhaps I'll send you a copy. The manuscript is very good and heartening, for it shows us our

43 Erich Baron.

world.'[8] For both Taut and Baron, romantic, chiliastic socialism was the contemporary equivalent to and replacement for religion. Taut called it 'Christianity in a new form',[9] and Baron compared it to the transcendental faith of the middle ages: 'Just as medieval man proceeded from religious confession to a higher consciousness, so the social sphere swells and climbs towards the divine – cosmic – artistic universe.'[10]

Obviously, the socialism of Landauer, Taut and Baron in 1916–17 was quite different from the socialism of the political parties. However, if one does compare 'romantic' and 'practical' socialism it becomes clear that they were not only dissimilar, but actually in direct opposition to each other.

Throughout the First World War and the German revolution, the Sozialdemokratische Partei Deutschlands (SPD) and its offshoot, the Unabhängige Sozialdemokratische Partei Deutschlands (USPD), adhered to the Erfurt Programme of 1891. The Erfurt Programme was firmly grounded on Marxist doctrine, and insisted that socialism would be the achievement of the working classes alone: all other classes were bound to property, and thus bound to support the existing social order. This first tenet of the SPD was totally rejected by Landauer, who spurned the orthodoxies of Marxism and the organized politics of the proletarian parties. Landauer damned Marxism as a blind faith in science: 'the man who produced this drug in his laboratory was called Karl Marx. Karl Marx, Professor, has given us a credulous faith in science instead of spiritual knowledge, politics and parties instead of the desire for civilization and culture.'[11] Marx, according to Landauer, was a philistine, and his political theory was nothing more than the philistine worship of technology and technological progress.[12] Landauer also dismissed the Marxist belief in a revolutionary proletariat. Far from being the revolutionary vanguard of society, Landauer identified the urban proletariat as the stronghold of philistinism and parochialism. 'If it came to revolution today, no part of the population would understand less about what was to be done than the industrial proletariat.'[13] In Landauer's analysis, not only did Marxism fail to offer a workable alternative to capitalism, it actually supported capitalism by accepting, as presuppositions, the centralized state and a centralized bureaucracy. This was apparently confirmed in August 1914, when the SPD voted unanimously in favour of war credits and acquiesced in the Kaiser's

Burgfrieden pact – a freezing of the political status quo for the duration of the war.

Landauer was in no doubt as to who should lead the 'romantic' socialists into battle against the philistines – the poets. 'We are poets, and we want to clear away the science-swindlers, the Marxists, the unfeeling, the hollow – those without *Geist*.'[14] This was not only highly antagonistic, it was also supremely élitistic. Only the especially gifted individual, the artist, said Landauer, could give birth to the *Geist* in the *Volk*. 'They were individuals, men of inner might, representatives of the *Volk*, who gave birth to *Geist* in the *Volk*.'[15] The unique role of the artist as a guide and leader of the spiritual development of society at large was also a theme with which Taut had concerned himself. His *Sturm* article of 1914, 'Eine Notwendigkeit', insisted that: 'Great art always exists first in the artist alone. The *Volk* may learn from it themselves, or wait until their teacher arrives.'[16] At the Werkbund conference, later in the same year, Taut attacked Muthesius's position as 'philistine' and 'unfelt' – an echo, perhaps, of Landauer's critique of Marx – and suggested that the future of the Werkbund should be entrusted to a creative élite. He said that instead of elevating the typical and the average to an undeserved pre-eminence, the Werkbund should foster and nurture the skills of the talented few at the top of the pile.

Art represents a pyramid, which widens towards its base. Above, at the apex, stand the most able – the artists with ideas. The broadening base means nothing more than a levelling down of these ideas. On no account can I understand the typical in any other way, and I find it exceedingly depressing that we cannot bring ourselves always to trust simply in the artists at the top.[17]

The sources for Taut's egoist view of the artist's role were Stirner and Nietzsche. Taut's son Heinrich recalls that his father was greatly influenced by Stirner's major work, *Der Einzige und sein Eigentum*, which he re-read on numerous occasions. Taut clearly identified strongly with the Stirnerian egoist, with the isolated leader whose life is sustained by the force of his own imagination and by an inviolable confidence in his own capacity for revolutionary human consciousness.[18]

He was also a convinced Nietzschean. As early as 1904 he wrote to his brother Max: 'I've read Nietzsche's *Zarathustra* over the last three months – a book of enormous and serious vitality. I've learnt a lot from it.'[19] Taut's existing inclination towards Stirner and Nietzsche would have been reinforced at Cologne in 1914 by his contact with Obrist and van de Velde.[20] A few years earlier, J. A. Lux had dubbed Obrist the Max Stirner of the applied arts. Van de Velde had made an intensive study of Nietzsche's writings in the 1880s, and after 1900 became a member of the group of Nietzsche devotees which had assembled around Count Kessler in Berlin. He remodelled the Nietzsche Archive in Weimar in 1903 and between 1910 and 1914 was involved with plans for a Nietzsche monument, also for Weimar. It is illuminating to compare the already quoted extract from Taut's Werkbund conference speech to Nietzsche's description of the artist in 'Wir Künstler'.

It is enough to love, to hate, to desire, simply to experience...we are immediately gripped by the spirit and the power of the dream, and we ascend the most hazardous paths with open eyes and indifferent to all dangers, high onto the roofs and towers of fantasy, without any dizziness, as if born to climb – we sleep walkers of the day! We artists! We concealers of naturalness! We moonstruck and God-struck ones! We deadly silent, indefatigable wanderers on heights that we do not perceive as heights, but as our plains, our places of safety.[21]

Nietzsche's vision of the artist as superman, as a man elevated above normal humanity, found an echo in Taut's pyramid image. It was later to provide the leitmotiv for *Alpine Architektur*.

A further source for the pyramid image was, as Franciscono has shown, Kandinsky's *Über das Geistige in der Kunst*.[22] At the head of the pyramid, said Taut, there should be a dictator. 'I therefore suggest that for all artistic questions, we should arrange to elect a recognized artist as a dictator, whose decision would be absolute...A dictatorship in artistic matters – I am quite certain,...that therein lies the only possible way in which good, artistic values might be promoted.'[23] Taut repeated this call for an artistic dictator in his open letter to the Werkbund conference at Bamberg in 1916. No text survives, but Gropius mentioned Taut's demand in a letter to Osthaus, written in June 1916. Gropius wrote that he found Taut's ideas excellent, but added: 'Only the suggestion of an artistic dictator is, in this form, unwise. I've begged him to moderate this passage in his paper.'[24] In the context of the liberal Werkbund, Taut's call for a dictator struck a jarring and discordant note. In Activist circles, however, it would hardly have raised an eyebrow.

The Activist programme, as formulated principally by Hiller, was vigorously élitist and anti-democratic. Like Taut, Hiller saw in a dictatorship the means of achieving concrete intellectual or social reforms. In an article published in the 1919 *Ziel* yearbook, Hiller praised the direct power of dictatorship and contrasted this strength to the weakness of liberalism. 'Dictatorship also belongs to the permitted means, indeed, it is the means par excellence. Do not tremble at the wrath of this word!...Dictatorship simply means reaching the goal by the most powerful methods – in contrast to flabby "anything-goes", to laissez-faire, to empty, tired liberalism.'[25] This paean to dictatorship was an extreme statement of the Activists' belief in the aristocratic role and status of the artist. The leading Activist theorist, Rudolf Leonhard, wrote in 1919–20: 'The majority of rebels were aristocrats: only aristocrats understand how to rebel; our ideal will be near, when all aristocrats become rebels.'[26] The belief in an aristocracy of *Geist* tied together several strands of the Activist ideology. It stood for the rejection of democracy, which was seen by the Activists as the opponent of *Geist* and of messianic idealism.[27] By its nature, the aristocratic spirit rejected the politics and the culture of the masses, thus endorsing Landauer's attack on the materialism and philistinism of Marxism and proletarian socialism.

In terms of the internal dynamics of Activism, the concept of an aristocracy endorsed the romantic picture of the artist or intellectual as the lone enlightened voice in the philistine crowd. At the same time as Hiller was writing in praise of dictatorship, Landauer was penning this hymn of praise to the poet. 'The poet is the leader in the choir. At the same time, however, he is the splendidly isolated figure who stands his ground against the multitude, like the solo tenor in the Ninth Symphony, who sings his own melody with inexorable momentum above the massed choir. He is the eternal rebel.'[28] This portrayal of the poet as both aristocratic and isolated corresponds exactly to Massimo Bontempelli's general observation that 'the avant-garde is by nature solitary and aristocratic; it loves the initiated and the ivory tower'.[29]

During the war years, Taut clearly cast himself in this role, as isolated, misunderstood, and undervalued. His frame of mind early in 1918 can be judged from a letter which he wrote to Max Taut from Bergisch-Gladbach.

The work at the Stellawerk has now become unbearable and I suspect that they want to get rid of me. But under no circumstances will I co-operate. Everything really looks so totally hopeless for us true architects that the way out appears ever nearer and easier. How loathsome politics now is! Stinking filth. But I *shan't* run away, my *Glanzwelt* lives inside me – even if I take it with me to the grave. Farewell, dear brother, keep your courage. You fit better in the world.[30]

This brief extract is typically avant-gardistic. Taut portrayed himself as a 'pure' artist, oppressed by the mundane world and by the dirty and unpalatable realities of politics. His response was also typically avant-gardistic: to take refuge in a private world, in a private utopia. The last sentence – 'You fit better in this world' – is pure agonism.

As Poggioli has shown, the tendency of the avant-garde towards aristocratic isolation was the response to the alienation – social, economic and political, which society at large imposes upon the avant-garde artist.[31] In his study of Expressionist literature, Walter Sokel has devoted an entire chapter to the theme of alienation. The chapter, entitled 'Poeta Dolorosus', traces the potent mix of Hegelianism and the Judeo-Christian belief in the persecuted prophet-saviour, which went into the Expressionist vision of the artist as isolated genius.[32]

The messianic appeals of the Activists were clearly derived from this Expressionist tradition. Hiller's description of the *Literat* as 'the prophet, the leader' and Taut's description of architecture as a 'priestly...divine calling' are indications that the Activists were casting themselves in the Expressionist role of prophet and saviour, and, by implication, offering themselves for persecution. There were differences, however, for the Activists lacked the fatalism of their Expressionist counterparts, and were thus unable to accept their isolation with the same resigned equanimity. Both Expressionism and Activism had chiliastic roots. As Sokel has written, in the context of Expressionism: 'The crucified is also the saviour. Persecuted at present, he will inherit the kingdom of the elect.'[33] But whereas the Expressionists saw no foreseeable end to their martyrdom, the Activists wanted paradise tomorrow, or, failing that, the next day. Thus the Activists identified themselves with the cult of prophetic genius, yet could not accept the isolation and impotence which went with it. Their solution to this problem was the *Bund* – the formalized group or council.

Shortly after the outbreak of war, Hiller suggested, in an article in *Zeit-Echo*,[34] that the intellectuals should abandon their fondly nurtured individuality and should work together to resolve the crisis brought about by the war. The natural leaders of intellect and *Geist* should form together into a *Bund*. He reiterated his plea in 'Philosophie des Ziels', his first Activist manifesto, in which he questioned the power of the individual against the folly of millions. 'The strong man is strongest when alone? Stupid, most dubious maxim! What is one strong man against millions of weak ones? But only twenty strong men, united in their ardour, would certainly be something against a billion weaklings who simply incorporate a common impotence.'[35] The sole hope for the *geistig* élite in combating the mass genocide was to speak as one united voice, as a *Bund*: 'Geistig men, let us form a *Bund*! This flare (the war is still blustering)...I will shoot this flare into your firmament. Let us form a *Bund*, so that those things over which we have been in agreement for millennia and of which nothing has yet been accomplished, will at last stream into life.'[36] The *Bund*, said Hiller, was the vehicle which would link *Geist* and *Macht*: 'What do we want? Paradise. What achieves it? *Geist*. What is needed in addition? Power. How is power to be won? By working together.'[37] Hiller's desire to order the forces of individualism into some form of coherent group reflects the complex relationship between the alienated, anarchically inclined artist, and the wider society. As Poggioli has noted:

Avant-garde individualism is not strictly libertarian, as its cult of the 'happy few' demonstrates. On one hand, the anarchistic state of mind presupposes the individualistic revolt of the 'unique' *against* society in the largest sense. On the other, it presupposes solidarity *within* a society in the restricted sense of that word – that is to say, solidarity within the community of rebels and libertarians.[38]

The idea of the *Bund*, however, was not only a typically avant-gardistic response to alienation, it was also a current concern of the German intelligentsia.

Hiller's immediate sources for the *Bund* would have included Simmel and Tönnies, as proponents of the antithesis of *Gesellschaft* and *Gemeinschaft*, and, more directly, Hans Blüher and Landauer. Blüher was the historian of the *Wandervogel* movement and subsequently a contributor to *Das Ziel*. This mixture of radical conservatism and romantic socialism is only one example of the appeal which the *Bund* held for both the radical right and the anarchist left. In the pre-war decade the *Bund* was promoted with equal enthusiasm by Avenarius, *Kunstwart* and the Dürerbund, by Diederichs and the *Tat* circle, and by Wyneken, Kropotkin and Landauer.

Hiller's most direct source was Landauer's Sozialistische Bund, which was founded in June 1908. But there were profound differences between the role assigned to the *Bund* by Landauer and that assigned by Hiller. To Landauer, the *Bund* represented the most innocent and natural form of social grouping, freed from any hierarchy or domination. *Bund* and *Gemeinschaft* were indistinguishable to Landauer. In *Aufruf zum Sozialismus* he defined the ideal society as: 'A federation of unions of *Bünden*; a commonwealth of communities of rural communes; a republic made up of republics of republics. Only there is freedom and order, only there is *Geist* – a *Geist* which means autonomy and community, association and independence.'[39] By forming together into groups with mutual interests, society could become self-regulating, said Landauer, without the need for any higher controls, without the state or the police. It was this anarchist view of the *Bund* which Taut adopted for his new city, in which, he said: 'There will be no conflict, for people of similar opinions will find each other.'[40] Although he was also opposed to the state, Hiller could not accept Landauer's idealist, anarchist solution as appropriate to the contemporary political crisis in Germany. Hiller's solution, which mediated between the formlessness of anarchy and the mediocrity and impotence of democracy, was an oligarchy of *geistig* leaders.

In an essay first written in 1917, Hiller offered his plans for the transformation of his belief in a *geistig* élite into a political programme. The essay was entitled 'Ein deutsches Herrenhaus'.[41] Hiller had taken both the idea and the title from the Berlin historian Kurt Breysig, who had suggested in 1912 that a *Herrenhaus* should be established, encompassing the religious, political and creative leaders of the nation.[42] Alfred Wolfenstein, a co-founder, with Hiller, of the Activist movement, wrote enthusiastically about this suggestion in *Die Aktion*.[43] Breysig's plan involved the established churches, political parties and cultural leaders. Hiller was more selective. He insisted that the *geistig* élite alone were the natural rulers of society: 'The more *geistig* the man, the more he is destined for power.'[44] The core of Hiller's argument was a long harangue against democracy, and on the impossibility of achieving a representative government via constituencies and democratic elections. Instead of the ponderous and inefficient system of parliamentary elections, Hiller suggested that the *geistig* élite should unite and proclaim themselves as the new leaders. 'This is history, albeit the history of the future. An upper chamber!...No one had appointed it, no one had elected it: one day the competent people met and said: we are it.'[45] Hiller thus translated the Expressionist idea of creative leadership into the programme for a new political élite.

The relationship of this élite to the mass of the population depended on the mutual resonance of *Geist* and *Volk*. As Hiller had already explained in 'Philosophie des Ziels':

The *geistig* man is a function of the *Volk*: in him the *Volk* is made aware of its needs, it thinks through him. For this reason, *Geist* can never be a tyrannical ruler. From the outset, his power is tacitly conferred on the *geistig* man by the *Volk*. It cannot do otherwise than appoint him as its leader, for his is the vitality of the *Volk*, its base and crown.[46]

Just as in Taut's city plan the *Kristallhaus* acted as the crown of the city, so Hiller's *geistig* man was to be the crown of the *Volk*. The *Volk*, however, was not synonymous with the masses – dismissed by Hiller with suitably aristocratic disdain as 'feeble-minded and immoral',[47] but, rather, represented the higher aspirations, the *Gemeinschaftswille*, of the people.

But the *Volk* had no powers of leadership. Adopting the pyramid analogy also favoured by Kandinsky and Taut, Hiller insisted that society could only be improved by example from above, not by grass-roots reform. 'It remains a mistake to try to cultivate the pyramid of human society from the base up. The more effective way is to work from the top.'[48] However, in order to articulate the mystical rapport between *Geist* and *Volk*, Hiller advocated a two-tier system. The lower one was to be the *Volkshaus*, which was to be a microcosm of the *Volk*, and responsible for the day-to-day administration of commerce, industry, and economic planning. It was also conceived as a 'source of information for the *Herrenhaus*'.[49] The function of the *Herrenhaus* was far more esoteric. Composed of the spontaneously self-chosen élite,[50] its mission was spiritual and philosophical, to ennoble society, to elevate the *Volk* to an ever-higher level of *Geistigkeit*.

The symbiosis of *Volk* and *Geist* through the *Volkshaus* and the *Herrenhaus* was given physical form by Taut with his plan for the *Stadtkrone*. The *Kristallhaus*, representing the spiritual strata of *Geist*, was supported by two *Volkshäuser*. Thus the realm of *Geist* was grounded on the firm base of the *Volk*, whilst the practical deliberations which would be conducted in the *Volkshaus* would take place in the reflected glow and inspiration streaming out of the spiritual focus – the *Kristallhaus* or *Herrenhaus*. As Taut explained: 'The *Volkshäuser* possess the full, harmonic tone of the human community. In them, *Geist* and soul should be elevated and matured, in order to transmit their wondrousness to all men.'[51]

Hiller's *bündisch* aspirations took a first step towards reality in the summer of 1917, with the foundation of the Bund zum Ziel. The group of Activists which had centred around Hiller and *Das Ziel* met between 10 and 12 August 1917, in a villa in Berlin-Westend, and formed themselves into a *Bund*. The *Leitsätze* (guiding principles) which were drawn up at the time stated the intentions of the Bund: 'The Bund zum Ziel is the active community of *geistig* orientated men, to whom *Geist* is not a game of perception or of pretty forms, but means ethical activity: a force which is not introspective, but rather concentrates on the transformation of reality, on changing the world.'[52] Hiller subsequently described these guiding principles as 'the outcome of a preliminary discussion of the (expanded) Ziel-Circle', but gave no indication as to who was actually there. All that is known is that the *Leitsätze* carried twenty-eight signatures. Hiller's subsequent reluctance to give names probably derived from the split in the Activist camp which occurred in the winter of 1917 as a direct result of the revolution in Russia.

The success of the Russian Revolution led a number of Activists away from their previously held, aristocratic positions and turned them into fervent advocates of proletarian revolution. A list of converts would include Becher, Frank, Rubiner and Taut's collaborator, Erich Baron, who abandoned the romantic socialism of the war years and, in 1925, became the General Secretary of the Gesellschaft der Freunde des neuen Rußland.[53]

Even before the war, the Expressionists had hailed the life on the Russian soil as a model of Christian *Gemeinschaft*. Sokel has noted the influence on Trakl, Kafka and Kornfeld of the 'mythical-demonic' Russia of Dostoyevsky, and saw in the works of Rubiner, Goll, Becher and Frank an echo of the Russia of Tolstoy and the village *mir*. Sokel commented: 'But within and beyond the Russian experience in either form lay that which both Dostoyevsky and Tolstoy proclaimed and the village community represented – the image of the fraternal way of life of apostolic Christianity.' He concluded: 'For the German Expressionists, Russia pointed the way back to Christ.'[54] This Expressionist infatuation with Russia, when combined with a successful revolution, gave a massive stimulus to the chiliastic expectations of the *Literaten* and intellectuals in Germany.

In the period between October 1917 and November 1918, however, there was little exact information to be had in Germany as to the true nature of structure of the new Russian society. As a result, an idealized picture of revolutionary Russia was created, a picture which was based more on wish-projection than on facts.

For example, Adolf Behne, ever susceptible to the fashion of the moment, leapt in during the winter of 1917 with an enthusiastic greeting to the new Russian *Volk*. In an article in the *Sozialistische Monatshefte*, he wrote: 'The conscience has awoken in Russia. The *Volk* has awoken in Russia. Both are the same...The fact that it was the *Volk* which first did the new, courageous and honest deed is profoundly gratifying. It points to the way which we have to go: from society to *Volk*, from classes and status to unity.'[55] As if to unite the revolutionary Russian *Volk* with the idealized view of the Orient nurtured by contemporary German intellectuals, Behne cited Ku Hung Ming's approval of the Russian people: 'the Russians, whom the Chinaman Ku Hung Ming named in his extraordinarily valuable book, as the best, healthiest, most amiable and most generous nation in Europe'.[56] Behne concluded his article: 'The awakening of the conscience in a great nation is an act of the deepest inner strength, which we may witness only with emotion.'[57] Behne followed this first piece up with a series of articles on Russian art and architecture which were published in the *Sozialistische Monatshefte* in 1918. The articles were little more than a series of potted essays on the history of Russian painting and design. At that stage, Behne had no knowledge of or information about recent Russian activity in the arts.[58]

More interesting than Behne's speculative articles, but still in a similarly idolatrous vein, was an account written by Taut of a visit to Kowno.[59] It was published in the *Sozialistische Monatshefte* in September 1918. In his earlier account of his visit to Constantinople, Taut had described the Orient as the 'true mother of Europe'.[60] By 1918, this maternal role was given over to Russia. Taut's first sentence began: 'At the threshold of Mother Russia'.[61] In Kowno, Taut was enraptured by the simplicity and naivety of the wooden buildings, and by the brightly coloured decorations on them. Although he admitted that Kowno was only on the fringes of Russia, he took the example of Kowno as representative of Russian culture as a whole.

> Certainly, all this is only at the periphery of the great Russian culture. But look at the brilliant ultramarine blue, red, brown, green and yellow painted shutters on the doors and windows. Everything is brightly and prettily painted in a naive, childlike manner – the marvellous architecture of the town hall also has this childlike charm. It is folk art: some shop signs have such artistic directness and are so full of expression, that they could have been painted by Henri Rousseau.[62]

Following on from his analysis of the *Roland* at Brandenburg and his account of Constantinople, Taut explained the roots of this folk art vitalistically. It was part of, and the direct result of true 'life': 'Only where there is life is there art: real life – not life hemmed in by abstractions.'[63] The moral was clearly drawn: 'The *Volksgeist* speaks clearly enough in everything: Live! Live for the moment! This living is everything, and itself remains art.'[64] This idealized picture of post-revolutionary Russia was one of an innocent and harmonious *Volk* striving via their simple, natural form of life towards *Geist*. Thus socialism in Russia was equated, at least at this stage, with the socialism of the Activists. The Russian Revolution was seen to have vindicated the Activist philosophy of a progression, through *Geist*, from *Volk* to paradise. In addition, the Russian culture was seen by German observers to combine both the 'fraternal way of life of apostolic Christianity' with the transcendental wisdom of the Orient, thus reinforcing both these models as paradigms for the eagerly awaited new age.

The chiliastic expectations stimulated by the revolution in Russia found apparent justification with the outbreak of revolution in Germany in November 1918, and the Activists moved quickly to exploit the new situation.

Part 3

November 1918–April 1919,
Activism and political engagement

11

The Politischer Rat geistiger Arbeiter and the Arbeitsrat für Kunst

Kurt Hiller called a second conference of the Bund zum Ziel for the 7 and 8 November 1918: it was held in the Nollendorfkasino, Berlin-Tiergarten. The purpose of the conference was to define the exact direction which the movement should take and thus stimulate concrete action and political involvement. A programme of demands and aims was drawn up and the title Bund zum Ziel was abandoned in favour of Aktivistenbund. What followed was best described by Hiller, in his own account of the conference and the days following it:

The next day brought the fall of the Kaiser, which seemed to us at the time to be the revolution. In a frenzy of optimism the group convened on 10 November in the Reichstag as the Rat geistiger Arbeiter – a name which was then widely misunderstood and even more widely abused. In order to differentiate itself from political neutrals, those without ethical direction, and from the professional interest groups of the 'intelligentsia', the group shortly afterwards adopted the name Politischer Rat geistiger Arbeiter [Political Council of *geistig* Workers].[1]

The change of name from Aktivistenbund to Politischer Rat geistiger Arbeiter was a response to the revolutionary fever of the moment and the success of the workers' and soldiers' councils, which had met on the same day in the Circus Busch, and had agreed on a radical programme of government by council rather than by a constituent assembly.

The intention of the Politischer Rat geistiger Arbeiter (RGA) was to align itself with the workers' and soldiers' councils and to gain political influence through the central revolutionary council. For a brief spell they appeared to be succeeding in their aim, principally through the influence of Hans-Georg von Beerfelde. Beerfelde was briefly at the head of the executive committee (*Vollzugsausschuss*) in the central revolutionary council. He was also sympathetic to the Activists and assigned a room in the Reichstag to them on 10 November. When he fell from power five days later, the RGA was evicted.[2]

The programme of the RGA was a manifesto-like reiteration of the Activist philosophy as it had first been outlined by Hiller in 1915 in 'Philosophie des Ziels'.[3] The principal targets of the programme were war and capitalism, which were seen to be intimately related. Other demands were for free sexuality, for the abandonment of the death penalty and for a fairer penal system, and for a radical reform of education. The kernel of the Activist education system was to be the

44 The workers' and
soldiers' councils in the
Reichstag, 26 December
1918.

'Kulturschule', whose function was described in the programme as:
'not so much schools for learning as schools for thinking, more to
indicate the way into the future than for the study of history, less
concerned with vocational training than with training for a life of ideas.
Removal of the dominating relationship of teacher to pupil. Extensive
participation of students in the administration of the school.'[4] Above the
schools, the universities would function as 'strongholds of *Geist*'.[5]

Following on from the principles outlined in Hiller's 'Ein deutsches
Herrenhaus', the RGA programme advocated a two-tier system of
government. The lower chamber was to be the *Reichstag*, based on free
elections and proportional representation.[6] Controlling the *Reichstag*
would be the *Rat der Geistigen*, whose function would be 'to remove the
danger of an encroachment by one-sided, economic viewpoints on
cultural politics, and to offset the damage caused by the torpor of party
bureaucracy'.[7] The *Rat der Geistigen*, like the *Herrenhaus*, would be
founded on autogenesis. The *geistig* élite would gather together and
simply declare itself to be the *Rat der Geistigen*. 'It will be created neither
by nomination nor by election, but by intrinsic right, which derives from
the duty of *Geist* to help. It will renew itself according to its own law.'[8]
The programme carried some sixty signatures. The signatories clearly
saw themselves as the base on which the *Rat der Geistigen* would be
founded. Most of them were drawn from literary circles – Kasimir
Edschmid, Otto Flake, Wilhelm Herzog, Kurt Hiller, Rudolf Kayser,
Rudolf Leonhard, Robert Musil, Heinrich Mann, René Schickele, Fritz
von Unruh. There were a number of educationalists and sociologists,
including Magnus Hirschfeld and Gustav Wyneken, one painter –
Ludwig Meidner, and one architect – Bruno Taut.

The Arbeitsrat für Kunst (AFK) was founded on the model of the RGA
towards the end of November, 1918. It seems certain that Taut was the
founder of the group. During the first six months of its existence, the

leaders of the AFK were Taut, Gropius, Behne and Valentiner, and it
has been variously suggested that either Behne or Gropius were
co-founders with Taut, or even that they founded the AFK without
Taut's initial involvement. Franciscono, for example, cites Lothar Lang
who named Behne as the progenitor of the group.[9] But Behne's name
was not on either of the lists of members which was published in
December 1918, and there is documentary evidence that Gropius joined
the already established group, and was not involved in its inception. In
a letter to Osthaus, written on 23 December, Gropius wrote: 'In the
Arbeitsrat für Kunst, which I have joined, there is at present a
sympathetically radical atmosphere, and productive ideas are being put
forward.'[10]

Thus Taut, rather than Behne or Gropius, was the founder of the AFK
and, from the outset, its ideological and political mentor. Taut's own
model, in turn, was the RGA. The initial structuring of the AFK reflected
Taut's credo that architecture could reconcile *Geist* and *Volk* and could
also unite the other arts under its aegis in order to achieve this
reconciliation. In accordance with this credo, the AFK was headed by
an 'architecture panel', led by Taut himself. Under the architecture
panel were several subordinate sections, each devoted to one branch of
the arts.

Taut's views on the role of architecture in the new socialist state can
be judged from an article which he wrote for the *Sozialistische Monatshefte*,
entitled 'An die sozialistische Regierung'. It appeared at the end of
November 1918 – more or less contemporaneously with the founding
of the AFK, and must have been written, therefore, in the early days
of the revolution, when the *Regierung* meant the central revolutionary
council. Of all Taut's writings, this article expressed most exactly the
Activist philosophy.

It began with the assertion that there was a higher life-force, which
should unite education, religion and art. 'A pure and noble conception
must reign over everything.'[11] This higher life-force must rise, said Taut,
Phoenix-like out of the dust of the old, materialist age, and must be given
a tangible form. 'The new rebuilding must be led clearly and resolutely.
A great design must guide all the forces involved – a ministry of *geistig*
affairs, new in its resolve and in its intellectual make-up, which will
influence education, teaching, the church and art in the new Germany.'[12]
Taut's 'ministry of *geistig* affairs' was intended as a formalized version
of Hiller's *Herrenhaus* and of the *Rat der Geistigen* of the RGA. But
whereas the RGA concentrated on the moral and ethical guidance of
the new society through a *geistig* élite, Taut was concerned with the
physical and material forms which the society would take. 'Rebuilding
is the watchword of the moment: the rebuilding of the material world
under the supreme control of the spiritual. The material world is *Geist*
which has become substance.'[13] The mission of the Activist architect
was to unite *Geist* and material in order to give *Geist* a physical
expression. Taut cited the contemporary need for 750,000 dwellings as
symbolic of the need to rebuild and reconstruct society. But even the

comparatively simple task of building houses should not be seen merely as a utilitarian necessity, but rather as one part of a larger programme of physical, and therefore spiritual, regeneration. Taut's language was particularly Activist at this point: 'The *geistig* leadership must define the aim, so that the movement doesn't get bogged down in crude materialism. The aim must be a new culture. The great movement would soon falter without a long-term objective, gleaming magnificently in the distance.'[14] But the Activist call was for activity, for practical action now: 'But we mustn't, as with the old ideals, merely praise them to heaven, we must begin.'[15] What was needed, said Taut, was a long-term spiritual aim on which a beginning could be made immediately. He did not see the contemporary shortage of capital or materials as a problem. On the contrary, the lack of material resources would act, inversely, as a stimulus to a greater expenditure of will and *Geist*. He quoted Kropotkin on the origins of Cologne Cathedral: 'Cologne Cathedral was begun with an annual expenditure of only 500 Marks.'[16] Just as the medieval church had embarked on massive cathedrals on an incremental basis, so the new régime should begin work on the first stages of a great *Volkshaus*, which would be the highest expression of *Geist* which has become substance', the focus for the new age of *Geist*.

It will be the duty of a true Minister of Culture to call this great project into life: a great *Volkshaus* on a large, open site, made up of several buildings for theatre, music and worship. The building will be conceived by the genuine artists of the period and will be both a symbol and, in its organic evolution, a manifestation and a focus for our age. All the arts will be united here under the wing of a new, crystal-clear architecture: it will be a symbol for science, for religion, for everything. Architecture is the plastic expression of the age, for all of us – all of us who work and dream are builders, builders of a new culture.[17]

The relationship between the *Volkhaus* and the much-needed housing followed the theories already established in *Die Stadtkrone*: the one would magnify the other.

Taut's vision of the unifying role of architecture in the rebuilding of the new society provided the basis for the first programme of the AFK: 'Art and *Volk* must form a unity. Art should no longer be the delight of the few, but the good fortune and the life of the masses. The aim is the fusion of the arts under the wing of a great architecture.'[18] The entire programme was founded on Activist presuppositions. Enemy number one was the state, which was to be relieved of its control over art and architectural education (AFK Programme, Demand no. 3). The Royal Academy of Arts, the Royal Academy of Building and the Royal Prussian Commission for Art were to be dissolved, and replaced by committees or councils of practising artists, who would be free from state control (Demand no. 2). In addition, the civil servants in the above institutions and the building inspectors (*Baupolizei*) would lose their former privileges (Demand no. 1). The pacifist base of Activism was represented by a demand to prevent the building of ill-conceived war memorials or museums (Demand no. 5).

Having taken control over architecture and the arts away from the old state apparatus, the AFK intended to seize control itself. Following the example of the Activists and the RGA, Taut's new group insisted that only the creative élite was competent to decide questions concerning the visual arts. Thanks to the mystical resonance between *Geist* – represented by the artist – and *Volk*, the artist alone was able to comprehend the visual needs of the new, harmonious society. 'From now on, the artist alone, as moulder of the sensibilities of the *Volk*, will be responsible for the visible fabric of the new state. He must determine the form-giving process, from the statue right down to the coin and the postage stamp.'[19] Taking its lead, once again, from the Activists, and from Taut's addresses to the Werkbund in 1914 and 1916, the AFK aspired to hold absolute control over the arts in the new state. The supreme authority in this dictatorship by a creative élite must be given to architecture.

This was the theme of the first *Flugschrift* of the AFK, Taut's 'Architektur-Programm', which was also written and published in December 1918. Architecture, said Taut, was uniquely suited to articulate and give form to the demands for a revolution based on *Geist*. 'The immediate vehicle of the *geistig* forces and moulder of the sensibilities of the general public, which today are slumbering and tomorrow will awake, is architecture.'[20] Following on from this first premise, Taut went on to detail his plans for experimental architecture, subsidized by the state and directly involving lay-participation, for *Volkshäuser* and *Siedlungen*, for planning architectural education and for the introduction of architects and architectural thinking into all spheres of the arts. All this led Taut to the conclusion that: 'The increased importance of the architect in public life through the holding of important posts and offices will result automatically from the implementation of this programme.'[21] In the short-term, however, the exact opposite was the case, and it was necessary for an architect, namely Taut, to achieve a position of political influence, in order to push through the programmes of the AFK.

It was clearly Taut's ambition from the outset that the AFK should have a direct political role as part of the Ministry of Culture such as he had described in his article 'An die sozialistische Regierung'. In a speech which he made in July 1919, Taut looked back on his early plans for the AFK and affirmed that he sought a direct governmental role: 'Initially, the Arbeitsrat für Kunst wished to exercise direct influence on the government.'[22] In the hope of achieving this, the AFK sent a deputation to Kulturminister Hoffmann (SPD) in the early days after the revolution. The meeting was a fiasco. Hermann Schmitz recorded the scene:

One example of a predictably unsuccessful frontal attack by the republican intelligentsia on the bastion of ministerial might, was the delightful scene of the reception, a few days after the abdication, of a deputation from the Arbeitsrat für Kunst in the new Ministry for Science, Art and Education. In spite of their urgency, the deputation from the group of artists and intellectuals, which had modelled itself on the workers' and soldiers' councils, unfortunately arrived a minute late. They were asked to wait behind a folding screen in the ante-room to Minister Hoffmann's office until the heads of the former Royal Museum – His Excellency Wilhelm von Bode and his successor, Privy Councillor Otto von Falke – who had just arrived with equal haste, were received by the Minister Hoffmann in order to have their positions ratified. The deputation, which was made up of Taut, Gropius and Valentiner, were then admitted to 'ten-commandments' Hoffman, who was surrounded by his advisers, and presented him with the comprehensive programme for the renewal of the official policy on art. Before the Minister had worked out how to reply, Nentwig, the Ministerial Director, turned to the revolutionary gentlemen with the request that they should specify their recommendations. As they were not in a position to do this, he dismissed them with the assurance that he would 'put their programme in the files, so that it might be given sympathetic consideration at the appropriate time'.[23]

The lack of a specific political programme reflected not merely muddled thinking, but also the recurrent Activist theme that *Geist* was incompatible with the existing political parties and the existing political bureaucracies.

During the war years, the Activists used the term socialism to describe an institutionalized idealism which derived from pacifism. The socialism of the Activists was neither an economic system nor a political movement in the usual sense of the term. In his essay 'Ortsbestimmung des Aktivismus', written in June 1918, Hiller insisted that the true socialism of *Geist* had nothing whatever to do with the parties.

'Socialism' – that is neither the mentality of trade union secretary Piefke, nor the crudeness of the expropriating mob, nor the doctrine of any cosy Marxists, who deny *Geist* and preach that progress will appear of its own accord thanks to the power of the economic system. Socialism is no party doctrine but a way of thinking; it is the focusing of the soul on fraternity.[24]

With the unexpected success of the revolution, the Activists were forced to come to terms with party political decisions. Not surprisingly, they opted for the USPD as the only vehicle through which they could exert influence on behalf of the politics of *Geist*.

Taut, like the other Activists, held initial hopes of achieving political influence through the USPD. Indeed, the founding manifesto of the *AFK* was first published on 12 December in *Die Freiheit*, the daily paper of the USPD. Of the USPD leaders, Taut was most attracted to Georg Ledebour.[25] Even within the USPD – a party which constantly vaunted its independence, Ledebour was a particularly independent spirit. From the beginning of the revolution he was against any co-operation with the SPD, was a vigorous advocate of the council system, and was equally vigorously opposed to a constituent assembly. After the congress of councils decided in favour of parliamentary government in December 1918, Ledebour joined the revolutionary committee, which called the general strike in January 1919 and demanded the overthrow of the Ebert-Scheidemann government and its replacement by the committee. The three presidents of the revolutionary committee were Scholze, Ledebour and Liebknecht. For his part in the January uprising Ledebour

45 Georg Ledebour speaking from the terrace of the Royal Palace, Berlin, January 1919.

was arrested on the night of 10–11 January and was tried in May for high treason. Thanks to the brilliance of his own defence, he was acquitted. He continued to work as a free-agent on the left of the USPD but to the right of the Spartacists. Significantly, he refused to join the KPD at the Halle Conference in October 1920, when the USPD joined the Third International.

Ledebour's position, on the libertarian left wing of the USPD, but opposed to Bolshevism, was also the position held by Taut during the revolutionary period. In his 'Architektur-Programm', Taut suggested that control over both public and private building should be the responsibility of a council made up of equal numbers of architects and laymen. The casting vote would rest with a chosen layman (Demand II C). This council would also be empowered to give architectural commissions or promote competitions (Demand IV B). Similarly, the adjacent disciplines, like town-planning, were to be entrusted to an advisory council (Demand IV C).

The political context of Taut's 'Architektur-Programm', however, did not derive exclusively from Ledebour's ideas on council government: the 'Programm' also contained a marked element of anarcho-socialism. In the context of the architecture councils, Taut said that: 'Only mutual aid makes a community fruitful and active. It is much more important than the number of votes, which means nothing without social cohesion.'[26] The obvious source is Kropotkin, whom Taut had already cited in 'An die sozialistische Regierung'. Taut's quotation was taken from Landauer's translation of Kropotkin's tract on mutual aid, published in 1904 as *Gegenseitige Hilfe in der Entwicklung*. On the same page as he mentioned the starting capital for Cologne Cathedral, Kropotkin described the medieval cathedrals in terms which Taut echoed in his description of the *Volkshaus*. 'A cathedral or a town hall was the symbol of the greatness of an organism: it was conceived by every single bricklayer and stone mason.' The cathedral was built 'to glorify the greatness of the victorious city, to symbolize the unity of the city's craftsmanship'.[27] Similarly, Taut wrote of the *Volkshaüser* that: 'The pride of the social republic should find a symbol in these *Volkshaüser*.'[28] Taut insisted, furthermore, that the *Volkshaüser* should not be built in the city, but on the land. 'They cannot stand in the city, for the city itself is rotten and will at some time disappear, just like the old institutions of power. The future lies on the newly accessible tracts of land, which can support themselves.'[29] Once again Taut's source was Kropotkin, whose tract *Das Feld, die Fabrik und die Werkstatt* was an appeal for a return to rural communities.

12

The politics of decentralization

In contrast to the Marxist theoreticians, who saw the struggle for socialism in terms of the industrial worker and in control of the industrial process, the anarcho-socialists saw the fight for socialism as a fight for land. As Landauer insisted in his *Aufruf zum Sozialismus*: 'The socialist struggle is a struggle for the soil; the social question is an agrarian question.'[1] Socialism on the land, said Landauer, could free itself from the money economy and could establish an equitable system of exchange, with capital replaced by mutual credit on the model of Proudhon. The virtues of the rural community were set in a markedly historicist context by Landauer. In idolizing the future socialism on the land, he also idolized the primitive communism of the middle ages. 'The socialist settler should simply move into the existing villages, and it will become clear that they can be rejuvenated once again, that the *Geist* which they possessed in the 15th and 16th centuries can also stir again today.'[2] The historicist golden age was to act as a model for the new age of the spirit.

Taut's advocacy of decentralization in his 'Architektur-Programm' linked the political principles of the left wing of the USPD to the mutualism and anarcho-socialism of Kropotkin and Landauer. There was a clear parallel between the council system of government and a decentralized programme for rebuilding. Both shunned the idea of a single central authority, or central focus. Just as Landauer rejected the notion of an elected parliamentary assembly, sitting in Berlin and administering the entire country, so Taut rejected the idea of the large city and the tyrannical influence which it imposed on the economic, cultural and political life of the nation.

It would be wrong, however, to suggest that the ideology of decentralization was the sole preserve of the radical USPD and anarcho-socialists. Before the war it had been advocated by the liberal reformers in the Dürerbund and had been the first presupposition of the Gartenstadtgesellschaft. Even Scheerbart wrote two essays which suggested that the coming of aerial warfare had put the great cities in the front line of any future war. His solution was to decentralize, to settle the population in small communities spread over the countryside. He added that it would be no great tragedy to abandon the cities, as they were the prime sources of human misery and degradation.[3]

Scheerbart's theories of vulnerability to air attack were not tested in the war. The cities, however, proved chronically vulnerable to the food shortages which resulted from the allied blockade. The starvation in the cities reinforced, on physical grounds, the anti-city lobby which had developed before the war on moral grounds. A number of right-wing, reformist groups flourished during the war, all espousing the cause of decentralization: for example, the Deutscher Schafferbund, the Greifenbund. The union of *Bund*-ish ideals and decentralization in the theories of nationalistic, anti-semitic and anti-intellectual groups exactly coincided with the espousal of almost identical theories by Landauer and by the Activists. For example, the stated intention of the Deutsche Siedlungsgemeinschaft was to return to the model of the 'traditional German farm', which was admired as the paradigm of the good society where money was less important than mutual aid, a sense of belonging, and the intense fellowship which unites a small and close-knit community. 'Fellowship – mutualism – is in the widest sense a power which is not only equal to money, but even far superior to it.'[4] Simplicity was to be the keystone of the whole movement: 'It is essential to point out that our settlements must be marked by a simplicity of the sort that has been developed by the *Wandervogel* and the *Neudeutsche Jugend* into a new German life-style.'[5] As in the pre-war schemes of the Gartenstadt-gesellschaft, the architectural mainstay of the decentralized *Siedlungen* was the self-contained house. The Siedlungsgemeinschaft recommended: 'We advise all those young men and women who live alone in the city to make a pilgrimage with like-minded fellows to the communal garden cities, and to acquire there a house of their own with a garden.'[6] To enlighten the prospective buyer on what form the housing would take, ground plans by Bruno Taut were included in the same article – obtained, presumably, from the Gartenstadtgesellschaft.

As we have already seen, the worsening economic situation stimulated a critical reappraisal of the architectural indulgence of the *Gründerzeit*. Muthesius's *Handarbeit und Massenerzeugnis* was one example of this reappraisal. He followed this in 1918 by a small book, *Kleinhaus und Kleinsiedlung*, in which he praised the economies of simple row-housing. Simplicity, to Multhesius, meant rural dwelling, founded on self-help and a high degree of autonomy.

These were ambitions which were by no means limited to the intelligentsia – either on the left or the right. Indeed, Muthesius's book was prefaced by a directive which Hindenburg had issued in June 1918: 'The well-being of the nation consists not in a small number of great capitalists, but in the highest possible number of able, independent, settled and contented citizens, who provide the state with that which it needs above all else: men healthy in body and soul.'[7] In 1915, the State of Prussia had officially endorsed the current interest in returning to the land by passing the 'Rentengutsgesetzgebung'. This act was designed to enable families of slender means to acquire small-holdings. The act offered generous credit with low interest and low premiums. Several colonies were set up on the land,[8] aided by the recent installation of electric current. The Gartenstadtgesellschaft were quick to note that

46 Heinrich Tessenow,
drawing of a terraced house,
1908.

the possibilities for decentralization were greatly enhanced by the
coming of electricity to rural areas. In 1915 the committee recognized
that:

Electricity, the great reformer, and in particular the long-range power-station,
gives the technical ability to improve the economically false distribution of the
population and of industrial activity in the German provinces through a planned
decentralization based on garden cities. Only through the union of agricultural,
handcraft and industrial activity, made possible by this form of community, can
the necessary potential for settlement be created in large areas of our country,
especially in the Ostmark.[9]

It is clear that decentralization and a return to the land was a vision
which preoccupied both the extreme right and the extreme left in the
political spectrum; the former following in the tradition of Riehl,
Lienhard, Bartels; the latter in the tradition of Proudhon and Kropotkin.

Just how unclear and, indeed, unhelpful the usual political distinctions
are in analysing the decentralist urge can be seen in the case of Heinrich
Tessenow, who was an important influence on Taut during the
revolutionary period. Tessenow's pre-war work linked him to the radical
conservative ideology of the *Heimatkunst* movement, and his designs
shared more affinity with those of Riemerschmid and Schultze-Naumburg
than with the early works of Bruno Taut. The war, however, affected
Tessenow in the same way that it affected Taut and literary Activists,

and the result was a book which was markedly Activist in spirit, and which fused together the ideology of Heimatkunst with the anarcho-socialism of Kropotkin.

The book, entitled *Handwerk und Kleinstadt*, was completed at Whitsun 1918 and published the following year. All the main Activist themes are to be found in it. Although the final German offensive was still making some headway at the time the book was completed, Tessenow was certain that the cataclysm was imminent and advised that plans should be drawn up for the new society which would have to be created out of the ruins of the Wilhelmine empire. The time for reconstruction was then – or never: a view which Tessenow expressed in chiliastic terms: 'The either–or was perhaps never more important than it is today; either we create something which is truly like the kingdom of heaven, or we create a hell.'[10] The earthly paradise was defined by Tessenow as a small town whose industries were predominantly based on *Handwerk*. As far as possible, the towns should be self-sufficient economically, and able to provide all the food necessary for their survival. As Tessenow noted: 'It is an ancient demand that every individual body should be as far as possible organic or autonomous, able to live on its own resources for as long as possible. In contrast, the large city fails in this demand, for it can hardly exist for a week without importing food from outside.'[11] In support of his theories on *Handwerk* and autonomy, Tessenow cited Kropotkin's *Landwirtschaft, Industrie und Handwerk*. 'This book has been translated into German by Gustav Landauer and is to be particularly recommended for its discussion of specific agricultural questions.'[12] Like Landauer, Baron and the Activists, Tessenow condemned the conception of the centralized state and the concomitant political system. Also like Landauer, Taut and Baron, he saw the war as the inevitable and ultimate expression of the repressive state. 'It is absolutely correct when it is said that war is simply politics with other weapons. All politics are from the outset warlike.'[13] The harmful influence of industrialization and the development of the modern state and its political and educational systems had distorted the development of man: *Geist* had been destroyed in favour of specialization. 'Today we are the most talented technicians and engineers, the most powerful warriors, most cold-blooded traders, sensitive painters, musicians and so on. We are great specialists, but we are not at all great, are not great men, for as specialists we lack harmony and diversity.'[14] To illustrate his idea of *Geist* – of a harmonious intellect, Tessenow produced an ingenious metaphor – a sphere. 'The human or pure *geistig* essence is unportrayable, but we do have a form which directly corresponds to the pure *geistig*, which is itself completely perfect as a form and is therefore analogous to the pure *geistig* essence: it is the sphere.'[15] According to this theory, the original, pure and simple man, the *Urmensch*, developed an outer aura as he developed his physical and intellectual abilities. When a man is in a state of harmony the outer aura is also spherical, as the antipodal forces which act on it – mental/physical, contemplative/active, feeling/intellect – are all in perfect balance. However, modern man, bemoaned Tessenow, had lost these balances and the outer sphere had been distorted in one direction or another, favouring one activity or specialization at the expense of its counterpart. By means of cross-sectional drawings of the central sphere and the surrounding aura, Tessenow portrayed the plight of twentieth-century man, and contrasted it with 'das große Ganze' – two perfect and concentric spheres: 'ever expanding until the infinity of space is permeated with *Geist* and we have thereby exculpated all wordly concerns'.[16] The circle and the sphere: recurring symbols for the millenarian dream of perfect peace and harmony.

Tessenow was at the centre of a libertarian cult which enjoyed a brief success in Berlin prior to the revolution. He then became a founder member of the Arbeitsrat für Kunst, and it seems likely that he excercised a strong influence on both the foundation programme and on Bruno Taut's 'Architektur-Programm'. Taut's insistence on decentralized *Siedlungen*, on *Volkshäuser* as pure symbols of *Geist*, on mutual aid and on 'the fundamental subordination of form and appearance to agricultural and practical considerations – no shrinking away from the simplest solution',[17] all conform exactly to the model for the future outlined by Tessenow in *Handwerk und Kleinstadt*.

13

The AFK, December 1918–April 1919

The AFK was an immediate success with progressive architects and artists. Walter Gropius, for example, was totally infatuated with Taut's ideas: he wrote to Osthaus about Taut: 'I regard him as quite extraordinarily able, and, as an individual, so far superior to the regrettably large number of architectural imposters (Behrens, Paul, Muthesius, etc.), that I await significant things from him…His "Architektur-Programm" is profoundly sympathetic to my own spirit.'[1] Osthaus was equally impressed. He wrote to Taut congratulating him on the 'Architektur-Programm': 'I have followed your involvement in the Arbeitsrat and have read your "Architektur-Programm" with the greatest of interest. I want to tell you that I find something expressed there which we need above all else.'[2] It is no coincidence that such unreserved support for Taut's Activist programme should have come from fellow-campaigners from the artists' group at the 1914 Werkbund debate. It is clear that at its inception the AFK was seen as an alternative and successor to the Werkbund. This was certainly Gropius's view, even though he was still a member of the *Vorstand* of the Werkbund. Contrasting the early AFK to the Werkbund, Gropius concluded, again in a letter to Osthaus: 'I regard the Werkbund as dead, nothing more can come out of it.'[3] A few weeks later, Gropius repeated this opinion: 'The Werkbund is not to be roused out of its terminal sleep, and I and many others are now transferring our energies to this new venture.'[4] That Gropius's view was widely held among his own generation of architects and artists can be seen from the contemporary membership lists of the AFK.[5]

The most successful of the AFK's proposals, in terms of gaining acceptance within the architectural profession, were those for decentralization and the building of *Siedlungen*. This success is easily understood, for as we have seen, the proposals were based on the pre-war precedents established by the various reform groups and the Gartenstadtgesellschaft, and were also particularly appropriate to the looming economic crisis in post-war Germany. Taut's own views on decentralization would have been endorsed by several founder-members of the AFK who had already been closely involved with housing programmes which offered alternatives to the tenement blocks in the cities. Besides Taut and Tessenow, the founder-members included Paul Schmitthenner, the architect of the Gartenstadt Staaken (1914–17), Paul Mebes, author of the influential

47 Paul Schmitthenner,
Gartenstadt Staaken,
1914–17.

book *Um 1800*,[6] Otto Bartning and W. C. Behrendt. All four were on
the editorial board and Behrendt was the editor of the magazine *Die
Volkswohnung*, which was founded in January 1919. The title, *Die
Volkswohnung*, was indicative of a vision of *Volk* and *Gemeinschaft* which
derived from Landauer's analysis. Indeed, Lindahl has dubbed *Die
Volkswohnung* 'the principal mouthpiece for romantic *Siedlungspolitik*'.[7]
The influence of Taut's views on decentralization and rural mutualism
is very clear in the early editions of the magazine. An article by Taut
on this theme, entitled 'Die Erde eine gute Wohnung', was published
in the fourth issue, in February 1919.

Three clear sources lay behind this article: Stirner, Kropotkin and
Landauer. Although Taut cites Rousseau's *Emile* as his authority, the
egoistic presuppositions of the article probably derived from Max Stirner,
who, as we have seen, had a strong influence on Taut at this time.[8] Just
as Stirner, in *Der Einzige und sien Eigentum*, claimed that the group is
an unnatural and unhealthy affiliation for the individual, so Taut
insisted: 'Of all animals, man is least able to live gregariously. Men who
are packed together like sheep soon die.'[9] To avoid this fate, Taut
advocated the policy of decentralization – the dissolution of the cities.
Taut cited the works of Migge[10] and Kropotkin to provide the economic
foundations for his argument.

Taut's plans did not imply the rejection of technology or of industrial
production. Rather than seeking to return to the pre-industrial idyll
nurtured by the Kunstwart group or the Dürerbund, Taut's decentralized
communities would still be dependent on industrial techniques. The
factories, however, would follow the *Siedlungen* onto the land, and would
themselves become reduced in scale. 'Industry would automatically
follow this pattern: it too would be dispersed in numerous plants in order
to serve the demand easily. The process would be speeded up by new
forms of transport.'[11] Far from turning his back on industry or advanced
technology, Taut wanted to redirect it in a manner appropriate, as he
felt, to the post-capitalist era, when industry would be freed from
'monopoly and centralization'.[12] As a contributory factor to this new

era of industrialization. Taut cited the Taylor system. In an extraordinarily influential book which was published in America in 1911 and in Germany in 1913, the American engineer Frederick Winslow Taylor suggested that industrial efficiency could be improved by studying the operation of the individual worker and eliminating any wastage of time or motion. Taut was clearly in favour of this system, and saw in it the means of minimizing repetitive work on the conveyor belt and of establishing a harmonious and efficient relationship between the workers and the machines. This would cut working hours and thus allow the workers to spend more time on the land. Taut described the hoped-for effect of resettling industry in small rural units:

> The accursed division of labour is beginning to be broken down and perhaps a completely new attitude towards the Taylor System will appear. The foreman will not then assess disconnected hand and arm movements, but will evaluate how long the strength of the worker, who is now more highly valued, can be kept useful through a healthy relationship of body and soul employed in harmonious work at the machine and, for half of the day, on the soil.[13]

It is extremely interesting that Taut welcomed the Taylor system at this early date,[14] and saw no conflict between the aims of the Taylor system and his own ideal of a rurally based society.

In the first copy of *Das Ziel*, Ludwig Rubiner had condemned Taylorism as the purest expression of *Nurkapitalismus*. As Rubiner explained: 'Taylor has worked out a system in America, with the aim of squeezing human potential dry.'[15] Taut, however, felt that in the post-capitalist economy, the Taylor system would not be used to increase output at the expense of the workers' freedom, but would actually offer them more freedom, by enabling them to produce the necessary goods in a shorter time.

This hypothesis assumed that the money economy would be replaced by a system of barter, like that already delineated by Landauer. As Landauer had insisted: 'The fundamental structure of socialist society is a union of economically autonomous communities which trade together on mutualist principles.'[16] Taking his lead from Landauer, Taut prophesied: 'The power of money will recede, will vanish – who needs to buy much on the land! One lives in nature, works in it, and leads a harmonious existence with a healthy balance between hand and brain, factory and the land.'[17] The net of settlements spread across the land exactly expressed Landauer's ideal of society as 'a federation of unions of *Bünden*, a commonwealth of communities of rural communes, a republic made up of republics of republics'.[18] The result, as described by Taut, would destroy national borders and the repressive conception of the state. 'The states and the powers of the state will vanish: a new form of government will take their place. For the city is the symbol of the power of the state, and this and everything which follows from it – politics, war, will never disappear until the cities have gone.'[19] In this article Taut gave a physical and spatial dimension to the programme of romantic socialism outlined by Landauer in *Aufruf zum Sozialismus*. Taut was later to illustrate these ideas in his book *Die Auflösung der Städte*, published in 1920 and subtitled *Die Erde eine Gute Wohnung*.

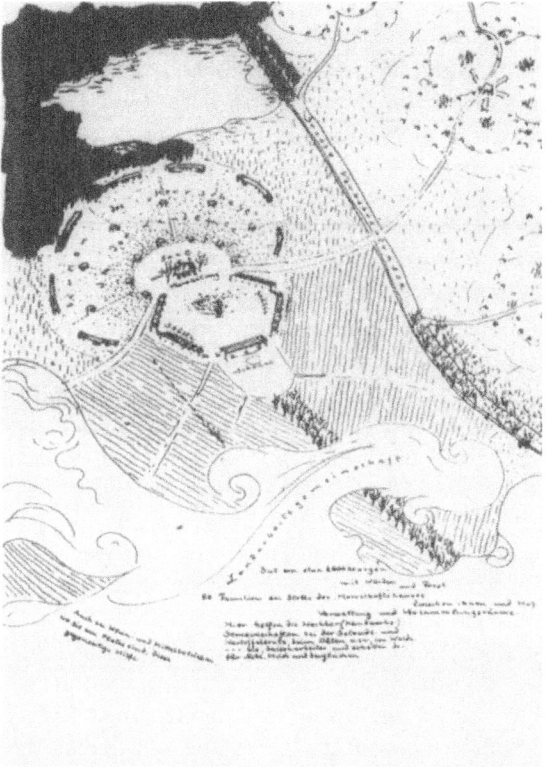

48 Bruno Taut, *Die Auflösung der Städte*, rural community. 'Here, the neighbouring communities c craftsmen help with the corr and potato harvest, with hoeing, and in the woods...for this they receive, as seasonal workers flour, milk and suchlike.'

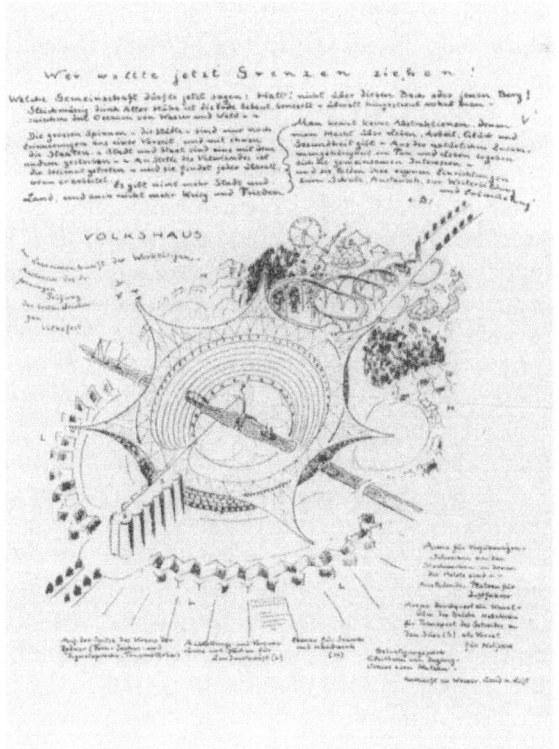

49 *Die Auflösung der Städte*, *Volkshaus*. 'Town and country no longer exist, there is no more war and peace. One knows no abstractions which give one power over life, work, good fortune and health. Mutual interests emerge from the natural fellowship of doing and living, and create their own organizations for protection and exchange, for further development and education...'.

Not only did Taut use *Die Volkswohnung* to publish his views on *Siedlungen*, he also used it to describe the simple architectural types and constructional methods which would be appropriate to the new *Siedlungen*. These were simple in the extreme; the fifth issue of the magazine carried an article by Taut on *Erdstampfbau*. Not only should the earth be a good dwelling, but the dwelling should be built of earth. Taut's advocacy of pressed earth for building was characteristically antagonistic. He began by attacking the constructional techniques which were taught in the schools of architecture. Citing a pamphlet written by Baurat Siebold at the end of 1918, Taut described the use of lime in the great constructions of Babylon and Egypt and went on to plead the case for buildings made of pressed earth. 'Yes – buildings of pressed earth! We are racking our brains at the moment over so-called economical building, but in doing so easily confuse "economical" with "meagre", and forget that meagre architecture was already the plague of the pre-war period.'[20] The building process, as described by Taut, was disarmingly simple: 'If the soil has no organic components and is not so oily or dry as to fall into clods – in other words if it is normal – then the earth excavated for the cellar and the foundations is not carried away: instead, the house is built with it.'[21] Taut added: 'Now this is no modern joke but a very old story.' This historicist belief in the application of old forms and types to the new situation was typically Activist, as was the insistently anti-academic tone of the piece. As Taut noted: 'Without the spectacles of the academic, the world looks a little different – not only in artistic but also in technical matters.'[22] In spite of its antagonistic tone, that aspect of Taut's architectural Activism which was concerned with *Siedlungen*, decentralization and simple building techniques was exactly in accord with the views of the Volkswohnung group, and was generally in line with current thinking on low cost building.[23]

Taut's conviction that the industrial era was over for Germany was reinforced in May 1919 when, under the terms of the Treaty of Versailles, Germany lost three-quarters of its iron-ore deposits and a quarter of its coal. In addition, enormous cash payments were imposed, and most of the merchant fleet confiscated. The treaty was signed on 28 June. On 6 July, the 'Richtlinien für die Behandlung der Zuschuß-anträge' were announced, specifying subsidies for the building of small houses and rural enterprises. In this way, the government itself sponsored the desire for autarchy, autonomy and self-sufficiency, a desire which naturally favoured primitivist solutions.

Autonomy, decentralization and simplicity represented, however, only one aspect of the Activist dialectic. Through a return to the simple life the *Volk* were to be purged of materialism, individualism and subjectivity, and were to be reintroduced to the ideals of the *Gemeinschaft*. But the *Gemeinschaft* was not seen as an end in itself. It was merely the form of society most receptive to an intensification of *Geist*. The *Gemeinschaft*, when infused with *Geist* would begin to move towards paradise. Without *Geist*, however, it was merely an economic and social system.

In an article published in *Das Kunstblatt* early in 1919 – 'Für die neue Baukunst!', Taut returned to the dialectic of *Volk* and *Geist*, of profane and sacred which he had first worked out in his article 'Architektur' for *Die Stadtkrone*. He insisted that the one should be clearly separated from the other. Only then could they enrich each other with their complementary resonances. Once again, Gothic and oriental models were taken as ideals.

In the Gothic age, the sacred was separated clearly and distinctly from the profane, and just because this distance was recognized, the houses of the period were beautiful. The passion which expressed itself in the satisfaction of daily needs through the most concise and always appropriate forms, was the same, in principle, as that which created the cathedrals in all their wonderful details.[24]

According to Taut and the AFK programmes it was the mission of the *geistig* élite of architects to articulate the complementary resonances of *Geist* and *Volk* around the focus of a *Kultusbau* which would unite all the other arts under its aegis. But where, asked Taut, were the architects? 'Only where are the architects? Don't they hear the call? They, the true moulders of an all-unifying art, where are they?'[25] The answer was: unmoved by the demands of Taut and the AFK to take over architectural and artistic control in the new state.

The success enjoyed by the AFK with the radical architects and artists was the direct consequence of the vigorous attacks which the AFK made on the art and architectural establishment. An equally predictable consequence was the wrath which the AFK thus attracted from the establishment and from the profession at large. Otto Burghardt wrote from Leipzig to the Werkbund, saying that Taut's views were unrepresentative of the majority of German architects and demanding that the Deutscher Architektenschaft should compose a counter-manifesto, giving the views of the majority.[26] The publisher Hugo Bruckmann, who had acted as an agent for the Arbeitsrat in Munich, and had passed on the 'Architektur-Programm' to the Bavarian press, commented wryly: 'I personally cannot suppress a mild shudder at the thought of such radical architects and such wild architecture.'[27] Another response from Munich, this time from the critic Walther Haas, indicated that Taut's programme was seen by non-Berliners as an example of in-bred Berlin avant-gardism, which bore no relation to the world outside. Haas wrote to Gropius in February 1919:

Dear Gropius, to me there is nothing more ridiculous than Bavarian particularism. When I can do something for the Berlin intelligentsia, then I do it gladly. I can't do anything, however, for things which are nothing but an expression of foundationless insolence, laughable presumptiousness, of some old song in a new form, such as emerges from Taut's programme, which you sent to me and which I already knew.

The spirit which speaks in it is exactly the same as that which seems to radiate from educated people, who try, by hanging together in a soft-shoe-shuffle, to dance away from all the misery. I don't mind if you think me as philistine as possible. (I find it good when the uneducated dance the shuffle. It is cheaper than smashing windows.)[28]

He dismissed completely Taut's plans for experimental buildings as being totally inappropriate to the economic crisis of the moment.

Is it then not clear to Taut how unspeakably badly things are going for us? Quite apart from the nonsense of not erecting trial façades on the actual site where the building will be built, one really asks oneself: has anyone made Taut wise to the fact that we have to pay the English 1000 million Marks in war-reparations. We should be happy in our people find any shelter at all. If I were a pastor, I would preach: 'make yourselves more humble at last; that means, "de-Berlinize" yourselves!'[29]

He concluded the letter with a final gibe against the unreality of the Berlin avant-garde. 'No, dear Gropius, one has too much humour here for things like Taut's programme. Nothing doing. One immediately feels that this is the mark of the Berliner...to be voluntarily humourless. In its place an involuntary drollery appears.'[30] Yet even within the circle of Berlin architects, the AFK was regarded with suspicion and some ridicule as a self-generating clique. The Activist faith in the autogenesis of the *geistig* élite was difficult to sustain in practice. Heinrich de Fries, who had collaborated with Behrens on the book *Vom sparsamen Bauen*, was attracted to the AFK as a means of realizing some of his ideas on simplicity and decentralization – ideas which corresponded, as we have seen, to those of Taut. His attempt to gain a position within the AFK was unsuccessful, however, and he wrote both an article for the *Rheinische Monatshefte*[31] and a letter to the *Vorstand* of the AFK denouncing the Arbeitsrat as a clique. In the letter he wrote: 'If the AFK is really supposed to be an association of radically minded artists, then why does a narrow group of friends strut around in the AFK to the exclusion of all those who are not known or are not acceptable to the members of this group?'[32] The letter concluded with de Fries's conviction that: 'the idea of an idealistic working community, which should be a glowing milestone on the path to a nobler artistic future, has already been destroyed in the bud by the personality politics of a few members'.[33] De Fries's complaints, although partly inspired by personal animosity, reflected the transformation of the AFK from a *kunstpolitische* pressure-group with aspirations to direct political power into an avant-gardistic *Kunstverein*.

Not only did the AFK fail in its specific ambitions to seize political control within the profession, it also failed in its more general aspirations to achieve a controlling influence over artistic questions in the government of the new republic.

We have already seen that the political failure of the AFK was almost immediate. Just as the RGA survived for only five days in the Reichstag, so the political ambitions which Taut had for the AFK were equally short-lived. The initial demands for artistic dictatorship by the AFK were instantly dismissed by the SPD minister Hoffmann. Similarly, the Activist plans for a decentralized socialist government based on the land, collapsed with the vote by the congress of workers' and soldiers' councils in favour of parliamentary government. This vote was taken on 20 December, and the resolution was passed by 400 to 50. The failure of the USPD at the congress reflected the division within its own membership, with the left tending towards the Spartacists and the right towards the SPD. The suppression of the January uprising by Noske's Friekorps culminated in the arrest of Taut's political mentor, Georg Ledebour, on 11 January, and, on 13 January, in the murders of the Spartacist leaders, Luxemburg and Liebknecht. The swing back to the right was also reflected in the election for the members of the constituent assembly, which was held on 17 January. The result was a substantial majority for the SPD, who gained 163 seats. By comparison, the USPD, as advocates of council government, won only twenty-two. With this vote and the subsequent meeting of the assembly at Weimar on 6 February, the attempt to transform the bourgeois democracy into a socialist democracy began to founder.

The reaction of the leaders of the AFK to the rapid collapse of their dreams was very characteristic for the avant-garde: a withdrawal into introspection, into the circle of the élite few. Writing to Osthaus early in February 1919, Gropius commented sadly:

Our only option now is to ignore the real world and to build for oneself a private, separate world. I believe that this is the correct course for each of us at the present moment. At some time unity must come of its own accord through intensive immersion in the individual personality. Socialism has been so sullied and so totally disgraced in these squalid times that it will need a long time before it can salve its honour.[34]

At exactly the same time as this letter was written, Behne penned an article for the *Sozialistische Monatshefte* which bitterly bemoaned the failure of the revolution.

We survey the achievements of our revolution with a feeling of sadness and of shame. What has happened in the ten weeks of the revolutionary period? Censorship and the state of siege have been lifted – a foregone conclusion. But otherwise the spirit of the old régime has returned to our people after a few short days of initial enthusiasm. Ideally, they want to set the old machine in motion again, only slightly repainted.[35]

After the failure of the political revolution, the function of the intellectual was to work for a moral revolution, which might, he suggested, be achieved together with the proletariat.[36] Like Gropius, Behne was withdrawing from the real political battleground into a make-believe world, where the *Volk* would again be united with the *geistig* élite and would join battle against the philistines.

Taut was profoundly affected by the failure of the revolution. His mood went from ecstatic intoxication to black despair between December 1918 and February 1919. In December he wrote in his article 'Ex Oriente Lux': 'The light illuminates all things. Everything finds its correct place in the sequence of subordination. Once again there is truthfulness, and a ray of the eternal light falls on the smallest hut. Brightness and purity in all things!'[37] By February he was complaining vehemently against the cool reception which his ideas had found in Germany. In a letter written to Osthaus on 11 February, he pondered on the idea of seeking a more sympathetic audience in America – the traditional refuge for frustrated European anarchists: 'Do you have contacts with America? I am coming more and more to the conclusion that there is no base for me here, and that perhaps there are people there who won't simply dismiss my ambitions as "fantasy".'[38] He added wistfully: 'I mean, there must surely be a place to be found for me in Boston or somewhere else.'[39] No place was to be found, however, and Taut remained in Berlin. Like Gropius and Behne, he withdrew into the frustrated agonism of the avant-garde. He wrote in March: 'The calling and the fate of the artist today is from the outset tragic. The man who is truly inspired by the urge to create stands isolated, left entirely to his own resources. He must laboriously grope for the threads which hold the mass of the people together and link the artist to the *Volk*.'[40] By then it was clear that Taut's plans for the Arbeitsrat as a vehicle for *Kunstpolitik* inside the government were dashed completely.

Taut was left bitter and frustrated. The direct result of this frustration was his resignation as head of the AFK. In mid-February Gropius wrote to Dr Valentiner, the third member of the deputation which had visited Hoffmann, fearing for the whole enterprise should Taut drop out. The letter was dated 18 February 1919. 'Taut will no longer work with the AFK. As I received an invitation to the meeting, I assume that you know about it. Something must now be done straight away, otherwise the entire, splendidly conceived enterprise will come to naught.'[41] As we shall see, Gropius himself took over the Arbeitsrat, and reconstituted it along lines which differed, especially in their political content, from Taut's original conception.

Taut himself reacted strongly against the various forms of socialism which were being bandied around in the early months of 1919. He returned to Hiller's thesis that the socialism of the Activist or the artist had nothing whatsoever to do with party politics. In an article published in the *Sozialistische Monatshefte* in March 1919, Taut defined 'Der Sozialismus des Künstlers'. As in 'Für die neue Baukunst', the artist was portrayed as isolated: 'Lonely, reclusive, looking like a vagrant in the sphere of common life, like the wandering Jew.'[42] Not only was the artist socially isolated, he was also betrayed by the materialistic forces within society, by the politics of power.

What does the world around us and the way it is ruled and governed mean to the artist? I certainly can't govern it. The world can only put the artist's body in chains, maim him, kill him – no, it can't kill him. Already before death he is a dead man. What are power politics to the artist? Let them rule in whichever form they want to. For him, ruling has only a cosmic worth. His world is not this world.[43]

The unity of *Kunst* and *Volk*, which had been the first presupposition of Taut's AFK was seen to be a chimera.

In a critique of the AFK published in February 1919, the conservative critic Karl Scheffler had attacked the AFK programme. '"Art and *Volk* must form a unity"...what is the point of such slogans if art is incapable of doing it and the *Volk* unable and unwilling.'[44] In the depressing days of March, Taut came to the same pessimistic conclusion.

'The artist goes sadly on producing new works, pleased to make his brothers happy, and they – they carry on just the same as before.'[45] The artist could unite with the *Volk* only after an absolute revolution of the *Geist*, not a compromised political revolution such as the revolution of November 1918. Taut's definition of a true revolution was taken directly from the Activist programmes of the war years.

As there is no path for the artist to take, only an existence to be lived out, so he must take the revolution as simple and absolute. He has no understanding of half measures, of taking one step forward and then one back. In the revolutionary idea he sees the removal of power – power in the form of the military and in those things which the military have to protect – money and all forms of authority, including that of the state. What terrifies the citizen (to avoid using here the polemical word 'bourgeois') is the absence of state, money and the military, which, because of his nature, he takes as given, as things on which he has always based his life.[46]

The three main targets of Landauer's *Aufruf zum Sozialismus* – the state, the military and the money economy were, said Taut, contrary to the spirit of the true artist.

One last glimmer of hope was held out to Taut in his crusade for a 'pure' revolution based on *Geist*. It came, appropriately, via Gustav Landauer.

By the end of December 1918, Landauer saw that the November revolution was in no way a socialist revolution – according to his own definition. In his preface to the second edition of *Aufruf zum Sozialismus*, dated 3 January 1919, he mourned the failure of the November revolution and damned the SPD and the USPD as incompetent, reactionary and *geistlos*.

A political revolution still had to come in Germany; now it has been thoroughly achieved...That the Marxist social-democratic parties in their various hues are incompetent in political practice, unable to reconstitute humanity in its rights and its social institutions, unable to create a realm of work and peace, and, at the same time, unable to comprehend theoretically the social realities, has been made absolutely clear. They have shown this most monstrously during the war, and also before and after it, from Germany to Russia, from enthusiasm for the war to the banal, uncreative tyranny of the present.[47]

Yet in spite of the collapse of the revolution under Ebert and the SPD, Landauer still had hopes of an anarcho-socialist revolution, which would reject the militaristic and managerial techniques of capitalism and embrace instead the system of mutualism already outlined by Kropotkin and himself.[48] The spirit which had inspired the Activists still lived in Landauer. His preface concluded: 'We should lead the way forward to socialism; how else can we lead other than by our example? Chaos is at hand; a new alertness and new vibrations manifest themselves; the spirits are awakening, the souls rise to the responsibility, the hands reach for action; may the rebirth come out of the revolution.'[49] Landauer's opportunity to lead by example came at the beginning of April, when a left-wing coup d'état succeeded to power in Bavaria, modelling itself on Béla Kun's soviet dictatorship in Hungary.

The new régime seized control on 6 April, and offered Landauer a

50 Gustav Landauer (with fur hat) at a demonstration in Munich on 16 February 1919.

cabinet position as Provisional Commissioner for the Education of the People, in effect, as Minister of Education. In this capacity Landauer sent invitations to Taut and to Tessenow, offering either one or both of them the position of *Bauminister* in the new government.

Only fragments have survived of the plans which Landauer drew up as People's Commissioner. From these fragments, however, it is clear that he had been influenced by Taut and by the programmes of the AFK in Berlin. In the rough draft of the *Kulturprogramm* which he wrote during the second half of April, Landauer adopted Taut's demand that all the arts should be united under the leadership of architecture. He wrote: 'The new era of human history should find its expression in the public buildings and monuments which will be built from now on. Young artists are to be widely promoted through official commissions. This applies to all the arts: painting and sculpture are, from the outset, to be incorporated into architecture.'[50] Having adopted Taut's plans, Landauer invited him to Munich to put them into practice.

Taut subsequently wrote to Osthaus: 'The proto-communist administration in Munich wanted to appoint Tessenow and myself (or one of us) as directors of the Bavarian building ministry – as some sort of ministers for building.'[51] At last, Taut had an opportunity to put into practice the ideas for a *Kultusministerium* which he had penned in 'An die sozialistische Regierung'. In his letter to Osthaus he looked back on his optimism at the time: 'I was looking forward to it in spite of the difficulties which I anticipated; perhaps I could have set some fresh ideas in motion.'[52] But the optimism was short-lived. On 1 May Munich fell to Noske's Freikorps and a white terror followed, in which Landauer was executed.

With the collapse of the proto-communist administration, the chili-

51 Wassili Luckhardt, *An die Freude*, 1919.

astic phase of activism came to an end. The contact, through Landauer, with the new régime in Munich had offered Taut a last, slim chance of putting into practice the Activist programmes which he had drawn up for the AFK. Now there was nothing. The result was, as he wrote to Osthaus: 'I'm left sitting alone, buried in the middle of Berlin at my drawing board, which is already more like a writing desk.'[53]

Part 4

April 1919–December 1920

14

The AFK under Walter Gropius

We have argued that Activism, both in its literary and architectural variants, sought to achieve concrete political and social ends through the benign dictatorship of a *geistig* élite which was guided by a rational intuition. The rational application of the will and the *Geist* was offered as a workable alternative to the introspective soul-searching of Expressionism. The failure of the self-elected élite to gain anything but the most transitory influence in the revolutionary period and the subsequent polarization of the Activist camp into pro-Bolshevik and anti-Bolshevik factions marked the end of the period of chiliastic expectation and the end of the phase of political Activism. New directions had to be found.

With the end of the chiliastic phase, the Activist avant-garde in architecture abandoned the fight on the wider political front, and limited its activities to the areas generally associated with the artistic avant-garde – the publication of programmes and manifestos, the organization of exhibitions. This complete change in emphasis can be clearly observed in the case of the Arbeitsrat für Kunst, which, in the early spring of 1919, was transformed from an aspiring political force into a pressure-group pursuing purely artistic aims.

After Taut's resignation, the AFK was reconstituted at a general meeting on 1 March. A three-tier system was established. The top tier, the *Geschäftsausschuß*, comprised the luminaries of the old Arbeitsrat and was directed by a three-man oligarchy consisting of Gropius (chairman), César Klein (vice-chairman) and Adolf Behne (secretary). Neither Bruno Taut nor Wilhelm Valentiner held a position in the new structure, but were ordinary members of the 'business committee'.[1] The second tier, called the 'artists' working committee', consisted of members who were active in Berlin,[2] while the third tier was for 'domestic and foreign friends of the Arbeitsrat für Kunst'.

The change in constitution and leadership was accompanied by a marked change in the political policy of the group. Taut's ambition for the Arbeitsrat to be a force in the arena of *Kulturpolitik* was formerly abandoned. Instead, the new Arbeitsrat was conceived by Gropius as a mechanism for bringing together the leading practitioners of the various arts, as a unifying focus for architects, artists, sculptors and theoreticians. This ambition was reflected in the choice of César Klein, a painter, for the post of vice-chairman.

In his critique of Taut's AFK, published at the beginning of February

52 Walter Gropius.

1919, Karl Scheffler wrote that the only possible virtue of the group might be that it could act as a common meeting ground for all the arts.

The single hopeful aspect of this business is that with the councils, something like a professional association has been established for the first time. Admittedly the association is still a caricature – not least because of its revolutionary gestures, but it nevertheless quietly points the way to a supra-political union, such as one might envisage in an ideal *Herrenhaus*.

Scheffler noted, however, that this ideal had not been achieved: 'It would appear that the members of the Arbeitsrat are themselves not aware of this opportunity.'[3] Under Gropius's reorganization the AFK matched Scheffler's ideal very closely, abandoning the unsuccessful role in *Kunstpolitik* in favour of a new function as a professional association as suggested by Scheffler.

In his first address to the AFK after the change of leadership, Gropius stated his position and outlined his plans for the group: 'In the main, I had to agree with Taut's misgivings, but had the feeling that we should continue quietly to spin our threads, in spite of all the nastiness in external politics.'[4] Caution and stealth were to replace the bangings on the revolutionary drum:

At first we gradually had to clarify what we wanted to do. The split between the two fundamentally different aims, which from the outset were disastrously intermingled – whether we should promote *Kunstpolitik* on a broader basis, or whether we should push for the success of a radical artistic credo by working together in a small minority group – this split has gradually resolved itself in favour of the latter conception. Now, for the first time, we actually have a clear foundation on which we can build, and I believe that we can be grateful that the tightness of our purse prevented us from pursuing a greater prominence.[5]

Working from this new, and distinctly revisionist platform, Gropius set about financing the new group.

Whereas Taut has sought to dissociate the AFK entirely from the art establishment of the old régime, and had based his plans and hopes on the political success of the workers' councils, Gropius was more pragmatic, and appealed for funds to the traditional patrons of the arts, the *haute bourgeoisie*, and the industrialists. The contrast between these two approaches could hardly be more marked. Even before the change of leadership had been ratified, Gropius was canvassing for financial support among the enlightened industrialists who had previously supported the arts via such bodies as the Werkbund. In late February he wrote begging letters to Benscheidt, the head of the Fagus works, to Walther Rathenau of AEG, and to Dr Robert Bosch. His appeals were surprisingly successful, given the name of the group: a success which probably owed more to his own reputation than to that of the AFK. Benscheidt gave 200 Marks with a hint of more to follow, while the firm of Fischbein and Mendel gave 1000 Marks in mid-March.[6] Gropius also turned to the rich art patrons of Berlin, whom he seduced shamelessly. He wrote on 11 March to Dr Valentiner, suggesting a social gathering for the benefit of two likely sympathizers, Princess Lichnowsky and Baby Friedländer: 'I have thought it over and feel that it would be advisable to invite Princess Lichnowsky and Baby Friedländer as guests on Saturday, so that we could warm them to our ideas more easily.'[7] It was Gropius's intention to build up a capital fund for the AFK to enable the group to pursue its programme. Chastened, no doubt, by the interview with Minister Hoffmann, Gropius saw little chance of attracting support from the state. On 13 March, Gropius wrote to Dr Friedrich Perzynski, a member of the Künstlerische Arbeitsgemeinschaft, describing the financial prospects of the group: 'I have attended to the matter of finance very energetically, and we have good prospects of collecting a capital sum this week, which will give us the necessary elbow-room for our plans.' He added: 'It is entirely clear to me, however, that no appreciable support for our efforts is to be expected from the present government.'[8] The AFK was thus entirely dependent on the traditional, bourgeois sources of patronage, and had abandoned the ideals of the November days in favour of a capital fund – a considerable *volte face*.

Yet despite the contrasting political assumptions of the AFK under Taut and Gropius, there was a notable continuity in the artistic programme of the group. Gropius was very strongly influenced at the time by Taut's Activist rhetoric and framed his own plans for the AFK in language which might have been written by Taut himself. In the typescript for an article written in March 1919, 'Der freie Volksstaat und die Kunst', Gropius offered the fundamental arguments of Taut and the Activists as his presuppositions. The state, he said 'must create a free flight-path for the creative spirit'.[9] He continued: 'We need a new spirituality in the entire *Volk*.'[10] Unlike Taut, he dissociated the sought-for *Geistigkeit* from any political revolution: 'Not the political, but only the completed *geistig* revolution can make us free.'[11] This cultural emancipation would evolve from a new base: 'New, intellectually untapped layers of the *Volk* are rising up out of the depths.'[12] Like Taut, Gropius insisted that the regeneration of the arts could only come via the spiritual guidance and leadership of architecture. In a passage which clearly reveals its source to be Taut's essay 'Architektur' from *Die Stadtkrone*,[13] Gropius insisted that the architect's destiny was to lead:

The 'arts' will find their way out of their lonely solitude and back into the womb of an all embracing architecture. For only through intimate collaboration and working together can an age generate that many-voiced orchestra which alone deserves the name of art. From time immemorial, the architect was called to conduct this orchestra. Architect, that means: Leader of the Arts.[14]

Also like Taut, Gropius planned to revive architecture through the example of a *Kultusbau*, but he differed in his views on how this might be achieved. Whereas Taut saw the construction of the *Kultusbau* or *Volkshaus* as the responsibility of the socialist state, Gropius conceived it as the product of a small group of artists and craftsmen working under the same conditions of intimacy and secrecy as the medieval masons. He concluded his article 'Der freie Volksstaat und die Kunst' with a plea for a return to the principle of the medieval *Bauhütte*:

The architect of yesterday was no longer the universal creator and mighty master of all artistic disciplines...His high office must once again find public recognition: he must establish this through that humanity which stands above the reality of the moment, through a burning interest in mutual work. Once the problems of the artist and the sculptor stir his mind as passionately as his own architectural problems, then architecture will again be filled with an architectonic spirit. The Gothic cathedral originated in the masonic lodges of the middle ages, in the close personal contact of artists of all degrees.[15]

In Gropius's conception, the *Bauhütte* would act as a focus for the progressive forces in the plastic arts, who would work together on the task of preparing for the second, spiritual revolution.

Gropius outlined his plans for a radical *Bauhütte* in a letter which he wrote to the painter Ludwig Meidner on 26 February 1919.

After initial unclarities, the AFK has finally struggled to the view that it can only follow its founding ideas profitably if the divisions between the individual artistic disciplines – architecture, painting, sculpture – are abandoned, and a joint, *absolutely radically* orientated working committee is elected. To begin with, this committee will quietly pursue preparatory work until, with some perhaps not too distant second revolution, the given moment appears in which to confront the public with the demands of the radical artists.

Gropius urged Meidner to attend the meeting on 1 March as a representative of the extreme left. His letter to Meidner concluded: 'This working committee is to be elected at the meeting on Saturday. Everything thereafter depends on the composition of the committee. We ask you urgently to take part in this meeting, so that the extreme left wing can be represented uncompromisingly in the election of the committee.'[16] It is difficult to define the political position of Gropius and Behne when they took over the leadership of the AFK. Behne was a member of the SPD, Gropius was in no party. A year later Behne explained the political standpoint of the AFK in a letter to the Bund sozialistischer Studenten. Relating the letter to Gropius he wrote: 'I made it clear from the start, that although we stand by socialism, we keep ourselves apart from party politics and are not attached to any party.'[17] It is clear that neither Gropius nor Behne were especially sympathetic to the KPD or the extreme left. When the painter Heinrich Vogeler, a member of the KPD, was arrested in May 1919, Behne wanted to expel him from the AFK. Gropius warned Behne against this, but saw no reason to make an official protest on behalf of the AFK.[18]

Indeed, the reorganization of the AFK under Gropius emphasized the vacuity of the equation which directly linked the political revolution with formal revolution in the arts. For under Gropius's leadership, the Arbeitsrat moved simultaneously to the right politically and to the left artistically.

When Gropius spoke of a 'radical' *Arbeitsausschuß*, the term related only to formal, artistic matters, and did not imply any identification with the radical left in politics. His artistic radicalism, however, was no less sectarian than its political counterpart. In a letter dated 6 March, Gropius asked Behne to take over the business side of the Arbeitsrat and described his plans for the AFK. Gropius's first step was to purge the AFK of all non-radical elements. He intended to turn the AFK into a small group of like-minded radical artists who would function in near-mystic secrecy like a medieval *Bauhütte*. The letter addressed Behne as 'Dear Eckhart',[19] a pseudonym suitably laden with medieval and mystical undertones:

Now the following: I intend to radicalize further. A coherent group must come out of this whole business, and even at the risk of causing offence, I want to show the door more or less gently to all the elements which don't fit in. This is even more necessary if we want to make a form of lodge out of it. Won't you, under these conditions, take over the business management of the whole enterprise? You are the only one who inwardly lives the idea which we are propagating and who adjusts all his steps accordingly.[20]

A month later he wrote to Professor Weiss, giving a more succinct account of his plans for a *Bauhütte* and relating the *Bauhütte* to the *Bauprojekte*, the *Kultusbau* on which the architects, painters and sculptors would work.

The original intention, before my time, to pursue cultural politics on a broad basis, proved itself to be a chimera. It became increasingly clear that something fruitful could only originate in a closed circle of artists, who commit themselves absolutely to positive projects. I made the proposal, therefore, that serious steps should finally be made to bring the three groups, architects, painters and sculptors together under one roof. As applications for admission were now arriving from all sides, we had to come to an understanding over who should belong to the working committee, i.e. that group of artists who would work together on the planned large-scale building projects.[21]

The new AFK, Gropius insisted, should be based on small groups, not on a centralized political platform. As he explained to the architect Carl Krayl: 'a large, centralized organization of artists will never succeed and has no purpose...small, lodge-like working groups, that's what we need'.[22] At the inception of the AFK, Taut had envisaged a fruitful symbiosis between the political revolution of November 1918 and a radical revolution in the plastic arts, led by architecture. Less than half a year later, Gropius had dismissed this relationship as a chimera.

As might be expected, the AFK was conspicuously more successful in its dealings with the Ministry after it had abandoned its claims to a direct political role or to artistic dictatorship. For example, Gropius approached Dr Busse, Haenisch's deputy at the *Kultusministerium*, on 13 March 1919, asking to speak to the minister in order to put forward the new programme of the AFK.[23] It is not clear exactly what the AFK's recommendations were, but an almost immediate success was achieved with the dissolution of the Preußische Landeskunstkommission. The *Lokal-Anzeiger* reported on 18 March: 'According to information in the journal *Die Glocke*, edited by Minister of Culture Hoffmann, the Preußische Landeskunstkommission has been disbanded. One of the demands of the Arbeitsrat für Kunst, Berlin, has thereby been satisfied.'[24] In Haenisch (USPD), Gropius found a more sympathetic ear than the earlier AFK deputation had found in Hoffmann (SPD). Indeed, in a speech at the beginning of February 1919, Haenisch had outlined his hopes for the future development of *Kulturpolitik* in terms which exactly matched Gropius's plans for the AFK. From the Activists, Haenisch adopted the idea of an aristocracy of *Geist*, but placed it in the context of socialist democracy, rather than in the Activist role of absolute dictator. 'I hope for the gradual emergence of a new spiritual and intellectual aristocracy on the basis of democracy and socialism.'[25] It was exactly such an artistic élite, founded on a democratic base, which Gropius was seeking to create out of Taut's original, Activist version of the *AFK*.

The differences between the two versions can be seen in the scale of their respective ambitions. Whereas the Activist élite sought to regenerate society and the state in all its aspects, the artistic élite of the *Bauhütte* was content to unite and reform the plastic arts along radical lines. The Arbeitsrat für Kunst under Gropius did not concern itself in its programmes with pacifism, political decentralization or the restructuring of art-administration and education. Instead, it concentrated on the funding of a *Bauprojekte*, the *Kultusbau* which would bring together the various talents of the *Bauhütte*. It was Gropius's intention that the AFK should set up the *Bauprojekte* as a magnet for radical artists. Once work was begun on the building, however, the formal organizational structure of the AFK would be made obsolete, and would be replaced by the *Bauhütte* which had been set up for the *Bauprojekte*. In a letter to Ewald Dülberg, written on 3 April 1919, Gropius explained this process:

I would like more and more to allow formal meetings to drop...instead, we are trying with all means to establish a joint, large-scale project – a utopian building project – on which architects, painters, and sculptors can work equally. If this working community flourishes healthily, then in God's name, the whole organization of the AFK can go to the devil.[26]

53 Max Pechstein (?), title illustration to the revised programme of the Arbeitsrat für Kunst, April 1919.

Gropius's conviction that the AFK should be restructured around the *Bauprojekt* and the artists' working committee was publicly announced in a new programme which was distributed in April to the press and to leading public figures. It was illustrated by a woodcut – probably by Max Pechstein – and, in addition to restating the demands of the group, listed the names of the members of the various committees. The programme concluded: 'The Arbeitsrat views, as the most important task for the near future, the consolidation of the closed group of artists in the working committee on the basis of the joint preparation of a comprehensive utopian building project, which will include architectural, sculptural and painterly elements in equal measure.'[27] Underlying the notion of the *Bauprojekt* was the vague assumption that its completion would benefit the arts and thus improve the society at large. Society would be improved by the sublime fusion of architecture, painting and sculpture and would be better prepared for the awaited second revolution, the *geistig* revolution. There was, however, no ambition to remodel the political framework of society, or to indulge in social engineering along the lines suggested by Landauer, Hiller or Taut.

Far from following in the anarcho-socialist tradition of Landauer and Taut, the AFK under Gropius was firmly grounded in the SPD version of socialist democracy. The plans for secrecy and exclusivity carried with them political associations which were even further to the right. The tradition of the *Bauhütte*, which had been substantially re-invented during the nineteenth century,[28] was very much the preserve of the radical conservatives in the early twentieth century. The articles on freemasonry in *Die Tat* by the brothers Horneffer were typical examples.[29]

Just as the radical conservatives like Horneffer sought to promote social reform within the strict confines of the educated bourgeoisie, so the new AFK under Gropius abandoned its previous pretentions to speak on behalf of the *Volk* and reverted to the customary role of the avant-garde. This role demanded the radical negation of a general culture by a specific alternative. In this unequal struggle, the new AFK was forced to take up an antagonistic stance. The radical views of the artists in the AFK were publicly set against the consensus of informed architectural and artistic opinion. Such a confrontation is incumbent upon all avant-garde movements. Whereas in November 1918, the RGA and the AFK were offering alternatives to a culture which had, as they thought, already destroyed itself, the AFK in the spring of 1919 was confronted with the truth that, far from being finished, the old culture was alive and vigorous.

15

◇◈◇

The Ausstellung für unbekannte Architekten

The open attack on the general culture, and, in particular, its architectural standards and institutions, was launched at the Ausstellung für unbekannte Architekten (Exhibition for Unknown Architects), held by the AFK in April 1919.

Taut had initially suggested the exhibition in January 1919 and had written to likely architects and artists asking for sketches and drawings. The idea was taken up by Gropius and Behne after the change of leadership and the exhibition was finally held in the Graphisches Kabinett J. B. Neumann on Kurfürstendamm, a notably un-proletarian location. Although Taut was the intitiator of the exhibition, he played no part in the selection of the exhibits. This was done by Gropius, Max Taut and Rudolf Salvisberg.

There was no catalogue. Instead, Gropius, Bruno Taut and Adolf Behne produced declamatory pieces which were printed and distributed free of charge – in the manner of a manifesto. All three statements were strongly antagonistic. Gropius and Taut both attacked the contemporary condition of German architecture. Gropius complained: 'For we walk through our streets and towns without crying for shame over such wastes of ugliness.'[1] The ugliness was the product, he said, of 'our function-cursed age'.[2] As Taut had done in his essay in *Die Stadtkrone*, Gropius distinguished between the sacred and the profane: 'A clear watershed, therefore, between dream and reality, between yearning for the stars and day-to-day work.'[3] He was supported, naturally, by Taut, who distinguished absolutely between architecture and the mere satisfaction of material needs: 'For "architecture" doesn't mean the cladding of thousands of functional objects – houses, offices, stations, market-halls, schools, water-towers, gasometers, fire-stations, factories and the like – in nice forms.'[4] This vituperative attack on the established canons of modernism, on the whole Werkbund aesthetic was aimed directly at the successful modernists of the pre-war years. Poelzig was particularly displeased by it, presumably as Taut had singled out water-towers and fire-stations as particular targets for his scorn.[5] Taut had already lampooned the cult of the artistic fire-station in his article 'Für die neue Baukunst'. Poelzig was so offended that he actually offered his resignation from the AFK, citing Taut's aggressiveness as one of his reasons. He wrote to Gropius on 21 April: 'I hereby resign from the Arbeitsrat für Kunst, Reason 1...Reason 2: the general attitude of Taut.

131

Having already provoked me in a thinly veiled way in *Das Kunstblatt*, I have just heard from Endell that Taut has baited me again in a similar manner in the manifesto to the Ausstellung unbekannter Architekten [*sic*].'[6] Two days later, in a letter to Osthaus, Taut commented with touching innocence:

Curious, how the Poelzig–Taut antithesis is now coming to a head. Poelzig believes that he was provoked by my article in *Kunstblatt*...and now he feels further attacked in my introduction to the Ausstellung unbek. Architekten. He now wants to resign from the Arbeitsrat on my account. What should I do? Polemics were and are quite alien to me and I simply feel that it is our duty to do everthing humanly possible to clear things up.[7]

Poelzig was under the impression that Taut was still the leader of the AFK and had to be reassured by Gropius that this was not the case. Although Poelzig was later to rejoin the Arbeitsrat,[8] at no time did he play an active part either in the meetings or the exhibitions of the group. His widow, Marlene Poelzig, recalls that Poelzig found the AFK too 'literary' and too 'intellectual' and felt that it had 'nothing to do with art'.[9] As a practising architect, Poelzig rejected the literary and polemical character of the AFK, a character which derived from its roots in literary Activism.

The polemical intention was also manifest in Behne's contribution, in which he attacked the art-buying public, saying that the AFK did not expect the snob to buy the drawings on display, and condemned the art-market: 'For whatever we do we must get away from spineless, passive art-consumerism.'[10] Antagonism such as this was the basic avant-garde position which had characterized the Activist movement from 1915 onwards. After the political ambitions of the movement had been frustrated, the antagonism was coupled with other avant-garde poses, which appeared for the first time in the spring of 1919. These poses, to use Poggioli's categories, were nihilism and agonism.

Nihilism, the desire to create a *tabula rasa* is clearly related to antagonism, indeed, Poggioli has defined it as a 'transcendental antagonism'.[11] It appeared in the Ausstellung für unbekannte Architekten in the desire of the organizers to break down and demolish all previously held views as to what was and was not architecture. By including a large number of works by non-architects, the AFK also posed the question of who was, and who was not an architect. As many painters as architects exhibited, including César Klein, Moriz Melzer, Arnold Topp, Wenzel Hablik, Gerhard Marcks, Fidus and Johannes Molzahn. The architectural visions of the painters shared two main influences: Cubism was one, the glass-worship of Scheerbart and Taut was the other. Two typical examples were Molzahn's suggestion for a glass *Kultusbau* and Hablik's design for an exhibition pavilion. Both were composed of faceted glass panes arranged fan-like around vertical axes. The reaction of the critics to such projects was entirely predictable. They applauded the rich fantasy, but denied that it had anything to do with architecture. Paul Westheim wrote in the *Frankfurter Zeitung*:

54 Johannes Molzahn, drawing exhibited at the Ausstellung für unbekannte Architekten, 1919.

Finsterlin, Molzahn, César Klein, Treichel and Topp are not architects who build on paper, they are artists who play an often delightful game with architectural props. A few arresting curves suffice to make theatrical or festival decorations, cinema coulisses and graphic illustrations. One is tempted to adapt Hebbel's quip about the bucket of water without the bucket: architectural fantasy without architecture.[12]

In a similar vein, W. C. Behrendt, a founder member of the AFK who had become a leader of the Sparsame Bauen movement, wrote in *Kunst und Künstler*:

The organisers therefore decided on a compromise, and began to recruit for the exhibition within their own circle, among painters and sculptors. What has come out of this are designs on paper, more or less daring fantasies, and

55 Wenzel Hablik, exhibition
building, 1919.

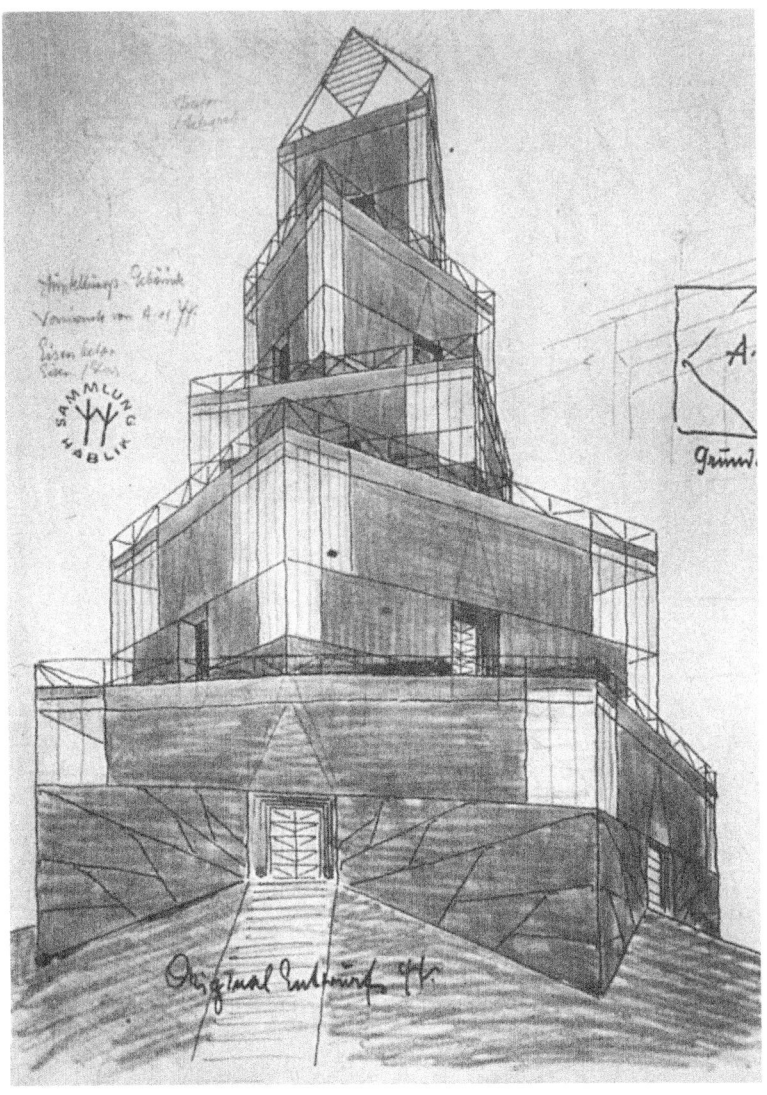

extravagant utopias. In isolated cases these are not without charm, at best
interesting, but for the most part devoid of any artistic value, more affected than
original.[13]

Walter Riezler commented on the drawings: 'They belong...in the
world of Kandinsky and the Cubists, and one would willingly hang one
or another of the drawings in one's room. But that is not the least
exoneration, if the exhibition is supposed to be concerned with designs
for buildings...No path leads from here to architecture.'[14] The most
intense critical outrage was provoked by the works of Hermann
Finsterlin and Jefim Golyscheff, who were neither architects nor
painters, in the accepted sense of the terms. Finsterlin had studied
chemistry, physics, medicine, philosophy and 'Indologie', while Goly-

56 Hermann Finsterlin,
designs for glass houses,
1919.

scheff, who was born in 1897, had been an infant prodigy as a violinist,
and had toured Russia, Rumania and Poland in 1905 as a soloist with
the Odessa Symphony Orchestra. He began drawing in 1907, stimulated
by his father who was a friend of Kandinsky, and moved to Berlin in
1909. He joined the 'artists' working committee' of the AFK in March
1919.

A whole room was given over to Finsterlin's polyp-like designs for
glass architecture. His designs were intended to shock: there was no
conception of structure – in spite of the presence of optimistic ground
plans and models. There was a strong erotic content, most noticeable
in the ejaculating tower of the *Fernsehturm*. Even the titles themselves
were calculated to upset: there was a *Haus des Monomanen* and a *Haus
des Psychometers*. The *Reichs-Anzeiger* critique commented: 'One sees
amazing designs which completely contradict the common notion of the
nature of architecture. H. Finsterlin portrays forms which resemble

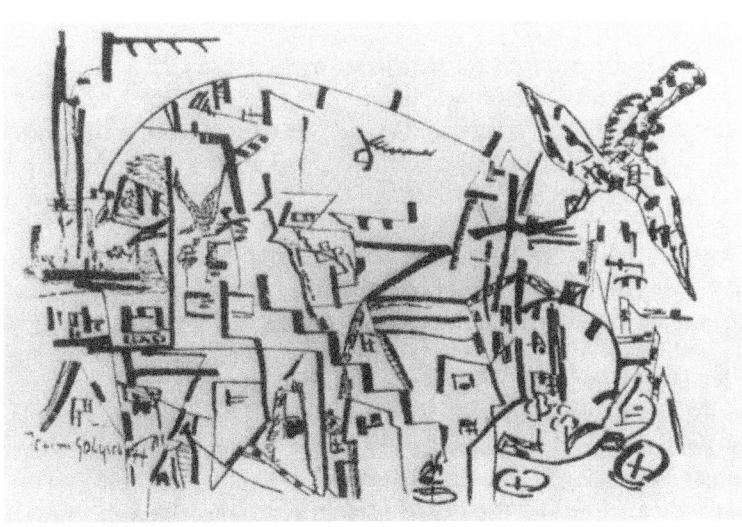

57 Hermann Finsterlin,
Fernsehturm, 1919.

58 Jefim Golyscheff,
drawing, 1919.

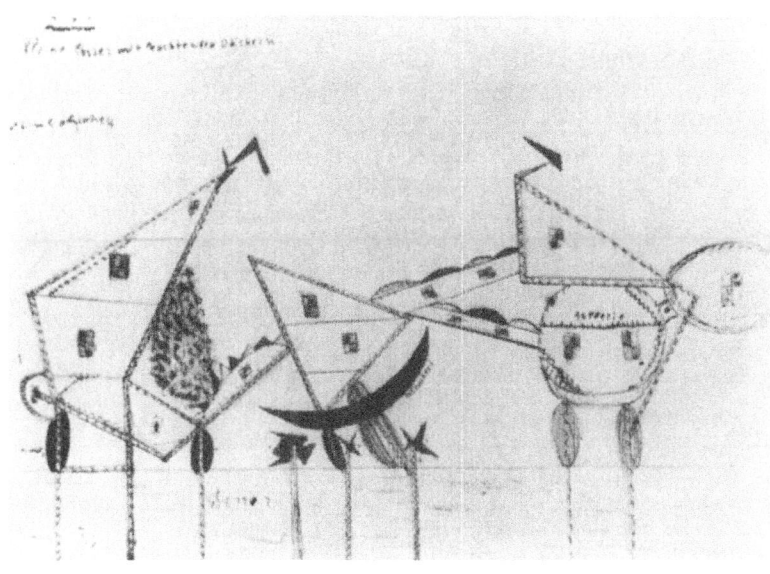

59 Jefim Golyscheff,
drawing, 1919, *Little houses
with illuminated roofs.*

mushrooms, stalactites or other curious natural forms.'[15] Finsterlin's
drawings appear to have shocked even the most sympathetic critics, and
the usually optimistic Behne, in his own review of the exhibition,
bemoaned Finsterlin's lack of appeal. 'It is a sign of the dreadful
earnestness of our age that educated people can derive so little pleasure
from these drawings, which are often delightful.'[16] Although entirely
different in their forms and graphic style, Golyscheff's drawings shared
with those of Finsterlin a totally nihilistic disregard for the conventions
of architecture and of gravity. His spidery, childlike drawings shunned
perspective or the notions of plan or elevation. Even Behne noted in
Golyscheff's works 'a complete lack of respect'.[17] Bringing both Finsterlin
and Golyscheff together as the *succès de scandale*, the critic Schikowski
wrote in *Vorwärts*:

> The misty peaks of extravagent fantasy are reached, however, by H. Finsterlin
> and Jefim Golyscheff. The former devises houses and devotional buildings,
> theatres and art-workshops, which rise out of labyrinthine ground plans and
> adopt the forms of organic bodies, flowers, mushrooms, polyps. The second, a
> young Russian musician, composes magical gardens which hang free in the air
> or under water, and houses with luminous roofs – all made of glass and
> reinforced concrete, the favoured materials of the modern architectural poets.[18]

The nihilistic intention of Gropius and his colleagues in including these
drawings in the exhibition can be adjudged from a letter which he
wrote to Golyscheff, telling him that his work had been selected for the
exhibition. 'We have hung a series of your fascinating drawings in the
Ausstellung für unbekannte Architekten – let the bourgeois think what
he will about them. We finally came to the conclusion that your works
should be included in the architectural section. They really are extreme
examples of what we want: utopia.'[19] By exhibiting Golyscheff's
drawings the AFK not only promoted anti-architecture, or architectural

nihilism, but also made a direct contact with the arch-nihilists of the period, the Berlin Dadaists.

Two exhibitions were held in the Graphisches Kabinett J. B. Neumann in April 1919. The second was the Ausstellung für unbekannte Architekten which was preceded by the first Berlin Dada-Ausstellung. In addition to the mutual interest which each exhibition must have generated for the other, there was a mutual link in Golyscheff, who exhibited at both. In his memoir of Berlin Dada, Hausmann recalled that he and Golyscheff organized this first exhibition – 'in the absence of Huelsenbeck'.[20] The Galerie Neumann had already been used on 18 February 1919 for a 'Dadarede' which was given by Huelsenbeck.

In the same memoir, Hausmann offered a select list of true members of the 'Dada-Club'. 'Besides, the programmes of the DADA-soirées show clearly that the only members were Hausmann, Huelsenbeck, Baader, Grosz, Heartfield, Mehring and Golyscheff.'[21] Hausmann has given the following account of Golyscheff's contribution to the Dada-Ausstellung.

One day in the spring of 1919 I met a young, free-thinking fellow called Jefim Golyscheff. While it is questionable if certain Dadaists were ever DADA, Golyscheff was. It wasn't necessary for him to be instructed in the aims of the DADA-Club, or rather, of DADA. He possessed all the necessary qualities of a true Dadaist.

Like Caesar, he came, he saw, he conquered...To the first DADA Exhibition in April 1919 he brought assemblages such as had never been seen before: things grafted together out of cans, small bottles, bits of cardboard, lumps of wood, scraps of plush and tufts of hair. An incredible optical spectacle: before then it had been impossible to show anything like this.

Naturally, all this found form in his fine, intelligent and sensitive hands. The first DADA Exhibition, in the Graphisches Kabinett closed with a large DADA-soirée, at which Golyscheff appeared with a young girl dressed in white. I can still see this scene as if it was today, as if nothing had changed. Golyscheff, with a weak smile, went up to the large grand piano and beckoned with a small movement of the hand to the innocent angel, who sat down and proclaimed with the voice of an electronic puppet:

    Anti-Symphony, 3 parts = musical war-guillotine
(a) Provocative shot in the arm
(b) Chaotic mouth-cavern or the submarine aeroplane
(c) Collapsible Hypo – F sharp – chondriac.[22]

The desire to shock was the prime mover behind the works which Golyscheff and Hausmann produced for the exhibition. As Hausmann recalled: 'For this occasion he and I made "technical drawings", as well as electric bells or a gasometer and such like, with the idea that the form should annoy the spectator, like the gasometer in the shape of the Venus de Milo.'[23] Golyscheff's assemblages, according to Hausmann, were in absolute opposition to the currently fashionable Expressionism which Walden and Sturm were selling to an enthusiastic public.[24]

In their attacks on Expressionism and in the modishness and indulgent introspection of the Sturm followers, the Dadaists carried on, in a more vigorous manner, from where the Activists had left off. Indeed, it has been suggested that Dadaism was a legitimate offspring of Activism.

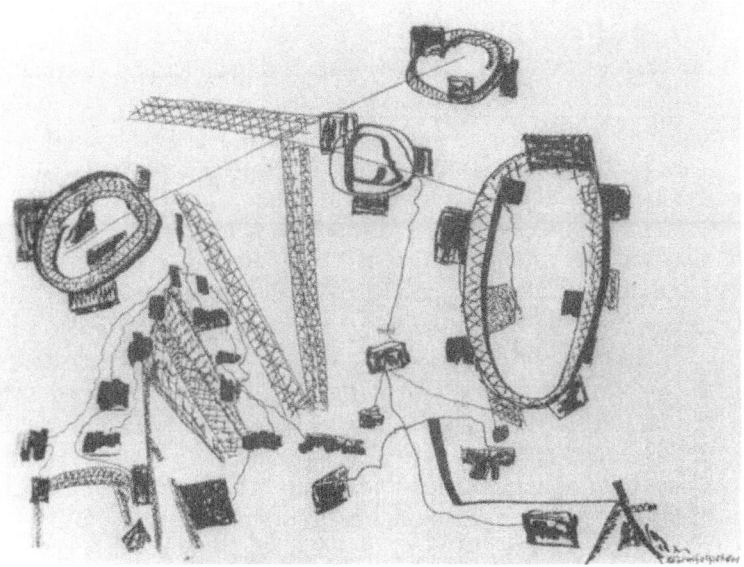

60 Jefim Golyscheff,
Technical drawing, 1919.

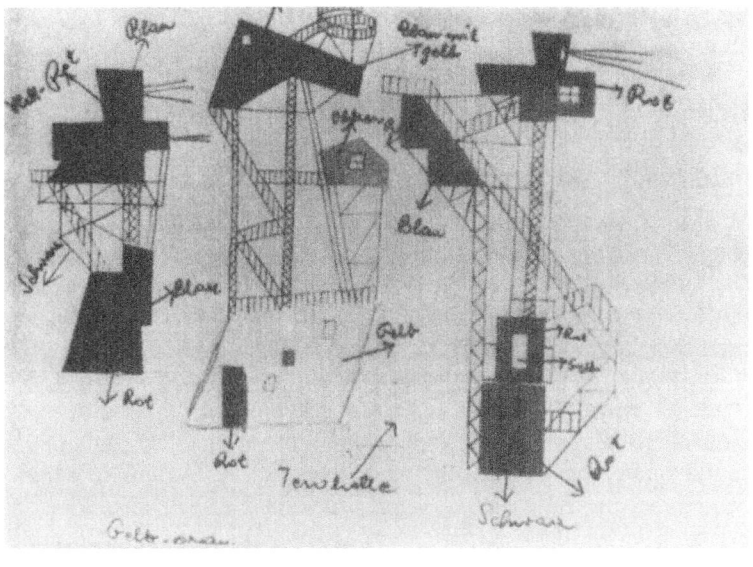

61 Raoul Hausmann,
Architecture fantastique, 1919.

Paulsen, for example, has claimed that in Switzerland and France, Dadaism was 'a mere appendage to Expressionism and Futurism', and only became politically aware after contact with German Activism. From this he concluded that: 'Dadaism proved itself in more than one point to be the ill-bred child of Activism.'[25] The Dadaists themselves would have denied this vigorously, for the Activists were the particular anathema of the 'Dada-Club'.

The Dadaists totally rejected the claims to leadership made by the self-appointed *geistig* élite. In 1917, Richard Huelsenbeck wrote in his essay 'Der neue Mensch': 'It is a false notion that an improvement of the world might be achieved via the power of the intellectuals.'[26] In an

obvious reference to Hiller's *Die Weisheit der Langenweile*, Huelsenbeck
continued: 'For we know the petty arrogances of the "Geistlings" and
of the converted literati, who carry their dyspeptic tenor through the
boring spaces of the reviews like a priceless babe-in-arms, without ever
having understood the wisdom of boredom.'[27] Hiller was again singled
out for vilification in the manifesto 'Was ist der Dadaismus und was
will er in Deutschland?', which was written in April or May 1919 by
Hausmann, Heulsenbeck and Golyscheff as a lampoon of the programmes
of the Activists. The three authors actually called themselves 'Der
dadaistische revolutionäre Zentralrat'. The manifesto called for: 'most
brutal battle against all schools of so-called *geistige Arbeiter* (Hiller,
Adler), against their concealed middle-classiness, and against Expressionism and the neo-classical culture as it is represented by Sturm.'[28]
Although the manifesto was intended as a lampoon of the programmes
of the RGA and the AFK, it did include the suggestion that a programme
of 'Socialization' should include the building of garden cities, 'which
advance mankind in the direction of freedom'.[29]

The disdain with which the Dadaists viewed the Activists appears to
have been mutual. Baader actually approached Hiller with the suggestion
that the Dadaists might contribute to the *Ziel* yearbook. Hiller's reply was
less than enthusiastic. He wrote to Baader:

There is no possibility of my including the crass rubbish of a Hausmann or the
talented trickery of a Huelsenbeck in my yearbook. The one I do appreciate is
the political cartoonist Grosz, but as a writer he doesn't come into question. I
give you the choice: either our exchange of notes will be published without
comment in the next *Ziel* (a nice advertisement for Dada, and free at that!) – or
none of it will be published.[30]

Baader appears to have chosen the latter option, as no writings by the
Dadaists ever appeared in the *Ziel* yearbooks.

In spite of the mutual antipathy between the Activists and the
Dadaists, certain general concordances did exist between the two
movements. Both were self-consciously internationalist. Dada in Berlin
could claim roots in Switzerland, France and America, while the
paradise of the Activists was also supra-national. As Otto Freundlich
wrote in 1917 in *Die Aktion*: 'The entire thrust of Activism, in all its
shades, is clearly internationalist. The actuality of national limitations
is either attacked or bluntly denied.'[31] We have already noted that both
movements developed in 1916–17 in rejection of positivist rationalism.
In addition, both opposed the introspection of Expressionism and sought,
in their various ways, to replace it with a cult of action, of vital activity.
For the Activists, as for the Dadaists, life rather than art was the goal
to be pursued.

In spite of all the eccentricities and excesses associated with the
'Dada-Club', the message of the Berlin Dadaists was very sober. Paulsen
has described it well: 'One no longer wants to improve the world, for
it has become clear, that the world is not to be improved. Instead, one
chooses to propagate life itself, life in its total dullness.'[32] With his

assemblages, Golyscheff was saying exactly this. The artist or intellectual should not become embroiled with dreams of paradise or utopia, but should reconcile himself with the mundanity of everyday life and with its bric-a-brac – bottles, tin-cans, hair. The apparent nihilism of the spring days of 1919 offered the chance to create a *tabula rasa* on which a new set of values could be worked out.

16

◇◇

Taut and the *Proletkult*

Although he was closely involved in April 1919 with the Ausstellung für unbekannte Architekten, with Golyscheff and the Dadaists, the impact of Dadaism on Taut's own writings does not appear, as we shall see, until the end of the year and the beginning of 1920. Instead of immediately pursuing the nihilist path after his disappointments in April and May, 1919, Taut swung vigorously away from the grandiose ambitions of November 1918, and placed his faith in a more didactic and incremental approach. Through a process of education and enlightenment, the ground would be prepared for a second, spiritual revolution, which would succeed where the political revolution had failed.

The idea of a second, spiritual revolution was a recurring topic in the spring of 1919, and was invoked by writers and theorists of all political persuasions. Thus Walther Rathenau, looking back over the revolutionary months, concluded: 'If it proves impossible to wrest the revolution out of the fetters of vested interests, of delusions and of claptrap, then we shall see an enlightened democracy of mendacity, of bad conscience and of oppression...Only the second revolution can save us, not the revolution of the Cossacks (i.e. the Soviet doctrine), but a revolution in our way of thinking.'[1] Likewise, we have seen that Gropius made the ultimate success of the restructured AFK dependent on a second revolution of *Geist*. In his article, 'Der freie Volksstaat und die Kunst', Gropius wrote: 'Not the political, but only the completed *geistig* revolution can make us free.'[2] In his speech to the AFK in March 1919, Gropius urged the group to be patient, to work in secrecy until the second, *geistig* revolution had prepared society for its message: 'We must have the courage to wait until there is a better *opinio communis*. Perhaps it will happen sooner than we expect.'[3] The faith in a second revolution carried with it the notion that it would be preceeded by a period of preparation, an interim period during which society would be primed and prepared for the revolutionary task.

This was Taut's theme in his contribution to the programme for the Ausstellung für unbekannte Architekten. At that moment, he insisted, there was no architecture: 'No, today there is as little architecture as there are few architects.'[4] It was impossible, said Taut, to create true architecture at the present time. All the architect could do was plan, to prepare for the future, to prepare for the coming of the second revolution.

In our profession today we cannot be creators, but are seekers and summoners. We shall not cease searching for that which can later take crystalline form. Neither shall we cease calling after companions who will join us on the difficult path, who in profoundest modesty accept that the things of today are merely the first rays of the dawn, and who will prepare themselves with selfless sacrifice for the rising of the new sun.[5]

This passage contains all the necessary elements for the avant-gardistic pose of agonism. It was necessary, said Taut, to suffer and make sacrifices at that time, in order to ensure the success, a distant success perhaps, of the second revolution. We shall discuss Taut's agonism later, for it coloured his writings strongly at the end of 1919. In the summer of 1919, however, Taut was preoccupied with the didactic task of preparation.

Unlike Rathenau, who rejected any type of revolution on the model of the 'Cossacks', or Gropius, who wished to avoid any direct involvement with politics, Taut adhered to his belief in a socialist *Kunstpolitik*. After the spring of 1919 his version of a socialist *Kunstpolitik* was strictly defined as a proletarian movement, modelled on the *Proletkult* which had been established in Soviet Russia. Taut thus followed the lead of Erich Baron, Rubiner, Becher and Frank, all of whom had left their previously held Activist position to become advocates of proletarian revolution.

After the rapid decline of the RGA, a number of former Activists turned to the Third International, formed in March 1919, and saw in it a new focal point for the revolutionary *Geist*. Before his death in 1920, Rubiner had become closely associated with the KPD. Similarly, Wilhelm Herzog, who, like Taut, had signed the RGA programme in November 1918, abandoned the élitist and anti-proletarian stance of Activism in the early months of 1919 and argued, in his literary journal *Das Forum*, that the most viable instrument of social change was the proletariat.

To Taut, the notion of the proletariat was loosely defined, and was virtually synonymous with the Activist notion of *Volk*, as an alternative group to the state or the political party. It did not correspond absolutely with the Bolshevik definition. Indeed, his views on Bolshevism seem to have been very ambivalent in 1919 and 1920. As a committed pacifist he found it hard to reconcile the ideal of revolution with the blood-letting which had been perpetrated in Russia in the name of the proletariat. Although drawn to the Third International, he must certainly have felt a strong sympathy for Hiller and the pacifist element of the old RGA. In the *Ziel-Jahrbuch* for 1919, Hiller totally condemned the sanguinary tactics of the Bolsheviks.[6] Like his political mentor, Georg Ledebour, Taut did not join the KPD after the Halle Conference, at which the USPD was dissolved in favour of a communist party aligned to the Third International.

Yet the idea of an international *Proletkunst* attracted Taut considerably. He made strenuous efforts as leader of the AFK to make contact with artist groups in Moscow. In January 1919, the AFK obtained a manifesto from the radical artists' group in Moscow through the intercession of Dr Ludwig Baehr, who also translated it. In response, Taut sent a telegram to Moscow on 26 January, on behalf of the AFK.

It read: 'We greet with great sympathy the endeavours of the Assembly of Plastic Artists in Moscow as described in the programme communicated to us by Ludwig Baehr, and are prepared to collaborate with it and with all artists of the hitherto divided nations. Der Arbeitsrat für Kunst. Bruno Taut, Walter Gropius, Max Pechstein.'[7] In 1919, direct contact was impossible as a result of the blockade. Nevertheless, a sporadic correspondence was established. The *Soldatenrat* in Moscow wrote back to the AFK sometime in March, 1919, prompting Taut to write another letter, which enclosed the programmes of the AFK. The tone of the letter was very Activistic. War and militarism were condemned: Taut assured the Moscow *Soldatenrat*: 'We have condemned with abhorrence the criminal deeds of the militarists. Those among us who swam for a while with the current under the influence of mass-suggestion, look back on this time full of shame and remorse.'[8] The letter went on to assure the Russians of the comradeship of the AFK and suggested an exchange of ideas, works and even personnel. Taut also suggested that the Russians and the AFK could collaborate on 'the preparation for the great work of love which, after the days of ugly hate, will once again lead Europe to beauty'. But, added Taut in the true Activist manner, ideas and manifestos were not enough. Action was the only valid programme: 'We place no value on words, we want to legitimate ourselves through our work.'[9] Through these contacts with the radical groups in Moscow, Taut was first introduced to the *Proletkult* which had been developed in Soviet Russia since 1917. Although, at this time, he would have had little or no information about the formal developments in architecture and art which had taken place in Russia since the revolution, he did at least have a good grasp of the theoretical and ideological precepts of the *Proletkult*. The admiration which he had expressed in September 1918 for the Russian *Volksgeist*[10] was transformed into admiration for the spirit of the *Proletkult*.

An early instance of this Russian influence can be seen in Taut's response to the AFK circular which was distributed in March 1919.[11] Almost all the members of the AFK agreed in their replies that some sort of working community should be established to bring together the practitioners of the various arts. Only Bruno Taut, however, specified that it should be a communist community. He suggested that: 'Kadinen should be placed at the disposal of the Arbeitsrat für Kunst for a communist artists' community, combining field and workshop.'[12] In his reply to the circular, Taut now excluded any possibility of a fruitful collaboration between the state and the radical artists. Indeed, he proposed that the state should be ignored as a controller or sponsor of architecture and the arts. Instead of working for the state, the radical artists should aim their efforts directly at the proletariat, and be sponsored by the workers' councils.[13] The re-education of the proletariat was the true mission of the radical artist.

It was in this light that Taut viewed the Ausstellung für unbekannte Architekten. In his review of the exhibition, written for the USPD paper *Freiheit*, Taut, alone amongst the critics, emphasized that the exhibition was intended for the proletariat. His review began: 'The wish which has already been expressed in the announcement in *Freiheit* should today, after the opening, be repeated: may many representatives of the progressive and revolutionary proletariat and also lots of women and children see this exhibition!'[14] Taut went on to explain the kinship which existed between the 'unknown architects' and the proletariat. Both existed at the fringes of bourgeois society, both attracted ridicule and scorn from the cultured bourgeois.

So we have here an exhibition by 'pitiable idealists': the revolutionary proletarian should be able to understand them best of all, for he is one himself. Without further ado he will accept the flowing and the limitless, exactly that which horrifies the bourgeois as 'anarchy'. Even in the spiritual realm, the bourgeois needs some form of '-archy' – rule, and is absolutely helpless when he finds no compartmentalization, no division between systems, no support from 'celebrated authorities'. We have no faith in the bourgeois world... and appeal, therefore, all the more strongly to the proletariat.[15]

Indeed, Taut asked the visitors to write down their responses to the exhibits. As he said in his review: 'What would be useful for all of us, however, would be if every proletarian, worker, craftsman, soldier, student etc., would write on a slip of paper: "I find that and that the most beautiful."'[16] The results of this survey were then published by Taut in *Freiheit* on 23 April in an article entitled 'Eine Volksabstimmung veranstaltet vom Arbeitsrat für Kunst'.

Such a direct appeal to the revolutionary spirit of the proletariat was in complete contradiction to the precepts of Landauer, Hiller and the Activists. Hiller had differentiated between the *Volk* and 'the feeble-minded and immoral mass'. *Geist*, as Hiller explained, was a function of the *Volk*, but had nothing to do with the masses, who were dismissed as non-revolutionary and reactionary. The success of the Bolshevik revolution, the apparent success of the communists in Hungary and northern Italy, and the gathering momentum behind the Third International seemed to disprove this Activist theory. Taut, certainly, became increasingly involved in the summer of 1919 with establishing a bridgehead between the intellectuals and the proletariat.

17

◇-◇

Taut's literary activity in the summer of 1919

Taut was joined in his didactic task by Behne and, to a lesser extent, by Gropius. Together they planned to bring out a new magazine which would, they hoped, spread the message of the AFK to a wider audience. This would seem to have been a contradiction of Gropius's plan to turn the AFK into a secret, almost masonic lodge, but was absolutely in accord with Taut's thinking at that time.[1] He described the project in a letter to Osthaus: 'Gropius, Behne and I are going to bring out a new magazine with the title *Bauen*...A prospectus will appear soon and will be distributed to the widest public – we want to win the layman over to our cause.'[2] The prospectus did appear: it was printed on red paper and distributed on Potsdamer Platz. It proposed that an ideal, fraternal form of socialism could be stimulated by architecture: 'Socialism and brotherliness will develop spontaneously through mutual activity, and a socialist – that is a truthful, brotherly attitude – will appear that much sooner, the more this mutual activity distances itself from everything practical, trifling and narrow-minded. One can only realize an ideal through devotion to an idea, through idealism.'[3] The goal would be a *Kultusbau* – as a symbol of peace and harmony. The act of building would forge a lasting unity not only between the architects, the painters and the sculptors, but also between the artists, the craftsmen and the masses, who would involve and identify themselves with the building project:

The true building is the mutual artistic labour of many men, not only of the architects, sculptors and painters, but also of the carpenters, bricklayers, stone masons and fitters. In the true building, all are involved to the same degree. Behind them stand the mass of the people, who follow the progress of the building and join in emotionally in the communal project. There are no underlings, simply collaborators. Each one contributes the best from his fantasy and sense of form, decorates the building through the love, devotion and innocence of his voluntary efforts.[4]

The magazine *Bauen* would be the first step towards this ideal. The prospectus was aggressively anti-academic and anti-bourgeois. The editors insisted: 'We are not talking about art like the other do, as if about a distant island...We propose to prepare the only soil out of which true art can grow...the people!'[5] The first copy of the magazine was planned for June 1919 and was to contain Taut's 'Haus des Himmels', a story by Scheerbart, and articles by Gropius and Wassili Luckhardt.

It did not appear, however, and no copies of *Bauen* were ever published. Instead, some of the material was used by Taut in the early numbers of his own magazine *Frühlicht*, which was launched in January 1920.

Although *Bauen* failed in its efforts to spread the message of the new, *geistig* movement in architecture to the wider public, Taut did achieve some success with the publication of *Alpine Architektur* in June 1919. It was published by Osthaus's Folkwang Verlag in a large, expensive format. The irony of this was not lost on Taut, who noted that the only market for his egalitarian visions was the same bourgeoisie against whom the polemic of the book was directed. He wrote to Osthaus: 'I find it very painful that these things, which exist in a pure and happy world, are now coming into contact with mammon.'[6] At this time, Taut had no source of income other than his writings. The irony of the luxury edition was compounded by the fact that Taut's finances depended almost entirely on the success of this expensive volume. Taut bemoaned this situation to Osthaus: 'It is a terrible pressure which weighs on me. Shouldn't the A.A., which cost me a lot of sacrifice, help to ease this pressure?'[7] While the Folkwang edition of *Alpine Architektur* was strictly aimed at the purses of the prosperous bourgeois, Taut did produce a more accessible version. It was entitled 'Rede des Bundeskanzlers von Europa am 24. April 1993 vor dem europäischen Parlament', and was published in the *Sozialistische Monatshefte*.[8] *Alpine Architektur* was first conceived by Taut as a symbolic alternative to militarism, nationalism and materialism. In the article he moved forward seventy years and showed the leader of a united Europe looking back on the period of achievement in which the proposals put forward in *Alpine Architektur* had been realized. The form of the article, a parliamentary speech, was taken from Scheerbart's short essay 'Der Architektenkongress. Eine Parlamentsgeschichte', which was written in 1914, and republished by Taut in *Frühlicht* in the autumn of 1921.

Taut continued his literary activities in the summer of 1919 with *Die Auflösung der Städte* (The Dissolution of the Cities), an expanded, illustrated version of his decentralist essay 'Die Erde eine gute Wohnung', which had been published in *Die Volkswohnung* in January 1919. Once again, the driving force behind the work was financial necessity. Writing to Osthaus in May 1919, Taut described his plans for the new book and asked if it would be possible to launch a subscription for the book to coincide with the publication of *Alpine Architektur*. 'I was thinking that with the appearance of A.A., we could put out a subscription to the new work; for I really don't know at present what I am going to live on for so long.'[9] While Taut's principles dictated that he should devote himself to the visual re-education of the wide mass of the public, the circumstances of the moment offered him only one means of earning his living – through the production of expensively produced folios which could only be afforded by the despised bourgeoisie.[10]

The scorn with which Taut viewed the cultured middle classes at this time can be seen in an article on the theatre, which Taut wrote in the summer of 1919. The article began with a scathing attack on the commercial theatres, which he described as 'capitalist department stores for the enjoyment of art'.[11] He portrayed the audience, rather ingenuously, as a crowd of racketeers:

as a war-profiteer, or at least as a superior citizen, one sits there stiffly, eyeing everyone and sizing them up. The safety curtain still closes off the store for art appreciation. When it goes up everything become pitch dark and, as in a peep show, whether one wants to or not one is forced to look at the platform on which the art objects are being sold.[12]

Returning to the *Kunstbauten* in his *Stadtkrone* project, Taut said that the theatre should not merely be used to amuse the bourgeoise, but, as in *Die Stadtkrone*, should be a focus for the *Volk* and the *Gemeinschaft*. This, he said, was a political and social function as much as an artistic one.

The first, greatest, and most difficult step in the emancipation of the theatre is not one for the artist but for the statesman. The theatre business must be lifted out of the capitalist mire, in which it threatens to sink and decay, and given an independent existence in the fresh air of the open society. It will then become the highest exaltation of the united masses and perhaps even an act of worship.[13]

Taut's differentiation between the statesman and the artist shows that he had rejected the notion of political leadership guided by a *geistig* élite which had formed the basis of the RGA programme.

Although Taut had abandoned the romantic socialism which he had followed during the war years, this article on the theatre still pursued the formal, artistic means for the articulation of *Geist* and *Volk* which he had initially worked out for the *Stadtkrone*. Just as he had sought to integrate the simple housing, representing the *Volk*, and the *Kristallhaus*, representing *Geist*, through the use of harmonious colours and an ascending building scale, so he sought to integrate the theatre audience with the *Glanzwelt* which was being depicted on the stage. As we have seen, Taut was almost obsessed with the schism between his private *Glanzwelt* and the barren reality around him. He wrote about it repeatedly in his war-time letters, and was still preoccupied with the idea in 1919. In the letter to Osthaus in which he mentioned his short-lived prospects in the *Räterepublik* in Munich and complained at the lack of any work, he added that he drew comfort from his writing and from the *Glanzwelt* which he was constructing on paper: 'I'm left sitting alone, buried in the middle of Berlin at my drawing board, which is already more like a writing desk. But I enjoy enormously the passionate night hours in which I build the new world as it should look after the dissolution of the cities.'[14] The theatre offered, in microcosm, the possibility of bringing the real world and the *Glanzwelt* together, if only for an hour or so.

In the hands of the architect, said Taut, lay the power to promote or to prevent this happy fusion.

Everything decisive in theatre design occurs at one point in the building – the acid test for the architect at one thin line on the ground plan, at the place where only a hanging cloth unveils a new *Glanzwelt* to the assembled throng – where the room is extended not only physically and spatially, but where this extension is, or at least should be, a spiritual extension, a spiritual inhalation and explosion in the heart – with one word, at the curtain.[15]

The proscenium arch, which rigidly separated the real world from the *Glanzwelt*, must be destroyed, said Taut. By redesigning the ground plan and by rethinking the lighting effects both on the stage and in the rest of the theatre, a new unity could be achieved – *Volk* and *Geist* could be fused as one. This was almost an Activist paradigm. Through the application of rational principles a more ideal state, an 'attainable paradise' could be reached. Now, however, the paradise in question was contained within the four walls of the theatre and was aimed specifically at the new *Volk*, the proletariat.

Taut suggested that the interior walls of the auditorium should be dissolved through the use of colour and glass: 'The walls are a radiant flux of intensive colour.'[16] The lighting in the auditorium should also be controlled during the performance to complement the lighting on stage. Both the stage and the auditorium would expand infinitely in all directions as a result of the correct use of light and colour, and one would merge with the other: 'The auditorium, through its articulation, extends itself into the stage, so that during the performance one senses no division. The auditorium must already appear limitless, but the stage must be truly limitless, not simply in its spiritual multiplicity, but sometimes without an actual end.'[17] Only in such a theatre, said Taut, could Stramm's *Geschehen* and Scheerbart's 'Stern–und Weltendramen' find a true context.

Taut's scheme for a dimensionless theatre anticipated, in many ways, Poelzig's conversion of the old Zirkus Schumann into the Großes Schauspielhaus. The conversion was commissioned by Max Reinhardt and was achieved with extraordinary speed in the late summer and autumn of 1919. Although, in his article, Taut specifically condemned 'Reinhardt's large-scale performances, which until now have flopped',[18] Poelzig's great burgundy-red auditorium and the combination of apron and panorama stage must have met with Taut's approval. The abolition of the proscenium, of coulisses and backdrops, as advocated by Taut, was to become a cliché in subsequent plans for a proletarian theatre. Gropius's Totaltheater, designed with and for Piscator in 1927 is the best known example.

'Zum neuen Theaterbau' was clearly related to Taut's current writing, for in August 1919 he began sketching the outline of a theatrical fantasy – similar in spirit to Scheerbart's cosmic dramas. He wrote to Osthaus on 2 August: 'I am busy today with a new idea, which fills me almost ecstatically with enthusiasm...It is an architectural drama, more correctly: pantomime. I hope to win Pfitzner to write a score of the symphony. It will be an absolutely splendid piece...music

62 Bruno Taut, *Der Weltbaumeister*, 1919, plate 3.

63 *Der Weltbaumeister*, plate 8.

and architecture, both abstract and both in the purest unison.'[19] The final version of this theatre piece was published by the Folkwang-Verlag in Hagen in 1920 as *Der Weltbaumeister*, subtitled *An Architectural Drama for Symphonic Music, dedicated to the Spirit of Paul Scheerbart*.[20] Thirty drawings portray the expansion of an architectural form which travels through infinite space before reaching paradise, where, predictably, it is metamorphized into a *Kristallhaus*. The parallel with his infinite theatre is very striking. If it had been made as a film, it is conceivable that the *Weltbaumeister* may have succeeded. The published series of black and white drawings, however, fail to do justice to Taut's vivid

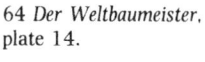

64 *Der Weltbaumeister*, plate 14.

65 *Der Weltbaumeister*, plate 25.

imagination. Much more interesting than the drawings was an essay which Taut wrote to describe his architectural symphony. The relationship between colour and music was portayed as resonant. The essay began: 'The colours ring, the forms resound – colours and forms carry the tone as pure, unfragmented elements of the universe.'[21] The relationship between the thus created work and the human observer was empathetic. 'Naturally, everything that man does remains anthropomorphic, and even a treatment which is conceived as totally cosmic must originate in human feelings and thought. Projection of our human existence into the universe, with the desire to lose ourselves there.'[22] In

66 Bruno Taut, *Bruckner IX Symphony – 3rd Movement*, 1919.

his article on the theatre and in *Der Weltbaumeister* Taut turned to empathy theory, as he had done in *Die Stadtkrone*, to explain the inexplicable relationships which he felt existed between *Volk* and *Geist*, between the human *Geist* and the cosmic '*All*'.

The endless theatre was envisaged by Taut as a means of bringing together *Geist* and *Volk*, the *Glanzwelt* and the everyday world. *Der Weltbaumeister* was intended as an abstract essay on the nature of *Geist*. In September 1919, Taut turned his attention firmly to the *Volk* as a founder member of the Bund für proletarische Kultur.

18

The Bund für proletarische Kultur

Taut's involvement with the Bund für proletarische Kultur (BPK) confirmed that after the collapse of the RGA and his resignation as leader of the Arbeitsrat für Kunst, Taut sided with the former Activists who had turned to the *Proletkult* during 1919. Among the founder members of the BPK were several members of the RGA, which had long been defunct. The writer Arthur Holitscher, who, with Friedrich Natteroth, initiated the BPK, had signed the programme of the Politischer Rat geistiger Arbeiter in November 1918. In September 1919 Holitscher's was the first name which appeared under the manifesto 'Aufruf zu einem Bund für proletarische Kultur', which was published in the *Räte-Zeitung*. The other signatories were, in order, Natteroth, Bruno Taut, Gertrud Eysoldt, Max Barthel, Hans Baluschek, Alfons Goldschmidt, H. B. Herfurth, the theatre-group Die Tribüne, Rudolf Leonhard and the Zentralarbeiterräte des Siemens-Konzerns.[1] Holitscher, Taut, Goldschmidt and Leonhard had all been members of the RGA.

The tone of the 'Aufruf' reflected this Activist background. Like the programme of the RGA, it called for a *geistig* revolution. 'A call for a new culture arises, for a spiritual revolution: a call for clarity, self-determination and revolutionary daring in the pursuit of economic and political targets.'[2] The authority on which the revolution was to be based, however, was no longer the *geistig* élite, but the revolutionary proletariat. 'You isolated beacons among the masses, you incorrigible idealists, who have for long been inspired by the importance of these ideas, but saw no way out of the chaos, we call to you: Join together! Appoint the most able minds at your work-places as representatives of your spiritual interests.'[3] The description of the revolutionary workers as 'incorrigible idealists' is very reminiscent of Taut's description of the 'unbekannte Architekten' in his review of the exhibition: 'So we have here an exhibition by "pitiable idealists"'.[4] This might suggest that Taut himself wrote the manifesto or, at least, directly contributed to its composition. That Taut's name should have appeared third in the list of signatories, after the two initiators of the group – Holitscher and Natteroth, indicates that he was closely involved with the formulation of the 'Aufruf'.

In response to the 'Aufruf', the Bund für proletarische Kultur was formally established, and attracted several interesting recruits to its ranks. One was Ludwig Rubiner, who had been a leading figure in

Hiller's movement until 1917, when he had abandoned Activism for
Bolshevism.[5] Another was the writer Leo Matthias, who had signed the
programme of the RGA in 1918. Three other founders had been
involved with the AFK. One was the painter Heinrich Vogeler, whom
Behne had wanted to expell from the AFK for setting up a 'red-guard'
within the group. Another was J. B. Neumann, the gallery owner, who
had been host to the Dada-Ausstellung and the Ausstellung für
unbekannte Architekten, and who had subsequently offered to run the
business side of the proposed magazine *Bauen*. The third, rather
surprisingly, was Behne himself.

The political stance of the group was, from the outset, closely linked
to the KPD. The 'Aufruf' exhorted: 'We must become a force which
will bring the power of capitalist corruption to its knees, together with
its lying press, its swindling of the people, its brain-washing politics. We
must use our volition to support the struggle of the revolutionary
parties.'[6] One of the founder members, Hermann Duncker, was an
influential functionary in the KPD, and the BPK was identified intimately
with the party. This can be seen from a letter which Käthe Kollwitz sent
to Max Barthel, declining his invitation to join the new group. Kollwitz
wrote:

Yesterday I was at the meeting of the Bund für Proletarische Kultur, and I have
decided not to join. The views which I had on this enterprise were reinforced
during the course of the meeting. To begin with, I am opposed to the idea that
the Bund für proletarische Kultur should be established on a party base. To join
would be much the same, as it were, as joining the Communist Party [KPD].
I cannot resolve, however, to join any party.[7]

Yet the Activist tag stuck to the BPK, and it was attacked from the left
for being just as bourgeois and élitist as the RGA had been. A critic in
the KPD paper *Freiheit* (not to be confused with the USPD paper of the
same name) asked: 'When will the literati, painters and sculptors finally
comprehend the basic condition of their work – that they have to learn
about revolution from the masses, that they are the recipients, who
should approach the class-conscious proletariat on bended knees. When
will they comprehend that they can at best be the tinder, but never the
spark.'[8] Franz Pfemfert, who was on the militant left of the KPD, at this
time wrote polemical pieces against the BPK and renamed it 'Der
Modebund für proletarische Kultur'.[9]

Pfemfert's criticism was probably justified, as Behne's presence in the
group indicates. Taut's political position at this time was clearly
confused. Although, as we have already seen, he was attracted to the
Proletkult he never joined the KPD. The eclecticism of Taut's political
thinking in the autumn of 1919 can be seen from the series of extracts
and quotations with which he prefaced *Die Auflösung der Städte*. Pride
of place was given to Kropotkin, with long extracts from *Gegenseitige
Hilfe in der Tier- und Menschenwelt* and *Das Feld, die Fabrik und die
Werkstatt*. Kropotkin's anarchistic and romantic socialism was supported
by extracts from Landauer's *Aufruf zum Sozialismus*. In absolute oppo-

sition, however, to the definition of socialism favoured by Kropotkin and Landauer, Taut also included 'The Statutes for the Socialization of the Land of the Soviet Republic of Russia', which described how the ownership of land became the sole prerogative of the state, and a short quotation from Lenin's *State and Revolution*. Between the two in the ideological spectrum appeared a quotation from Ludwig Rubiner and the 'Principles' of Barbusse's Clarté group, a group which specifically refused to align itself with the Third International.

It is clear that even in the autumn of 1919, Taut's *Glanzwelt* was still substantially built on the romantic socialist foundations laid by Kropotkin and Landauer. His practical involvement with the BPK in the day-to-day world is therefore especially noteworthy. Whereas in November 1918 the real world and the *Glanzwelt* became temporarily confused, by the late summer of 1919 Taut had once again unravelled the two threads. If the dream of an ideal world was still based on Landauer, Taut now realized that direct practical action could best be achieved from the springboard offered by the KPD and the radical workers. It is significant that when *Die Auflösung der Städte* was published in 1920 the frontispiece spoke of the book as 'only a utopia' which might be achieved in the third millennium A.D.[10]

The practical achievements of the BPK were entirely related to the theatre. The Theater des Bundes für proletarische Theater was set up in October 1919 and began with a production of Ernst Toller's *Die Wandlung*. This was followed by the first production of *Freiheit* by Herbert Kranz, given in the Philharmonie in December 1919. It is not known whether Taut was involved with these productions or not. Certainly, any contribution which he could have made to the work of the BPK would have had to have been in the context of the theatre, for the group did not involve itself with any architectural projects.

The importance of Taut's membership in the group is considerable, despite the lack of any architectural results. It signalled a return to political reality. However modish Pfemfert may have found the participation of ex-Activists in proletarian *Kulturpolitik*, this participation marked the transformation of the Activist impulse into a practical desire to work for the cultural needs of an identifiable segment of the population – the proletariat. Most important of all, the involvement of the former Activists in the BPK was a resolution of the paradox on which Activism and the RGA had foundered: namely, the desire to act as a political force while shunning the established political system and the established parties.

19

The Werkbund conference:
September 1919

The return to political reality which the BPK represented was paralleled
by the return of the radicals to the Werkbund, also in September 1919.
One might say that the BPK was to the Politische Rat geistiger Arbeiter
as the Werkbund was to the Arbeitsrat für Kunst. By returning to the
Werkbund, however, the radicals did not abandon the principles on
which they had based the AFK. Instead, the Werkbund itself underwent
a drastic reorganization in order to assimilate this new and radical wing.

As we have already seen, the Arbeitsrat für Kunst was initially
conceived as a radical alternative to the Werkbund.[1] The hostility which
the radical architects felt against the Werkbund lingered on into 1919,
and was not lessened by the collapse of the political ambitions of the
AFK in the spring of that year. Throughout the period of the revolution
both Taut and Gropius had been on the *Vorstand* of the Werkbund, but
had been very hostile towards its passivity and impotence. As Gropius
explained to the committee at the end of June 1919: 'At the outbreak
of the revolution, the Werkbund should have put itself in the vanguard.
It let this moment slip, however, and now the feeling against it is
extraordinarily strong.'[2] Gropius's condemnation of the Werkbund
provoked Behrens to an equally vigorous retort, which compared Taut
and Gropius to the much-maligned Centre Party politician Matthias
Erzberger. Behrens said that, like Erzberger, Taut and Gropius were
intent on acquiring power and influence, but would not know what to
do with the power after they had got it.[3]

Taut continued the attack at the next meeting of the committee, a
month later. The response from the other members of the committee
was predictably chilly. In a despairing letter, Taut described to Gropius
what had happened, for Gropius had not attended the meeting. 'You
will also get the minutes of the meeting and see from them how
everything went. I can only say that I was completely isolated there and
didn't find the least support even from Poelzig. Everywhere only injured
feelings and so on.'[4] Two days later, he wrote on the same theme to
Osthaus. 'I regret very much that you were not there, and consider the
Werkbund a lost cause.'[5] Yet Taut did not feel able to completely
abandon the Werkbund without making an attempt to reform it
according to the pattern which had been derived from the Activists and
made concrete in the AFK.

At the beginning of August 1919 he penned a 'Freundschaftsbau-

Protokoll' which was intended as a call to action for the Werkbund. No copy of this 'Protokoll' has survived, but it is reasonable to assume that it was a suggestion that the Werkbund should support the building of *Volkshäuser*, or should establish a *Bauprojekt* similar to that formulated by the AFK. The tone of the 'Protokoll' was clearly agonistic. Gone were the optimistic and wild demands of the early days of the AFK, to be replaced by avant-garde agonism, by the expectation of ridicule and failure. Osthaus acknowledged this trait in his response to Taut's 'Protokoll': 'Today I can return the protocol to you. Thank you for your concern. It reads like a drama – the tragedy of our movement is in it. I gladly return your proclamation, endorsed with my signature.'[6] Taut appears to have also tried to pursue the *Volkshaus* idea independently of both the AFK and the Werkbund. In the same month as the 'Protokoll' was written – August 1919 – Taut established a new group, the Volkshaus-Bund. He described its aims as follows: 'The "Bund" pursues the aim of erecting *Volkshaüser* everywhere.'[7] Little came out of this group, although there was talk in the autumn of 1919 of joining up with the AFK.[8]

It was the Werkbund rather than the Volkshaus-Bund which appeared to hold out the most promise in August and September 1919. At the final meeting of the old committee, held at the end of August in anticipation of the elections at the Stuttgart conference in September 1919, Gropius and Taut joined forces in a further offensive. Osthaus described it in a letter to August Endell, written on 25 August. 'You did not attend the last committee meeting of the Werkbund, but will have read the minutes. Gropius and Taut made a very passionate attack.'[9] The gist of this attack can be gained from an enthusiastic letter of support which Osthaus subsequently wrote to Taut. It is clear that Taut's proposals were absolutely in keeping with his Activist pedigree. Osthaus wrote: 'I was very pleased by your performance at the last committee meeting, especially by your suggestion for a council of artists, which I had also thought to make at Stuttgart – though more in the sense of a council of *geistig* leaders [*Rat geistiger Führer*].'[10] Taut's belief in the right of the artistic élite to take over control of the Werkbund was now finding support. What had been considered as dangerous élitism at the Werkbund conferences of 1914 and 1916 had become, as a result of the polemics of the RGA and the AFK, an acceptable notion. Osthaus urged Taut not to abandon the Werkbund just at the point when his views might gain final acceptance. 'Otherwise I wanted to stress that the true concept behind the Werkbund is in no way obsolete, but in fact even today still remains to be realized.' He added: 'I am preparing a long paper on these ideas for the discussion at Stuttgart.'[11] A Werkbund conference was to be held in Stuttgart two weeks later: from 6–9 September.

Taut welcomed Osthaus's support, but doubted whether the Werkbund, in its form at that time, was able or willing to adopt a new programme which would emphasize the interests of the artists within the Werkbund rather than those of the businessmen and industrialists. He wrote to

Osthaus on 27 August: 'I was very pleased by your letter, but the WB
certainly won't change its constitution. So we have no choice but to form
an uncompromising bloc within the committee.'[12] This plan was very
successful. As a result of the elections at Stuttgart, Poelzig replaced Peter
Bruckmann as chairman. Behrens and Bruno Paul, both leading
members of the anti-Taut/Gropius lobby, lost their positions on the
committee, which now included Otto Bartning, Gropius, César Klein,
Osthaus, Taut and van de Velde. Of this group, all but van de Velde had
been members of the AFK, and, as we have noted already, Taut was
the founder of the AFK, while Gropius and Klein were chairman and
vice-chairman respectively after the shake-up in March.[13]

The impact of the radical artists on the Stuttgart conference was
considerable. The ghost of the AFK and of Taut's Activism lurked
conspicuously behind several of the principal speeches. Indeed, it was
originally planned by the committee that the main address should be
given by Taut himself – a measure of the ascendency of the radical
faction within the committee. Taut initially agreed to speak. A month
before the conference, however, he stood down in favour of Hans
Poelzig.[14]

It is clear from Taut's letters before the Stuttgart meeting that Poelzig
had not supported the Taut/Gropius line as vigorously as Taut would
have wished. At Stuttgart, however, Poelzig threw his weight behind
the Taut/Gropius/Osthaus lobby. Almost at the beginning of his speech,
Poelzig echoed Osthaus's very Activist view that the Werkbund should
aim to be a *Rat geistiger Führer*. Poelzig insisted: 'The Werkbund must
remember that it was conceived as a spiritual and not an economic
movement. As a result of the Werkbund's various political and economic
undertakings, this spirit has now been buried, and it is time to bring it
to light again in all its pureness.'[15] Poelzig's description of what the
Werkbund should be was strongly reminiscent of Hiller's definition of
the role of the *Herrenhaus*. It should be concerned solely with 'pure' and
geistig matters and should spurn any contact with vulgar politics or
business. The two *geistig* pillars on which the Werkbund should be based,
said Poelzig, were art and craftsmanship. 'Art and craftsmanship are the
two foundations on which the activity of the Werkbund should be
based...By craftsmanship I mean something quite different from
hand-finishing in some branch of industry.'[16] In contrast to the *geistig*
qualities offered by craftsmanship, Poelzig felt that 'Business and
industry have, in the majority of cases, simply prostituted art.'[17] Poelzig
coupled this Activist indifference to the real, material world with the
historicism which had been a major element in Landauer's writings and
which had been adopted by Bruno Taut in his essay in *Die Stadtkrone*.
As Poelzig put it: 'Spread out in front of us lie the artistic treasures of
the millennia. We cannot shut our eyes to them.'[18] As Taut had done
in *Die Stadtkrone*, Poelzig favoured the Orient and the European middle
ages as the finest models of the architecture of *Geist*. However, the
preference for these models should not, he said, completely preclude the
appreciation of classical architecture.

Although I personally do not dispute at all the increasingly great influence which oriental and medieval art is going to exercise on our own art and particularly our architecture, and although I accept that a regeneration of our art is only possible in the spirit of medieval art, I nevertheless feel that the study of antiquity can still heighten our perception of architectural ornament and rhythm: qualities which are accessible to us as never before.[19]

From this historicist starting point – the same starting point as Taut had used in *Die Stadtkrone*, Poelzig went on to endorse all the important arguments which Taut had outlined in *Die Stadtkrone*. Architecture, said Poelzig, was not merely a rarified product of the *Geist*, but depended for its validity on a mutual resonance with the *Volk*. 'Architecture is the product of the spiritual disposition of a nation...We must once again realize that great art also demands inspiring content and must be in close touch with the soul of the people if it is not to degenerate as art.'[20] This resonant relationship between *Geist* and *Volk* was exactly that which had been advocated by Landauer, by Taut and by the literary Activists.

Also like the Activists, Poelzig insisted that such a harmony between *Geist* and *Volk* could only be achieved after a spiritual revolution. This was the second revolution which had inspired Gropius's revamped conception of the *AFK*. Once the revolution had been achieved, the results would have an eternal significance: all the arts would be united under the leadership of architecture. In one succinct sentence, Poelzig managed to condense three of Taut's main themes: chiliasm, the need for a *geistig* revolution and the mission of architecture as leader of the arts. 'But we cannot conjure up an architecture as *ars magna* out of nothing: it will appear only when a concerted, large-scale revolutionizing of the soul has taken place, and where the conviction has prevailed that we must create for eternity.'[21] From this definition of architecture as '*ars magna*', Poelzig went on to say that art and design education should also be revived according to architectonic principles: 'only architecture provides a thorough training in all the arts'.[22] He thus reiterated a point which Taut had first made in 1914 in his article 'Eine Notwendigkeit', and which had been developed to become the basis of the AFK's demands for a new system of art education, and, ultimately, the basis of Gropius's Bauhaus programme. As Gropius had already done at Weimar, Poelzig proposed that the existing academies and schools of art should be transformed into training workshops, which would be firmly grounded on the discipline of craftsmanship.[23]

The return to simple first principles, which had been espoused by both Taut and Behne in *Die Stadtkrone* and *Wiederkehr der Kunst*, would be facilitated, said Poelzig, by the enforced poverty of the post-war era.

The war has made us poor, poorer than we can realize at the moment. The soil in which we must plant will be barren. If we do not lose heart, however, this barren soil can lead to recovery, by rejecting everything diseased and excessively luxuriant, which threatened to overgrow our creative work.[24]

Once again, Poelzig was endorsing an aspect of the AFK programme, namely, the demand for decentralization and simplicity, which derived from Taut and Tessenow, and found its principal mouthpiece in *Die Volkswohnung*.

Not only did Poelzig base his plan for the Werkbund on the Activist programmes which had been drawn up by Taut, such as *Die Stadtkrone* or the early manifestos of the AFK, but he also made this debt explicit at the conclusion of his address. 'But the genuinely inspired youth anticipate the future. The truth from which we shall benefit is contained in the demands of the young, demands which all ultimately strive after spirituality and ecstasy, and pursue the architectural nexus of all the arts.'[25] Poelzig thus aligned himself with the radical block in the committee in their confrontation with the surviving members of the older generation.

Poelzig was followed by Osthaus, who attempted to reconcile the warring parties for fear of a repetition of the battle at Cologne in 1914. He explained, rather laboriously, that each side was misrepresenting the other side: the radicals by accusing the conservatives of merely promoting 'good taste', the conservatives by portaying the radicals as destructive revolutionaries.[26] In truth, said Osthaus, the ideals of Taut and Gropius were exactly those of the founding fathers of the Werkbund. 'They dream of cathedrals and thereby basically mean the moral regeneration of humanity. They thus lead our movement back to its innermost essence.'[27] Having established this rather precarious link between the aims of the AFK and those of the early Werkbund, Osthaus then moved onto the offensive. His lyrical definition of architecture was that of Taut and the AFK:

Building only becomes art when we forget the roof over our heads, when the columns become prayer, when the domes become a soaring, spiritual hymn. All forms of craftsmanship depend on the right building, just as the building itself depends on the pure aspirations of the soul. At this moment, therefore, it is not fantasy to dream of cathedrals.[28]

Osthaus declined to give details of the exact role which he felt the Werkbund should play in this regeneration of architecture, although he indicated internationalism and education as the two main directions to be pursued. The task of the Werkbund, like that of the *Herrenhaus*, was to offer *geistig* leadership – 'For where there is the true *Geist*, the rest will come of its own accord.'[29] In conclusion, Osthaus invoked the quintessential historicist image – the golden age. He asked: 'Am I painting utopia? Am I portraying a golden age which has long disappeared? The golden age never existed and was never lost, but has hovered as an ethical imperative over every age.'[30] It would have been unthinkable for Osthaus to have delivered this speech to the Werkbund conferences in 1914 or 1916. His suggestions, that the Werkbund should concentrate on *geistig* education and should aim at utopia or a new golden age, show how deeply the Werkbund had been infiltrated by the tenets of Activism, and of the AFK.

A contemporaneous article by Osthaus, which was published in the *Mitteilungen des Deutschen Werkbundes*, spelled even more clearly

Osthaus's debt to Activism. The capitalistic age, he said, had elevated profit above form. In order to restore respect for form to its proper status, the artist must be given pride of place in the plans to restructure society. Osthaus's view of the artist was that of the Activists – the artist was moved by intuition, not calculation. 'The call must therefore be: artists to the front. What is going to be built must be composed as poetry. Everything which is merely calculated is dissipation, is, indeed, one more blow of the axe at the roots of our culture.'[31] Osthaus went on to advocate a panel of experts, which would be responsible for commissions for public building – a recommendation which had already been made by the AFK and which was to be adopted again by the Werkbund under Poelzig. Also from Taut and the AFK came the idea of *Volkshäuser*. Osthaus suggested: 'It would of course be pleasing if the best that is created remains open for everyone's enjoyment. *Volkshäuser* as places both of the highest attainment and of community life could achieve this.'[32] The conclusion of the article was a reiteration of the Activist belief in talent. Osthaus said that progress through work must be based on three qualities: *Geist*, taste and talent. He went on: 'It was the fault of the capitalist economic system that they left this trinity out of their reckoning.'[33] If the post-war economy was to survive, it would have to revive this trinity. Artistic talent, felt Osthaus, could compensate for the material shortages which beset the emerging republic.

It is clear that the addresses given by Poelzig and Osthaus at Stuttgart, and Osthaus's article 'Die Kunst im Aufbau der neuen Lebensform' all rested heavily on earlier writings by Taut and on the Activist presuppositions of the AFK. It is perhaps significant that the issue of the *Mitteilungen des Deutschen Werkbundes* which carried the report of the conference also contained a prospectus for *Die Stadtkrone*. Indeed, the last sentence of this issue read: 'Enclosed with this issue is a prospectus for Bruno Taut's book *Die Stadtkrone*, published by Eugen Diederichs in Jena, which we strongly commend to notice.'[34] Although the capture of the Werkbund was the most notable achievment of Taut and the architectural Activists,[35] it was of less significance to Taut in 1919 than it would have been if it had occurred in 1916.

By 1919 the vision of the 'cathedral of a new humanity' had been with Taut for at least seven years. Just as the Werkbund was grudgingly accepting the heterodoxies of Activism, Taut himself was moving on to a new, more incremental approach to architecture.

Although Taut did not speak at the conference, having stood down in favour of Poelzig, his views on the Werkbund's future role can be found in a contemporary text, entitled 'Für den Werkbund'. This is either the text of Taut's undelivered address, in which case it must have been written before the end of July, or it is the text of a policy statement, which Taut produced during or after the Stuttgart conference. Either way, it offers a clear account of Taut's position in the late summer of 1919. Paradoxically, his more incremental, less holistic approach aligned him with the conservative majority in the Werkbund. Peter Bruckmann, for example, commented after Osthaus's speech: 'It would be nice if Osthaus's dreams should ever become reality, but for the moment we can only deal with things close at hand.'[36] In his essay 'Für den Werkbund' Taut agreed with Bruckmann that the immediate work in hand was more important at that time than discussions or propaganda. Taut wrote:

> The idea behind the formation of the Bund is pure and admirable, and happily even appears in the name itself – '"Werk"-Bund'. The objective, therefore, is not speeches or doctrines but the finished work, ever and always the finished work, and not business, marketing, propaganda or indoctrination...All the energies of the Werkbund must be directed towards work and to nothing else.[37]

At no point in his address did Taut summon ideal images of Gothic cathedrals or oriental temples. The 'attainable paradise' of the Activists was to be found, felt Taut, through the rational combination of three qualities: work, materials and form.

As he had done at the Bamberg conference in 1916, Taut suggested that the immediate task of the Werkbund should be to build up a collection of materials which would act as a guide for architects, indicating what new techniques and potentials were at their disposal. 'One of the next tasks of the Werkbund would be to assemble a collection of materials, chosen according to the most rigorous and therefore stringent criteria.'[38] But, wrote Taut, work plus materials needed form for their completion. Therefore a free, unfettered and informed art education was necessary, and the Werkbund should lead the way. 'The training of the visual and auditory faculties, the emancipation and opening up of the senses, this is one of the greatest tasks of the Bund.'[39] Taut did not expand in any detail on what form the ideal art education should take. He had, however, recently published his views on architectural education in an article in *Bauwelt*, and one can assume that his plans for the Werkbund would have followed the pattern described in the article. It was provocatively titled 'Zuviel Gerede vom Architektur-Unterricht' (Too much talk about architectural education). Taut's polemic was directed against 'the flood of writings on the reform of universities and schools of art'.[40] While excepting from censure the seminal writings of Theodor Fischer and his own 'Architektur-Programm', Taut condemned the rest of the current plans for reform as conservative attempts to maintain the status quo while appearing to make radical changes. His own solution was drastically simple: 'The current university racket with its box-like compartmentalization must definitely be done away with.'[41] Just as the Werkbund should concentrate on work rather than on theorizing, so, said Taut, architectural education should be based on practical site experience. The aspiring architect should first work as an apprentice bricklayer or carpenter in order to prepare himself for his ultimate role as an architect, as 'leader of the craftsmen'.[42] The 'art' of architecture would then follow on naturally from this practical education: it could not, said Taut, be learned as an academic discipline. 'One cannot learn art. "Lika" asked in one of Scheerbart's stories: "How do I learn to write poetry?"

"Ninny! Simply try and you can do it.''[43] Historical models and precedents should be discovered through practical activity in building, not through academic learning, and the application of historical types should also follow this rule. 'The by nature uncomplicated technician will not have Greek, Italian or Gothic art thrust upon him. He will continue to be useful without these pretensions, and will find his niche in the building industry according to his talents.' Taut added: 'The best people in the industry today are the overseers, managers and others who have come from this background, and, in addition, a few notable architects whose careers have been guided from the start by a lucky star.'[44] As we have already seen, Taut had replaced, by the summer of 1919, the Activist notion of *Volk* with the more tangible notion of the proletariat. In a similar way, the mystical relationship between the 'divine calling' of the architect and the *Volksseele* was replaced by the direct involvement of the architect in the practical work of education. The authority of the architect was then founded not on a metaphysical concept of a higher *Geist* but on his status as 'leader of the craftsmen'. In his essay 'Für den Werkbund', Taut amplified this point: the only acceptable authority was one based on activity, on work.

By damning the academies and the slavish study of historical precedents, Taut clearly felt that he was freeing architecture from the constraints of the past. This emancipation from the doctrines of the past should, he said, be the ambition of the Werkbund. 'So let the Werkbund be the forum in the struggle for the new: free from doctrines...*Heimatkunst*...tradition...Functionalism or whatever.'[45] The Werkbund should create the *tabula rasa* on which the future would be worked out. The creation of the *tabula rasa* was the task of youth: 'If this conviction prevails, then its organization will reveal itself of its own accord. At the head must stand an artist who is in the ascendency rather than in decline. The Werkbund today is ripe for such a rejuvenation, in which alone its salvation lies.'[46] From his essay 'Für den Werkbund', written in the late summer or early autumn of 1919, it is clear that Taut felt that the *tabula rasa* had been achieved. The time had now come to move away from the polemical campaign of Activism and to establish, by actual building, the outlines for the new architecture.

20

◇◇

Autumn and winter 1919: unrealized projects

Taut's maxim, that the Werkbund should be concerned with practical work, was given formal expression in a series of recommendations and demands which Poelzig, on behalf of the committee, made in October 1919.[1] It was suggested by the Werkbund that official building activity should be divided into artistic production and administration.[2] The latter was to be the exclusive preserve of a reduced number of building inspectors, who would have no direct control over the former. Control over artistic matters should be vested, said the Werkbund, in 'building councils'.

Building councils should be formed and used, as it were, as provincial and local authorities. They would advise the Minister for Science, Art and Education from time to time, especially on small building projects in the countryside (schools, foresters' houses), and, if necessary, offer him suggestions for the choice of appropriate designers.[3]

Naturally, the Werkbund wished to be closely involved with any such reorganization of public building. Poelzig's appeal, which went unheeded by the Prussian Assembly, indicates the immediate influence which the AFK radicals had on the Werkbund. In contrast, however, to the earlier demands of the Arbeitsrat for absolute artistic control under the new régime, the Werkbund, more pragmatically, limited its immediate suggestions to small-scale projects: schools and foresters' houses were singled out.

In contrast, the Arbeitsrat was still intent on its plans for the *Bauprojekt*. It is interesting to note that in the autumn of 1919 the small-scale, decentralist schemes of the AFK had largely been carried over by Taut, Gropius and Klein to the Werkbund, whilst the more fantastic projects were still being discussed by the same people in the meetings of the AFK. The AFK, however, was becoming increasingly enfeebled. Like the RGA, which only survived into the early months of 1919, the AFK was intimately identified with the chiliastic Activism of November 1918. Once this chiliastic phase had run its course, the Arbeitsrat became more and more anachronistic. The rise of the *Proletkult* demanded the demise of the AFK, grounded, as it was, on Hiller's élitist Activism.

Just as the Werkbund had accepted Taut's Activism at the point which he himself was revising his own position, so the AFK continued to attract new members during the summer of 1919, although the group had, by that time, lost its impetus.[4] In spite of the new members, the meetings during the summer were poorly attended and two of them, on 6 June and 13 August, were cancelled due to lack of numbers.[5] Financially, the group was also in a weak condition. In a circular of 1 November 1919, Behne reported a deficit of over 2000 Marks, and added: 'We cannot accomplish our mission, if we do not obtain greater resources.'[6] In the same circular in which he described the finances of the AFK, Behne announced that the meeting planned for 15 November would consider the *Bauprojekt*.

The meeting was actually held on 18 November. Various proposals were offered for shoring up the sagging AFK. César Klein suggested that the AFK should be merged with the Novembergruppe, with the Arbeitsrat as the directing intelligence of the enlarged group and the Novembergruppe as an exhibiting body, which was what it had become in any case.[7] Gropius felt that it would be better to unite with the Werkbund, and intimated that money could be forthcoming for the AFK's *Bauprojekt*. The protocol of the meeting of 18 November reported: 'Gropius mentioned that he had attempted a similar merger with the Werkbund, which has changed considerably since reconstituting its committee, in order to gain access to its funds. There are prospects of a transferral of 10,000 Marks.[8] When questioned whether the business interests in the Werkbund would swamp the AFK, Gropius described the changes which had occurred at Stuttgart. In the words of the protocol: 'Gropius has no fears of this happening, given the current composition of the committee, which includes Taut, Klein, Poelzig, Bartning and Osthaus, as well as himself. The artistic interests have gained the upper hand over the political interests, particularly Jäckh's, with which the AFK clearly has nothing in common.'[9] Nothing, however, came of the suggested union of the AFK and Werkbund. Indeed, by seizing effective control of the Werkbund in September, the leading figures in the AFK had already made it clear where they thought the better prospects lay. Describing to the AFK, his attempts to prevent a rift from dividing the two groups, Gropius noted: 'Important considerations advised against provoking a sharp division, for the strength of the Werkbund has become considerable, and much can be achieved with it if it is competently led.'[10] But if the Werkbund had much to offer the AFK, the obverse was not the case, especially as the leading talents of the AFK were already on the committee of the Werkbund. All the AFK had to offer were increasing debts and an unrealizable *Bauprojekt*. Not suprisingly, no formal merger was ever achieved.

One last hope for the *Bauprojekt*, which was suggested by Behne and supported by P. R. Henning and Bruno Taut, was that the Arbeitsrat should seek to involve itself in the rebuilding programme in France, and should design *Volkshäuser* for the devastated towns and villages in the battle zone, as part of the programme of reparations. As Behne explained at the meeting of 18 November:

This project, which should be pursued absolutely independently of the goverment, will bring together various things which belong within the scope of the AFK. Estates must be built for at least 100,000 workers, whose activity in France will extend over some ten years. It is planned that every 1000 workers will be accommodated in a workers' village. They will need *Volkshäuser*, libraries, theatres, baths, and amusement parks...The link which we desire with the people and the workers could be achieved through this project.[11]

This grandiose plan came, however, to nothing. Hastened, ironically in this instance, by the conditions of the Treaty of Versailles, which had been announced in May 1919, and which were beginning to bite by the autumn, the Mark weakened progressively as the year went on. In November 1918, one American dollar bought 12·5 Marks. By the end of 1919 a dollar bought 82 Marks. There was little prospect of building in Germany itself, let alone in France.

Taut acknowledged the gathering financial crisis in an article published in September 1919 – 'Aufruf zum farbigen Bauen'. This was the first time, in all his published writings since November 1918, that Taut made any reference whatsoever to the current economic situation. Whereas, at the end of 1918, Taut had insisted that *Kultusbauten* were more important than housing, and had driven Walther Haas to desperation with the impracticability of the 'Architektur-Programm', he was now, in September 1919, prepared to frame his suggestions for future action in terms of economic reality.

When the 'Aufruf' first appeared in *Bauwelt*, it was signed by Hugo Zehder, the editor of the magazine, *1919, Neue Blätter für Kunst und Dichtung*. However, its author was clearly Bruno Taut. Taut proclaimed:

We do not want to build any more joyless houses, or see them built...Colour is not expensive like moulded decorations and sculptures, but colour means a joyful existence. As it can be provided with limited resources, we should, in the present time of need, particularly urge its use on all buildings which must now be constructed.[12]

In an article published in July 1919, Gropius had also stressed the cheapness of coloured decoration and its appropriateness to the prevailing economic climate. He wrote this in relationship to furniture, but his message was equally applicable to architecture. And just as Taut had done in his 'Eindruck aus Kowno', Gropius identified the joyful use of colour with the Orient and with the Russian *Volk*. Now, in the post-revolutionary era, Gropius felt that the revival of this *Volk* tradition would result from the growing class pride of the proletariat. He thus linked colour directly with the *Proletkult*.

The common people want colour. The more their class pride develops, the more will they scorn the imitation of the rich bourgeois, and will devise their own style for their own sort of life. This instinct among the common people will be the foundation for the new art. Where today traditional art is still alive among the people – in the Orient, in Russia, still here in part in southern Germany – then there, on house and costume, glows colour.[13]

For Gropius, colour did not only offer an opportunity to brighten up the grey *Alltag*, but could also play a polemical role, as a protest against the greyness and poverty to which the nation had been reduced. 'Especially today, as a joyful protest against the external austerity and poverty which fate has forced upon us, we should muster the courage to brighten up the greyness of our shabby surroundings – houses, furniture, clothes – with cheerful colours. The happy result would be a great impact achieved with the slenderest of means.'[14] Purification and regeneration through the enforced return to simplicity was, as we have seen, the theme of Poelzig's address to the Werkbund at Stuttgart. Poelzig also advocated the use of colour in architecture. He noted in his address: 'Even in exterior design, many young architects wish to re-assign a role to colour as a pioneering and form-giving element. They are right to do so.'[15] The current preoccupation with colour found a direct expression by the incorporation in the Werkbund conference of the Erster Deutscher Farbentag.

The principal contribution to the Farbentag was made by Dr Wilhelm Ostwald, who, as he had already done on a smaller scale at Bamberg in 1916, gave a lecture on his system of colour-harmonies. Ostwald's *Farbenlehre* was an attempt to produce an exact system which could be used to match colours harmoniously. His first presupposition, as expressed in *Die Harmonie der Farben*, was that: 'only those colours whose characteristics share certain simple relations will appear har-monious or related'.[16] The members of the Werkbund were not entirely convinced of the validity of Ostwald's quasi-scientific system, or of its applicability to questions of design. Especially critical were the Freie Gruppe für Farbkunst des Deutschen Werkbundes, a group which already existed within the Werkbund, and which was led by the art critic Dr Hans Hildebrandt.[17] This group was supported by the radical faction. A year later the Freie Gruppe für Farbkunst brought out a special number of the *Mitteilungen*, now entitled *Werk* – in response, perhaps, to Taut's address at Stuttgart. The special number included an article by Klee attacking pseudo-scientific colour theories and an extract from Kandinsky's *Über das Geistige in der Kunst*.

Such a rejection of Ostwald's attempt to turn colour harmonization into an exact science was exactly in keeping with the Activist spirit, the spirit of the early AFK, which still affected the radical group in the revived Werkbund. Indeed, Taut harked back to the anti-positivist strain in Activism in his speech at Stuttgart, in which he insisted that the Werkbund should build on intuition, not on fixed dogmas or the arid nationalism of the positivists. 'Everything which makes one happy is ultimately based on the impulsive, on the incomplete and non-final, on that which kindles hope.'[18] The 'Aufruf zum farbigen Bauen' was the offshoot of this lobby in the Werkbund, which advocated intuitive use of colour in architecture and design, untrammeled by any optical or physical theories. Certainly, from Taut's many writings on colour and from his coloured illustrations to *Alpine Architektur* and *Die Auflösung der Städte*, no consistent colour theory can be adduced.[19]

The 'Aufruf zum farbigen Bauen' was signed by all the leading figures in the Werkbund, including the conservative faction. It is a measure of the success of Taut's penetration into the Werkbund that eminent members of the older generation of designers, such as Bruno Möhring, Paul Schmitthenner, Heinrich Straumer and Bruno Paul should have aligned themselves alongside Taut's group of radicals and fantasists. Not only did the list of signatories include the radical group in the Werkbund – Taut, Gropius, Osthaus – but it also included the group of young designers who were later to contribute to the Gläserne Kette correspondence: Paul Goesch, Jakobus Göttel, Hans Scharoun and Taut's brother Max.[20]

We have postulated that Activism represented an attempt to bring together the practicality of the pre-war reform movement with the aesthetic and psychological impulses of Expressionism. The 'Aufruf' must be taken as evidence of the success of this ambition, for it brought together representatives of various diverse groups and movements, all of whom, for their own reasons, had an interest in colour. There were the conservatives in the Werkbund, who, like Avenarius, saw colour as an integral part of the *Heimatkunst* programme. The Gartenstadt movement was represented in the 'Aufruf' by Bernhard Kampffmeyer, and Adolf Otto, respectively the chairman and the general secretary of the Gartenstadtgesellschaft. Both Taut and Göttel had designed estates for the Gartenstadtgesellschaft – Taut at Falkenberg, Göttel at Bonn, and both used colour on the facades. Taut was also the apostle of Scheerbart's lyrical visions of a coloured glass paradise, while through Taut and Behne, another signatory, a direct link ran back to the painters in the Sturm group.[21] The more mystical approach to colour was represented by Paul Goesch, who was a follower of Steiner's theosophical cult, with its carefully worked out theories on the interrelationship of form, colour and the moral condition of man.[22]

With all the factions of the Werkbund united behind the call for colour and with a dominant voice in the committee of the Werkbund, the prospects for Taut's Activism seemed very good in the early autumn of 1919. Yet nothing was achieved. A contributory reason for the lack of progress along the lines proposed by Taut was the inability of the Werkbund to adapt to its new role. Although Poelzig's recommendations to the Prussian Assembly reflected the influence of Taut's Activism, the Werkbund wavered between radicalism and its established role as an arbiter of official taste. The copy of the *Mitteilungen des Deutschen Werkbundes* published on 1 November 1919 announced that the heraldic artist Hupp had been commissioned by the committee to prepare drawings for a new German Eagle. Behne seized on this as typical of the lingering conservatism within the Werkbund. He wrote in the *Sozialistische Monatshefte*:

If only the Werkbund had suggested a new symbol instead of the disgraced bird of prey! It is also sad that the Werkbund bulletin [*Mitteilungen des Deutschen Werkbundes*] still comes out in a layout which is as un-*geistig* as possible. Such arty typefaces, arty spacings, arty advertisements in the text are exactly what the Werkbund should be fighting against: superficial culture of the worst sort.

Behne begged: 'Let the committee at long last give us a sign that the Werkbund has an aim, that it is a promoter of art and not a medical corps.'[23] Looking back on the period from the summer of 1921, Gropius was inclined to blame Poelzig for the Werkbund's lack of resolve in the months directly following the Stuttgart conference. In a letter to Otto Bartning, who had joined the committee at Stuttgart, Gropius commented retrospectively: 'There was only one opportunity to drag the Werkbund forwards. This could have been done when Poelzig took over the chairmanship, if he had used the power of the Werkbund clearly and uncompromisingly on behalf of the younger members. This he did not do.'[24] Poelzig's inability to break with the business interests in the Werkbund and to side wholeheartedly with Taut and his followers reflected the worsening financial situation both in the Werkbund itself and in the country at large. In his Stuttgart address he had proclaimed: 'Let us support the young in their economic struggle so that they do not abandon hope...and sell off their principles...The Werkbund must become the conscience of the nation.'[25] Before it could assert itself as the conscience of the nation, the Werkbund became a victim, temporarily at least, of the nation's ills. For the Werkbund could not hope to further the ambitions of the new generation of architects if nothing was being built.

In spite of the revolution and the political uncertainties, building activity had not collapsed completely at the end of the war. It was only around September 1919 that the economic squeeze brought building to a virtual halt. In Berlin, for example, there were eighteen building starts in the first quarter of 1919. By the last quarter of 1919, the number had dropped to nine, and had fallen to five in the first quarter of 1920.[26] At exactly the moment when Taut was urging the Werkbund to turn its attention to practical activity and to *Werk*, there was less and less work to be done.

For Taut, the only hope of work around the end of 1919 and beginning of 1920 came from Osthaus, who asked him at the end of November if he would be interested in designing a complex of buildings for the Hohenhagen site which would include the existing Folkwang Museum, a new school and the necessary dormitories, workshops and halls. Osthaus admitted from the outset that there was little prospect of completing the project in its entirety. As he wrote in the letter in which he first introduced the idea to Taut: 'since the construction of all the principal elements is inconceivable in the near future, and even a complete design for the individual buildings cannot be considered, a percentage fee, as is customary, is out of the question'.[27] In a subsequent article, describing Taut's completed plans for the *Folkwang-Schule*, Osthaus reiterated the ideal nature of the project. 'Naturally it is an ideal project, whose direct implementation is not planned. But it is not an ideal project in the sense of a utopia, of a baseless game of idle architectural fantasy...The implementation is hampered only by the current state of the building market.'[28] Taut's plan followed closely from Osthaus's initial concept, as described in the letter of 22 November.

It would be a question of uniting the two establishments of the Folkwang Museum with the school, its living quarters, workshops and public rooms into a *Stadtkrone*...I have in mind a cloister-like layout in the sense of a perimeter

67 Bruno Taut,
Folkwang-Schule project,
1919–20.

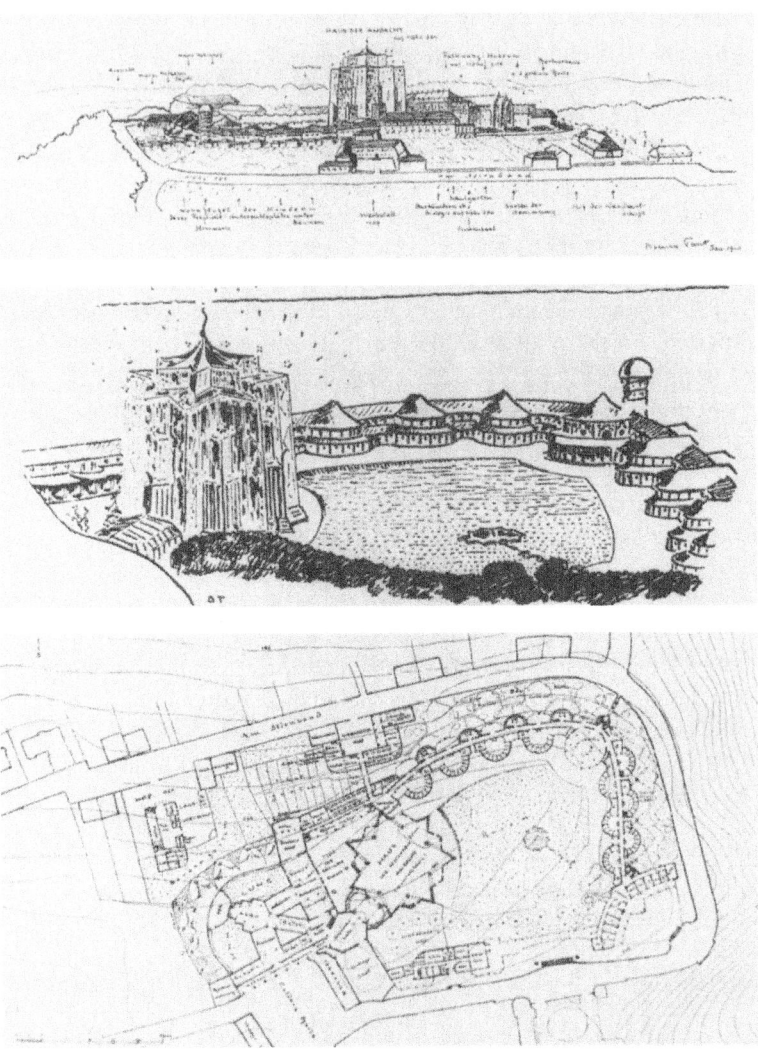

building with a varied silhouette encircling a large inner courtyard or park. The idea thus came to me to ask you, as the father of all *Stadtkronen*, to collaborate.[29]

Taut took to the scheme enthusiastically and produced a plan which closely followed Osthaus's original suggestions. The everyday buildings, the dormitories and workshops, were extremely simple. As Osthaus noted: 'All the functional buildings will be designed in an absolutely straightforward manner.'[30] The dormitories were semi-circular in plan, ranged along a central, connecting walkway. The centrepiece of the complex, which rose high above the school and museum, was the House of Devotion, a glass temple in the tradition of the *Kristallhaus* and the *Volkshaus*. Taut intended that it be decorated by the artists and sculptors in the Arbeitsrat für Kunst.[31]

The *Folkwang-Schule* project might be seen as a paradigm of archi-

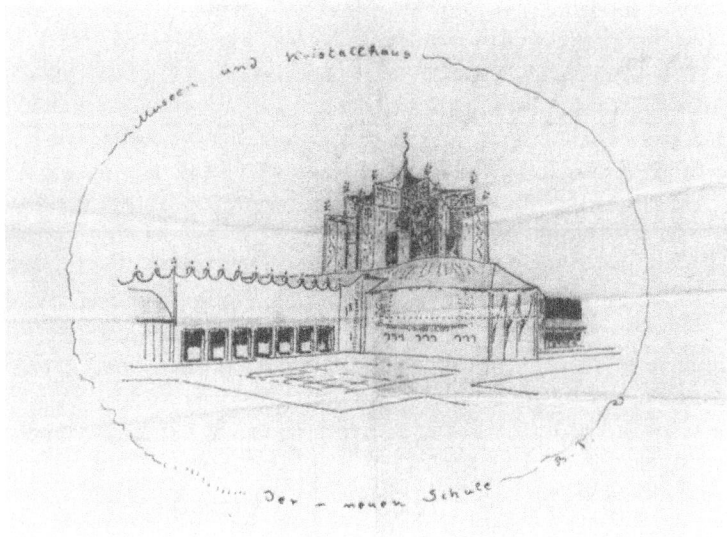

68 *Folkwang-Schule* project, 1919–20, museum and *Kristallhaus.*

tectural Activism. It was the realization of an educational programme which Osthaus had outlined in his address to the Werkbund at Stuttgart.

The point on which I want to lay emphasis is the general education of the young people. It is, of course, imperative to make propaganda for our objectives. We would be spared the effort, however, if we were a well-educated nation. Children leave the schools today thoroughly miseducated, crippled in body and soul. We must insist that the schools, too, should concentrate on beauty and happiness. During the first six school years rhythmic gymnastics and manual dexterity should provide the framework of the tuition: manual dexterity in the context of a working community...The formal abstractions of the academic disciplines are absolutely secondary considerations.[32]

The references to rhythmic gymnastics clearly link Osthaus's programme to the pre-war reform movement, to Jaques-Dalcroze's music school at Hellerau, and to the Duncan School in New York, with which Osthaus, on behalf of the Werkbund had established a link in 1914, shortly before the outbreak of the war.[33] The description of the school as a working community and the rejection of abstract academic disciplines points, however, to another source: Gustav Wyneken.

Wyneken's educational theories were based on the notion of a progressive collective *Geist*, which strove to overcome materialism. In his seminal book, *Schule und Jugendkultur* (1913), Wyneken defined *Geist* as follows: '*Geist* is by nature social, so established by nature as to develop in the world into a collective *Geist* for the purpose of its own fulfilment, for the purpose of developing its intrinsic essence.'[34] As we have already seen, Wyneken felt that the development from *Volk* to *Geist*, called by him 'this process of objectification', was the only true development open to man.[35] The ideal vehicle for this development was the school, and Wyneken established his own experimental school, the Freie Schulgemeinde at Wickersdorf in 1906. The school, he believed, offered the ideal opportunity to fuse the individual consciousness into a common cultural community.

Wyneken's educational theories prefigured much of the ideology of Hiller's Activism. Socialism was defined in terms of *Gemeinschaft*. The goal was a *geistig* community, and the natural leaders of this community were, according to Wyneken, the specially gifted or talented children.[36]

Although Hiller had reservations about Wyneken's Activism, which he felt over-emphasized aesthetic values at the expense of political ones,[37] Hiller published a series of articles by Wyneken in *Das Ziel*. The most important, as an influence on Osthaus, would have been the article 'Schöpferische Erziehung', which appeared in *Das Ziel I*.[38] All the educational tenets which Osthaus discussed in his Stuttgart address can also be found in this article.

An even more direct link between Wyneken's Activist theories on education and the *Folkwang-Schule* was made through Taut himself. He wrote to Osthaus on 16 December 1919, saying that before he decided on the general layout of the school, he first wanted to consult Wyneken, adding: 'for I see ever more clearly that even for the smallest beginnings, one must have a picture in front of one's eyes of how the whole thing should someday be arranged'.[39] Taut's final plan had much in common with the plan for the new city and *Die Stadtkrone*, which was, as we have suggested, a model for the 'attainable paradise' of the Activists. In both plans the intimate yet antipodal relationship of *Geist* and *Volk* was expressed through the contrast of fantastic and primitive architectural forms. The *Kristallhaus* was set against the simplest of housing. In *Die Stadtkrone*, Taut arranged the profane buildings concentrically around the *Kristallhaus*. For the *Folkwang-Schule* plan he established axes to pull together the various elements of the plan. One ran from the entrance portal across the gymnastics lawn to the stage of the House of Devotion. Another ran from the entrance, along the easterly row of dormitories to the observatory, where it turned back towards the House of Devotion, once again along a row of dormitories. The entrance from the outside world, the House of Devotion, the dormitories and the observatory – described by Taut as a symbol of the future – were thus dynamically related. He said to Osthaus, in describing his ground-plan:

I have tried to bind the axes together dynamically, as I generally believe that they must derive spontaneously out of the dynamic of the plan. I feel that on these grounds alone I am able to justify some arbitrariness in the plan. The plan should possess the greatest possible wealth of relationships – organic, dynamic and scenic.[40]

By breaking down the dormitories into small units and linking them axially, Taut gave a model for the ideal Activist society – Landauer's 'commonwealth of communities'. The workshops, gardens and fields which surrounded the museum and the House of Devotion would offer the children the chance not merely to learn, but also to live. As Wyneken insisted in a lecture given in August 1919: 'The vigorous life, which is freshly bestowed on us in our youth, should be the ultimate principle'.[41] Taut's concept of the education which the *Folkwang-Schule* should offer was entirely in accord with Wyneken's strictures.

This can be seen from a surviving manuscript by Taut, which described the aims of the school.

Every child must draw from his experience of practical activity and construct his abstract categories. The child will start on the farm, in the garden and in the workshop. Out of his own dexterity and craftsmanship, from observation of his own body as well as of the living essence of the external world, from men, animals and plants, the child will derive his self-awareness.[42]

Taut was so excited by the project that he launched a one-man crusade to attract interest and collect money for the project. He approached the former Prussian Minister of Finance, Hugo Simon, and the two current *Kunstwarte*, Redslob and Waetzoldt for financial support.[43] In addition, copies of plans for the school were given to Dr Valentiner by Taut to be passed on to one Herr Kaesback – 'who has better contacts with the financial circles'.[44]

Besides giving lectures about the *Folkwang-Schule* and trying to raise money for the building, Taut made an even stronger affirmation of his belief in the project and its educational aims. An experimental school was set up by Osthaus in January 1920 as forerunner of the new *Folkwang-Schule*, and Taut sent his own son, Heinrich, to the school for three months. The school was housed in Osthaus's own villa, the 'Haus Hohenhof', which was adjacent to the site for the new school. The director of the school was Dr Fritz Klatt. The educational methods were very liberal and formal tuition was optional.[45] In spite of the good intentions behind the project the school was not a success, and closed at the beginning of December 1920.[46]

A similar fate befell the plans for the new *Folkwang-Schule*. The continued inflation, coupled with the collapse of the building market and the political disturbances in the Ruhr area, prevented any further progress beyond the planning stages. Early in May 1920, Osthaus acknowledged this in a letter to Taut. He wrote: 'Whether we can build is very questionable... The city has approved the grant, the government's answer is still pending.'[47] No further financial support was forthcoming, and the project was formally abandoned.

21

The Gläserne Kette

We have noted that the chiliastic phase of Activism, together with the immediate political ambitions of the Activists, finally collapsed in April and May 1919, and have suggested that two alternatives offered themselves to the Activists. One was Dadaism or a variant on it, the other was a return to incremental and didactic methods, aimed at small-scale reforms. Taut initially opted for the latter alternative, as witnessed by his involvement with the BPK, the proletarian theatre movement, the Werkbund and the Farbiges Bauen movement. The fact that even these modest projects had failed to produce any results by the end of the year, prompted Taut to revert to the other alternative, the nihilist and Dadaist alternative. Along with the contacts with the Dadaists, which Taut had first made in the spring of 1919, Taut also revived some of the theoretical and fantastical projects with which he had been occupied in the immediate post-revolutionary period. Thus the six months which began in December 1919 were months of intense theoretical activity. As Taut commented in January 1920: 'Writing seems just as important for us today as designing.'[1] The letters and drawings produced by Taut and his circle during this period acted both as a coda to Activism and as an overture to the subsequent upsurge of Functionalism and *Sachlichkeit* in German architecture.

The intensity of Taut's writing activity at this time was in total contrast to his enforced inactivity as a designer. The short-lived plans for the *Folkwang-Schule* offered only momentary relief in the prevailing gloom. Taut's reaction to this enforced inactivity was predictably agonistic. In a letter which he wrote to Osthaus prior to the first mention by Osthaus of the *Folkwang-Schule* project, Taut complained that there was no call for the true architect, which he still defined Activistically as a dictator in the realm of culture. While the 'true' architects were being ignored, said Taut, the designers who catered for the transient tastes of the moment were overworked.

And the architects? Oh, they don't have it so bad. They often earn an awful lot if they are nice and well-behaved. Furniture and everything else gets bought, everything that is apart from ideas...The Architect, that is he who determines cultural values, who should dictate our manner of life, he is boycotted. My drawing board here in the office remains empty, every day the same nothing. My brother employs three men, all of whom complain that they will die of overwork, and I hang in the air as an 'imaginary architect'.[2]

Taut's agonistic reaction to this predicament was to say that he would not compromise simply in order to gain commissions. In 1914, he had insisted that he would not compromise with the militarists and the nationalists, for he was convinced that his mission lay with architecture. He now repeated this passionate, and typically avant-gardistic belief in his mission. The letter continued:

It is quite clear to me that this situation is inevitable, and I am not depressed by it. I will have nothing to do with the tangled things which are struggling with all their might for survival...No, I believe firmly in my mission...I am convinced that the very fact of my existence, the fact that I specifically am as I am, is proof enough. If I see the light, then it exists, and I must produce it.[3]

As with all avant-garde agonism, there was in Taut's sense of mission a strong note of futurism. The only hope for the realization of Taut's *Glanzwelt* lay with the younger generation and with the future. As he commented to Osthaus: 'It is good that I am finding support from some architects with similar views, and splendid that the very young, the twenty-year-olds, believe in me as they do. If they were the people dispensing commissions today, I wouldn't have to wait for long.'[4] Such sentiments conform exactly to Bontempelli's description of the agonist strain in avant-gardism. As Bontempelli has noted: 'the very spirit of avant-garde movements is that of sacrifice and conservation of the self for those who come after'.[5] This sense of self-immolation and sacrifice can be discerned very clearly in Taut's letter to Osthaus, which was strongly reminiscent of the war-time letters in which he indicated that he would rather die than abandon his pacifist principles. Sacrifice, said Taut, was the inevitable fate of the *geistig* leader: 'My torch often dazzles me, but I will carry it – I must, even if I am destroyed in the process.'[6] At the end of 1919, Taut sought to share the burden of self-sacrifice. Rather than suffer alone, he sought to share his agonism with fellow-sufferers. The three interrelated avant-gardistic attitudes which we have noted in his letter to Osthaus – agonism, futurism and the cult of youth – were to become the driving force behind the group which Taut formed in December 1919, and which has subsequently been named 'Die gläserne Kette'.

On 24 November 1919, Taut wrote to the group of architects and artists who had exhibited at the Ausstellung für unbekannte Architekten and suggested that they form a circle for the mutual exchange of ideas and criticism. The current pause in building activity could thus be turned to good use, said Taut, in preparing the ground for future action.

Dear Work-Friends!
I want to make this proposal to you: today there is almost nothing to build, and if we can build anywhere, then we do it in order to live. Or are you lucky enough to be working on a nice commission? My practice almost makes me ill, and it is basically the same for all of you. Speaking honestly, it is quite good that nothing is being built today. Things will have time to ripen, we shall gather our strength and when building begins again, then we shall know our objectives and shall be strong enough to protect our movement against botching and degeneration.

Let us consciously be 'imaginary architects'! We believe that only a complete revolution can lead us to work. The bourgeois, including our 'Herr Colleague', quite rightly suspect in us the forces of revolution. Break up and dissolve all former principles! Dung! And we are a bud in fresh humus.[7]

The agonist predeliction for rejection and failure was built-in from the outset. Taut added prophetically: 'May this be a magnet, the icy kernel of an avalanche! If it comes to nothing, if I am deluding myself, then at least it will be a beautiful souvenir for each of us.'[8] Among those initially approached by Taut, only Gropius and Behne expressed misgivings. Gropius joined but took no part in the correspondence. Behne declined to join. Taut had asked those willing to contribute to sign his letter and return it to him, along with an appropriate pseudonym. A second letter was sent out on 19 December, with a full list of members, giving both names and pseudonyms. The list read:

Pseudonym	*Name and Address*
Anfang	Carl Krayl, Tuttlingen.
Tancred	Paul Goesch, Berlin-Friedenau.
Hannes	Hans Scharoun, Insterburg.
Mass	Walter Gropius, Weimar.
Stellarius	Jakobus Göttel, Köln.
Antischmitz	Hans Hansen, Köln.
W. H.	Wenzel Halblik, Itzehoe.
'kein Name'	Max Taut, Berlin.
Berxbach 7	Wilhelm Brückmann, Emden.
Prometh	Hermann Finsterlin, Schönau bei Berchtesgaden.
Zacken	Wassili Luckhardt, Berlin-Charlottenburg.
Angkor	Hans Luckhardt, Berlin-Charlottenburg.
Glas	Bruno Taut, Berlin.[9]

The pseudonyms reveal very clearly the avant-gardistic presuppositions which lay behind the group.

Krayl, as 'Anfang', emphasized the new beginning, the *tabula rasa*, while Goesch (Tancred), and Hans Luckhardt (Angkor), linked themselves to the New Jerusalem and the Burmese temples respectively. Gropius (Mass), Wassili Luckhardt (Zacken), and Taut himself all chose names which reflected their architectural credos, with 'Zacken' an illusion to the spiky crystalline forms which Luckhardt favoured at the time. 'Stellarius', Göttel's chosen pseudonym derived from the group's antecedents in the astral novels of Scheerbart and Taut's cosmic architecture as described in *Alpine Architecture* and later in *Der Weltbaumeister*. Two of the members, Scharoun and Hablik, preferred variants of their ordinary names, while Taut's pragmatic brother Max refused to use a pseudonym at all. The two remaining members, Hansen and Finsterlin, both chose names which represented avant-gardistic poses. Hansen's 'Antischmitz' stood for the artist's antagonistic stand against the accepted Forms of society, against the values of the ubiquitous Herr Schmitz. Finsterlin's stood for agonism, casting himself as Prometheus, as the intellectual turned leader, who sacrificed himself for mankind.

The very idea of pseudonyms was agonistic, for it conjured up an aura of secrecy and mystery, which, Taut said, was necessary to defend the group from intrusions from the hostile world. In his very first letter Taut suggested that the secrecy he desired could be achieved through the use of a private language. 'The circle of at least presumed mutual understanding and the use of terse language will make it easier for us to be difficult to understand for outsiders. Nevertheless we must have a mutual obligation not to reveal anything to uncomprehending eyes.'[10] Linguistic obscurity such as this is very typical of the avant-garde. Poggioli has spoken of the 'conventional and willful obscurity which the avant-garde shows off to distinguish itself as a group'.[11] Also typical, was the desire to keep the activities of the group secret until the suitable moment had been reached when the group, which formerly had been despised and alienated, finally achieved the recognition and acclaim due to it. Replying to Finsterlin's first letter, Taut reaffirmed the need for secrecy and for the quiet communion of the spirit rather than for frantic group activity. '"Prometh" is right: we must guard the bud carefully. No great "actions" therefore: only occasional publications. It must never be called the "group". Don't let it be suffocated or profaned by bustling activity. Only appear in public for the purpose of attracting kindred spirits. Thus is my "dawn" to be understood.'[12] This represented a considerable move away from the position which Taut had held a year previously, in the dawn of the political revolution. The political Activism and *Kulturpolitik* of November 1918 had been replaced by a withdrawal into agonism and secrecy. This change of heart reflected not only the changed political situation, but also the influence of Walter Gropius, who had striven to restructure both the Arbeitsrat and also the Bauhaus as quasi-masonic lodges in which the artists and architects could be united amongst themselves, yet remain separated from the mass of the people. The similarity between Taut's position at the end of 1919 and that of Gropius during the previous spring can be seen by comparing Taut's admonition to secrecy and cautiousness with Gropius's address, delivered to the Arbeitsrat early in March, in which he urged the members to be patient and bide their time.

I look upon our *Bund* as a conspiratorial brotherhood. If we want to achieve something great, then we must adhere to our programme in every respect and tolerate no compromises – particularly amongst ourselves. Initially we would rather achieve nothing, for any shifting of our position is the beginning of the end. We must have faith in our ability to wait patiently until the day comes when we can step out in public – vehemently and fully prepared. I consider the close union amongst ourselves to be the most important and most valuable aspect of our group, much more important than external propaganda.[13]

For Taut, as for Gropius, the way forward now lay not in public declamations and conspicuous gestures, but in the inner workings of the closed exclusive group.

At no time did Taut assign a political role to the group, nor did he mention politics in any of his letters. In its agonist phase, Taut's avant-garde was conceived as a means of preparing for the coming *geistig* revolution, the second revolution summonsed up in the spring of 1919 as a substitute for the failed political revolution. As no political programme was to lead to the *geistig* revolution, no time-scale could be established for its realization. All that was certain, according to the agonist programme, was that the sacrifices made now would be justified by the ultimate success of the avant-garde and the second revolution.

Apart from political ambitions, all the presuppositions of Taut's war-time Activism resurfaced in the Gläserne Kette letters. As we have indicated, the new group provided a coda to Taut's Activism. In this coda the principal themes were reassembled as a recapitulation. These themes, the call for a leader, agonism and the Prometheus myth, and the final glory of the revolution can all be identified in a poem written by Karl Liebknecht in 1917 which Taut circulated at the outset of the correspondence.

> Storm, my companion,
> you call me!
> Still I can do nothing,
> still I am in chains!
> Yes, I am also storm,
> part of you;
> and the day will come again
> when I shall break the chains.
> I shall rage anew,
> rage through the worlds,
> storm around the earth.
> Storm through the lands,
> storm mankind,
> his brain and heart,
> storm-wind, I am like you![14]

This poem expresses clearly the sense of preparation, sacrifice and expectation, which characterizes avant-garde agonism. In the Gläserne Kette letters, the sense of preparation was inseparable from the conviction that architecture was, at that moment, going through an interregnum. Taut's initial letters all carried a sense of uncertainty. They affirmed the loss of traditional values, but offered no guidance as to how new ones might be created.[15]

We have already noted that Carl Krayl's pseudonym 'Anfang' represented the desire to begin again, to demolish the old values and begin afresh with a *tabula rasa*. This desire was fundamental to the Gläserne Kette group. It found its strongest expression in the works of Taut and of Krayl himself, both of whom produced letters and drawings in the early months of 1920 which had a close affinity to the contemporary iconcoclasm of the Dadaists.

Taut had been in contact with Golyscheff and the Dadaists before and during the Ausstellung für unbekannte Architekten in April 1919. One of Golyscheff's exhibits in that exhibition was a model of a large hook, on which houses for 200 families were suspended. This model subsequently found its way to Taut's office in Magdeburg, where he worked as City Architect between 1921 and 1924, with Krayl as his assistant.[16] This would suggest that either Taut, or Krayl, or both were

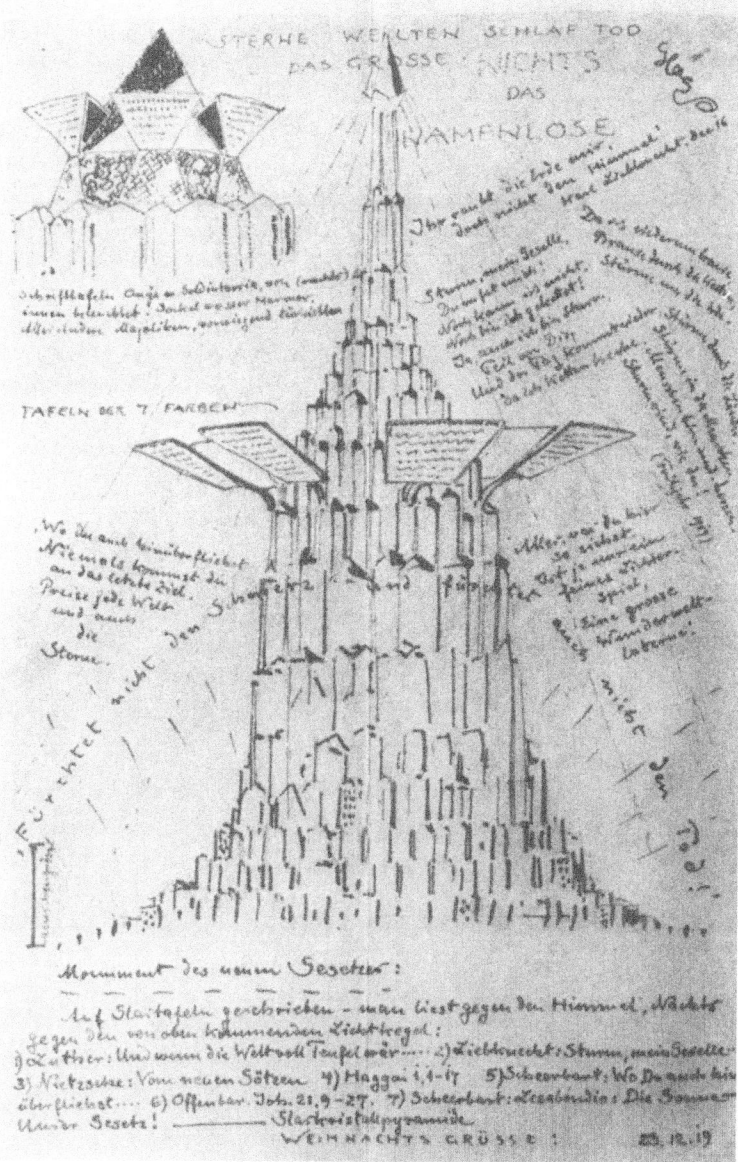

69 Bruno Taut, letter to the Gläserne Kette, 23 December 1919.

attracted to Golyscheff's architectural nihilism, a fact which is confirmed by their own work late in 1919 and early in 1920.

Krayl paraphrased Golyscheff's hanging village in a drawing which he sent to the Gläserne Kette group, entitled *Einen Licht Gruss aus meinem Sternenhaus*. Like Golyscheff's suspended village, the *Sternenhaus* was set high above the earth, supported on a crane-like cantilevered arm. Not only did Krayl's idea derive from Golyscheff, but also his manner of drawing, which was very ingenuous; both the *Sternenhaus* itself and the lollipop trees on the ground were made to resemble the playful drawings of children.

The same insistence on play and on infantilism can be seen in Taut's

70 Carl Krayl, drawing,
1920.

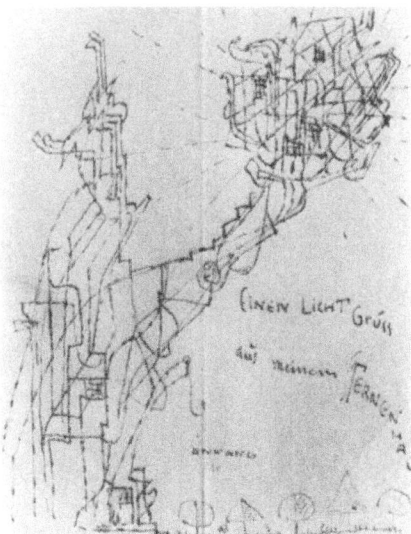

71 Raoul Hausmann and
Johannes Baader (with rose
in pipe), 1919.

early contributions to the Gläserne Kette. Like Krayl, he was influenced
by Golyscheff and was probably acquainted with Baader and Hausmann,
whose regular meeting place was the Café Josty in Potsdamerplatz.[17]
Taut was also a regular at the Café Josty, which was just around the
corner from his office in Linkstraße,[18] and it is unlikely that he could
have avoided meeting the café's most notorious patrons. As well as these
contacts with the contemporary Dadaists, Taut was also immersed in
the works of Scheerbart, whom the Dadaists themselves acknowledged
as a proto-Dadaist, and whose poetry had been adopted by them as a
model.[19] In one of his earliest letters to the group, Taut, quoting

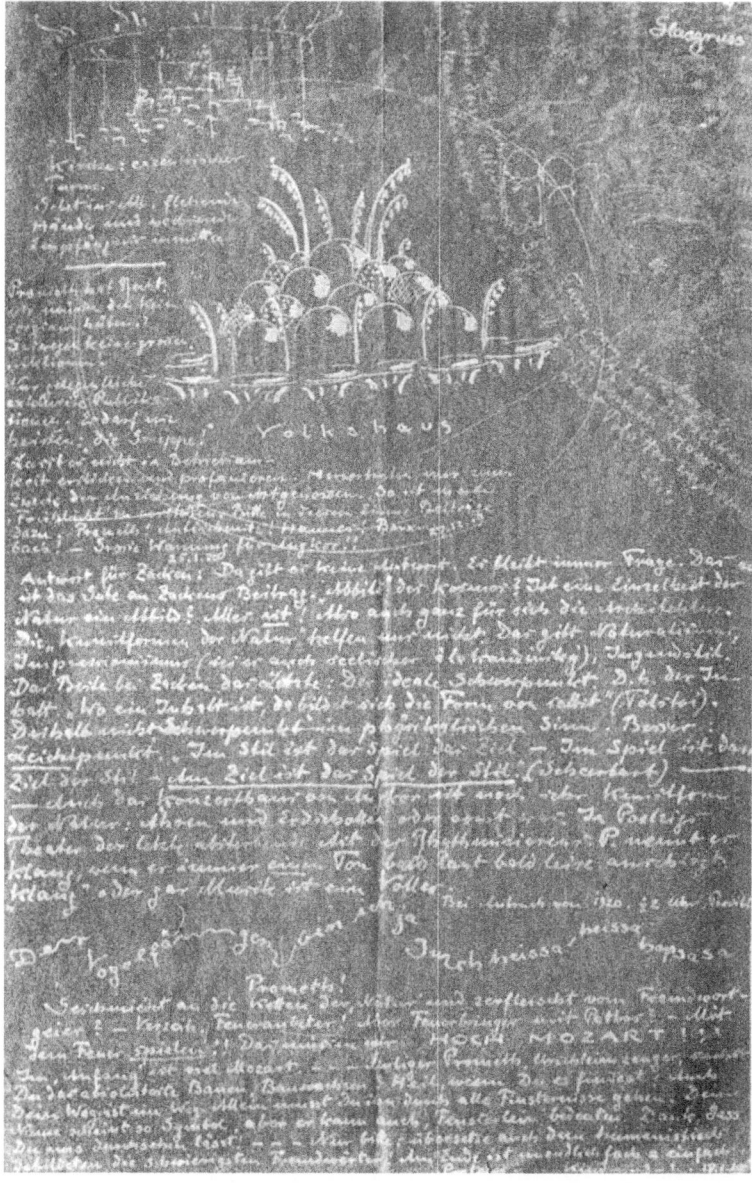

72 Bruno Taut, letter to the Gläserne Kette, 27 December 1919.

Scheerbart, said that the aim of the group was the game, the game was the aim:

> Im Stil ist das Spiel das Ziel –
> Im Spiel ist das Ziel der Stil –
> Am Ziel ist das Spiel der Stil.

> In style is the game the aim –
> In the game is the aim the style –
> In the end is the game the style.[20]

A drawing by Taut of the same date was of a *Bewegungsspiel fürs*

73 Bruno Taut,
Bewegungsspiel, 1919.

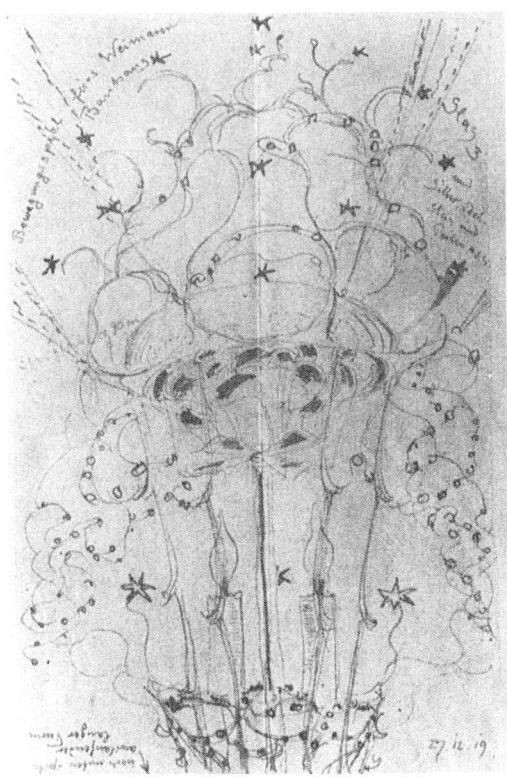

74 Paul Goesch,
architectural fantasy, *c.*
1920.

75 Paul Goesch, architectural fantasy, *c.* 1920.

Weimarer Bauhaus. It appears to be a design for a mobile, shaped like an ice-cream cone, with the point on the ground. At the top of the cone Taut indicated arabesques and stars, which were to be made up of silver, pearls and precious stones. As in Krayl's *Sternenhaus*, the drawing style is free in the extreme, and the childlike pleasure in simple line is elevated above any concern for content.

Paul Goesch, too, circulated drawings around the group, which combined a naive obsession with ornament and detail with the clumsy outlines and delight in colour which characterizes childrens' painting. In his architectural fantasies the surfaces were broken down into a mass of interlacing patterns and colours which served both to destroy the solidity of the larger forms and to suggest complex sub-structures within the larger elements. In his drawing of two columns and a lintel, for example, the columns appear to be made up of fragments of old columns, blocks and arches, which might have been taken from a scrap-heap. Other architectural jokes show temples made up of coloured layers, like liquorice-allsorts, and a gothicky arcade which is literally dripping with vegetable ornamentation.

The naivety and infantilism of the Gläserne Kette was not, however, simply a flight from reality or a means of escaping from the problems of the new republic. There was a more purposeful, nihilistic intention, which saw in infantilism the means of creating the sought-after *tabula rasa*. Poggioli has noted the connection between infantilism and nihilism,

saying that in Dadaism, nihilism 'took the form of an intransigent
puerility, an extreme infantilism'.[21] Poggioli concludes: 'there existed
in the avant-garde mentality a nihilism and an infantilism which
functioned reciprocally'.[22] This combination can be seen in the already
cited letter in which Taut included Scheerbart's riddle on the function
of style and the aim of the game. Later in the letter, while praising Krayl's
contributions, Taut brought together nihilism and infantilism with one
felicitous image: 'Play with fire!! That's what we must do. Hurrah for
Mozart!! There's a lot of Mozart in "Anfang".'[23] Dadaism and nihilism,
however, are impotent gestures when limited to the circle of believers.
In order to use these weapons to their full effect, Taut needed a public
platform. This was provided by his magazine *Frühlicht*, which was
launched contemporaneously with the Gläserne Kette, and appeared in
fourteen editions in Berlin between January and July 1920.

77 Paul Goesch,
architectural fantasy, *c.*
1920.

78 Paul Goesch,
architectural fantasy, *c.*
1920.

Taut was approached by the Zirkelverlag in October 1919, and asked
if he would be interested in acting as joint editor of a new architectural
magazine. Initially he declined, as he still had hopes for the magazine
Bauen which had been first mooted in the previous spring. Taut was also
concerned lest the proposed magazine should conflict with one which
Osthaus was thinking of launching.[24] Osthaus, however, offered no

79 Paul Goesch,
architectural fantasy, *c.*
1920.

objections, and Taut joined the editorial board of the new journal,
entitled *Stadtbaukunst alter und neuer Zeit*, along with Cornelius Gurlitt
and Bruno Möhring. It was another measure of the success of the radical
group at Stuttgart and of the 'Aufruf zum farbigen Bauen' that
Möhring, a leading representative of the conservative faction in the
Werkbund, was prepared to work on the same journal as Taut – the
leader of the radicals.

Taut explained this unlikely alliance to Osthaus in very historicist
terms. Möhring represented the past, Taut, the future. The present was
of little interest. 'It is a journal which will be read almost entirely by
architects. The way we see it, the emphasis will not be on the present,
but almost entirely on the past and the future.'[25] In this historicist
idolization of past and future, Taut was reponsible for the future, and
in order to dissociate his section from that of Gurlitt and Möhring, Taut
was allocated a supplement at the end of each issue. From the outset
it was clearly Taut's intention to antagonize the readership, which was
composed mainly of architects. As Taut confided to Osthaus: 'So I shall
be solely responsible for a special section with its own title – I'm thinking
of *Frühlicht* – in which…well you know already what will happen

80 Paul Goesch, paraphrase
of Berlin Cathedral, 1920.

there.'[26] The letter concluded in a Dadaistic vein, with a final salute to
Scheerbart. 'But, as I say, shouldn't one do something against "Serios-
ism" with happiness and laughter from all sides? Hurrah for Paul
Scheerbart!'[27] Scheerbart and Dadaism were to prove the twin supports
on which the new magazine was based.[28]

The very first copy began with Taut's manifesto 'Nieder der Seriosismus', a blast against the sacred cows of architecture.

Oh, our concepts: space, home, style! Phew, how these concepts stink! Destroy
them! Liquidate them! Nothing should remain! Scatter the schools, let the
professorial wigs fly, we want to play catch with them. Blow, blow! Let the dusty,
matted, patched up world of concepts, ideologies and systems feel our cold north
wind! Death to the concept-lice! Death to everything fusty! Death to everything
called title, dignity, authority! Down with everything serious![29]

This Scheerbartian beginning was followed by an extract from Behne's
Wiederdehr der Kunst, which hailed Scheerbart as the progenitor of the
new age of glass architecture. The third issue, furthermore, was almost
entirely devoted to the letters which Taut and Scheerbart had exchanged
in 1914, when Taut was designing the Glashaus for the Werkbund
exhibition and Scheerbart was writing *Glasarchitektur*. The illustrations
were chosen to amplify the iconoclastic, Dadaistic and Scheerbartian
tone of the text. Of the twenty-three drawings in the first four issues,
thirteen were by Goesch and five were by Krayl. The Dadaistic intention
was made clear in the third issue, by the inclusion of Krayl's suggestion
for the *House of a Dadaist*, a scribbled composition of triangles and
circles, which may have resembled the 'technical drawings', and tin-can
and wood assemblages which Golyscheff and Hausmann had exhibited
at the Dada exhibition at Neumann's gallery in April 1919.

The infantilism of the Gläserne Kette group cannot, however, be
categorized merely as nihilism: it carried other implications. The return

81 Carl Krayl, hanging
house, 1920.

82 Carl Krayl, *House of a
Dadaist*, 1920.

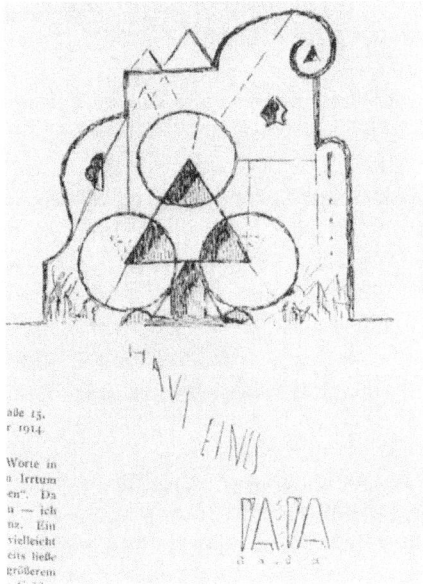

to childishness was not only promoted for its destructive qualities,[30] but also seen as a return to innocence and purity. The innocence of the child was to be the model for the purity of the *tabula rasa*. The theme of childhood innocence was one which preoccupied the former Activists in 1919 and 1920 after the disillusionment of the political revolution. In an article in the second edition of *Die Erhebung*, the successor to *Das Ziel* to which Taut also contributed, Rudolf Kayser prefaced his thoughts on *Kinderland* with a quotation from *Zarathustra*. 'Innocent and forgotten is the child, a new beginning, a wheel rolling out of itself, a first movement, a sacred affirmation.'[31] The former Activists who wrote for *Die Erhebung* tended to link this idolization of innocence with a simplistic historical analysis which contrasted a lost age of innocence, purity and *Gemeinschaft* against the recent age of industrialism and materialism. The sources for this analysis were the writings of Landauer and the eschatological fantasies of Hiller and the war-time Activists. Thus in *Die Erhebung II*, Hermann Schüller, in an article entitled 'Naivität und Gemeinschaft' could write: 'What is meant by naivety? The purity of the physical life and the naivety of the soul are interrelated...The capitalist, conscience-less, adventurist form of production destroys the naive...In families and schools based on individualism, the naive development of man, which is a mutualist attribute of nature, is violated.'[32] That Taut subscribed to this view of a new socialism, which was to be founded on simplicity and 'the purity of the physical life', has already been noted in the context of the *Folkwang-Schule*. It was a view which was also shared, initially at least, by the members of the Gläserne Kette. Writing to Gropius in May 1919, Krayl suggested that the AFK should publish a magazine devoted to ideal visions and plans for the future. The magazine, said Krayl, would bring together architecture, painting and sculpture, and would offer an alternative to the existing journals. Citing *Moderne Bauformen* and *Deutsche Kunst und Dekoration* as examples of obsolete publications, he asserted: 'The age of the artistic directions represented by these journals is over. We, however, want to look into the distant future and show what is to come.'[33] In the new age, he said, architecture would once again become 'pure', and the resultant social order would be one of 'pure' socialism. 'This time will come, for our own age of materialism in every form is tired, spent, devoid of ideas, exhausted to the point of collapse. Nothing else can follow other than a release from the bonds of the materialist age, therefore *pure* socialism.'[34] Gropius and the AFK did not respond to Krayl's suggestion when it was first made, but almost a year later Taut's Gläserne Kette and *Frühlicht* offered the young architects ample opportunities to express their views on the 'pure' architecture and the 'pure' society of the future.

The Gläserne Kette's obsession with innocence and purity stemmed directly from the avant-gardistic pose of agonism. Confronted by an unsympathetic and hostile world, the artist seeks refuge from reality in a pure and perfect alternative. Poggioli has noted this relationship, commenting:

83 Hans Scharoun, letter to
the Gläserne Kette, no date.

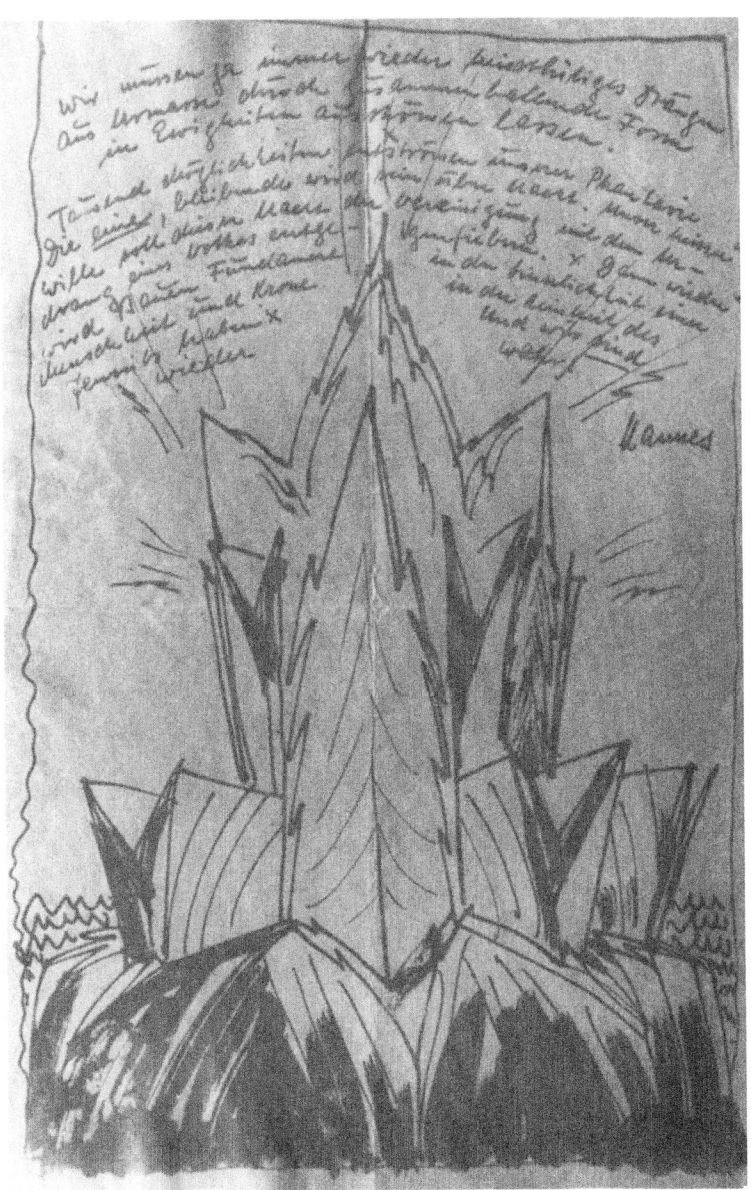

The modern mystique of purity aspires to abolish the discursive and syntactic
element, to liberate art from any connection with psychological and empirical
reality, to reduce every work to the intimate laws of its own genre or means;
in the literal sense of the terms, it is the ultra-ism or hyperbolism, an extension
of the agonistic spirit to the realms of style and form.[35]

It became clear that agonism provides the link which unites the two
apparently irreconcilable poles of the Gläserne Kette – infantilism and
purism.

True to the chiliastic and historicist antecedents in Taut's earlier
writings, the Gläserne Kette looked backwards in time for models of the

'pure' future. This retrospective glance, however, did not stop at the Gothic age or at the oriental temples, but returned to the very paradigm of man's innocence, to the primeval state of man before the Fall. As Hans Luckhardt noted: 'I have the impression that "Glas" wants to promote architectural development in the direction of the religious and the primitive – that he only has eyes for the coming spiritualization of mankind through faith.'[36] Architecture was to rediscover the link between the primeval slime and eternity – both seen as absolute states of purity. Hans Scharoun demanded:

We must of course again and again let hot-blooded thrusting out of the primeval slime stream out through concentrated form into eternity. A thousand possibilities flow out of our fantasy. The one which remains will come into being overnight. Our ardent will should rage feverishly towards this night of unification with the primeval urge of the *Volk*. Then once again will building have its foundation in the sensuality of mankind and its crown in the purity of the beyond. And once again we shall be rooted in reality.[37]

In abandoning medievalism and orientalism in favour of absolute primitivism and the pure *Urform*, the Gläserne Kette shrugged off the vestiges of German romanticism which lingered in Taut's earlier gothicophilia, and aligned themselves more directly with the contemporary avant-garde in painting – especially with Cubism.

Also linked to Cubism, on a morphological level at least, was the Gläserne Kette's favoured symbol of primitive purity, the crystal. Within the group, the most vigorous advocate of the crystal as a paradigm of innocent purity was Wassili Luckhardt. In January 1920 he wrote:

In front of me lies a crystal geode which has broken away from the earth's crust. Many many pyramids and prismatic forms have, as it were, grown out of the earth's crust and radiate in the sunshine. All are varied in size and shape, each one, however, is built according to the same constructional law. With these forms, doesn't one already have the impression of architectonic creation – don't these structures seem to summon up the creating hand of man, which shapes a meaningful entity out of the chaos of these original forms?[38]

Wassili Luckhardt also produced the most striking image of crystalline purity. His 1920 drawing *Kristall* was reminiscent of Taut's Glashaus at Cologne, but, unlike the Glashaus had no polemical function. Luckhardt's drawing was not conceived as an advertisement for glass architecture, but as a symbol of avant-garde purism.

With the exception of Goesch and Finsterlin, all the members of the group produced variations on the crystalline theme. Krayl, the arch-Dadaist, offered a *Kosmischer Bau*, which brought together three current symbols of primeval innocence – the mountains, the crystal and the new dawn.

This combination, which derived directly from Taut's *Alpine Architecture*, also appeared frequently in the drawings of Hablik. His *Museum im Hochgebirge*, to be made of glass and precious metals, recalls the geode in Luckhardt's letter.[39] Similarly prismatic forms were used in his design for a *Berg-Dom* and for various monoliths and towers, all to be set in the mountains. On a more modest scale, Max Taut used crystalline forms

84 Wassili Luckhardt,
Kristall, c. 1920.

85 Carl Krayl, *Kosmischer
Bau,* 1920.

86 Wenzel Hablik, *Museum im Hochgebirge*, *c.* 1920.

87 Wenzel Hablik, *Berg-Dom*, *c.* 1920.

88 Wenzel Hablik, tower, *c.* 1920.

for his design for a monument on the Kreuzberg in Berlin and in his project for *Betonhallen*. Likewise Hans Scharoun in his designs for a *Volkshäuser* relied on simple geometric forms, based on crystalline models. His *3 × 3 dimensionales Glashaus* is a good example.

The crystal, however, was not the only symbol of purity summonsed up by the group. The crystalline analogy for the *Urform* was paralleled by an organic analogy. In a subsequent article, Behne cited this analogy as the kernel of the new architecture. 'The contemplation of the roots is especially important for us. Our works must grow organically out of

89 Max Taut, proposed monument on the Kreuzberg, Berlin, 1920.

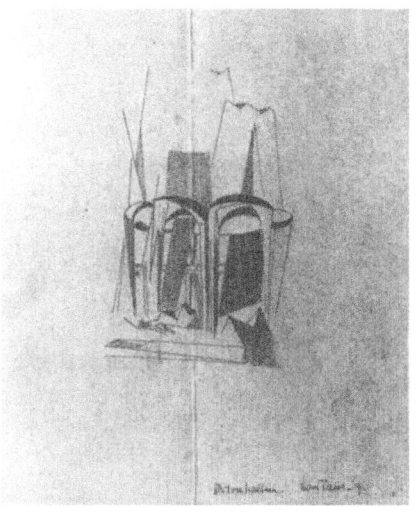

90 Max Taut, *Betonhallen*, 1919.

the simple, primitive cell.'[40] Hablik turned to the theme of an organically developing architecture, which he saw as means of returning to primal nature. In a letter of July 1920, he described his dream of building like the plants and insects.

Just a hint: the supple structure of grasses and flowers, for example, that are almost all rooted in the ground in star formation according to an inherent law (which can be noticed particularly clearly on high mountains or in the naked sands of the dunes), the spheric structure of heavenly bodies – the hard, sharp-edged, complicated and simple forms of crystals, animals, man – what beautiful creations – and yet evolved according to precise laws...It seems to me immaterial which symbols we make use of to find an expression for the living strength in us. Be it the cell-proliferation of greenfly glands – or oak apples – beetles' buildings, sharp-edged crystals, the perspectives and labyrinths of snails – palm or fern fronds, victoria regia, orchids or stinkwort, sea urchins or cacti, mammals, birds, or the palaces of the human body – created by the bacillus of lust for mental or manual whoring...Since, unlike the lice and wasps, we have not yet learned to stimulate a substance so that it forms itself, we are left with a choice of materials that are already separated from self-creative life.[41]

91 Hans Scharoun, *3 × 3
dimensionales Glashaus*, 1920.

92 Wenzel Hablik, glass
fantasy, 1920.

His illustratory drawings combined natural and artificial vegetation – the latter made up of metal, stone and glass. Both crystalline and organic forms were combined by Hablik in this modern-day Garden of Eden.

In his search for a self-forming substance which could approximate to the building-materials of the plant and animal world, Hablik alighted on glass. He hit upon the idea of fusing sand in its natural location to make glass buildings. A letter to the Gläserne Kette showed a glass spiral which he planned for the sand-dunes on Sylt. He developed the concept further in the scenario for a proposed film, entitled *Erbauen eines Glashauses am Meere*.

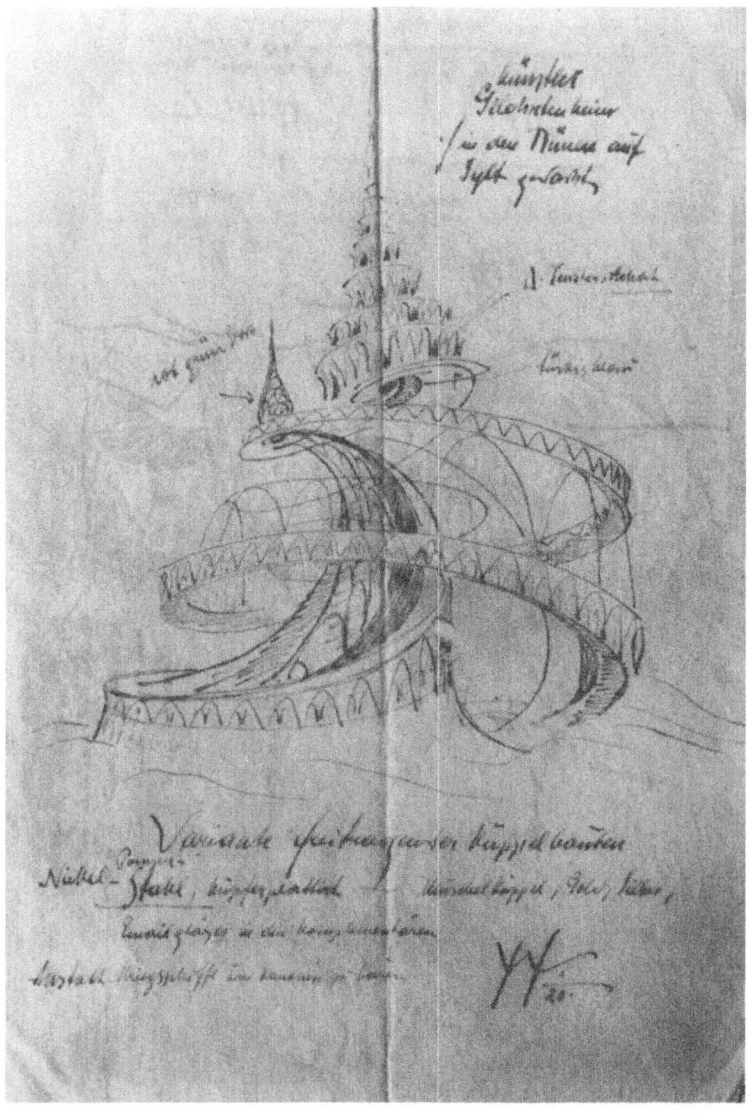

93 Wenzel Hablik, home for artists and scholars in the dunes on Sylt, 1920.

His description combined both the desire to synthesize the *Urform* from earth and fire, with the excitement of high technology – the very paradigm of the two ideologies of primitivism and fantasy. The conversion of sand into glass was to be achieved with the aid of ships, airships, aeroplanes, gas-pumps and complex electrical systems. Hablik's account is very exciting:

Already, stately forms are arising, gigantic, scintillating glass domes, serrated and pinnacled – spheres and strips – cones and flowery cylinders – a glistening, a shimmering, a shower of sparks. The inmost depths of craters congeal into a molten foundation, and spatial structures radiate leapfrogging from the centre. The mighty airship is launched forth, seven aeroplanes part from it and orbit the building site.[42]

94 Wenzel Hablik, crystal
house, 1920.

In a drawing of a *Siedlung*, Hablik admitted the close connection between
the primitive purity of fused-glass and infantilism. Around the drawing
he inscribed the legend: 'Yes! We may even be childish, and play in the
sand like children!'

A similar process of fusion would have been necessary to construct
the designs which Finsterlin submitted to the group. His vision of the
Urform derived not from the crystal but directly from the amoeba in the
primeval slime.[43] All of his drawings followed the pattern which he had
established at the Ausstellung für unbekannte Architekten, showing
polyp-like houses, and vegetable constructions intended to be made of
glass.

Although Taut repeatedly extolled Finsterlin's written contributions,[44]
he had reservations over the imitation of natural types, which he saw
as a dangerous formalism. He was joined in these reservations by other
contributors, notably Hans Luckhardt.[45] Indeed, Taut feared that any
imitations of organic or vegetable forms might lead to some form of
neo-Jugendstil. As he wrote to the group in its early days: 'Style not
through the pursuit of form (van de Velde), but through a philosophy
of life, through religion.'[46] In his article in *Die Erhebung*, Taut reiterated
this point: 'The "problem of form" has never existed. Where it seemed
to appear, it was the result of inner bleakness. Building will come of itself
in anyone who has a philosophy of life, that means whoever has love
and warmth.'[47] Not the architect himself, but the architect's faith would
produce the forms appropriate to the new age. This religious faith was
dubbed by Taut 'the great, all-embracing element'. He wrote in *Die
Erhebung*: 'The great, all-embracing element is discernible. We flutter
around it like amoebae, like coral polyps or salt atoms at the creation

95 Wenzel Hablik, *Siedlung,*
c. 1920.

96 Hermann Finsterlin,
Traum aus Glas, 1920.

of rock or crystal.'[48] Mankind was likened to the basic crystal salts and
amoebae, which would be united together in one divine construction
by a mutual faith in some higher authority. The authority in this case,
was religious. Taut wrote: 'Our architectural aspirations are merely
aspirations for religion.'[49] The architect's role was thus prophetic and
apostolic – to spread the faith amongst the laity. Taut compared the

97 Hermann Finsterlin,
house for the arts, 1920

98 Hermann Finsterlin,
Wahlhallen, 1920.

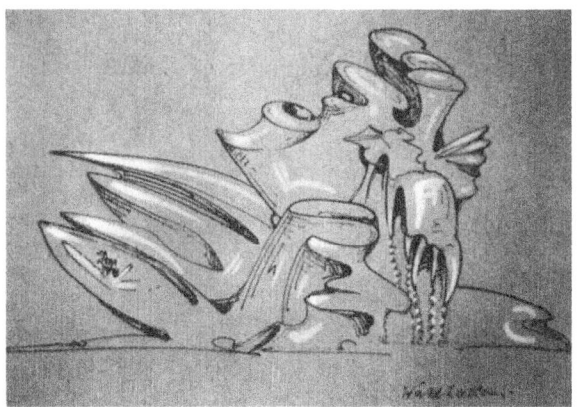

twelve other members of the Gläserne Kette to the twelve apostles and
assigned to himself, rather immodestly, the role of Christ. 'Numbers:
3, 5, 7, 12. Contrast: 2, 4. Both united in 12. In 13 the highest fortune:
1 leads (Christ).'[50] This view of the architect's relationship to society was
still the élitist, Activist view first formulated during the war years. The
architect was the *geistig* leader who articulated the strivings of the *Volk*
towards an ideal *Gemeinschaft*. Taut used exactly these terms in the
article in *Die Erhebung*. 'The feeling for *Gemeinschaft* has, on a new scale,
become liberated. Thus the call for architecture, for architecture is
nothing else than the crystallization of the feeling for *Gemeinschaft*. The
people call to us architects: be leaders!'[51] Through the intercession of
the Christ-like figure of the architect, a pure architecture and a
correspondingly pure society were to be achieved.

The actual process involved was akin to transfiguration. In the letter
in which he likened himself to Christ, Taut declared, 'Highest fortune,
transfiguration.'[52] Towards the end of the correspondence Taut referred
back to this, stating: 'In no way can one reach the cosmos by following
the simple path which we perceive through our limited conception of
the senses. Every explanation or clarification is nonsense, only transfiguration remains.'[53] The hoped-for transfiguration was essentially

chiliastic. Man would be freed from the chains of progress and intellect, and would return to his *Urnatur*, his primeval, innocent state of harmony and brotherhood. Just as in Christian theology, the transfiguration was a prophetic sign, an apocalyptic event which pointed to the future transfiguration of all Christians through Christ, so the transfiguration envisaged by Taut and his followers anticipated the transfiguration of all mankind through architecture.[54]

The theme of transfiguration was a variant on the Activist belief in the transformation of the *Volkswille* into pure *Geist* through the mediation of the *Literat*. Both variations – that of Hiller and that of the Gläserne Kette – insisted that the subjective, earthly spirit could only reach the higher realm of pure objectivity when guided by a *geistig* leader – by the *Literat* or architect. In one of his drawings for the Gläserne Kette, Scharoun gave pictorial form to this process. The subjective realms of *Volk* and *Geist* (*ich*, *Ich*) were protrayed as two intersecting cones. The point of objectification (*Du*), where the two fused together, was at the centre of a great work of architecture – the *Volkshaus*.

Scharoun's *Volkhaus* can be taken as a typical product of the Gläserne Kette. It was constrained by Taut's dictum that form could not be arrived at by design but only through faith and *Weltanschauung*. The form was thus made subservient to the content, expressing only the most general notions about glass and colour. Implicit in these material qualities were the various avant-gardistic themes which we have already discussed – agonism, purism, nihilism, infantilism and the desire for a *tabula rasa*. These in turn, were related to the content of the drawing, which can best be described as the expression of a quasi-religious faith in social regeneration, in the *Gemeinschaftsgefühl*. This is exactly as Taut would have wished it.

There could, however, be no formal development away from these symbolic statements of purity and innocence. Once Wassili Luckhardt had protrayed his faith in the *Gemeinschaftsgefühl* as a crystal, what was he to do next? Similarly, what was Krayl to do after he had playfully destroyed the notion of architectural rigidity and substance with his spidery drawings. Was he to destroy it all over again? By adopting an agonist, nihilist and purist stance against the current practices in architecture, the members of the Gläserne Kette had established a new starting point, a *tabula rasa*, but, at the same time, had also removed themselves from what was generally accepted to be the realm of architecture.

This was certainly the view of their critics. In response to the articles and drawings in *Frühlicht*, Heinrich de Fries penned a vitriolic article, which he fashioned as a speech to an 'imaginary assembly of young architects'. It was published in *Das Kunstblatt* In March 1920, and represented a typical reaction from a progressive architect to the excesses of the Gläserne Kette group. De Fries began by asking the 'imaginary' architects what they actually had to offer to the proletariat, saying that propaganda and self-advertisement were all very well, but

99 Hans Scharoun, idea for
a *Volkshaus*, 1920.

where were the concrete suggestions and models for the new architecture? Unlike Taut, who had suggested to his companions that writing
was as important at that time as drawing, de Fries insisted that anything
other than concrete suggestions for building were irrelevant, and had
nothing whatsoever to do with architecture.

In the course of the meeting a great many stirring words have alluded to the
large number of designs and no small number of manifestos which the last year
has produced. I am acquainted with the bulk of the designs and with the
majority of the manifestos. They are essentially made up of bad graphics and
superlative cliché writing which, in the course of the year, have repeated
themselves again and again without ever changing a word. They are not
concerned with architecture...

Beams of light, plant motifs and jewellery boxes look very nice when drawn in
a small format, but to offer them as buildings after magnifying their scale is
simply nonsense. And when some of you, gentlemen, turn coloured light fittings
made of American coloured glass upside down and magnify them beyond
measure in order to depict a *Volkshaus* of the future, then I must ask you to
have patience with my lack of comprehension.[55]

As if in defiant response to such attacks, the Gläserne Kette group organised an exhibition of their work, which was held under the auspices of the Arbeitsrat für Kunst. Like the Ausstellung für unbekannte Architekten, the new exhibition was held in the Graphische Kabinett J. B. Neumann, on Kurfürstendamm. It opened on 3 May 1920, and was called Neues Bauen.

The drawings exhibited were all by members of the Gläserne Kette, with the single exception of a design for a villa by Fritz Kaldenbach, which was exhibited posthumously. An introduction to the drawings was written by Adolf Behne. In it, he launched a vigorous attack on Heinrich de Fries, condemning him and his associates for advocating subsistence-level housing, and adding that the members of the Gläserne Kette would have nothing to do with any such building programme.

There is no shortage of serious and genuine attempts to alleviate the current plight. Bruno Möhring, Peter Behrens, and Hugo [sic] de Fries have made suggestions for the construction of dwellings of a newer and better type. But the shack, the two-storey house and also Behrens's *Siedlung* dismay us and prove to us that only a wretched substitute for housing is possible as long as the existence minimum remains too low. No, we cannot collaborate with such

101 Bruno Taut, Siedlung
Ruhland, 1920.

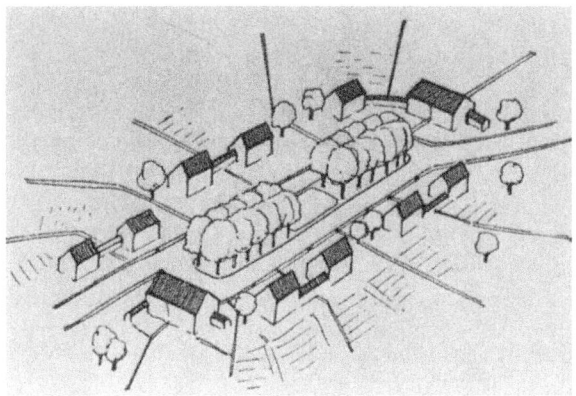

102 Siedlung Ruhland,
house elevation and section.

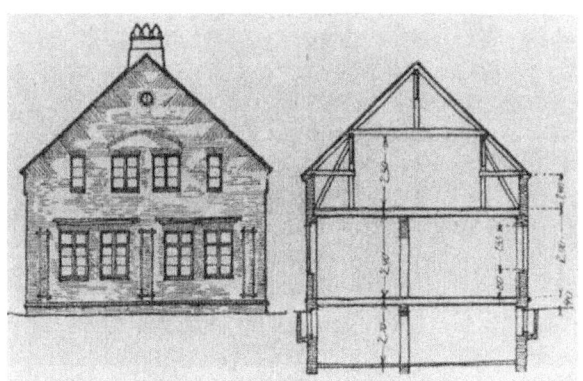

103 Max Taut, project for a
wooden bungalow, 1920.

schemes to build burrows and cells, mass barracks and stables for our fellow men.

When the time comes to build houses fit for humans, then we shall be there. Until then, we would merely be the tools of the racketeers and exploiters. Let them get on with their business alone. We don't fit in with them. When the world is once again ruled with understanding and generosity, then we shall help it to build.[56]

Such an uncompromisingly purist position was, however, difficult to sustain. Although Behne was echoing the ideal, avant-gardistic intentions of the group, he was contradicted by actual events. For in 1920, several members of the group were occupied on the design of very basic housing.

In the spring of 1920, Bruno Taut drew up plans and designs for a *Siedlung* for agricultural and factory workers at Ruhland, a village thirty miles north of Dresden. The client was a housing association. In his account of the development of the project, Taut wrote that both he and the residents agreed that the housing should be of the simplest type possible. 'Following directly from the wishes of the residents, which exactly correspond with my own convictions, I have given the houses the sparest of outlines, with a king post supporting the simplest of roofs'[57] Also in the summer of 1920, Taut's brother Max was submitting his designs for very primitive housing to the 'Wohnlauben-Wettbewerb' in Spandau. Max Taut offered two designs for wooden bungalows, both with three beds and a small shed for animals. The materials were absolutely basic: the walls were of wooden sandwich construction, filled with coke-ash, and the roofs were to be covered with rubberized paper. At an estimated 12,000 Marks per dwelling, Taut's huts were almost three times cheaper per square metre than a conventional apartment house.

As if to reconcile such primitive huts with the grandiose projects being discussed by the Gläserne Kette, Bruno Taut took the opportunity, in 'Architektur neuer Gemeinschaft', to reiterate the Activist view on the need to differentiate *Volk* from *Geist*, the hut from the temple, the *Praktiker* from the *Phantast*. He also emphasized, as the Activists had done, and as he had done in *Die Stadtkrone*, that *Volk* and *Geist* although distinct from each other, were mystically related. As Taut wrote: 'A fixed chain extends from the stable to the star, and one can exchange one end for the other at will...It is a chain in which everything small becomes great and everything great becomes small, that is, humanly possible, if the connection exists within us.'[58] The architects' *geistig* purpose was to delineate this succession from stable to star. Only then, said Taut, would the hut be given true meaning and context. 'Whoever builds a stable doesn't have to be able to build a *Kristallhaus*. But he won't build it as correctly and simply as is appropriate if he doesn't know on which rung on the ladder to heaven his stable belongs. We must construct this ladder.'[59] This idealist view of a direct progression from the most humble to the most elevated, the basis of the perfect social and spiritual *Gemeinschaft*, was the touchstone of war-time Activism. It was the agonistic and purist reaction against the war. Now, five years later, it had become an anachronism.

The revolutionary peace had been notable more for sectarianism than for expressions of brotherhood and *Gemeinschaft*, and although the need for some form of religious or quasi-religious focus was still felt, it was clear by 1920 that the Activist notion of *Geist* was inadequate to the task. Although Taut was still reiterating the Activist faith in *Geist* and *Gemeinschaft* in *Die Erhebung*, this reiteration, as we have already noted, took on the nature of a coda. For in the early months of 1920 Taut himself was beginning to question his faith in the Activist paradise.

As early as February 1920, Taut wrote to Osthaus, saying that he was trying to finish his *Auflösung der Städte* as quickly as possible. He then stated: 'With that, "utopias" should come to an end, and I hope that I shall have some opportunities to work with my ideas in the realm of the practical.'[60] He confirmed his withdrawal from the realms of the fantastic in a letter which he wrote to the Gläserne Kette in the middle of April, even before the opening of the Neues Bauen exhibition. 'I am now finished with intuitive works, I might almost hope for ever. Concrete matters, hard objects must now strike me.'[61] Later in the month, Taut wrote to Osthaus, asking permission to publish his plans for the *Folkwang-Schule*. The purpose of this, was to dispel the myth that he was a pure fantasist, with no feeling for reality. As he bemoaned in the letter: 'This is very important to me, as there is a story spreading around about me, that I can only design utopias.'[62] One direct result of Taut's campaign to disembarrass himself of this utopian tag was his decision, after the Neues Bauen exhibition had finished in Berlin, to withdraw his works from it. It had been arranged that the exhibition would travel on to other venues, but Taut wanted no further part in it. Hans Luckhardt explained why he did this in a contemporary letter to the Gläserne Kette. '"Glas" no longer wants to exhibit his works, because in this form they appear to him too liable to evaluation as graphic art, with the cultural ideas pushed into the background.'[63] By concerning themselves more with the formal aspects of Taut's drawings rather than with their content, the critics and visitors to the exhibition indicated to Taut the fragility of his Activist thesis that form was secondary to and dependent on a mystical and beneficient *Geist*.

By the autumn, Taut had become hardened in his resolve to abandon the clouds and the stars in favour of the earth. He wrote in a letter dated 5 October 1920: 'In a word, I no longer want to draw utopias *in principio*, but absolutely palpable utopias, which "stand with both feet firmly on the ground".'[64] The letter continued with a series of practical suggestions which clearly spelt out the end of the phase of agonism. Taut analysed the function of the architect and defined three specific duties. The first was to build. He added: 'there is little of that at present'. The second was to 'create the new shape of culture (the so-called pure Utopia)', and the third was to 'awaken the demand for building'. He now considered the third task to be the most important and proposed that the group set about promoting their ideas and visions in a form which should be as clear and understandable as possible.

The third task seems to me to be the most necessary and the most important, especially as the second grows out of it. To carry it out one should not use pointers and rough drafts which are understood by the ordinary man as at best tasty titbits – I am now satisfied of this from our two exhibitions – but it should have such an obvious clarity that anyone, any child, any worker can understand it...This means conceiving entirely new methods of presenting our designs, not, as previously, simply ground plans, which make architecture seem a purely technical matter, but plans of a kind which are unbelievably understandable. They should neither be a series of sketches like mine, which are really book illustrations, nor the drawings of 'Prometh' or 'Anfang', not even Hannes's 'tasteful' water colours, nor plaster models, nor the slightly dry art of 'Angkor' and 'Zacken', none of the romantic Expressionism of 'Tancred' and no dreams à la 'Berxbach'. No, absolutely no studio art. What to us are the rungs for the ascent into the lonely starry night are – pearls cast before swine. No pearls that belong in jewellery boxes.[65]

Taut appeared by now to agree with Heinrich de Fries that the decorative qualities appropriate to the jewellery-box had little to do with architecture. His comment on casting pearls before swine was very indicative of the evolution of Taut's *Kunstpolitik*. In November 1918 he was insisting that 'Art and *Volk* must form a unity.' By October 1920 he had abandoned his idealistic belief in any resonance which might exist between the artist and the people, and was prepared to admit, more realistically perhaps, that it was up to the artist and the architect to persuade and convert the public at large to the new cause.

Having demolished the subjectivity and the 'artiness' of the Gläserne Kette, Taut went on to describe a possible successor, a group called Die Bauwandlung, which had been set up in Darmstadt and hoped to gain sponsorship for a planned exhibition from the town of Darmstadt itself, and from the State of Hessen. The new group was the brainchild of a local architect, Emmanuel Josef Margold. Margold had enlisted the support of Poelzig, Gropius and Bruno Taut, while such prestigious names as van de Velde, Endell, Obrist, Bonatz and Pankok were also mentioned in connection with the exhibition, which was scheduled for the following spring. Taut hoped to enroll the entire Gläserne Kette en bloc into Die Bauwandlung. He clearly viewed the project with considerable enthusiasm, seeing in it, perhaps, a fruitful way out of the impasse of subjectivity and self-indulgence which was stifling the Gläserne Kette. At the very end of his letter, he intimated very clearly that his continued interest in the Gläserne Kette circle depended on the success of the new group, and of the proposed exhibition. 'If, however, nothing comes out of it all, then I shall be reduced to passivity in this matter, and, like the rest of us, will go my own way.' He concluded with a valediction which revealed a flagging conviction in the group – 'Still with the eternal belief in fire!'[66]

Frühlicht ceased to be published with *Stadtbaukunst alter und neuer Zeit* after the second July edition of 1920. Taut had argued with Gurlitt over an article by Paul Goesch which touched on sexual matters, and had used the dispute to terminate his contract. He subsequently wrote to the Gläserne Kette, saying that he was pleased to be rid of the responsibility. A similar feeling may have coloured his relations with the

Gläserne Kette itself. He pinned his hopes for the group on its successful absorption into Die Bauwandlung. On this premise the exchange of letters continued while the negotiations for the new group were being made. During this time, the new member, Alfred Brust, suggested that they should all compose some form of apologia, stating their creeds, and both Taut and Finsterlin responded with rather tortured offerings. The plans for Die Bauwandlung came to nothing, and, as he had warned, Taut decided to go his own way.

A copy exists of one, last letter, dated Christmas 1920. It was unsigned, but was probably written either by Hans Scharoun or by Bruno Taut. The fragmentary, telegraphic style of the writing, however, has more in common with Taut's earlier letters than with those of Scharoun. Whoever it was written by, the letter gives a fascinating insight into the uncertainty and pessimism which was felt by the writer at the end of 1920.

The dominant tone of the letter is one of resignation and impotence. Out of all the ambitions and hopes of November 1918, nothing had been realized. The writer was depressed that so little could have resulted out of so much optimism. He wrote: 'Our age has one great strength: it wishes for better things. The great and the humble, faith and tragedy simultaneously. To wish for better but to be unable to do anything, to achieve nothing – this is the meaning of the age.'[67] As a symptom of this hopelessness, the writer cited the vulgarization and decline of the Expressionist impulse: 'Out of step with the age: death of Expressionism. Absorbed into literariness and vaudeville'[68] Not only was the writer disillusioned with Expressionism, he was also disenchanted with politics. The brief confluence in 1918 of political revolution and artistic radicalism was seen to have been fortuitous and fruitless: 'Strangle the "beautiful soul" of politics. Collaboration with politics pointless. Politics is in its essence mundane, materialistic. The devil's work of mechanization: bourgeois, capitalism.'[69] Neither capitalism nor Bolshevism appeared to offer feasible alternatives to the contemporary crisis. Both, felt the writer, were destined to failure and chaos:

Socialization: political consequences, inexorable death of the industrial state (from the standpoint of industry uneconomic, senseless).

Enforced death of too many. Safety-valve against over-population: hunger, plague, civil-war.

Chaos. Decline of the West.

Consequence of the East, Bolshevism: quicker, more conscious disintegration than in the West. Also chaos.[70]

What was left? Merely the hopes of 1916. The letter concluded with a reiteration of the ideal progression, by which European culture would develop, via the example of the northern Gothic, into a worthier, oriental model. In 1916, this sequence was held up as a feasible alternative to continued European strife. By 1920, the writer himself sadly dismissed it as utopian. 'Beginning of the West. Cultural shift from south to north. Demise; shift from Occident to Orient. —: utopian.'[71]

◇◇

22

Taut and the theatre

As befits a movement which had its roots in the Freie Volksbühne circle, Taut's architectural Activism and his dreams of a *Glanzwelt* did find a partial realization in the theatre. As we have seen, Taut wrote extensively on the theatre in the summer of 1919 and, in the same period, conceived *Der Weltbaumeister*.

Taut planned a performance of *Der Weltbaumeister* to coincide with the launching in Darmstadt of the Bauwandlung, the intended successor to the Gläserne Kette. The new group hoped to hold an exhibition in the Mathildenhöhe at the beginning of 1921 and Taut proposed to stage a performance of *Der Weltbaumeister* at the opening of this exhibition. The music for the performance had been composed by Heinz Tiessen, to whom Taut wrote in October 1920:

Given your liking for the *Weltbaumeister*, nothing needs to be said between us about the intimate connection between music and architecture. You will therefore understand my efforts to have your *Weltbaumeister* played on the occasion of the exhibition, perhaps even in it. This would give a special liveliness, would get rid of those who are lukewarm, and stir and attract other, unknown forces.[1]

The group was never formed, however, and neither the exhibition nor the performance took place.

Although *Der Weltbaumeister* remained unperformed, Taut was also involved in several other theatrical projects in the autumn of 1920 and early in 1921. From July 1920 onwards, he was in correspondence with the eminent director Ludwig Berger. Taut was very enthusiastic about Berger's writings on the theatre. In one of his early letters to Berger he wrote: 'My thanks, having read your *Spielgeist*. It is vision, symbol and form fused together into an indivisible unity...I was very pleased to see the importance which you attribute to the architectonic.'[2] In a series of increasingly sycophantic letters, Taut suggested to Berger that they should work together on a new production. As a suitable vehicle for their collaboration, Taut put forward Alfred Brust's play *Der singende Fisch*, set in India. Brust was a member of the Gläserne Kette and had fallen into financial difficulties. By putting on his play, Taut hoped to ease Brust's problems and, at the same time, realize his ambition to work with Berger. In December 1920 he wrote to Berger:

Alfred Brust has just sent me a cry for help. He will have to work as a waiter or something if no help comes by 1 Jan...I myself am trying everything possible, but perhaps some idea will occur to you. Couldn't, for example, *Der singende Fisch* still be included in the winter programme, thereby making it possible to give Brust an advance?[3]

Berger, it seems, rejected this proposal and by the end of the year, relations between Taut and Berger appear to have become strained.

At the same time as he was courting Berger, Taut himself was being courted by Felix Holländer, who asked Taut to collaborate with him on a large-scale production of *Die Rauber* by Schiller. This time, Taut declined, saying: 'The large space makes the intimacy of Shakespeare just as impossible as the youthful pathos of Schiller, which would degenerate into a hollow tirade. In addition, the impossible realism.'[4] As an alternative, Taut suggested *The Birds*, by Aristophanes. Taut's plan was to put on a play as a masque. He felt that it would find a sympathetic reception, for, as he explained: 'I believe that the mood of this work would be very topical in our present circumstances, for the two Athenians, just as we also want to do sometimes, leave the filth of their surroundings for a better world.'[5] This scheme to create a theatrical *Glanzwelt*, like the project for *Der Weltbaumeister*, came to nothing.

Taut did collaborate, however, on one play which actually was produced. It was another Schiller piece – *Die Jungfrau von Orleans*. It was performed in the Deutsches Theater in February 1921 with Helene Thimig, Agnes Straub, Paul Hartmann and Werner Krauss in the leading roles. The director was Karl-Heinz Martin and the sets, costumes and lighting were designed by Bruno Taut. This collaboration with Martin was clearly seen by Taut as second-best to working with Berger on the Brust play. Indeed, Taut wrote wistfully to Berger in a garbled, New Year's greeting: 'I am now working with your colleague Martin, but I mean, we two together...'[6] Nevertheless, the work with Martin finally gave Taut the opportunity to put some of his theories on stage design into practice.

As a substitute for the proscenium Taut constructed an arch-like frame of glass prisms. On the stage, behind the arch, he built catwalks, ramps and cubiform platforms. The coulisses and backdrops were likewise painted in a quasi-Cubist manner, with Cubistic trees in papier-mâché. Lighting also played an important role. Not only did Taut use the coloured light naturalistically to portray such scenes as the dying red rays of the sun over Reims, he also used it symbolically. Thus the evil Isabeau was swathed in purple light and the transfiguration of Joan was bathed in celestial blue.

By substituting a glittering glass arch for the conventional proscenium, Taut hoped to break down the division between the stage and the auditorium. As he had advocated in the article 'Zum neuen Theaterbau', Taut's set sought to free the drama and the audience from the conventional restraints imposed by traditional theatre practice. The drama and the audience should flow together into a single unity, aided by the effects of light and colour. As Taut wrote in the programme notes to the play: 'The production must derive as a natural consequence from the spiritual format of the drama, so that during the performance it

104 Bruno Taut, design for a production of Schiller's *Die Jungfrau von Orleans* at the Deutsches Theater, Berlin, 1921.

retires into the background behind the dramatic proceedings, allowing the spectator to forget its existence.'[7] Critical opinion was divided as to how successful he had been in achieving this intention.

The critic of the *Börsen-Courier* admitted that the sets were highly original, but wondered whether Martin and Taut had chosen the right piece for their experiments. He felt that the ardour and vigour of Schiller's writing could stand by themselves, without the need for elaborate staging. Ludwig Sternaux, in the *Lokal-Anzeiger*, was particularly disturbed by the glass arch. He wrote:

The zig-zag frame of coloured glass, which glistened in formless caprice around the stage opening, here protruding like arrowheads, there climbing and falling like a cascade – this bizarre, unreal frame which was supposed to differentiate sharply between the wonder-world and the everyday world, tended more to disturb than to conjure up the desired mood.[8]

Perhaps Sternaux misunderstood Taut's intention, that the arch should draw the audience towards the stage like iron filings to a magnet. Only then, when they were completely in the drama, would they forget the everyday world.

In the *Berliner-Zeitung*, Norbert Falk praised the lighting effects, even though he saw in them an element of kitsch. His critique reported: 'Although this stage lighting becomes schematic and, in its succession of rapid changes, almost approaches the displays of "Bengal Lights", it achieves in part some very fine and extraordinarily pictorial effects.'[9] The wittiest review of the production appeared in the *Berliner Tageblatt*.

The writer, Fritz Engel, was also left unconvinced by Taut's set, and, in particular, by the glass arch. He commented:

The set, designed by Bruno Taut, is taciturn, ponderous, conceived in an unreal Gothic, and shot with glittering light which, playing like a rainbow and dancing like a will-o'-the-wisp, blurs all realities. Before the curtain goes up one sees framed glass pictures on the left and right of the forestage. One is startled. Has Schultze, the glazier's boy, built his trial piece here for his master's test, and why here of all places? When the curtain rises it becomes clear that these are part of an arch, which is supposed to span the scene magically. I am prepared to do without it. One sees similar things on the verandahs of restaurants in the summer. It is an unnecessary distraction.[10]

The comparative lack of acclaim which Taut's sets attracted from the critics may perhaps explain why Taut did not pursue this direction. The *Jungfrau von Orleans* was to remain the only stage production with which Taut was directly involved. Taut's experiments were left to others to pursue, most notably Erwin Piscator, who founded the Proletarische Theater, Bühne der revolutionären Arbeiter Groß-Berlins with Hermann Schüller, a colleague of Taut's in the RGA and the Bund für proletarische Kultur.

The fact that Taut should have been involved in the theatre at all, however, shows that the private and radical *Glanzwelt* of 1916 had, by 1921, become acceptable on the commercial stage. This process of popularization, although a measure of Taut's success as polemicist, was an important contributory factor to the decline and demise of Taut's Activist movement.

23

◇-◇

The end of an avant-garde

The question which was raised in the introduction must now be answered: why did Taut's Activist movement end so suddenly, and why at that particular time?

Clearly there is a connection between contemporary developments in German politics and the fortunes of the avant-garde groups which had been established in 1918 with specific, if unrealistic political intentions. The Marxist critic Georg Lukács has explained the collapse of Expressionism entirely in terms of the political context. In his celebrated essay '"Größe und Verfall" des Expressionismus', written in 1934, Lukács characterized Expressionism as the artistic exegesis of the political ideology of the USPD and of the anarcho-socialists who loosely adhered to the USPD line.[1] According to Lukács, both the USPD and their Expressionist counterparts actively worked against the success of a proletarian revolution and sought to disguise their true, revisionist intentions behind a facade of 'pseudo-activism' and declamatory polemics. When the battle was joined with the counter-revolutionary forces, said Lukács, then the inconsistencies of both the USPD and of Expressionism were exposed. He commented:

The hard struggles of the early revolutionary years and the first defeats of the revolution in Germany emphasized ever more clearly the actual affinity between revolutionary phrases and the whining of the capitulators. Thus ended – not merely by chance at the same time as the USPD was dissolved – the period in which Expressionism had been the dominant literary current in Germany.[2]

The chronology of Lukács's account corresponds closely to the actual demise of Taut's Activist movement. The USPD collapsed at the Halle Conference in October 1920, Taut's movement was concluded with the end of the Gläserne Kette correspondence in December 1920.

Lukács's comments are particularly relevant to the Activist movement. His essay, despite its title, was not a critique of the wider Expressionist movement but limited itself almost exclusively to the Activist offshoot. In his efforts to reveal the true nature of Expressionism, Lukács included numerous quotations, most of which were taken from the Activists and the Activist yearbooks. According to Lukács, the USPD and, by implication, the Activists had worked directly against a proletarian revolution over the period 1914–19. The USPD, he said: 'developed out of the former "Marxist centre", with the stated ideological intention of diverting the masses away from the path of revolution.'³ The revisionism which Lukács noted in the USPD was clearly endorsed in the writings of the Activists. As we have seen, the political ideology of Activism was élitist, undemocratic, anti-Marxist and anti-proletarian. The driving force behind the Activist revolution would not be the proletariat but the *geistig* leader, the bourgeois *Literat* or architect.

How did Activism and, in particular, the architecture of Activism, express this revisionist tendency? The core of Activist architecture was the magnificent collective symbol. It appeared in various guises as *Kristallhaus*, *Kultusbau*, *Volkshaus* or *Tempel*. The function of this symbol of harmony and *Gemeinschaft* was to unify the warring factions in society and, by a process akin to religious transfiguration, to elevate them above mean subjectivism and individualism and so to bring them to a new level of 'pure' and 'objective' existence. The revolution thus accomplished would be a spiritual rather than an economic or social revolution. It would, as we have already noted, be inspired not by class interests or by Marxist demagogy, but by the guidance of the *geistig* leader.

The values of the Activist élite were not the values of the proletariat but rather the traditional values of the liberal bourgeoisie: good taste, aesthetic delight, appreciation of beauty, respect for creative genius. The Activists, however, sought to establish these values as absolute and unchallengeable norms. They claimed for these specifically bourgeois values the status of objective truths. The legitimacy of the Activist claims for an objective *Geist* which can be perceived solely by the gifted élite was questioned by Lukács, who wrote: 'It is exaggerated subjectivism which poses here with the empty gestures of objectivity.'⁴ The Activists' infatuation with objectivity was given formal expression in the cult of purism, which was a dominant theme in both literary and architectural Activism.

The absolute and objective essence of *Geist* was naturally seen to be pure. The myth of purity permeated every aspect of Activism. Politically, the Activists dreamt of a non-materialist, pure form of socialism; Taut wrote of 'socialism in the non-political, supra-political sense', Krayl of 'a release from the bonds of the materialist age, therefore *pure* socialism'.

In the realm of architecture, the insistence on purity was given powerful expression through appeals to glass and crystal, earth and fire. The glass architecture was located in areas of unsullied purity. Taut and his followers favoured mountainous sites, high above the discord and chaos of the materialist, brick and stone culture below. Although such calls for purism and for a return to the pure essence can work effectively as manifestos or calls to action, they can give no indication as which direction the future should take. Purism is essentially empty. As Lukács commented in his critique: 'The "pure essence", freed from all qualifications, is of necessity empty.'⁵ In the political context, however, emptiness is not synonymous with impotence: by refusing to offer alternatives, the empty gestures of purism reinforce the status quo.

Lukács has rightly condemned the notion of pure socialism as 'the total emptying of the concept of revolution'.[6]

The fact that purism should exercise a negative influence in politics is not especially remarkable. We have already noted the close correspondence in the avant-garde psychology between purism and nihilism. The negative qualities of both can be clearly seen in the life-cycle of purist and nihilist symbolism.

We have noted that purism and nihilism are favoured modes of expression for avant-garde agonism. A presupposition for agonism is a sense of doomed transience. As Hans Luckhardt wrote of Krayl's nihilistic drawings: 'I sometimes feel that the works of "Anfang" are rather strongly focused on Dadaism...Dadaism is primarily a manifestation of disgust and weariness with civilization and belongs to the many complexes of ideas which appear in a period of transition.'[7] These comments would have been equally applicable to his brother's drawings of pure, crystalline forms.

The aesthetics of purism and nihilism are closely akin to those of the joke: the purist or nihilist statement, like the joke, is self-destructive. It cannot be effectively repeated. In being once used, the purist symbol, the nihilist blast and the joke all destroy themselves. Thus both Krayl's scrawls and Wassili Luckhardt's crystal could work only once as potent critiques of contemporary architecture.

While transcience is a built-in pressuposition of avant-garde, and self-destruction is the natural consequence of purism and nihilism, a third factor which affects the life-span of an avant-garde group is less predictable: this factor might be called the absorption rate. We have already argued, in the context of the AFK and the Ausstellung für unbekannte Architekten, that avant-garde antagonism represents the radical negation of a general culture by a specific one. In this confrontation the principal advantage of the general culture is its ability to absorb the radical alternative, and to adopt the alternative as its own. Thus, while the agonistic and nihilistic aspects of avant-gardism are self-limiting, the longevity of the antagonistic aspect is dependent upon the assimilating ability of the general culture, of society at large. Paradoxically, the more appealing and successful the avant-garde group is in converting the wider society to its point of view, the shorter is its life as a genuinely avant-garde group.

Although it attracted considerable scorn and abuse, Taut's Activist movement was remarkably successful, especially within the confines of the architectural establishment. We have seen how the Arbeitsrat für Kunst attracted all the leading radicals in architecture into its ranks in December 1918. As well as the leading figures from the artists' group at the 1914 Werkbund conference – Taut, Gropius, Poelzig, Osthaus – the AFK also drew together the main figures in the primitivist, decentralist lobby – Tessenow, Mebes, Schmitthenner, Behrendt – and, via *Die Volkswohnung*, articulated the contemporary urge towards decentralization and resettlement on the land.

These immediate successes were followed by the take-over of the

Werkbund by the AFK radicals in September 1919, and by the 'Aufruf zum farbigen Bauen', which brought together, for the first time, the old and the new generations within the Werkbund. Having converted the architectural establishment to the cause of coloured architecture, Taut and Krayl went on, in 1921 and 1922, to convert the public at large with the programme of facade painting which Taut initiated as City Architect at Magdeburg.[8]

Success debilitates the radical voice of the avant-garde. Thus the demands of the AFK and of the Volkswohnung group ceased to be radical demands when they gained official acceptance. This happened in July 1919, when the government's 'Richtlinien für die Behandlung der Zuschußanträge' were announced, specifying subsidies for the building of small houses and rural enterprises. Similarly, the achievement of the leaders of the AFK in winning a block of seats on the committee of the Werkbund had a debilitating effect on the AFK itself. No longer could it be considered an antagonistic avant-gardistic faction if its leaders were also the leaders of an established institution like the Werkbund.[9] As a result, the views of the AFK on coloured architecture or the direct involvement of artists and architects in governmental decision-making ceased to be considered extreme or radical after they had been endorsed by the Werkbund.

Poggioli has noted that the 'tragic position' of avant-garde art is that it must fight on two fronts simultaneously: against the bourgeois culture of which is is an offspring and against popular culture. We have seen that the Activist avant-garde in architecture was defused and enfeebled by the traditional cultural establishment – in this case, the Werkbund. An even greater threat, however, is posed by popular culture. Stripped of its uniqueness and its power to shock or surprise, the voice of the avant-garde is rendered inaudible in the chanting of the masses who have taken up its call. This is exactly what happened to the architectural Activists.

In 1920 and 1921 'Expressionism' became the popular style of the moment, especially in Berlin. The symbols of purity and *Geist* which Taut had coined during the war years and which had found a last refuge in the Gläserne Kette letters now exploded onto the street. The popular culture reacted to the attacks of the avant-garde by adopting the symbols of the avant-garde as its own and putting them to new use.

In the June 1920 edition of *Das Kunstblatt*, Paul Westheim criticized the spread of this enfeebled and watered-down 'Expressionism': 'The Expressionist academy, Expressionist fashion, Expressionist fellow-travellers, that catchphrase Expressionism with which the smart art dealers and smooth art critics practise their propaganda; would that it was already at an end!'[10] The most extreme example of this adoption of the garb of the former radicals was offered by the Skala-Tanzkasino, a Berlin restaurant and night-club which was remodelled in 1920 by the architect Walter Würzbach and the sculptor Rudolf Belling. They skilfully assembled the motifs of Taut and his group – spirals, spiky crystals, curvaceous forms, and, of course, glass, to dress up the night-club in a grotesque pastiche of Activist architecture.

105 Walter Würzbach and
Rudolf Belling,
Skala-Tanzkasino, Berlin,
1920.

It would be wrong, however, to imply that the former Activists were above this process of popularization. César Klein, for example, collaborated with Walter Würzbach in 1920 on the interior decoration of a house in Berlin which provided the archetype for the fourth-rate formalistic 'modernism' which was to blossom in Germany in the mid-twenties. As in the Skala-Tanzkasino, the purist crystalline symbols of the Gläserne Kette were liberally adopted for furniture and wall-paintings. Even Wassili Luckhardt, the arch-purist of the Gläserne Kette, was prepared to compromise: in 1922–3 he erected, with the help of Belling, a giant crystal-shaped advertisement on the Avus, the motor racing track in Berlin.

The nadir of this tendency was reached in the early 1920s at the Lunapark, a fairground at Halensee, Berlin. The roller-coaster appeared in various guises, two of which – the *Albulabahn* and *Der gläserne See* – could have been designed by Wassili Luckhardt and Finsterlin respectively, during their Gläserne Kette phase. The *Albulabahn* was surrounded by a mass of crystalline spikes and zig-zags, while the *Gläserne See* swirled and heaved like one of Finsterlin's glass houses.

By the end of 1920, 'Expressionism' had established itself in every aspect of popular taste and design. Its popularity on the streets and in the dance-halls rose in inverse proportion to its decline in favour

106 César Klein and Walter Würzbach, bedroom, Potsdamer Straße 113, Berlin, 1920.

107 Wassili Luckhardt and Rudolf Belling, advertisement on the Avus, Berlin, 1922–3.

108 Lunapark, Halensee,
Berlin – *Albulabahn*, 1920.

amongst the literati. Hans von Wedderkop noted this in an editorial in
Der Querschnitt, entitled 'Shimmi greift ein'.

Wilhelm Hausenstein and Wilhelm Worringer recently killed off Expressionism –
earnestly, briefly and to the point. This treatment, however, was only concerned
with deliberately displayed Expressionism, the most powerful exponent of
modern feeling. While these vigorous pioneers have thus supposedly foundered,
Expressionism as a whole is now beginning to penetrate into the unconscious
soul of the people. Whoever has seen the 'Shimmi' in the Skala is convinced
of this.[11]

The reaction of the architects to the mass appropriation of their icons
of purity, primeval innocence and *Geist* was exactly that of the literati.

Taut was one of the first to abandon the compromised ideals of
Activism. We have seen that he began to question the worth of intuitive
architecture in the spring of 1920 and firmly resolved to abandon Utopia
by October of the same year. Behne followed. In his writings from 1920
and 1921 one can clearly see the growing scorn, with which an
avant-gardist views his most recently abandoned dogma. He was
especially vituperative in his attacks on popular 'Expressionism'. Writing
to Gropius about the Skala-Palast, he concluded: 'But in the last analysis
it is not architecture but masquerade.'[12] This distinction between
architecture and masquerade was not one which he would have drawn
a year earlier.

A few weeks after he had written to Gropius, Behne composed an

109 Lunapark, Halensee, Berlin – *Der gläserne See,* 1921.

article in which he specifically dissociated the currently popular 'Expressionist' style from the ideals of the former avant-garde and reconstituted these ideals to fit the new situation. In January 1921 he wrote:

The aim is a building and thereby an art which no longer knows anything of Expressionism. An architecture which aspires to be Expressionistic, in the sense of the currently popular Expressionism, would be atrocious. Examples of it are not entirely lacking in racketeering dance halls. We have nothing in common with this...The aim is objectively won form, which will rise above the smoke-screen of subjective emotion.[13]

Out of the ruins of the previous avant-garde Behne extracted a new direction and new goals. As the rule of the spiritual élite and the dictatorship of *Geist* had proved a chimera, so the architectural radicals transferred their chiliastic faith to a new form of mysticism – the mysticism of function, efficiency and Taylorism.

At the very moment that the gothicky and crystalline symbols of the Activist period were being assimilated into the mass culture, the members of Taut's architectural avant-garde were staking out fresh territory in the land of Functionalism. Simultaneously, they were denying any further connection with the visions of 1918: visions which had been sullied by association with the Skala-Palast. The 'pure' essence was defenceless and impotent against the attacks of the 'Shimmi'. The 'nullity of content',[14] the emptiness of purism and nihilism was exposed through contact with vulgar reality.

This process of confrontation and decline was an internal struggle, conducted exclusively within the confines of the local culture. The decline of architectural Activism came of its own volition, not as the result of the importation of L'Esprit Nouveau from France, De Stijl from Holland or Constructivism from Russia. In spite of the efforts of the AFK to discover what direction the new architecture outside Germany was taking, it is clear that little meaningful contact had been achieved by the end of 1920, at which time Activism was already dead. Behne was very conscious of the isolation of German architecture. In January 1921, in the article which condemned popular Expressionism and called for 'objectively won form', Behne confessed: 'In this we can learn a lot from Europe, and we hope to build the bridges soon.'[15] The Activists played an important part in setting up these bridges. Indeed, almost all significant contact which was made with foreign architects in the period 1919–20 was made by sometime members of the AFK.

Behne was a lively advocate of pan-Europeanism in the arts, and published several articles on this theme in 1919.[16] On a more direct level, we have seen that Taut, on behalf of the AFK, sought to establish contact with the radical Russian groups in the early months of 1919. In October 1920 he mentioned in a letter to the Gläserne Kette that he might visit Russia in the winter of 1920/1: nothing came of this plan, however. At the same time as Taut was first trying to establish a link with the Russians, he was also corresponding with Theo Wijdeveld, the influential Dutch architect and editor of the magazine *Wendingen*. The AFK sent Wijdeveld a copy of Taut's 'Architektur-Programm' and received an enthusiastic response. Wijdeveld wrote: 'It was with great interest that I became acquainted with Bruno Taut's 'Architektur-Programm'...In Holland, too, the time has become ripe to put forward a similar programme, and I would be very obliged to you if you could send me everything which has already appeared on the subject, or will appear.'[17] This early contact with the Dutch led, in October 1920, to an extended visit to Holland by Behne. During this visit he had discussions with Wijdeveld, Berlage, Kromhout and van Doesburg, and he subsequently wrote a long article about the new developments in Holland.[18]

The AFK had also been active in seeking to re-establish contact with the French and achieved some success through René Schickele and Barbusse. Taut also had links with the group of former Activists who published the 'Aufruf an die revolutionäre französische geistige Jugend' in August 1919. This group, like the Clarté group to which it appealed, was in favour of the proletarian movement but sought to be independent of any control or interference from Moscow. Among the signatories to the 'Aufruf' were Fritz von Unruh, Georg Kaiser, Rubiner, Toller, Leonhard, Max Pechstein, Schickelé and Alfred Wolfenstein. Although Taut did not sign the original 'Aufruf', it is clear from subsequent letters to Osthaus that he was involved with this campaign and attended meetings of the group, which appears to have been led by Leonhard – a colleague of Taut's in the BPK.[20]

The French connection was also pursued in the context of architecture. The former Activists responded enthusiastically to the appearance of *L'Esprit Nouveau*. In a letter to Behne, Gropius wrote of the need for a German edition and went on to recommend to Behne the work of the magazine's editors, Ozenfant and Jeanneret.

I have written to the editors with the suggestion that they should publish a German edition. I am convinced that they would find plenty of buyers for it in Germany. We have nothing to compare with it. May I draw your attention to two new works by Ozenfant and Jeanneret, who publish extraordinarily interesting pictures in *Esprit Nouveau*.[21]

Taut was equally enthusiastic about the new developments outside Germany. In the second series of *Frühlicht*, published in Magdeburg in 1921 and 1922, Taut introduced his readers to the work of Gaudi, Oud, Tatlin, Rodchenko and Sant'Elia.

The fact that the Activist architects themselves made the first contacts with the evolving Functionalist movement in Europe confirms Poggioli's hypothesis that: 'The crisis of the avant-garde is not, so to speak, a crisis of rule, but only of succession: the king is dead, long live the king!'[22] The body of Activism, with its crystalline trappings, gothicky contours and cosmic aspirations, expired during 1920. The spirit and the ideology of Activism survived, however, and was incorporated into the new avant-garde of Functionalism.

Conclusion

To maintain the Functionalist succession, which ran from the Crystal Palace to the International Movement, the early historians of the modern movement tried to isolate the Expressionist phase and extract it from the clear path of progress. Not only did they put the 'unhealthy' work of Taut and his contemporaries into isolation, they also insisted that the fantasy architecture of 1916–20 had nothing whatever to do with what came before or afterwards. Any connection with pre-war architecture was conveniently severed by the war itself, and the only connection allowed with Functionalism was the total defeat which the virus of Expressionism suffered at the cleansing hands of Functionalism.

This view was reinforced by the former Activists themselves, who, as we have seen, went to great pains to dissociate themselves from the dogmas of the expired movement. This process was well under way by the end of 1920. It gathered momentum throughout the decade. In *Bauen*, which was published in 1927, Taut commented wryly: 'To speak of spiritualization is also impossible today. One can no longer decently and without irony utter such words as spiritualization, ennoblement, and immersion in *Geist*.'[1] Two years later, he wrote even more critically of the Activist phase. In line with Giedion's subsequent analysis, Taut dismissed the dreams of 1918 as symptoms of an illness – of *Geistesstörung*.[2] Yet despite such refutations, the Activist phase was intimately linked to its forerunners and successors. It was not an isolated or inexplicable phenomenon, nor was it unimportant for the subsequent development of modern architecture in Germany.

The most striking similarity between architectural Activism and the progressive architecture of the pre-war period was political. The ideology of Activism, like that of the reform movement, wavered between revisionist socialism and anarcho-socialism. Both were anti-Marxist, anti-popularist and deterministic in that in both instances, the architect was assigned the task of reforming society through the application of a specific canon of taste and behaviour.

The success of the architect in this task would, it was hoped, divert the restless urban proletariat away from political revolution towards a happier, decentralized existence on the land. Ultimate control over this dispersed population would still be exercised by the traditional controllers, the educated bourgeoisie.

The desire to avert political revolution through architectural controls

223

or diversions recurred throughout the formative years of the modern movement. A sequence can be traced from Ebenezer Howard's first tract, subtitled 'A Peaceful Path to Real Reform', via the markedly revisionist Deutsche Gartenstadtgesellschaft to Le Corbusier's *Vers une Architecture*, with its celebrated conclusion: 'Architecture ou révolution. On peut éviter la révolution'.

The Activist interlude made an important contribution to this tradition. It was based on the assumption that the *geistig* architect could reform and remodel society and could produce harmony and happiness, thus obviating the need for political revolution. The belief in an all-seeing and all-healing architecture was fundamental to the development of the modern movement. The Charter of Athens, composed in 1933 by the leading figures in the modern movement, made this claim quite clearly with its assertion: 'L'architecture est à la clef de tout.'[3] During the Activist phase architecture was elevated to a lofty and quasi-religious status by the architects themselves. As Functionalism developed, they adhered to this definition, but with different supporting arguments. For both the Activist and the Functionalist architect, however, the goal was the same – the reachable man-made paradise, which would be created by the architect or by the *geistig* leader rather than by political revolution.

If reformist socialism provided the political base for architectural modernism in Germany, then it is clear that no direct connections should be drawn between the political revolution in 1918 and the architectural revolution which occurred over the following five years.[4] Any confluence between artistic and political radicalism is brief and fortuitous. As Poggioli has noted: 'the identification of artistic revolution with the social revolution is…no more than purely rhetorical, an empty commonplace'.[5] For three or four days in November 1918 the paths of the Activists and the political revolution crossed. No lasting relationship was established, however. As the subsequent history of the AFK made clear, artistic radicalism is by no means incompatible with a move to the political centre.

Although the political demands of Taut's group were little more than empty gestures, it is indisputable that the Activist group worked as a genuinely radical avant-garde within the context of architecture and the plastic arts. Massimo Bontempelli has defined the function of the avant-garde as follows: 'In sum, the avant-garde had the function of creating the primitive, or, better, primordial conditions out of which is then born the creater found at the beginning of a new series.'[6] Adopting this definition, it could be suggested that the period of architectural Activism was a period of polemic and preparation for the coming architectural revolution – it was not the revolution itself. Taut himself suggested this in his 'Architektur-Programm', when he wrote:

The immediate vehicle of the *geistig* forces and moulder of the sensibilities of the general public, which today are slumbering and tomorrow will awake, is architecture. Only a completed *geistig* revolution will create this architecture. But this revolution, this architecture will not come of their own accord. Both must be *willed* – the architects of today must prepare the way for the new architecture.[7]

Gropius reiterated the point in his contribution to the manifesto of the Ausstellung für unbekannte Architekten, saying: 'There *are* no architects today, we are all simply preparing the way for someone who will once again deserve the name of architect.'[8] The obvious fact that many of the leading Activists and fantasists became outstanding exponents of Functionalism design would suggest that the Activist interregnum did act as a fruitful period of preparation for the Functionalist revolution.

Traces of what was to come can be detected during the Activist phase. Activism was not against technology: Taut's dream of building in the Alps presupposed a highly developed technology. The same is true of Hablik's scheme to fuse houses out of sand, with the help of airships, aeroplanes, gas and electricity. Such wild schemes may have prepared the way, in part, for the infatuation with technology which was to follow. Lewis Mumford has noted the importance of fantasy in the evolution of technology: 'to have dreamed so riotously was to make the technics that followed less incredible and hence less impossible'.[9] On a more sober level, Taut advocated the Taylor System as early as February 1919 in his article 'Die Erde eine gute Wohnung' and his call was taken up by Hans Luckhardt in a letter written to the Gläserne Kette in May 1920. In this letter, Luckhardt suggested, prophetically, that the group should abandon its mystical beliefs and should concentrate on the *Geist* of the future, automation.[10]

Yet despite these pointers and threads which linked Activism to Functionalism, the contrasts between the two tendencies are, at first glance, far more striking than the similarities. In formal terms there is little in common between Taut's drawings of 1916–19 and his housing schemes in the mid-twenties. It is difficult to link the mountain temples and phallic observatories with the austere housing which followed a mere half-decade later. Similarly stark contrasts between the drawings of the Activist phase and the buildings of the mid-twenties can be found in the work of Taut's colleagues in the Arbeitsrat für Kunst. What, then, were the connections: how did the succession from Activism to Functionalism manifest itself?

As we have already noted, the ultimate aim of both movements was the same: a man-made paradise. This paradise would be conceived by the architect and would, by implication, remain under the ultimate control of the architect. Where the Functionalist differed from the Activist, however, was in the source of his authority. The Activist architect based his authority on his status as *geistig* leader, who was uniquely qualified to reconcile and bring into harmony the 'objective' truths of *Geist* with the demands of the *Volkswille*. Under the new régime of Functionalism the architect played exactly the same role, but with a slightly modified script. The 'objective' truths of *Geist* were replaced by the 'objective' laws of function and technology. The *Volkswille* was similarly transformed into the *Zeitwille* – the will of the age.

In 1916 Taut cited the *Volkswille* as the source of the architect's authority: 'With total abandon the architect immerses himself in the soul of the *Volk* and discovers both himself and his noble calling by striving to give material expression to that which slumbers in every soul.'[11] Under the role of Functionalism the *Volkswille* was given a new, temporal quality. Thus Mies van der Rohe wrote in 1924: 'Architecture is always the *Zeitwille* given spatial form, nothing else.'[12] One year later, Gropius wrote of the need to give 'objective' expression to the *Zeitwille*: 'The will which characterizes our age strives for a unified vision of the world. It presupposes a yearning to free *geistig* values from their individual limitations and to raise them to the status of *objective truths*.'[13] Who was best qualified to give 'objective' expression to the *Zeitwille*? The answer, just as in the Activist model, was the architect.

The Activist architect claimed for himself the ability to comprehend and unite painting, sculpture, architecture and perhaps music, and to use the resulting *Kultusbau* for the benefit of the community. Although these claims were far-reaching to the point of immodesty, the subsequent claims of the Functionalists were even wider-reaching. The Functionalist architect placed himself at the centre of a complex made up not merely of the plastic arts, but also of economics, engineering, sociology, psychology and the emerging science of urbanism. The artist/intellectual was replaced by the artist/technocrat. Thus Taut claimed in 1927: 'After great catastrophes it is always the builders who must go to the front. Whoever is otherwise active in economic, industrial and even political life belongs in his precepts and principal concerns to the staff of these builders.'[14] Later in the same book, Taut reiterated this picture of the architect as all-comprehending polymath, as the point of unification between the arts and the natural sciences: 'There is no division here between the artist on one side and the technician and constructor or calculator on the other side; instead, one is here inseparably bound up with the other.'[15] Architecture was the nexus which pulled together the various skills and disciplines necessary for the construction of the new society. Describing the new architecture, Ludwig Hilberseimer put this argument very clearly: 'Manufacturing techniques, business management, economic and social factors exercise a considerable influence. But standing dominant above all is the creative will of the architect.'[16] At the centre of these various disciplines the architect worked as a controlling and unifying spirit. Just as the Activist architects had hoped to effect social unification through *Geist*, now the Functionalists were appealing to the unifying power of the new 'objective', absolute technology.

In the hands of the architects, technology proved to be a far more potent force than *Geist* had been. Although the Activists had claimed that *Geist* was an immanent force in man, it remained a complicated and ill-defined abstraction, a concept which was inaccessible to all but the favoured few. Far from uniting humanity, the Activist *Geist* divided it into those who understood the notion of *Geist* and those who did not. In contrast, technology and the fruits of technology were visible, accessible and tangible.

A ready-made vocabulary of form was one aspect of this visibility, and one which made technology especially attractive as a guiding spirit for architecture. Activism had been bedevilled by the lack of a formal language. The Activist dogma, as formulated by Taut, was that form would be the automatic outcome of faith in *Geist* – form follows faith. This proved to be a chimera, as the diversity of the Gläserne Kette drawings made clear. The problem was resolved by the switch to Functionalism. Here, without doubt, form did follow function. The logic of function demanded Euclidean forms. The cult of purism, which in Activism had led to sterile crystal-worship, achieved a new significance. The new purism of function generated a vocabulary of forms and justified them on grounds of reproducibility and economics.

The search, however, was not merely for form, but for process. According to the tenets of Activism, the static *Volkswille* would find expression, via the architect, in a static monument – the *Kultusbau*. In contrast, and in keeping with the temporal nature of the *Zeitwille* which inspired it, Functionalist architecture was concerned with process, with the secular development from the single room to the entire city. As Hilberseimer described it: 'A city building, being a cell, and the city organism, being part of a whole, must both display essential architectonic characteristics that are conditioned by the nature of the entity "city".'[17] In this dynamic conception of architecture the anology with ships, planes and motor-cars was especially attractive. The important development from form to process clearly distinguished Functionalist from Activist architecture. This move from static, collective symbolism to dynamic process was alluded to by Mies van der Rohe in his observation: 'All the aspirations of our age are directed towards the profane. The efforts of the mystics will remain mere episodes.'[18]

The shift from *Geist* to technology, from static form to dynamic process carried with it important implications in the realm of social engineering. The ambition of the Activists was not merely to build *Kultusbauten*, but also thereby to improve society by creating better social and moral conditions. This was seen to be the unique facility of the architect. As Taut wrote during the Activist phase: 'To be an architect literally means to be a leader. Today the architect must be leader in everything, the one who leads forward into a more beautiful, lucid future.'[19] This crudely deterministic theory was adopted in its entirely by the ideologues of Functionalism. Thus Taut himself wrote in 1929: 'The architect will become an ethical and social creator.' He explained how housing design would improve the lives of the inhabitants, who: 'through the design of the house will be led to a better attitude in their social intercourse and their mutual relationships'. Through its creations, said Taut: 'Architecture will thus become the creator of new social forms.'[20] Clearly, the Activist and Functionalist ideologies were related in that both sought to use architecture as a vehicle for moral and social reform.

The means differed, however. As we have seen, the reforming zeal of Activism was focused into static images of *Geist* – the *Kultusbau* or *Volkshaus*. The élitist urge to guide society from above was encapsulated in these symbols of collective *Geist*. The *Kultusbau* was conceived as a beacon, which would generate around itself a new and morally superior society. It would achieve this power simply through its architectural and physical beauty. Even if a *Kultusbau* had been built, it seems highly improbable that the expectations of Taut and his followers would have been fulfilled. Aesthetic contemplation is not a potent stimulus to social or political action. The Activist dreams to manipulate and improve society by appeals to *Geist* were doomed to failure, for *Geist* – or its physical realization, the *Kultusbau* – had no power to persuade or to command or to compel.

In contrast, technology, supported by the logic of function, possesses an immanent tendency towards control and manipulation. The demands of function are not open to debate: they are perceived as incontestable and irrefutable. The logic of function is an absolute imperative. It is absolute not only in the specific instance, but also in the general context. As Hilberseimer insisted, the true application of Functionalism demanded that the simplest cell, the room, should be reformed along Functionalist lines. But a functionally perfect room is incompatible with a non-functional house. So the house must be conceived anew. The Functionalist house, it follows, can only function correctly in the Functionalist street, and the Functionalist street in the Functionalist city. The logic of function therefore demands that the city and thereby society be remodelled from the smallest cell outwards.

This Functionalist chain parallels the Activist chain, which ran from the single glass temple to the cosmos. The difference between the two paradigms, however, is that the Activist chain was based on the repetition of static symbols: one glass temple followed by two, then five, then fifty. The Functionalist chain, as one would expect, was based on a dynamic and irreversible process. By reforming one room according to Functionalist principles, one was committed to reforming the entire city.

In the ideology of Functionalism, the architects found the manipulative power which they had failed to achieve through the static, Activist *Geist*. Whereas the Activist *Geist* had utterly failed to convert or improve society, the logic of function offered limitless opportunities for social manipulation. The Activist ideology was, as we have seen, élitist and anti-democratic. It proposed a self-chosen élite, which would guide and control the lives of the masses. This dream became reality when the political ideology of Activism was married to the logic of Functionalism. The political legacy of Activism was an important component in the evolution of the modern movement in Germany. Taut noted this himself in a letter which he wrote to Wenzel Hablik from Magdeburg in 1922: 'As you know, the correspondence between the friends has long since died out. The *geistig* band remains, however...From my collaborators here I have learnt that there are more of us than we think.'[21]

Appendix 1

◇◆

Programme of the Politischer Rat geistiger Arbeiter, Berlin, November 1918. In *Das Ziel III* (Leipzig, 1919), pp. 219–23.

The guiding star for all future politics must be the inviolability of life. It is our duty to sanctify the Creation, to protect creativity, to banish slavery in every form from the face of the earth.

The Politischer Rat geistiger Arbeiter, therefore, will fight above all against the subjugation of the people by military service, and against all oppression of the workers by the capitalist system. The Politischer Rat geistiger Arbeiter stands for freedom and social justice. In its determination to achieve the most rapid and radical enforcement of the dictates of human reason, the Politischer Rat geistiger Arbeiter condemns the procrastinators, the half-hearted and the cautious, and welcomes all revolutionary methods which do not lead to anarchy; that is to the destruction of cultural values and to the brutal tyranny of the few. In this conviction, the Politischer Rat geistiger Arbeiter demands:

I

As guarantees for the absolute prevention of war:
– A league of nations and a parliament of nations, invested with compulsory powers of arbitration, and, in accordance with the demand for pacifism, an international agreement on the abolition of military service in all lands, and a ban on military installations. International action against those who disturb the peace to be taken only by means of economic measures.
– A systematic transformation of attitudes, to be achieved in particular through a fundamental change in the teaching of history. This must be controlled by independent people's committees.

II

– Promotion of the process of selection through the fair distribution of wealth.
– Blue collar and white collar workers to be paid the full proceeds of their labours, not diminished by the 'surplus value' which the capitalist entrepreneur has hitherto pocketed.
– Progressive shortening of working hours according to the current development of production techniques: a large-scale housing programme; unemployment insurance. The abolition of all indirect taxation, rapidly progressive income tax and death duties. Socialization of the land; confiscation of assets above a certain point; the conversion of capitalist concerns into workers' co-operatives.
– Protection of the interests of the consumer.

III

– Sexual freedom within the limits of the obligation to respect the wishes of those who are reluctant and to protect the inexperience of youth. Limitation of the

229

criminal law to the protection of personal rights; complete acknowledgement of the rights of all men and women over their own bodies. The severe punishment of deliberate or negligent transmission of venereal diseases. Full legal and social rights not only for illegitimate children, but also for unmarried mothers.

IV

– Abolition of the death penalty; the right of the convicted person to voluntary death. Killing on the express and earnest request of the victim to be exempt from prosecution.
– Humanization of imprisonment; without exception compulsory activity instead of forced labour.

V

– Radical reform of public education.
– Comprehensive schools: non-mechanical selection of the most talented children from all classes for the:
– 'Culture School': no charge for attending. Their task, to be not so much schools for learning as schools for thinking, more to indicate the way into the future than for the study of history, less concerned with vocational training than with training for a life of ideas. Removal of the dominating relationship of teacher to pupil. Extensive participation of students in the administration of the school. Supervision of tuition by panels of outstanding university teachers. Study of the ancient languages optional. Abolition of the *Abitur* examination. Graduation from the 'Culture School' entitles the student to attend:
– the University. The University should once again become a stronghold of *Geist* through separation from the colleges of applied science, through the incorporation of theology in the faculty of philosophy, through open lectureships, election of professors by panels of students who themselves are chosen according to a secret, proportional ballot, through the elimination of enforced drinking and duelling, through unrestricted freedom for all members of the university community to engage in political discussion and action, and by dismissing the grey-beards from the faculty.
– In addition to the University there would be as many 'People's Colleges' as possible, open to everyone.
– The press should be purged of the filth of corruption, of incitement to nationalism and of feuilletonistic brainwashing. Press councils, made up of experienced journalists of a *geistig* inclination, to pass judgement on any improper journalistic activity.
– Freedom of the press, freedom of union and assembly. Freedom from government interference for schools, academic research, philosophic doctrine and art.

VI

– Separation of Church and state, elimination of confessional instruction in all schools. In its place, moral instruction, philosophical propaedeutics.

VII

– The safeguarding and consolidation of the greater German social republic. Dissolution of special federal bodies; extensive self administration for German ethnic groups, as well as for the co-operative communities and their controlling bodies.

– The *Reichstag*: to be elected on a non-constituent basis. Equal direct and secret voting rights for all nationals of both sexes who are over twenty years old. Women eligible for election. Three year legislative period.

– In addition to the *Reichstag*, to remove the danger of an encroachment by one-sided economic arguments on cultural policies, and to offset the damage caused by the torpor of party bureaucracy:

– The Council of *Geistige* [*Der Rat der Geistigen*]. It will be created neither by nomination nor by election, but by intrinsic right, which derives from the duty of *Geist* to help. It will renew itself according to its own law.

– The Government: in the hands of a committee of delegates of the *Reichstag* and the Council of *Geistige*; before the Council assembles, in the hands of the former.

– The President of the German Republic: to be elected for a limited period of office by the *Reichstag*, following the non-binding advice of the Council; by the *Reichstag* alone until the Council is convened.

The Politischer Rat geistiger Arbeiter believes that a policy of freedom, justice and reason is to be most rapidly realized and most efficiently secured under this constitution, which perfects the democratic idea and ensures leadership by the most able.

The Politischer Rat geistiger Arbeiter seeks to bring together all people who agree with its objectives. Comrades, support us! Help us push through the radical programme in cultural politics within the context of the social republic.

The following, among others, have endorsed the spirit of the above programme: Lou Andreas-Salomé (Hannover), Lucian Bernhard, Bund der geistig Tätigen, Vienna (Chairman: Dr Franz Kobler), Dr Richard Nicolaus Graf Coudenhove (Pöstlingberg bei Linz a.D.), Kasimir Edschmid (Darmstadt), W. E. Axel von Fielitz, Dr Hans W. Fischer (Hamburg), Otto Flake (Zürich), Dr Alfred H. Fried (Berne), Dr Manfred Georg, Dr Alfons Goldschmidt, Prof. Dr Albert Görland (Hamburg), Willi Handl, Wilhelm Herzog, Werner Richard Heymann, Dr Kurt Hiller, S.-R. Dr Magnus Hirschfeld, Arthur Holitscher, Willy Jaeckel, Dr Rudolf Kayser, Annette Kolb (Berne), Berta Lask, Moritz Lederer (Mannheim), Rudolf Leonhard, Dr Leo Matthias, Dr Walter Meckauer (Breslau), Ludwig Meidner, Moritz Melzer, Carlo Mierendorff (Darmstadt), Alexander Moissi, Robert Müller (Vienna), Max Freiherr von Münchhausen (Burg i. Spreewald), Dr Robert Musil (Vienna), Hans Natonek (Leipzig), Heinrich Nienkamp, Dr Kurt Peschke, Dr Kurt Pinthus, Politischer Rat geistiger Arbeiter, Munich (Chairman: Heinrich Mann), Hermann Rahtjen (Bremen), Dr Hans Reichenbach, Walter Rilla (Breslau), René Schickele (Berne), Hermann Schüller, Egmont Seyerlen, Dr Hugo Sinzheimer (Frankfurt a.M.), Dr Martin Sommerfeld (Munich), Franz H. Staerk (Sigmaringen), Dr Friedrich Sternthal (Dresden), Dr Helene Stöcker, Bruno Taut, Dr Frank Thieß, Fritz von Unruh, Prof. Dr J. M. Verweyen (Bonn), Gustav von Wangenheim, Carl M. Weber (Coblenz), Prof. Dr Eduard Wechssler (Marburg), Dr Armin T. Wagner, J.-R. Dr Johannes Werthauer, Willi Wolfradt, Kurt Wolff (Leipzig), Dr Gustav Wyneken, Paul Zech.

Appendix 2

◇◇

Arbeitsrat für Kunst – Programme, December 1918, in
Mitteilungen des deutschen Werkbundes, 1918, no. 4,
pp. 14–15.

In the conviction that the political upheaval must be used to free art from the guardianship under which it has existed for decades, a group of like-thinking artists and art-lovers has formed itself in Berlin. The aim of the group is to bring together all the dispersed and thus fragmented energies which wish to transcend one-sided professional interests, in order to participate vigorously in the reconstruction of our entire artistic life. In the closest contact with the governmental authorities and with groups of a similar tendency, such as the Kunstkammer in Munich, Dresden, etc., the Arbeitsrat für Kunst hopes to realize its immediate objectives in the not too distant future. These objectives are indicated in the following summary of the group's programme:

Above all stands the leading principle: Art and *Volk* must form a unity. Art should no longer be the delight of the few, but the good fortune and the life of the masses. The aim is the fusion of the arts under the wing of a great architecture. From now on, the artist alone, as moulder of the sensibilities of the *Volk*, will be responsible for the visible fabric of the new state. He must determine the form-giving process, from the statue right down to the coin and the postage stamp.

In the first instance, six demands are made on this basis:

1. Recognition of the public nature of all building activity, the national removal of all privileges enjoyed by civil servants. The joint administration of complete city-sections, city-blocks and estates, without encroaching upon the freedom of the individual unit. New tasks: *Volkshäuser*, as places where all the arts are offered to the people. Permanent experimental sites, for assessing and improving architectural effects.

2. The dissolution of the Royal Academy of Arts, the Royal Academy of Building and the Royal Prussian Commission for Art in their present form. The replacement of these bodies...by groups which are derived from within the ranks of working artists, free from governmental influence. The conversion of exclusive art exhibitions into free exhibitions.

3. The freeing of the entire education for architecture, sculpture, painting and the crafts from the guardianship of the state. Transformation of art and craft education from the base up. The provision of government funds for this and for apprentice training in workshops.

4. The revitalization of the museums as educational institutions for the people. The organization of constantly changing exhibitions, made accessible to the entire population with the help of lectures and guided tours. Dissemination of academic material in purpose-built depositories. The separate establishment of study collections for craftsmen, ordered according to techniques. Fair distribution of government funds for the acquisition of old and new works.

5. The removal of all artistically worthless monuments and the demolition of all buildings whose artistic value is disproportionate to the value of their

raw materials, which might be used elsewhere. The prevention of hastily planned war memorials, and the immediate cessation of work on the war museums planned for Berlin and elsewhere in Germany.

6. The creation of a state agency for the cultivation of the arts within the framework of future legislation.

This summons carries the signatures of the following: Otto Bartning, Rudolf Bauer, W. C. Behrendt, Joseph Bloch, Theo v. Brockhusen, A. E. Brinckmann, Heinz Braune, Ewald Dülberg, Martin Elsässer, August Grisebach, Walter Gropius, Wilhelm Hausenstein, Franz Heckendorf, Carl Georg Heise, Fritz Hellwag, Ernst Herzfeld, Willy Jaeckel, Walter Kaesbach, César Klein, Käthe Kollwitz, Leo v. König, Bruno Krauskopf, Mechtilde Lichnowsky, Paul Mebes, Hans Meid, Herbert Mueller, Julius Meier-Graefe, Heinrich Nauen, Wilhelm Niemeyer, Rudolf Oldenbourg, Karl Ernst Osthaus, Friedrich Paulsen, Max Pechstein, Friedrich Perzynski, Hans Poelzig, E. Pottner, Heinrich Richter, Chr. Rohlfs, John Schikowski, E. E. Schlieper, Paul Schmitthenner, Hermann Schmitz, Rich. L. F. Schulz, Erik-Ernst Schwabach, Prussian Finance Minister Hugo Simon, Willy Steger, Georg Swarzenski, Georg Tappert, Bruno Taut, Max Taut, Heinrich Tessenow, Arnold Topp, Wilhelm R. Valentiner, Hermann Voss, Ludwig Wolde, Wilhelm Worringer. Statements of support should be sent to the Arbeitsrat für Kunst, Berlin NW 40, In den Zelten 19.

Appendix 3

◇◇◇

Bruno Taut, 'Architecktur-Programm', December 1918, in *Mitteilungen des deutschen Werkbundes*, 1918, no. 4, pp. 16–19.

Art! – that is a great thing, when it exists. Today this art does not exist. The fragmented tendencies can only find their way back to a single unity under the wings of a new architecture, with each individual discipline playing its part in the building process. Then there will be no division between the applied arts and sculpture or painting, everything will be one: architecture.

The immediate vehicle of the *geistig* forces and moulder of the sensibilities of the general public, which today are slumbering and tomorrow will awake, is architecture. Only a completed *geistig* revolution will create this architecture. But this revolution, this architecture, will not come of their own accord. Both must be *willed* – the architects of today must prepare the way for the new architecture. To be feasible, their work for the future must be publicly supported. Therefore:

I Support and concentration of the imaginative forces among architects.

(a) Support for so-called 'utopias', for architectural ideas which, transcending the formal, strive to concentrate the energies of the *Volk* in buildings as symbols of a better future, thereby demonstrating the cosmic character of architecture. The provision of public funds in the form of grants to radically inclined architects to enable them to carry out such projects. Financial assistance for publishing activities, for the construction of models, and:
(b) for a well-situated experimental site (in Berlin: the Tempelhofer Feld), on which architects can erect large-scale models of their ideas. Here, too, new architectural effects, such as glass as a building material, should be tried out, perfected and exhibited to the masses as full-scale temporary constructions or as individual building elements. The layman, the woman, and the child will lead the architect further than the inhibited specialist. Costs could be balanced by melting down public monuments, demolishing triumphal avenues etc., as well as by participation of industries connected with the experimental buildings.
(c) The decision on the distribution of financial means to rest with a council made up half of creative architects, half of radically minded laymen. If no agreement can be reached, the final decision to be taken by a layman chosen from the council.

II *Volkshäuser*

(a) Work should begin on great *Volkshäuser*, not in the towns but on the open land, joined to housing developments. Groups of buildings for theatre and music, with lodging houses and the like. Prospect of a long period of construction, therefore a beginning should be made according to a grand-scale plan but with limited means.
(b) Architects to be chosen not be competition, but in accordance with I(c).

234

(c) If building comes to a halt, it should be given new incentives during the pauses by means of designs for extensions in accordance with I(a)–(c).

The pride of the social republic should find an expression in these *Volkshäuser*. They should be the first attempt at the unification of the powers of the *Volk* and the artists. They cannot stand in the city, for the city itself is rotten and will at some time disappear, just like the old institutions of power. The future lies on the newly accessible tracts of land, which can support themselves.

III Housing developments

(a) Uniform direction in the sense that one architect will establish overall principles according to which he will examine all projects and buildings, without thereby impeding personal freedom. This architect to have the right of veto.
(b) As II(b).
(c) The fundamental subordination of form and appearance to agricultural and practical considerations; no shrinking away from the simplest solutions – nor from colour.

IV Other buildings

(a) For street development and, according to circumstances, for whole city districts, the same applies as for III(a) and (b).
(b) No distinction between public and private buildings. As long as there are freelance architects there will be only freelance architects. Until there are state potters there need not be state architects. Public and private buildings can be built by anyone; commissions in line with I(c) or through competitions which are not anonymous, but in which participants are invited by a council in accordance with I(c) and awarded prizes; no unpaid designs. Unknown architects will apply to the council for an invitation. Anonymity is made worthless by the recognizable artistic handwriting of successful architects.
(c) Building officials, such as municipal building advisers and the like, to be concerned only with local building control, demolition and financial supervision, with purely technical functions. The intermediate areas, like town planning, to be controlled by an advisory council of architects.
(d) *No* titles and dignities for architects (doctor, professor, councillor, excellency, etc.).
(e) In everything, preference to be given to the creative; no control over the architect once he has been commissioned.
(f) In the event of public opposition, decision by a council in accordance with II(c), which can be established by an architects' corporation.
(g) Authority in this and other matters, and state recognition, to be given only to such architects' corporations in which the principle of mutual aid is thoroughly applied. They should assert their influence on the *Baupolizei* [the police who enforce the building regulations]. Only mutual aid can make a community fertile and active. It is much more important than the number of votes, which means nothing without social cohesion. It excludes inartistic and hence unfair competition.

V Architectural education

(a) Corporations in accordance with IV(g) to have the power to decide on the building, constitution and supervision of technical schools; teachers to be chosen in collaboration with the students. Practical work on the building site.
(b) In the technical schools no artistic but only technical tuition. Unity in technical schools.

(c) Artistic education in the offices of practising architects, according to the choice of the students and the architects themselves.

(d) General education according to inclination and previous knowledge in people's colleges and universities.

VI Architecture and the other arts

(a) Exhibitions to be designed by architects in cheerful forms; lightweight buildings on public squares and busy sites to appeal to the popular taste, almost like a fair.

(b) The most extensive inclusion of painters and sculptors on all building work in order to direct them away from salon art; the stimulation of mutual interest between architect and 'artist'. In accordance with this principle:

(c) The introduction of students of architecture to the creative, 'new art'. Only the architect whose view takes in the whole domain of art, and who understands the radical endeavours of painting and sculpture is of any significance. He alone will help bring about the unity of the whole.

The increased importance of the architect in public life through the holding of important posts and offices will result automatically from the implementation of this programme.

Note: Taut made minor alterations to his original text for the second edition of the 'Architektur-Programm', which was published as a pamphlet by the AFK at Christmas 1918.

Notes

Introduction

1 Adolf Behne, 'Expressionistische Architektur', *Der Sturm*, V, no. 19/20 (January 1915), p. 135.
2 Wolfgang Pehnt, *Die Architektur des Expressionismus* (Stuttgart, 1973), pp. 194–5.
3 Marcel Franciscono, *Walter Gropius and the Creation of the Bauhaus in Weimar* (Urbana, 1971), p. 240.
4 *Ibid.*, p. 5.
5 Franco Borsi & Giovanni Klaus König, *Architettura dell'Espressionismo* (Genoa, 1967), p. 58. 'But in spite of the cultural activities of the Arbeitsrat für Kunst and the experiments conducted in the secret letters of the Gläserne Kette, there were still urgent professional needs. In response to these needs, the Ring was established on the initiative of Bruno Taut. It was set up spontaneously and without formality by a group of architects who belonged to the Arbeitsrat für Kunst.'
6 *Ibid.* 'L'Esprit Nouveau had won.'
7 Norbert Huse, '*Neues Bauen*' *1918 bis 1933* (Munich, 1975), p. 49.
8 *Ibid.*
9 Plus one minor scheme, the partially completed Werksiedlung der Oheim-Grube, Katowice, 1915.

1. Reformism and Expressionism

1 Renato Poggioli, *The Theory of the Avant-Garde* (Cambridge, Mass., 1968), p. 27.
2 It would seem that Taut joined the Choriner Kreis in 1903, after he had started working in the Office of Bruno Möhring in Berlin. Taut's movements before 1918 are still far from clear. The new edition of Kurt Junghanns's monograph promises to offer some clarification on Taut's early life and work.
3 For a detailed history of the Deutsche Gartenstadtgesellschaft see: Kristiana Hartmann, *Deutsche Gartenstadtbewegung* (Munich, 1976).
4 Bruno Wille, *Aus Traum und Tag* (Berlin, 1920), quoted: Janos Frecot, Johann Friedrich Geist, Diethart Kerbs, *Fidus 1868–1948* (Munich, 1972), p. 86.
5 Heinrich Hart, quoted: Albert Soergel, *Dichtung und Dichter der Zeit* (Leipzig, 1911), p. 205.
6 Soergel, *Dichtung und Dichter der Zeit* p. 600.
7 Deutsche Gartenstadtgesellschaft, *Programme*, quoted: Hans Kampffmeyer, *Die Gartenstadtbewegung* (Leipzig, 1909), p. 47.
8 See: *Gartenstadt*, VII, no. 9 (September 1913), p. 165.

9 F. Staudinger, 'Gartenstadt und Genossenschaft', *Gartenstadt*, III, no. 2 (February 1909), p. 20.

10 Kampffmeyer, *Gartenstadtbewegung*, p. 103.

11 Kurt Pinthus, *Menschheitsdämmerung* (Berlin, 1920), new edition (Hamburg, 1959), p. 26.

12 The list of exhibitors at the Erste Deutsche Herbstsalon, held at the Sturm gallery in 1913, included Henri Rousseau – in memoriam, Archipenko, Arp, Boccioni, Carrà, Chagall, Delaunay, Ernst, Feininger, Gleizes, Goncerova, Kandinsky, Klee, Kokoschka, Kubin, Larionov, Léger, Macke, Marc, Marcoussis, Moilliet, Mondrian, Picabia, Gabriele Münter, Russolo and Severini.

13 Walter H. Sokel, *The Writer in Extremis* (Stanford, 1959), p. 111.

14 August Stramm, 'Verzweifelt', *Der Sturm*, V, no. 17/18 (December 1914), p. 115. A literal translation of this poem reads:

Despair

A shrill stone blares overhead
Night greys shuddering at glass
The ages stop
I
Stone.
You glassing
from afar.

15 Wassily Kandinsky, 'Über die Formfrage' (1912), in *Essays über Kunst und Künstler*, edited by Max Bill (Stuttgart, 1955), p. 18.

16 Heinrich Hart, 'Weltpfingsten, Gedichte eines Idealisten' (1872), in Hart, *Gesammelte Werke* (Berlin, 1907), I, pp. 1–4.

17 Kurt Heynicke, 'Aufbruch', in Pinthus, p. 224.

18 Wassily Kandinsky, *Concerning the Spiritual in Art*, translated by Michael Sadleir and others (New York, 1966), p. 77.

19 Julius Hart, 'Alles ist mein', in Albert Soergel & Kurt Hohoff, *Dichtung und Dichter der Zeit* (Düsseldorf, 1961), I, p. 237.

20 Hermann Muthesius, 'Wo stehen wir?', lecture delivered to the annual assembly of the DWB, Dresden, 1911, in *Jahrbuch des Deutschen Werkbundes 1912* (Jena, 1912), p. 25.

21 Karl Scheffler, *Die Architektur der Großstadt* (Berlin, 1913), p. 63.

22 Pinthus, p. 28.

23 Ferdinand Avenarius, *Der Kunstwart*, XXVI, no. 8 (1913), p. 81.

2. Bruno Taut: 1900–1914

1 Bruno Taut, letter to Max Taut, 2 Mar. 1902, in Tilmann Buddensieg, 'Schinkel wird nicht erwähnt: Bruno Taut zum ersten Mal in Berlin', *Neue Heimat Monatshefte*, XXVII, no. 5 (May 1980), pp. 14–19.

2 *Ibid.*

3 *Ibid.*

4 *Ibid.*

5 Bruno Taut, diary entry 17 Mar. 1905, in H. Taut, 'Tagebuchauszüge 1904–1907' (unpublished, Lehnitz, DDR), quoted Hartmann, p. 123.

6 Adolf Behne, 'Das Monument des Eisens von Taut und Hoffmann auf der Internationalen Baufachausstellung in Leipzig', *Das Kunstgewerbeblatt*, XXV, no. 2 (February 1914), pp. 86–8.

7 Adolf Behne, 'Bruno Taut', *Der Sturm*, IV, no. 198–9 (February 1914), p. 182. Behne's jibe at puritanism in architecture may have been aimed at Adolf Loos. Loos had lectured in Berlin in 1910 and extracts from the lecture were printed in *Der Sturm*. (Adolf Loos, 'Über Architektur', *Der Sturm*, I, no. 42 (December 1910).)

8 Behne, 'Bruno Taut'.

9 *Ibid.*

10 *Ibid.*

11 Tilmann Buddensieg, 'Berlin, Kottbusser Damm', *Frankfurter Allgemeine Zeitung*, 30 April 1977.

12 Bruno Taut, 'Eine Notwendigkeit', *Der Sturm*, IV, no. 196/7 (February 1914), pp. 174–5.

13 Bruno Taut, 'Das Problem des Opernbaues', *Sozialistische Monatshefte*, 20, I, no. 6 (26 March 1914), p. 357.

14 For a detailed account of the Falkenberg project see Hartmann, pp. 104–21.

15 Bruno Taut, 'Drei Siedlungen', *Wasmuths Monatshefte für Baukunst*, IV, no. 5/6 (1919/20), p. 183.

16 Behne made exactly this point in 'Die Bedeutung der Farbe in Falkenberg', *Gartenstadt*, VII, no. 12 (December 1912), p. 250. 'Just as the relationship between the garden city and the residents keeps the middle course between freedom and constraint, so the coloured house mediates between the repeated house-type and the single house.'

17 Taut, 'Drei Siedlungen', p. 183.

18 Ferdinand Avenarius, 'Farbige Häuser', *Der Kunstwart*, XIII, no. 13 (April 1900), pp. 37–8.

19 Bruno Taut, 'Theodor Goecke: Ein Nachruf', *Die Bauwelt* X, no. 34 (21 August 1919), p. 13.

20 For a full account of 'Das graue Tuch' see Rosemarie Haag Bletter, 'Paul Scheerbart's Architectural Fantasies', *Journal of the Society of Architectural Historians*, XXXIV, no. 2 (May 1975), pp. 83–97.

21 Paul Scheerbart, letters and postcards to Herwarth Walden, Sturm-Archiv, Handschriftabteilung, Staatsbibliothek Preussischer Kulturbesitz, West Berlin.

22 Paul Scheerbart, 'Das Ozeansanatorium für Heukranke', *Der Sturm*, III, no. 123/4 (August 1912), pp. 128–30.

23 Taut, 'Eine Notwendigkeit', pp. 174–5.

24 Scheerbart, letter to Taut, 8 Feb. 1914, in *Frühlicht*, 3 (February 1920). Reprinted in Taut, *Frühlicht* (Berlin, 1963), p. 19.

25 For a literal translation of these aphorisms see Paul Scheerbart & Bruno Taut, *Glass Architecture and Alpine Architecture*, edited by Dennis Sharp (London 1972), p. 14. The following versions, kindly suggested to me by Brad Robinson, although less literal, are closer in spirit to Scheerbart's doggerel.

1 Life sans glass?
   A pretty pass!

2 Brick will ever pass away,
   Where tinted glass will thrive and stay.

3 Glass in tints:
   Hate relents.

4 A colourful future
   Only in the glass culture.

5 Life without a crystal palace?
   Friendless as an empty chalice.

6 A glass house cannot conflagrate,
   Unneeded here the fire brigade.

7 Listen to my joyful sermon:
   A house of glass stays free of vermin.

  8 Materials inflammable
     Belong among the damnable.

  9 A double glass wall
     Will make diamonds pall.

  10 Light bestrides the universe
      And brightens crystals none the worse.

  11 Wax ecstatic!
      Glass is prismatic!

  12 Flight from colour?
      All the duller!

  13 Glass makes everything bright,
      Use it on the site.

  14 Glass will form the future city,
      Brick will just engender pity.

26 Scheerbart, letter to Herwarth Walden, 21 April 1914, Sturm-Archiv. Scheerbart dedicated the book to Taut, and Taut dedicated the Glashaus to Scheerbart.
27 In Ernst Lichtblau, *Die Wagnerschule: Arbeiten aus den Jahren 1905/1906 und 1906/1907* (Leipzig, 1910). Taut's idea of a *Stadtkrone* might also have a source in the Wagnerschule. At the turn of the century, Josef Plečnik produced a series of drawings entitled *Studies for a Stadtkrone*. See Marco Pozzetto, *Joze Plečnik e la Scuola di Otto Wagner*, (Turin, 1968), p. 44.
28 By 1914 Berg had already designed the Jahrhunderthalle at Breslau in concrete, and the Königliche Preußische Materialsprüfungsamt had tested glass bricks.
29 Taut, 'Eine Notwendigkeit', p. 175.
30 Paul Scheerbart, 'Der Architektenkongress: Eine Parlamentsgeschichte', *Frühlicht* (Magdeburg Edition), no. 1 (August 1921).
31 Taut, 'Eine Notwendigkeit', p. 175.
32 Bruno Taut, *Glashaus: Werkbundausstellung Cöln 1914* (Cologne, 1914).
33 *Ibid.*
34 Bruno Taut, 'Aeusserungen über die Gartenstadt Falkenberg bei Grünau', in Hartmann, p. 178.
35 Taut, 'Eine Notwendigkeit', p. 175.
36 *Ibid.*

3. Pacifism

  1 Thomas Mann, *Briefe 1889–1936* (Frankfurt, 1961), p. 115.
  2 Karl Ernst Osthaus, letter to Walter Gropius, 22 Oct. 1915, KEO-Archiv, Kü 344/251.
  3 Adolf Behne, 'Der Haß der Neutralen', *Die Tat*, VII, no. 4 (July 1915), pp. 340–1.
  4 Taut, letter to Charlotte Wollgast, 3 Sept. 1914, Collection Heinrich Taut, Lehnitz (DDR).
  5 *Ibid.*
  6 *Ibid.*
  7 *Ibid.*
  8 *Ibid.*
  9 *Ibid.*
  10 Taut, letter to Max Taut, 5 Mar. 1915, from 'Auszüge aus Briefen von Bruno Taut an Max Taut', Heinrich Taut Collection.

11 Taut, letter to Max Taut, 11 Oct. 1917, from *ibid.*

12 Taut, letter to Max Taut, 6 Mar. 1916, from *ibid.*

13 Taut, letter to Max Taut, 5 Mar. 1915, from *ibid.*

14 The official report of the conference made no reference to Taut's contribution.

15 Osthaus, letter to Gropius, 20 June 1916, KEO, Kü 344/263.

16 Gropius, letter to Osthaus, 25 June 1916, KEO, Kü 344/265.

17 'Protokoll der gemeinsamen Sitzung des Vorstandes mit dem Ausschuss in Bamberg am 13. 6. 1916.' KEO, DWB 211/15.

18 Osthaus, letter to Gropius, 20 June 1916, KEO, Kü 344/263.

19 Hans Poelzig, letter to Fritz Hellwag, quoted in part in Hellwag, letter to Osthaus, 2 July 1916, KEO, DWB 197/4. The Burgfrieden, or Civic Truce pact was proclaimed by the Kaiser on 4 August 1914. It demanded the unity of all Germans regardless of political allegiances or confessional barriers.

20 Bruno Taut, *Die Stadtkrone* (Jena, 1919), p. 57.

21 Bruno Taut, 'Die Vererdung. Zum Problem des Totenkults', *Die Werkstatt der Kunst*, XVI, no. 18 (29 January 1917), p. 220.

22 *Ibid.*, pp. 220–1.

23 Taut, *Stadtkrone*, p. 57.

24 Friedrich Nietzsche, *Schopenhauer als Erzieher*, in Taut, *Stadtkrone*, p. 57.

25 Bruno Taut, 'Krieger-Ehrung', in (1) Deutsche Gartenstadtgesellschaft, *Unseren Kriegsinvaliden Heim und Werkstatt in Gartensiedlungen*, (Leipzig, 1915), pp. 76–7. (2) *Das Kunstgewerbeblatt*, XXVI, no. 9 (June 1915), pp. 174–6. (3) *Die Tat*, VII, no. 3 (June 1915), pp. 257–9.

4. Regeneration

1 Taut, 'Krieger-Ehrung', *Das Kunstgewerbeblatt*, p. 175.

2 Taut, 'Vererdung', p. 222.

3 *Ibid.*, p. 221.

4 *Ibid.*

5 Taut, 'Krieger-Ehrung', *Das Kunstgewerbeblatt*, p. 176.

6 *Ibid.*

7 Bruno Taut, 'Gartenstadt Falkenberg', in *Unseren Kriegsinvaliden Heim*, p. 52.

8 *Ibid.*

9 *Ibid.*

10 Taut, 'Krieger-Ehrung', *Das Kunstgewerbeblatt*, p. 176.

5. Chiliastic expectations – the *Gemeinschaft*

1 Norman Cohn, *The Pursuit of the Millennium* (London, 1970), p. 15.

2 Paul Scheerbart, 'Das neue Leben', in Taut, *Stadtkrone*, p. 11.

3 *Ibid.*

4 Taut, *Stadtkrone*, p. 59.

5 *Ibid.*

6 *Ibid.*

7 *Ibid.*, pp. 59–60.

8 These translations were published as:

   (1) Peter Kropotkin (trans. Gustav Landauer), *Gegenseitige Hilfe in der Entwicklung* (Leipzig, 1904).

   (2) Peter Kropotkin, *Landwirtschaft, Industrie und Handwerk* (Berlin, 1904).

9 See, for example: Gustav Landauer, *Volk und Land: Dreißig Sozialistische Thesen* (1907), and *Die Revolution* (1907).

10 Gustav Landauer, 'Die zwölf Artikel des sozialistischen Bundes', *Der Sozialist*, II, no. 14 (10 July 1910).

11 Gustav Landauer, *Aufruf zum Sozialismus*, second edition (Berlin, 1919), p. 19. Taut included this quotation in *Die Auflösung der Städte oder die Erde eine Gute Wohnung* (Hagen, 1920).

6. *Geist* and *Volk*

1 Martin Buber, *Daniel* (1913), in Hermann Friedmann & Otto Mann, *Deutsche Literatur im 20. Jahrhundert*, fifth edition (Berne, 1967), p. 299.
2 Landauer, *Aufruf*, p. 3.
3 *Ibid.*, pp. 9–10.
4 *Ibid.*, p. 98.
5 Taut, *Stadtkrone*, p. 52.
6 Adolf Behne, 'Wiedergeburt der Baukunst', in Taut, *Stadtkrone*, pp. 130–1.
7 Adolf Behne, *Die Wiederkehr der Kunst* (Leipzig, 1919), p. 13.
8 Bruno Taut, 'Ex Oriente Lux', *Das hohe Ufer*, I, no. 1 (January 1919), p. 17. In the same article Taut quoted Scheerbart's poem *Indianerlied* (originally published in *Katerpoesie*, 1908).

> 'Throttle the European!
> throttle him!
> Throttle him! Throttle him!
> Throttle him dead!'
> – sings St Paul.

9 Martin Buber, *Von Geist des Judentums* (Munich, 1916), pp. 18–19.
10 Taut cited Meister Eckhart in *Die Stadtkrone*, using this edition, see *Stadtkrone*, p. 69.
11 Some examples of the new interest in the Orient were: Bernhard Kellerman, *Ein Spaziergang in Japan* (1910); Alfred Döblin, *Die drei Sprünge des Wang-lun* (1915); Waldemar Bonsel, *Indienfahrt* (1916); Ku Hung Ming, *Der Geist des chinesischen Volkes und der Ausweg aus dem Krieg* (1916); Hermann Graf Keyserling, *Das Reisetagebuch eines Philosophen* (1919); and the German translation of Gauguin's *Noa Noa* (1912). Gauguin's path to the Orient was followed by several German painters, including Pechstein, Nolde, Hofer and by Taut's subsequent collaborator, Wenzel Hablik.
12 Wilhelm Worringer, *Formprobleme der Gotik*, thirteenth to seventeenth edition (Munich, 1922), p. 12.
13 *Ibid.*, pp. 24–5.
14 Adolf Behne, 'Deutsche Expressionisten', *Der Sturm*, V, no. 17/18 (December 1914), p. 114.
15 Karl Scheffler, *Der Geist der Gotik* (Leipzig, 1917), p. 45.
16 Worringer, *Formprobleme*, p. 69.
17 Paul Fechter, *Der Expressionismus* (Munich, 1914), pp. 3–4.
18 *Ibid.*, p. 4.
19 Georg Simmel, 'Deutschlands innere Wandlung' (1914), in Summel, *Der Krieg und die geistigen Entscheidungen* (Munich, 1917), p. 10.
20 Erich Baron, 'Aufbau', in Taut, *Stadtkrone*, p. 109.

7. The role of the Activist

1 Taut, *Stadtkrone*, p. 51.
2 Behne, 'Wiedergeburt', in Taut, *Stadtkrone*, p. 115.
3 Behne, *Die Wiederkehr der Kunst*, p. 56.

4 *Ibid.*, p. 92.

5 *Ibid.*, p. 64.

6 *Ibid.*, p. 39.

7 *Ibid.*, pp. 58–9.

8 Kurt Hiller. 'Philosophie des Ziels', in *Das Ziel Aufrüfe zu tätigem Geist* [hereafter *Ziel* I] (Berlin, 1916), p. 214. See also Kurt Hiller, 'Ortsbestimmung des Aktivismus', in *Die Erhebung. Jahrbuch für neue Dichtung und Wertung* [hereafter *Erhebung* I] (Berlin, 1919), p. 371: 'The Activist is in all circumstances a pacifist.'

9 Baron wrote his essay 'Aufbau' in the autumn of 1917, see Chapter 10.

10 Baron, 'Aufbau', in *Stadtkrone*, p. 101: 'the hot-blooded prophets of the committed *Geist*'.

11 In order of publication, the Activist yearbooks were:

1. *Das Ziel. Aufrüfe zu tätigem Geist* ed. Kurt Hiller (Munich & Berlin, 1916).

2. *Tätiger Geist! Zweites der Ziel-Jahrbücher* ed. Kurt Hiller (Munich & Berlin, 1918).

3. *Das Ziel. Jahrbücher für geistige Politik III* ed. Kurt Hiller (Leipzig, 1919).

4. *Das Ziel. Jahrbücher für geistige Politik IV* ed. Kurt Hiller (Munich, 1920).

5. *Die Erhebung. Jahrbuch für neue Dichtung und Wertung* ed. Alfred Wolfenstein (Berlin, 1919).

6. *Die Erhebung. Jahrbuch für neue Dichtung und Wertung: Zweites Buch* ed. Alfred Wolfenstein (Berlin, 1920).

7. *Geistige Politik! Fünftes der Ziel-Jahrbücher* ed. Kurt Hiller (Leipzig & Vienna, 1924).

12 Hiller, *Ziel I*, p. 222.

13 *Ibid.*, pp. 187–217.

14 *Ibid.*, p. 196.

15 *Ibid.*, p. 198.

16 *Ibid.*, p. 199. In his pioneering work *Expressionismus und Aktivismus*, Wolfgang Paulsen offered the following contrast: 'The Expressionist creates the world for *himself* – the Activist, in contrast, for the new society, the new order, for paradise.' Wolfgang Paulsen, *Expressionismus und Aktivisumus: eine typologische Untersuchung* (Berne, 1935), p. 70.

17 Hiller, *Ziel I*, p. 201.

18 *Ibid.*, p. 199.

19 Taut, *Stadtkrone*, pp. 59–60.

20 Landauer, *Aufruf*, p. 22.

21 Gustav Landauer, *Ein Weg Deutschen Geistes* (Munich, 1916), p. 15.

22 Heinrich Mann, 'Geist und Tat', *Ziel I*, p. 8.

23 Ludwig Rubiner, 'Hören Sie!', *Die Aktion*, VI, no. 27/8 (8 July 1916), p. 380.

24 Hiller, 'Ortsbestimmung des Aktivismus', pp. 367, 369. Once again, a direct source can be found in Landauer, who wrote: '*Geist* means comprehension of the totality of daily existence, *Geist* means the union of the separate, of objects, ideas and men. *Geist* means enthusiasm, a fiery spirit, courage and pugnacity in the periods of transition. *Geist* means doing and building.' See: Landauer, *Aufruf*, p. 23.

25 Kurt Hiller, 'Der Bund des Geistigen' (1915), in Hiller, *Geist werde Herr – Kundgebung eines Aktivisten vor, in und nach dem Kriege* (Berlin, 1920), p. 57.

26 See Georg Simmel, *Brücke und Tür*, essays, (Stuttgart, 1957), p. 94.

27 Gustav Wyneken, *Schule und Jugendkultur* (Jena, 1913), p. 5.

28 Taut, *Stadtkrone*, p. 60.

29 Hiller, *Ziel I*, p. 209.

30 Taut, *Stadtkrone*, p. 52.

31 *Ibid.*, p. 51.

8. The rationalism of intuition

1 Taut, letter to Max Taut, 30 Oct. 1915 and 5 Nov. 1915, Heinrich Taut Collection.

2 For example, Hans Arp wrote in *Der Sturm* in 1913 of 'crystalline amphorae on the mountain peaks', Hans Arp, 'Von der letzen Malerei', *Der Sturm*, III, no. 188/9 (December 1913), p. 140. Compare also, Otto Kohtz, writing in 1909 under the obvious influence of Scheerbart:

> Perhaps the day will come, when men will have the power to build not only castles and gardens, as at Versailles, but to play with the mountains like a child with sand. Works of art could be built as high as the Himalayas, created out of fantasy like a jeweller's casket, fretted like lacework. Stone could be used like precious metal, woods and meadows like jewels, the glaciers as pearls, and the water like crystal.

In: Otto Kohtz, *Gedanken über Architektur* (Berlin, 1909), p. 4.

3 Bruno Taut, *Alpine Architektur* (Hagen, 1919), no. 11.

4 *Ibid.*, no. 16.

5 *Ibid.*, no. 16.

6 *Ibid.*, no. 4.

7 Allan C. Greenberg, 'Artists and the Weimar Republic: Dada and the Bauhaus 1917–25' (unpublished Ph.D., University of Illinois, 1967), p. 84.

8 Max Brod, 'Aktivismus und Rationalismus', *Tätiger Geist! Zweites der Ziel-Jahrbücher* [hereafter *Ziel II*] (Munich & Berlin, 1918). pp. 61–2.

9 See Paulsen, *Expressionismus und Aktivismus* p. 13. 'The notion of rationalism appears in Activist writings roughly as often as the notion of "God" appears in the writings of the Expressionists. Here again, the intellectual affinities of the Activists are revealed.'

10 Brod, 'Aktivismus und Rationalismus', p. 62.

11 *Ibid.*

12 Paulsen, *Expressionismus und Aktivismus* p. 59.

13 This connection is discussed in greater detail in the Conclusion.

14 Hiller, 'Ortsbestimmung des Aktivismus', p. 366.

15 It is interesting to note that Behne reviewed both Worringer's *Abstraktion und Einfühlung* and the *Jahrbuch des Deutschen Werkbundes, 1913* in the same article: 'Moderne Kunstbücher', *Die Tat*, V, no. 9 (December 1913), pp. 936–42. Of the former, Behne wrote: '"A Contribution to the Psychology of Style" is the subtitle of this book, which appeared, as is rarely the case, at exactly the moment at which it was necessary.'

16 Wassily Kandinsky, 'Malerei als reine Kunst', *Der Sturm*, IV, no. 178/9 (September 1913), pp. 98–9, in Herwarth Walden, *Expressionismus* (Berlin, 1918), p. 12.

17 See Johann Gustav Droysen, *Grundriß der Historik* (Leipzig, 1868).

18 Taut, *Stadtkrone*, pp. 51–2.

19 *Ibid.*, p. 52.

20 *Ibid.*

21 Bruno Taut, 'Der Roland von Brandenburg', *Das Kunstgewerbeblatt*, XXVII, no. 6, (March 1916), p. 111.

22 *Ibid.*, p. 112.

23 *Ibid.* Behne made exactly the same claim the following year for Cubism, but substituting 'life' for 'nature': 'Cubism does not wish to offer a banal enumeration and psychological interpretation of the body and its workings from a particular external standpoint, it wants to be life itself.' See Adolf Behne, 'Biologie und Kubismus', *Die Tat*, IX, no. 8 (November 1917), pp. 703–4.

24 Taut, *Stadtkrone*, p. 50.
25 Theodor Lipps, *Ästhetik*, second edition (Leipzig, 1914), I, p. 159.
26 Taut, *Stadtkrone*, p. 87.
27 See Chapter 7, n. 15.

9. The new city and the resonance of *Geist* and *Volk*

1 Taut, *Stadtkrone*, pp. 63–4.
2 *Ibid.*, p. 64.
3 See Chapter 6, n. 16.
4 Taut, *Stadtkrone*, p. 67.
5 *Ibid.*, p. 69.
6 Bruno Taut, 'Reiseeindrücke aus Konstantinopel', *Das Kunstgewerbeblatt*, XXVIII, no. 3 (December 1916), p. 50.
7 *Ibid.*
8 Taut, *Stadtkrone*, p. 70.
9 By the end of 1917, the average adult ration was only 1000 calories per day, with bread rationed to 70 ounces and fats to 2 ounces per person per week.
10 Paul Westheim, 'Bauluxus', *Sozialistische Monatshefte*, 23, XLIX, no. 20/1 (10 October 1917), p. 1103.
11 See Taut, *Stadtkrone*, p. 56. 'Recently the opulent provision of modern town halls with towers and monumental architecture has been justifiably abandoned, both on grounds of economy and because it contradicts the spirit of the building.'
12 Adolf Behne, 'Kritik des Werkbundes', *Die Tat*, IX, no. 1 (August 1917), pp. 430–8, in *Werkbund Archiv Jahrbuch 1* (Berlin, 1972), p. 120.
13 *Ibid.*, p. 126.
14 *Ibid.*, p. 120.
15 *Ibid.*, p. 128.
16 Kurt Hiller, *Die Weisheit der Langenweile*, I (Leipzig, 1913), in Lewis D. Wurgaft, 'The Activist Movement: Cultural Politics on the German Left, 1914–1933' (unpublished PhD, Harvard University, 1970), p. 38.
17 As was Ebenezer Howard's proposed city. His *Garden Cities of Tomorrow* was first published in German in 1907 as *Gartenstädte in Sicht*.
18 See Theodor Fritsch, *Die Stadt der Zukunft* (Leipzig, 1896), pp. 14–15: 'At the centre one could conceive a mighty edifice, perhaps a vast domed structure as a cathedral, temple to the arts, a magnificent governmental palace or something similar.' Taut would certainly have known of Fritsch's plans through his work for the Gartenstadtgesellschaft.
19 See Fidus, *Tempelkunst* (Berlin, 1914). In the 1890s Fidus was a close friend of Scheerbart in the circle of anarchists and socialist bohemians which also included Willy Lentrodt, Richard Dehmel and Franz Evers. Fidus must have figured in the discussions on architecture held by Taut and Scheerbart in 1914. The existence of a Taut–Fidus connection was confirmed in 1919, when Fidus exhibited his designs for temples at the Arbeitsrat für Kunst exhibition – Unbekannte Architekten – organized by Taut, Behne and Gropius.
20 Kohtz's very rhetorical introduction to his folio of drawings prefigured Taut's own views on mere functionality, as expressed in 'Eine Notwendigkeit' and *Die Stadtkrone*. See Kohtz, *Gedanken über Architektur*, p. 3.
21 August Horneffer, 'Das heilige Haus', *Die Tat*, III, no. 2 (February 1912), p. 547.
22 *Ibid.*, p. 559.
23 Ernst Horneffer, 'Die Freimauerei und die religiöse Krise der Gegenwart',

Die Tat, IV, no. 7 (October 1912), pp. 307–34, and *Die Tat*, IV, no. 8 (November 1912), pp. 382–402.

24 *Ibid.*, p. 395.
25 *Ibid.*
26 Taut, *Stadtkrone*, p. 69.
27 See Wilhelm Ostwald, 'Die wissenschaftlichen Grundlagen zum rationellen Farbatlas', *Mitteilungen des Deutschen Werkbundes*, no. 5 (July 1916), pp. 18–26.
28 Kurt Hiller, *Der Aufbruch zum Paradies* (Munich, 1922), p. 56.
29 Hiller, 'Philosophie des Ziels', pp. 196–7.

10. The politics of Activism

1 Taut, *Stadtkrone*, p. 66. Compare this with Landauer's complaint, written in 1911, of the contemporary class society: 'In this age of ours, no market place or high domed space, no temple or meeting house is the communal meeting place for all men.' *Aufruf*, p. 18.
2 Taut, *Stadtkrone*, p. 66.
3 *Ibid.*, p. 67.
4 Taut's close friendship with Baron lasted until 1933. In his later diaries, written in Japan in the mid-1930s, Taut repeatedly mentioned his debt to 'E.B.'.
5 Landauer, *Aufruf*, p. 22.
6 Baron, 'Aufbau', in Taut, *Stadtkrone*, p. 104. Compare Landauer's definition of socialism as: 'an attempt to create a new reality with the help of an ideal'. *Aufruf*, p. 1.
7 In his article 'Die Vererdung', Taut wrote of: 'a belief in human existence as part of the totality of nature, a belief present in all men today, one might say, through their belief in socialism'. 'Die Veredung', p. 222.
8 Taut, letter to Max Taut, 11 Oct. 1917. Heinrich Taut Collection.
9 Taut, *Stadtkrone*, p. 59.
10 Baron, 'Aufbau', in Taut, *Stadtkrone*, p. 108.
11 Landauer, *Aufruf*, p. 23.
12 *Ibid.*, p. 48: 'the father of Marxism is steam'.
13 *Ibid.*, p. 142.
14 *Ibid.*, p. 34.
15 *Ibid.*, pp. 6–7.
16 Taut, 'Eine Notwendigkeit', p. 175.
17 Taut, address to the Werkbund conference, 4 July, 1914, in *7. Jahresversammlung des Deutschen Werkbundes von 2. bis 6. Juli 1914 in Köln* (Jena, 1914), p. 75.
18 Taut's isolation was noted by Gropius in a letter which he wrote to Behne in December 1919, in the context of the Gläserne Kette: 'I realize that Bruno doesn't fit into any group. His destiny is to remain alone and he should acknowledge this and draw the consequences.' Gropius, letter to Behne, 29 Dec. 1919, in Franciscono, *Bauhaus*, pp. 99–100.
19 Taut, letter to Max Taut, 8 June 1904, Heinrich Taut Collection.
20 Taut may also have known a critique of Protagoras, Nietzsche and Stirner which was published in 1914: Benedict Lachmann, *Protagoras, Nietzsche, Stirner: ein Beitrag zur Philosophie des Individualismus und Egoismus* (Berlin, 1914).
21 Friedrich Nietzsche, 'Wir Künstler', in 'Die fröhliche Wissenschaft', *Werke* (Leipzig, 1906), IV, p. 59.
22 Franciscono, *Bauhaus*, p. 99. In 'Eine Notwendigkeit' Taut singled out the 'geistvollen Kompositionen Kandinskys' for special praise.

23 Taut, Address to Werkbund conference 1914, pp. 75–6.
24 Gropius, letter to Osthaus, 25 June 1916, KEO, Kü 344/265.
25 Kurt Hiller, 'Überlegungen zur Eschatologie und Methodologie des Aktivismus', *Das Ziel. Jahrbücher für geistige Politik III* [hereafter *Ziel III*] (Leipzig, 1919), p. 214.
26 Rudolf Leonhard, *Alles und Nichts!* (Berlin, 1920), p. 66.
27 Hiller, 'Überlegungen', p. 213. 'Democracy is the political science of relativism – in German: the total lack of ideas.'
28 Gustav Landauer, 'Eine Ansprache an die Dichter', *Erhebung I*, p. 303. Besides Landauer himself, an important source for the Activists' belief in an aristocracy of *Geist* was the social theorist Hans Blüher, a friend of both Landauer and Buber. See, for example, Blüher, 'Die Untaten des Bürgerlichen Typus', *Ziel I*, pp. 9–11.
29 See Poggioli, *Avant-Garde*, p. 39.
30 Taut, letter to Max Taut, 30 Jan. 1918, Heinrich Taut Collection.
31 Poggioli, *Avant-Garde*, p. 99.
32 Sokel, *Writer in Extremis*, pp. 52–82.
33 *Ibid.*, p. 63.
34 Kurt Hiller, 'Wir', *Zeit-Echo*, no. 9 (1915), pp. 132–4.
35 Hiller, 'Philosophie des Ziels', p. 203.
36 *Ibid.*
37 *Ibid.*
38 Poggioli, *Avant-Garde*, pp. 30–1.
39 Landauer, *Aufruf*, p. 131.
40 Taut, *Stadtkrone*, p. 66.
41 Kurt Hiller, 'Ein deutsches Herrenhaus', published: (1) *Ziel II*, pp. 379–425. (2) *Der neue Geist* (Leipzig, 1918).
42 Kurt Breysig, *Von Gegenwart und von Zukunft des Deutschen Menschen* (Berlin, 1912).
43 See Alfred Wolfenstein, 'Herrenhaus der Zukunft', *Die Aktion*, (Jahrgang 1912), no. 31 (31 July 1912), pp. 967–8.
44 Hiller, 'Herrenhaus', *Ziel II*, p. 393.
45 *Ibid.*, p. 415.
46 Hiller, 'Philosophie des Ziels', pp. 204–5.
47 *Ibid.*, p. 205.
48 *Ibid.*
49 Hiller, 'Herrenhaus', *Ziel II*, p. 417.
50 *Ibid.*
51 Taut, *Stadtkrone*, p. 67.
52 Bund zum Ziel, 'Leitsätze', in *Ziel III*, p. 218.
53 He was also editor of the magazine *Das neue Rußland*.
54 Sokel, *Writer in Extremis*, p. 155.
55 Adolf Behne, 'Ist das Schwäche?', *Sozialistische Monatshefte*, 23, XLIX, no. 25/6 (19 December 1917), p. 1286.
56 *Ibid.*, p. 1287. See also Chapter 6, n. 11.
57 *Ibid.*, p. 1287.
58 Adolf Behne, 'Die russische Kunst und die europäische Kunstgeschichte', *Sozialistische Monatshefte*, 24, LI (16 July 1918), pp. 691–4; 'Die Einheit der russischen Kunst', *Sozialistische Monatshefte*, 24, LI (6 August 1918), pp. 745–8; 'Die russische Kirche', *Sozialistische Monatshefte*, 24, LI (20 August 1918), pp. 790–4; 'Die Überwindung des Tektonischen in der russischen Baukunst', *Sozialistische Monatshefte*, 24, LI (3 September 1918), pp. 833–7.
59 Exactly why Taut was in Kowno at this time is unknown. His son can offer no reason for the visit, but does recall that his father bought two paintings by Chagall while he was there.

60 Taut, 'Reiseeindrücke aus Konstantinopel', p. 49.
61 Bruno Taut, 'Eindrücke aus Kowno', *Sozialistische Monatshefte*, 24, LI (24 September 1918), p. 897.
62 *Ibid.*, p. 898.
63 *Ibid.*, p. 899.
64 *Ibid.*, p. 900.

11. The Politischer Rat geistiger Arbeiter and the Arbeitsrat für Kunst

1 Anon., 'Anhang: Dokumente', *Ziel III*, p. 219. Although unsigned, the report is almost certainly by Hiller, as both spokesman for the Activists and as editor of *Das Ziel*.
2 See Kurt Hiller, *Leben gegen die Zeit* (Hamburg, 1969), pp. 129–30; and Johannes Fischart, 'Hans Georg von Beerfelde', *Die Weltbühne*, XIV, no. 47 (21 November 1918), pp. 478–83. The same issue of *Die Weltbühne* carried the programme of the RGA.
3 For a translation of the programme, see Appendix 1.
4 Anon., 'Anhang: Dokumente', p. 221.
5 *Ibid.*, p. 221. During the war years the Activists had considered founding an independent university. Rudolf Leonhard discussed this idea seriously with Gustav Landauer in 1915, but nothing came of the plan. See Charles B. Maurer, *Call to Revolution: the Mystical Anarchism of Gustav Landauer* (Detroit, 1971), p. 138.
6 Hiller was later to rechristen this *Reichstag* as *Zentralrat* of the *Arbeiterräte*. He maintained, however, that the *Arbeiterräte* should be chosen through elections. See Hiller, 'Überlegungen', pp. 208–9.
7 *Ibid.*, p. 222.
8 *Ibid.* The validity of the Activists' faith in autogenesis was questioned by Ernst Bloch. In an article published in Friedrich Burschell's weekly newspaper *Revolution*, Bloch described the RGA as follows: 'Impetuous ladies and literature-loving men are joining together. With the Reichstag behind them and with business prospects in the foreground, they announce their position as *Rat geistiger Arbeiter*. No one has comissioned this council, no one even considers its members to be in any way representative or competent.' Ernst Bloch, 'Zur Deutschen Revolution', *Revolution*, II (30 November 1918), p. 11.
9 See Franciscono, Bauhaus, p. 128, quoting Lothar Lang, *Das Bauhaus 1919–1933* (Berlin, 1965), p. 19.
10 Gropius, letter to Osthaus, 23 Dec. 1918, KEO, Kü 346/282.
11 Bruno Taut, 'An die sozialistische Regierung', *Sozialistische Monatshefte*, 24, LI (26 November 1918), pp. 1050–1.
12 *Ibid.*, p. 1051.
13 *Ibid.*
14 *Ibid.*
15 *Ibid.*
16 *Ibid.*
17 *Ibid.*
18 Programme of the AFK, December 1918, in *Mitteilungen des Deutschen Werkbundes*, 1918, no. 4, pp. 14–15, and *Die Bauwelt* (26 December 1918). For the full text see Appendix 2.
19 Programme of the AFK, December 1918, in *Mitteilungen des Deutschen Werkbundes*, 1918, no. 4, p. 14.
20 Taut, 'Architektur-Programm', in *Mitteilungen des Deutschen Werkbundes*, 1918, no. 4, p. 16. For the full text see Appendix 3.
21 *Ibid.*, p. 19.

22 Taut, 'Protokoll der Vorstandssitzung des Werkbundes vom 30 Juli, 1919', in Herta Hesse-Frielinghaus, August Hoff, Walter Erben & others, *Karl Ernst Osthaus* (Recklinghausen, 1971), p. 476.

23 Hermann Schmitz, *Revolution der Gesinnung: Preußische Kulturpolitik und Volksgemeinschaft seit dem 9. November 1918* (Neubabelsberg, 1931), pp. 50–1. The absence of Behne from this deputation confirms that he was not involved in the Arbeitsrat at its inception and was certainly not the founder of the group.

24 Hiller, 'Ortsbestimmung des Aktivismus', p. 363.

25 Ledebour was one of two leading politicians who strongly influenced Taut, both personally and politically, during the 1920s. The other was Clara Zetkin.

26 Taut, 'Architektur-Programm', p. 18.

27 Kropotkin, *Gegenseitige Hilfe*, p. 217.

28 Taut, 'Architektur-Programm', p. 17.

29 *Ibid.*

12. The politics of decentralization

1 Landauer, *Aufruf*, p. 142.

2 *Ibid.*, p. 149.

3 See Paul Scheerbart, 'Dynamitkrieg und Dezentralisation', *Gegenwart*, LXXVI (27 November 1909), pp. 905–8, and 'Die Entwicklung der Stadt', *Gegenwart*, LXXVII (18 June 1910), pp. 497–8.

4 Alfred Riebau, *Die Neudeutsche Siedlung* (Leipzig, 1916), p. 10.

5 *Ibid.*, p. 14.

6 Deutsche Siedlungs Gemeinschaft, *Die Eroberung unseres Vaterlandes* (Leipzig, 1916), p. 32.

7 Paul Hindenburg, 'Verfügung vom 17. Juni 1918', in Herman Muthesius, *Kleinhaus und Kleinsiedlung* (Munich, 1918), Preface.

8 For example: Kolonie Raschko (Kreis Adelnau), Kolonie Luisenthal (Kreis Schildberg), Rentengutskolonie 'Vogelsang bei Widenau (Westfalen), Gartenstadt Neumünster-Holstein.

9 Deutsche Gartenstadtgesellschaft, '*Unseren Kriegsinvaliden Heim*', p. 27.

10 Heinrich Tessenow, *Handwerk und Kleinstadt* (Berlin, 1919), p. 4.

11 *Ibid.*, p. 37.

12 *Ibid.*, p. 40.

13 *Ibid.*, p. 80.

14 *Ibid.*, pp. 65–6.

15 *Ibid.*, p. 67.

16 *Ibid.*, p. 76.

17 Taut, 'Architektur-Programm', p. 17.

13. The AFK, December 1918–April 1919

1 Gropius, letter to Osthaus, 2 Feb. 1919, KEO Kü 347/290. The Bauhaus-Archiv contains the rough draft of a letter from Gropius to an unnamed correspondent, which probably refers to one or both of the early AFK programmes. It is written on the back of an unrelated letter, dated 2 Dec. 1918, BA, GN 1. 1. 5.

> A splendid work! A dawn on the dark horizon of our age. I go further: it is a joy to feel, to share in, and to burn with the fire of this *Geist*! *This* is revolution, a new light of faith, the nascent crystal of a new humanity, a resuscitation from a long and deadly war-narcosis! I am inspired, and have sent him [Taut?] a jubilant letter.

2 Osthaus, letter to Taut, 3 Feb. 1919, KEO, Kü 351/1.
3 Gropius, letter to Osthaus, 23 Dec. 1918, KEO, Kü 346/282.
4 Gropius, letter to Osthaus, 2 Feb. 1919, KEO, Kü 347/290.
5 For a facsimile of the membership lists of the AFK after Gropius's reconstruction, see *Arbeitsrat für Kunst 1918–1921*, exhibition catalogue (Berlin, 1980), p. 89.
6 Paul Mebes, *Um 1800*, first published in 1908, was an account of the simple and rationalist domestic architecture which had been developed for the expanding territories of East Prussia and on the Baltic during the years of hardship caused by the Napoleonic wars. The parallel with the crisis of 1918 was not lost on the readers and the book enjoyed considerable success in the immediate post-war years, being reprinted in 1918 and again in 1920.
7 Göran Lindahl, 'Von der Zukunftskathedrale bis zur Wohnmaschine', *Idea and Form* (Uppsala Studies in History of Art), I (1959), p. 280.
8 See p. 85.
9 Bruno Taut, 'Die Erde eine gute Wohnung', *Die Volkswohnung*, I, no. 4 (24 February 1919), p. 45.
10 Leberecht Migge, *Jedermann Selbstversorger* (Jena, 1918).
11 Taut, 'Die Erde eine gute Wohnung', p. 47.
12 *Ibid.*, p. 46. His source for this was given as Kropotkin's *Landwirtschaft, Industrie und Handwerk*.
13 Taut, 'Die Erde eine gute Wohnung', p. 46.
14 Frederick Winslow Taylor's book *The Principles of Scientific Management* (New York and London, 1911) first appeared in German translation in 1913 as *Die Grundsätze wissenschaftlicher Betriebsführung*, translated by Rudolf Roesler (Munich and Berlin, 1913).
15 Ludwig Rubiner, 'Die Änderung der Welt', *Ziel I*, p. 118.
16 Landauer, *Aufruf*, p. 130.
17 Taut, 'Die Erde eine gute Wohnung', p. 47.
18 Landauer, *Aufruf*, p. 131.
19 Taut, 'Die Erde eine gute Wohnung', p. 48.
20 Bruno Taut, 'Alte Bauweisen in neuzeitlicher Form', *Die Volkswohnung*, I, no. 5 (10 March 1919), p. 69.
21 *Ibid.*, p. 69.
22 *Ibid.*, p. 70.
23 See, for example, Carl Ballod, *Die Ackerstadt und die städtische Selbstversorgung* (Berlin, 1918); and Peter Behrens and Heinrich de Fries, *Vom sparsamen Bauen* (Berlin, 1919).
24 Bruno Taut, 'Für die neue Baukunst!', *Das Kunstblatt*, III, no. 1 (January 1919), pp. 22, 24.
25 *Ibid.*, p. 18.
26 Otto Paul Burghardt, letter to Gropius, 2 Feb. 1919, BA, GN 10. 10. 232. Gropius replied in the Activist and élitist tone which he had adopted from Taut:
> 'In our opinion, it is absolutely impossible to arrive at a programme which represents the entire architectural profession. If it were possible, it would certainly be very uninteresting, for strong ideas immediately become watered-down compromises in the hands of the broad mass of the profession. It is exactly against this mass that we are fighting. The mass can certainly agree on economic points and try to promote them, but never on artistic principles.'

Gropius to Burghardt, 6 Mar. 1919, BA, GN 10. 10. 231.
27 Hugo Bruckmann, letter to Friedrich Perzynski, quoted: Charlotte Luke, letter to Taut, n.d., BA, GN 10. 4. 102.
28 Walther Haas, letter to Gropius, 9 Feb. 1919, BA, GN 1. 1. pp. 8–11.

29 *Ibid.*
30 *Ibid.*
31 See *Rheinische Monatshefte*, 24 Mar. 1919.
32 Heinrich de Fries, letter to AFK committee, 24 Mar. 1919, BA, GN 10. 11. 269–70.
33 *Ibid.*
34 Gropius, letter to Osthaus, 2 Feb. 1919, KEO, Kü 347/290.
35 Adolf Behne, 'Unsere moralische Krisis', *Sozialistische Monatshefte*, 25, LII (20 January 1919), p. 34.
36 *Ibid.*, p. 38.
37 Taut, 'Ex Oriente Lux', p. 18.
38 Taut, letter to Osthaus, 11 Feb. 1919, KEO, FV 74.
39 *Ibid.*
40 Taut, 'Für die neue Baukunst!', p. 16.
41 Gropius, letter to Dr Valentiner, 18 Feb. 1919, BA, GN 10. 19. 471.
42 Bruno Taut, 'Der Sozialismus des Künstlers', *Sozialistische Monatshefte*, 25, LII (24 March 1919), p. 259.
43 *Ibid.*, p. 260.
44 Karl Scheffler, 'Die Kunst und die Revolution', *Kunst und Künstler*, XVII, no. 5 (1 February 1919), p. 166.
45 Taut, 'Der Sozialismus des Künstlers', p. 260.
46 *Ibid.*, p. 261.
47 Landauer, *Aufruf*, p. VII.
48 See *ibid.*, pp. XV–XVI.
49 *Ibid.*, p. XVII.
50 Landauer, 'Entwurf zu einem Kulturprogramm' (April 1919), original MS in Landauer Collection, Jewish National and University Library, Jerusalem. Unfortunately there is no record of the correspondence between Landauer and Taut in this collection.
51 Taut, letter to Osthaus, 16 May 1919, KEO, Kü 351/4.
52 *Ibid.*
53 *Ibid.*

14. The AFK under Walter Gropius

1 The other members of the 'business committee' were Otto Bartning, Hermann Hasler, Erich Heckel, Georg Kolbe, Gerhard Marcks, Ludwig Meidner, Max Pechstein, Hermann Richter-Berlin, Karl Schmidt-Rottluff and Max Taut.
2 Rudolf Belling, Artur Degner, Lyonel Feininger, Otto Freundlich, Jefim Golyscheff, August Grisebach, Erwin Hass, Paul Rudolf Henning, Jakob Hirsch, Walter Kaesbach, Moritz Melzer, Otto Müller, Franz Mutzenbecher, Emil Nolde, Friedrich Perzynski, Richard Scheibe, Fritz Stuckenberg, Georg Tappert and Arnold Topp.
3 Scheffler, 'Die Kunst und die Revolution', p. 166.
4 Gropius, address to the AFK, 22 Mar. 1919, BA, GN 2/3.
5 *Ibid.*
6 For letters to these and other potential sponsors, see BA, GN 10. 4. 105, 10. 10. 218, 10. 11. 252, 10. 17. 411.
7 Gropius, letter to Valentiner, 11 Mar. 1919, BA, GN 10. 16. 468.
8 Gropius, letter to Friedrich Perzynski, 13 Mar. 1919, BA, GN 10. 16. 379.
9 Walter Gropius, 'Der freie Volksstaat und die Kunst', BA, GN 2/3. This article may have remained unpublished. It is substantially similar to another article by Gropius: 'Baukunst im freien Volksstaat', *Deutscher Revolutions – Almanach für das Jahr 1919* (Berlin, 1919), pp. 134–6.

10 Gropius, 'Der freie Volksstaat und die Kunst'.
11 *Ibid.*
12 *Ibid.*
13 *Die Stadtkrone* was published by the Eugen Diederichs Verlag, Jena, in February 1919. An extract from Taut's essay in *Die Stadtkrone* was subsequently printed in *Das hohe Ufer*, I, no. 5 (May 1919), pp. 125–6.
14 Gropius, 'Der freie Volksstaat und die Kunst'.
15 *Ibid.*
16 Gropius, letter to Ludwig Meidner, 26 Feb. 1919, BA, GN 10. 15. 352.
17 Behne, letter to Gropius, 5 Feb. 1920, BA, GN 10. 8. 183.
18 See Gropius, letter to Behne, 22 May 1919, BA, GN 10. 8. 188.
19 Taut quoted directly from Eckhart's writings in *Die Stadtkrone*: 'For were I but pure and untrammeled, God would yield Himself to me from His high seat and dwell within me.' *Stadtkrone*, p. 69. On the subject of pseudonyms within the Arbeitsrat, see Franciscono, *Bauhaus*, pp. 106–7.
20 Gropius, letter to Behne, 6 Mar. 1919, BA, GN 10. 9. 195.
21 Gropius, letter to Professor Weiss, 9 April 1919, BA, GN 10. 19. 481.
22 Gropius, letter to Carl Krayl, 14 April 1919, BA, GN 10. 14. 323.
23 Gropius, letter to Dr Busse, 13 Mar. 1919, BA, GN 10. 10. 234.

> Dear Sir, among other things, the Arbeitsrat für Kunst has on its programme: 'contact with trade unions or workers'. From our ranks, a whole list of noteworthy suggestions have been made, indicating how this aim could be achieved. We would like to get in contact with you and would ask you to tell us when you could meet a commission from the Arbeitsrat.

24 'Das Ende der Preußischen Landeskunstkommission', *Lokal-Anzeiger*, Berlin, 18 Mar. 1919.
25 Konrad Haenisch, *Sozialdemokratische Kulturpolitik* (Berlin, 1919), p. 13.
26 Gropius, letter to Ewald Dülberg, 3 April 1919, BA, GN 10. 11. 239.
27 For facsimiles of this and other AFK publications see *Arbeitsrat für Kunst 1918–1921*, exhibition catalogue (Berlin, 1980).
28 For example, Karl Heideloff, *Die Bauhütte des Mittelalters in Deutschland* (Nürnberg, 1844); and Ferdinand Janner, *Die Bauhütte des deutschen Mittelalters* (Leipzig, 1876).
29 See Chapter 9, nn. 21–3.

15. The Ausstellung für unbekannte Architekten

1 Gropius, *Ausstellung für unbekannte Architekten* (Berlin, 1919).
2 *Ibid.*
3 *Ibid.*
4 Taut, *ibid.*
5 During the preceding decade, Poelzig had designed a water-tower (Posen, 1911), a chemical factory (Luban, 1911–12), a gasworks (Dresden-Reick, 1916), and a project for a fire-station for Dresden (1916).
6 Poelzig, letter to Gropius, 21 April 1919, BA, GN 10. 17. 400–2.
7 Taut, letter to Osthaus, 23 April 1919, KEO, Kü 351/2.
8 Poelzig was listed among the new members in the 'Bericht der Geschäftsführung', dated 1 Nov. 1919, see BA, GN 10. 50.
9 Marlene Poelzig, conversation with author, Hamburg, May 1974.
10 Behne, *Ausstellung für unbekannte Architekten*.
11 Poggioli, *Avant-Garde*, p. 26.
12 Paul Westheim, 'Architektonische Phantasie zu der Ausstellung für unbekannte Architekten', *Frankfurter Zeitung*, 30 May 1919.

13 W. C. Behrendt, 'Berlin', *Kunst und Künstler*, XVII, no. 8 (1 May 1919), p. 339.

14 Walter Riezler, 'Revolution und Baukunst', *Mitteilungen des Deutschen Werkbundes*, 1919, no. 1, p. 20.

15 E. Pl. *Reichs-Anzeiger* (Berlin), April 1919.

16 Adolf Behne, 'Unbekannte Architekten', *Sozialistische Monatshefte*, 25, LII (28 April 1919), p. 422.

17 In Eberhard Steneberg, *Russische Kunst Berlin 1919–1932* (Berlin, 1969), p. 10.

18 John Schikowski, 'Architektenträume', *Vorwärts*, 29 Mar. 1919.

19 Gropius, letter to Jefim Golyscheff, 22 Mar. 1919, BA, GN 10. 12. 278. In a subsequent letter to Behne, dated 22 May 1919, Gropius described Golyscheff as 'brilliant and uninhibited...a marvellous fellow'. BA, GN 10. 8. 188.

20 See Raoul Hausmann, 'Dada empört sich, regt sich und stirbt in Berlin!', *Am Anfang war Dada* (Steinbach/Gießen, 1972), p. 20.

21 Hausmann, 'Nachhall', *Am Anfang war Dada*, p. 153.

22 Raoul Hausmann, in *Phases*, II (Paris, 1967), quoted in translation by the author in Steneberg, *Russische Kunst*, pp. 10–11.

23 Hausmann, *Am Anfang war Dada*, p. 77. One of Hausmann's 'technical drawings' from this occasion, entitled *Architecture Fantastique*, shows the clear influence of the architectural fantasies which Golyscheff produced for the Ausstellung für unbekannte Architekten.

24 *Ibid.*, p. 20.

25 Paulsen, *Expressionismus und Aktivismus*, p. 63.

26 Richard Huelsenbeck, 'Der neue Mensch' (1917), in Huelsenbeck, *Dada: eine literarische Dokumentation* (Hamburg, 1964), pp. 61–2.

27 *Ibid.*, p. 61.

28 Raoul Hausmann, Richard Huelsenbeck, Jefim Golyscheff, 'Was ist der Dadaismus und was will er in Deutschland?', *Der Dada*, I (June 1919). At a Dada evening on 12 March 1919, Hausmann and Baader launched a make-believe group in parody of the RGA. It was called the 'Anationalen Rat der unbezahlten Arbeiter'.

29 *Ibid.*

30 Hiller, letter to Johannes Baader, n.d. [spring 1919]. Hannah Höch-Nachlaß, Berlin.

31 Otto Freundlich, 'Das kommende Reich', *Die Aktion*, VII, no. 45/6 (17 November 1917), p. 600–2.

32 Paulsen, p. 64.

16. Taut and the *Proletkult*

1 Walter Rathenau, in Schmitz, *Preußische Kulturpolitik*, p. 11.

2 Gropius, 'Der freie Volksstaat und die Kunst'.

3 Gropius, address to AFK, March 1919.

4 Taut, *Ausstellung für unbekannte Architekten*.

5 *Ibid.*

6 See Kurt Hiller, 'Anti-Kain', *Ziel III*, p. 24: 'The Bolshevik wants war; although not war between nations but the international war of class against class – the sanguinary war afresh, with all the old, terrible weapons.' See also Walter Rilla, 'Der Irrtum Lenins', *Ziel III*, pp. 63–9.

7 Taut and others, 'Telegramm nach Moskau', 26 Jan. 1919, BA, GN 10. 3. 93.

8 Arbeitsrat für Kunst, letter to the Moscow *Soldatenrat*, 25 Mar. 1919, BA, GN 10. 3. 93.

9 *Ibid.*

10 See Taut, 'Eindrücke aus Kowno', p. 900.

11 On 8 March 1919, the new leadership of the AFK composed a series of questions which they sent to the members of the group, asking for their responses. These responses were then published as a book in November 1919, under the title: *Ja! Stimmen des Arbeitsrates für Kunst in Berlin*. The questions were principally those which had been raised in the original manifesto of the group and in Taut's 'Architektur-Programm', concerning the teaching of art and architecture, the relationship of the arts to *Handwerk*, of the artist and socialist state, and of the artist and the people. Specific questions were also asked about how future *Siedlungen* should be built, and on the use of colour in the cityscape. Examples of work by members of the Arbeitsrat accompanied the text, and included architectural projects and completed buildings by Gropius, Bruno Taut, Paul Goesch, Hermann Finsterlin, Wenzel Hablik, Max Taut, Hans Poelzig, Paul Mebes, Hans and Wassili Luckhardt, Werner Scheibe and Wilhelm Brückmann. Some of these drawings had already been exhibited at the Ausstellung für unbekannte Architekten, in April 1919.

12 Taut, in *Ja! Stimmen des Arbeitsrates für Kunst in Berlin* (Berlin, 1919), p. 102. For a facsimile of *Ja!*, see *Arbeitsrat für Kunst*, exhibition catalogue (Berlin, 1980), pp. 11–76.

13 See Taut, in *Ja!*, p. 100.

14 Bruno Taut, 'Idealisten', *Freiheit*, 28 March 1919.

15 *Ibid.*

16 *Ibid.*

17. Taut's literary activity in the summer of 1919

1 By this time Gropius had already been called to Weimar and was in the process of realizing his vision of an artists' community – the Bauhaus. His activity in the AFK and on the proposed magazine was much reduced after April 1919, and the leading role was taken over by Behne.

2 Taut, letter to Osthaus, 24 April 1919, KEO, Kü 351/3.

3 Adolf Behne (ed.), *Bauen*, prospectus (Berlin, June 1919).

4 *Ibid.*

5 *Ibid.*

6 Taut, letter to Osthaus, 16 May 1919, KEO, Kü 351/4.

7 *Ibid.*

8 Taut, 'Rede des Bundeskanzlers von Europa am 24. April 1993 vor dem europäischen Parlament', *Sozialistische Monatshefte*, 25, LIII (25 August 1919), pp. 816–19.

9 Taut, letter to Osthaus, 16 May 1919, KEO, Kü 351/4.

10 Taut's market, had it existed in recent times, would have fallen into the 'radical chic' category. That such a category existed in 1919 can be seen in a short note in the June 1919 edition of *Kunst und Künstler*. The note read: 'In Vienna, a publisher has brought out a luxury edition of the Communist Manifesto, printed on hand-made paper in an edition of one hundred copies. Whether or not the sheets have been signed by the Viennese communist leaders was unfortunately not to be ascertained.' *Kunst und Künstler*, no. 9 (1 June 1919), p. 377.

11 Bruno Taut, 'Zum neuen Theaterbau', *Das hohe Ufer*, I, no. 8 (August 1919), p. 204.

12 *Ibid.*

13 *Ibid.*

14 Taut, letter to Osthaus, 16 May 1919, KEO, Kü 351/4.

15 Taut, 'Zum neuen Theaterbau', pp. 204–5.

16 *Ibid.*, p. 206.

17 *Ibid.*, p. 208.

18 *Ibid.*, p. 205.

19 Taut, letter to Osthaus, 2 Aug. 1919, KEO, Kü 351/8.

20 Taut also drew a parallel between symphonic music and architecture in one of the drawings for the Haus des Himmels, which he originally intended to publish in June 1919 in the first issue of *Bauen*. The drawing was entitled *Bruckner IX Symphony – 3rd Movement*. He admired Bruckner's works enormously; as early as 1906 he wrote to his brother Max: 'I have heard a great symphony by Bruckner: a modern master, a mighty work.' Letter to Max Taut, 1 Mar. 1906, Heinrich Taut Collection.

21 Taut, 'Der Weltbaumeister', carbon copy of typescript, KEO, Kü 74/1. This essay was published in *Der Weltbaumeister* under the title 'Über Bühne und Musik: Nachwort zum Architekturschauspiel'.

22 *Ibid.*

18. The Bund für Proletarische Kultur

1 Holitscher, Natteroth and Baluschek were writers, Barthel was a poet, Gertrud Eysoldt an actress, Goldschmidt an economist and H. B. Herfurth was the vice-chairman of the state department for the unemployed. Looking back from 1928 Holitscher described the foundation of the BPK as follows:

> In that first summer of the German revolution I was sought out by a young proletarian and invited to organize a Bund für proletarische Kultur. We were to adopt and implement under German conditions what the 'Prolet-movement' was aiming at in Russia. It was primarily petty work, of little importance, but it was taken very seriously by our sundry group – some more middle class radicals, prepared to make sacrifices, had joined the young proletarian and myself.

Arthur Holitscher, *Mein Leben in dieser Zeit* (Potsdam, 1928), II, p. 183.

2 'Aufruf zu einem Bund für proletarische Kultur', *Räte-Zeitung*, I, no. 41 (September 1919).

3 *Ibid.*

4 Taut, 'Idealisten', *Freiheit*, 28 March 1919.

5 See *Das Ziel. Jahrbücher für geistige Politik IV* [hereafter *Ziel IV*] (Munich, 1920), pp. 53–9, for Hiller's obituary for Rubiner, who died in 1920. Hiller emphasized the importance of Rubiner's contribution to the Activist movement and regretted the ideological differences which had estranged him from Activism.

6 'Aufruf zu einem Bund für proletarische Kultur'.

7 Käthe Kollwitz, letter to Max Barthel, quoted: Max Barthel, *Kein Bedarf an Weltgeschichte: Geschichte eines Lebens* (Wiesbaden, 1950), p. 52.

8 'Militarist' (pseud.), 'Proletarische Kultur', *Freiheit*, I, no. 170 (22 September 1919).

9 See Franz Pfemfert, 'Kleine Aktion', *Die Aktion*, X, no. 11/12 (20 March 1920), p. 155.

10 Taut, *Die Auflösung der Städte*, Frontispiece: 'Naturally it is only a utopia…or an (indeed rather precipitate) paraphrase of the 3rd millennium AD.'

19. The Werkbund conference: September 1919

1 See Chapter 13, nn. 3 and 4.
2 'Protokoll der Vorstandssitzung des DWB vom 30.6.1919', in Hesse-Frielinghaus, *Osthaus*, pp. 471, 506 n. 59.
3 See *ibid.*, p. 506 n. 59.
4 Taut, letter to Gropius, 31 July 1919, KEO, Kü 351/7.
5 Taut, letter to Osthaus, 2 Aug. 1919, KEO, Kü 351/8.
6 Osthaus, letter to Taut, 11 Aug. 1919, KEO, Kü 351/12.
7 Taut, unsigned carbon copy of letter to Gropius, 22 Aug. 1919, KEO, Kü 351.
8 See Adolf Behne, 'Arbeitsrat für Kunst, Bericht der Geschäftsführung, 1. November 1919', BA, GN 10/50: 'The Deutscher Volkshausbund, Berlin, invites the AFK to take out joint membership. Perhaps Bruno Taut can say something about this on 15 November.'
9 Osthaus, letter to August Endell, 25 Aug. 1919, KEO, Kü 374/182.
10 Osthaus, letter to Taut, 25 Aug. 1919, KEO, Kü 351/2.
11 *Ibid.*
12 Taut, letter to Osthaus, 27 Aug. 1919, KEO, Kü 351.
13 The entire committee, as elected at Stuttgart consisted of Bartning, Bertsch, Bruckmann, Feinhals, Gropius, Kautzsch, Klein, Leipart, Osthaus, Poelzig, Poeschel, Pankok, Riemerschmid, Schirmer, Schmidt (Hellerau), 'Museumsdirektor' Schmidt (Frankfurt), Schulz, 'Ministerialdirektor a. D.' Simons, Taut, Wienbeck, van der Velde.
14 Taut, letter to the Werkbund committee, 31 July 1919. See Joan Campbell, *The German Werkbund* (Princeton 1978), p. 132, n. 80.
15 Hans Poelzig, 'Werkbundaufgaben', *Mitteilungen des Deutschen Werkbundes*, 1919, no. 4, p. 110.
16 *Ibid.*, p. 110.
17 *Ibid.*, p. 111.
18 *Ibid.*, p. 116.
19 *Ibid.*
20 *Ibid.*, p. 117.
21 *Ibid.*
22 *Ibid.*, p. 119.
23 See *ibid.*, pp. 120–2.
24 *Ibid.*, p. 124.
25 *Ibid.*
26 See Karl Ernst Osthaus, 'Deutscher Werkbund', *Das hohe Ufer*, I, no. 10 (October 1919), pp. 237–8.
27 *Ibid.*, p. 243.
28 *Ibid.*, pp. 243–4.
29 *Ibid.*, p. 244.
30 *Ibid.*, p. 245.
31 Osthaus, 'Die Kunst im Aufbau der neuen Lebensform', *Mitteilungen des Deutschen Werkbundes*, 1918, no. 5/6, p. 3.
32 *Ibid.*, p. 4.
33 *Ibid.*, p. 5.
34 *Mitteilungen des Deutschen Werkbundes*, 1919, no. 4, p. 139.
35 A measure of this success was the resignation, after the elections at Stuttgart, of Dr Ernst Jäckh from the position of chairman of the commercial section. Jäckh was the most vigorous spokesman for the industrial and business interests in the Werkbund and had been the *eminence grise* behind the Muthesius faction at the 1914 conference. His departure confirmed the

ascendancy of the artists over the businessmen in the Werkbund. As August Endell wrote to Osthaus at the time: 'That Jäckh wants to go is financially no good sign – the rats are leaving the ship. What now – "W.B."?' Endell, letter to Osthaus, 27 Sept. 1919, KEO, Kü 374/185.

36 Peter Bruckmann, *Mitteilungen des Deutschen Werkbundes*, 1919, no. 4, p. 128.
37 Bruno Taut, 'Für den Werkbund' (Summer/Autumn 1919), typescript, Bauakademie der DDR, East Berlin.
38 *Ibid.*
39 *Ibid.*
40 Bruno Taut, 'Zuviel Gerede vom Architektur-Unterricht', *Die Bauwelt*, X, no. 32 (7 August 1919), p. 9.
41 *Ibid.*, p. 10.
42 *Ibid.*, p. 9.
43 *Ibid.*
44 *Ibid.*, p. 10.
45 Taut, 'Für den Werkbund'.
46 *Ibid.*

20. Autumn and winter 1919: unrealized projects

1 The first meeting of the new committee was on 18 October 1919.
2 See Hans Poelzig, 'Staatliches Bauwesen', *Das hohe Ufer*, I, no. 12 (December 1919), p. 283.
3 *Ibid.*, p. 284.
4 The list of new members published on 1 November 1919 included Paul Goesch, Adolf Meyer, Hans Poelzig – who had rejoined, Adolf Allwohn, Ludwig Hilberseimer, Hans and Wassili Luckhardt, Paul Mebes, Jakobus Göttel and Viking Eggeling. See 'Arbeitsrat für Kunst, Bericht der Geschäftsführung, 1. November 1919', BA, GN 10/50.
5 See *ibid.*
6 *Ibid.*
7 See 'Protokoll der Sitzung des Geschäftsausschusses und der künstlerischen Arbeitsgemeinschaft des Arbeitsrates für Kunst...am Dienstag, d. 18. November 1919', BA, GN 10. 10. 42–7. p. 3.
8 *Ibid.*, p. 3.
9 *Ibid.*, p. 4.
10 *Ibid.*
11 *Ibid.*
12 Hugo Zehder, 'Aufruf zum farbigen Bauen!', *Die Bauwelt*, X, no. 38 (18 September 1919), p. 11. The 'Aufruf' was signed only by Zehder, although it had clearly been written by Taut and was later published under Taut's own name in *Das hohe Ufer*, I, no. 11 (November 1919), p. 272, and in *Frühlicht* (Magdeburg edition), no. 1 (Autumn 1921).
13 Walter Gropius, '"Sparsamer Hausrat" und falsche Dürftigkeit', *Das hohe Ufer*, I, no. 7 (July 1919), p. 180.
14 *Ibid.*
15 Poelzig, 'Werkbundaufgaben', p. 117.
16 Wilhelm Ostwald, *Die Harmonie der Farben* (Leipzig, 1918), p. 1.
17 See Walter Riezler, 'Die Grenzen von Ostwald's Farbenlehre', Deutscher Werkbund, *'Erster Deutscher Farbentag' auf der 9. Jahresversammlung des Deutschen Werkbundes in Stuttgart am 9. September 1919* (Berlin, 1919), p. 42.
18 Taut, 'Für den Werkbund'.

19 This has been confirmed by Hans J. Rieger in 'Die farbige Stadt' (unpublished PhD., Zurich University, 1976), pp. 58–60.

20 In March 1919, Scharoun won first prize in a competition organized by the city of Prenzlau, for a site beside the Sankt Marien-Kirche. Adolf Behne reported the result in a contemporary article: 'The first prize was awarded to the student Scharoun, who proposes a group of houses with varied heights and with colour variations...It should be noted with pleasure that a young architect is once again using colour as an expressive medium and, what is more, wins a prize thereby.' Behne, 'Farbfreudigkeit', *Sozialistische Monatshefte* 25, LII (7 July 1919), p. 684.

21 There was little reference to colour in the writings of the literary Activists, although Rubiner suggested that the new colour sense which evolved in the 1880s and 1890s derived from the clouds of coloured dust which circled the earth after the eruption of Krakatoa in 1882. See Rubiner, 'Die Änderung der Welt', p. 107.

22 See Rudolf Steiner, 'Von der Aura des Menschen' (1904), *Lucifer-Gnosis 1903–1908* (Dornach, 1960).

23 Adolf Behne, 'Werkbund', *Sozialistische Monatshefte*, 26, LIV (26 January 1920), p. 68.

24 Gropius, letter to Otto Bartning, 2 June 1921, BA, GN 10. 5. 124.

25 Poelzig, 'Werkbundaufgaben', p. 124.

26 Statistics from *Zentralblatt für das deutsche Baugewerbe*, XIX, no. 28 (16 July 1920), p. 294.

27 Osthaus, letter to Taut, 22 Nov. 1919, KEO, Kü 352/13.

28 Karl Ernst Osthaus, 'Die Folkwang Schule', *Genius*, II (1920), p. 201.

29 Osthaus, letter to Taut, 22 Nov. 1919, KEO, Kü 352/13.

30 Osthaus, 'Die Folkwang-Schule', p. 205.

31 See Hesse-Frielinghaus, *Osthaus*, pp. 481–9 for a full history of the *Folkwang-Schule* project.

32 Osthaus, 'Deutscher Werkbund', pp. 244–5.

33 See *ibid.*, p. 243.

34 Wyneken, *Schule und Jugendkultur*, p. 6.

35 *Ibid.*, p. 5.

36 See *ibid.*, p. 26.

37 For Hiller's critique of Wyneken's theories, see Kurt Hiller, *Gustav Wynekens Erziehungslehre und der Aktivismus* (Hanover, 1919).

38 Gustav Wyneken, 'Schöpferische Erziehung', *Ziel I*, pp. 121–34.

39 Taut, letter to Osthaus, 16 Dec. 1919, KEO, Kü 352/20.

40 Taut, letter to Osthaus, 24 Jan. 1920, KEO, Kü 353/26.

41 Gustav Wyneken, 'Der Anfang eines neuen Schullebens', *Das hohe Ufer*, I, no. 9 (September 1919), pp. 215–20.

42 Taut, 'Die Folkwangschule in Hagen Westf.', manuscript, KEO, Kü 353/33. At the same time as Taut and Wyneken were discussing what form the *Folkwang-Schule* should take, another former activist, Rudolf Kayser, was advocating a similar scheme. In an article in *Die Erhebung. Jahrbuch für neue Dichtung und Wertung: Zweites Buch* [hereafter *Erhebung II*] (Berlin, 1920), written at the end of 1919 or the beginning of 1920, Kayser suggested that special schools should be established on the land in order to promote in the new generation the *geistig* receptivity which the Activists had failed to awake in their own generation. 'The schools should be on the land and on the outskirts of the cities...far from all restraints, radiant with physical nakedness and movement, brotherly, sisterly, working, thinking, playing: this generation must succeed in reaching what was denied to us.' Rudolf Kayser, 'Kinderland', *Erhebung II* (Berlin, 1920), p. 286.

43 See Taut, letters to Osthaus, 22 Jan. 1920; 19 Feb. 1920; 5 Mar. 1920; KEO, Kü 353/27; 354/33; 354/39a.

44 Taut, letter to Osthaus, 9 Feb. 1920, KEO, Kü 354/34.

45 Klatt described his methods in *Die schöpferische Pause* (Jena, 1921). The book was very successful; 21,000 copies were sold between 1921 and 1928.

46 Heinrich Taut recalls that the school was dreadful. The staff were unqualified and there was little tuition. There was complete freedom to do nothing, and the food was inedible. The pupils' discontent was aggravated by the school's insistence that they should dance naked in the cold hall of the villa in order to find freedom of expression. As the pupils were of both sexes and aged thirteen and fourteen, this apparently led to embarrassment rather than freedom.

47 Osthaus, letter to Taut, 5 May 1920, KEO, Kü 354/42.

21. The Gläserne Kette

1 Taut, letter to the Gläserne Kette [hereafter GK], 28 Jan. 1920. In *Die gläserne Kette. Visionäre Architekturen aus dem Kreis um Bruno Taut 1919–1920*, exhibition catalogue. (Leverkusen and Berlin, 1963), p. 23. [Hereafter *Cat. GK*.]

2 Taut, letter to Osthaus, 14 Nov. 1919, KEO, Kü 352/12.

3 *Ibid.*

4 *Ibid.*

5 Bontempelli, quoted Poggioli, *Avant-Garde*, p. 67.

6 Taut, letter to Osthaus, 14 Nov. 1919, KEO, Kü 352/12.

7 Taut, letter to GK, 24 Nov. 1919. *Cat. GK*. p. 10.

8 *Ibid.*

9 *Ibid.*, p. 11.

10 *Ibid.*, p. 10.

11 Poggioli, *Avant-Garde*, p. 152.

12 Taut, letter to GK, 27 Dec. 1919, *Cat. GK*, p. 13.

13 Gropius, address to the AFK, March 1919.

14 In Taut, letter to GK, 23 Dec. 1919, *Cat. GK*, p. 12. This poem is incorrectly transcribed in the Gläserne Kette catalogue: it is also falsely attributed to Taut himself and incorrectly dated.

15 This characteristic of late Activism was commented on at the time by the critic Willi Wolfradt – one of the founders of the RGA. He called it *Zwischenkulturlichkeit* – the condition of being between two cultural eras. See Willi Wolfradt. 'Zwischen den Kulturen', *Die neue Rundschau*, XXX, no. 10 (October 1919), pp. 1188–1206.

16 See Steneberg, *Russische Kunst*, p. 12.

17 See Hausmann, *Am Anfang war Dada*, p. 58: 'One afternoon I was sitting with Baader in the Café Josty on Potsdamerplatz (Josty was the headquarters for Baader and myself).'

18 At this time Taut ate lunch almost every day at the Café Josty. The surviving correspondence of the radical takeover of the Werkbund in the autumn of 1919 shows that the same café was used as a meeting place by the Gropius/Taut faction. For example, Gropius wrote to Osthaus: 'Dear Osthaus! Poelzig, Taut, Klein, Bartning, Tessenow and Pankok will be at the Café Josty at 9 am on the 18 October, where we want to reach an agreement on the tactics for the meeting.' Gropius, letter to Osthaus, 9 Oct. 1919, KEO, Kü 347/309.

19 Compare, for example, Scheerbart's *KIKAKOKU* (1897), with Hugo Ball's *Lautgedichte* or the simultaneous poetry of Huelsenbeck and Tzara.

20 Taut, letter to GK, 27 Dec. 1919, *Cat. GK*, p. 19.

21 Poggioli, *Avant-Garde*, p. 62.

22 *Ibid.*, p. 62.

23 Taut, letter to GK, 18 Jan. 1920, *Cat. GK*, p. 19.

24 Taut, letter to Osthaus, 23 Oct. 1919, KEO, Kü 351/8.

25 Taut, letter to Osthaus, 25 Oct. 1919, KEO, Kü 351/9.

26 *Ibid.*

27 *Ibid.*

28 There was also a plan at this time that Taut should illustrate a selection of the works of Scheerbart for publication by the Folkwang Verlag. The project failed, however, as Scheerbart's widow refused to give the Folkwang Verlag the copyright permission. Taut explained why to Herr Fuhrmann, an employee of the Verlag: 'During his life Scheerbart always had to find a different publisher for each new work, in order to bring it out on terms which hardly brought him enough to support the barest existence. It is therefore quite understandable if the widow Scheerbart sees red when she hears the word "publisher".' Taut, letter to Fuhrmann, n.d., KEO, Kü 352/14.

29 Taut, 'Nieder der Seriosismus!', *Frühlicht*, 1 (January 1920), in *Stadtbaukunst* I, no. 1 (January 1920), p. 13.

30 As Poggioli has noted: 'the taste for destruction seems innate in the soul of a child'. *Avant-Garde*, p. 62.

31 Quoted: Rudolf Kayser, 'Kinderland', *Erhebung II*, p. 283.

32 Hermann Schüller, 'Naivität und Gemeinschaft', *Erhebung II*, p. 293.

33 Krayl, letter to Gropius, 2 May 1919, BA, GN 10. 14. pp. 326–7.

34 *Ibid.*

35 Poggioli, *Avant-Garde*, p. 201.

36 Hans Luckhardt, letter to GK, 31 May 1920, *Cat. GK*, p. 44.

37 Hans Scharoun, letter to GK, n.d., *Cat. GK*, p. 24.

38 Wassili Luckhardt, letter to GK, n.d. (January 1920), *Cat. GK*, pp. 18–19.

39 Hablik was a keen collector of crystalline stones, and his large collection is still kept in his former house in Itzehoe.

40 Adolf Behne, 'Die Zukunft unserer Architektur', *Sozialistische Monatshefte*, 27, LVI (31 January 1921), p. 90. Behne went on to say, 'It is unmistakable that the reappraisal has begun: the love of children's drawings, of primitive art, the works of a Paul Klee, a Paul Goesch, and of the younger architects.' (He then listed the names of Bruno Taut and the other twelve members of the Gläserne Kette.)

41 Wenzel Hablik, letter to GK, 28 July 1920, BA, GN 10, pp. 452–6.

42 Hablik, 'Erbauen eine Glashauses am Meere', letter to GK, 22 July 1920, *Cat. GK*, p. 58.

43 There is an interesting parallel between Finsterlin's preference for the polyp over the crystal and the Billionaire's exaltation of the coral over the cross in Kaiser's play *Die Koralle* (1917).

44 See, for example, Taut, letter to GK, 31 May 1920, *Cat. GK*, p. 41: 'Immerse yourselves, friends, in the intricately formulated reasoning of our "Prometh", and all of you will perhaps breathe a sigh of relief.'

45 See Hans Luckhardt, letter to GK, 30 Mar. 1920; *ibid.*, p. 38.

46 Taut, letter to GK, 26 Dec. 1919; *ibid.*, p. 12.

47 Bruno Taut, 'Architektur neuer Gemeinschaft', *Erhebung II*, pp. 278–9.

48 *Ibid.*, p. 271.

49 Taut, letter to GK, 15 April 1920, *Cat. GK*, p. 39.

50 Taut, letter to GK, 26 Dec. 1919, *Cat. GK*, p. 12. Christ, like Prometheus, represented an agonist ideal: the intellectual leader who was willing to sacrifice himself for mankind.

51 Taut, 'Architektur neuer Gemeinschaft', pp. 270–1. That such ideas were compatible at this time with the *Proletkult* can be seen from an article by Arthur Holitscher, also in *Erhebung II*. Holitscher, a co-founder of the BPK wrote: 'The leader is the man whose inner essence contains this core of strength and humility, this hard and pure crystal. Purity and radicalism. The pure radical.' Holitscher, 'Das Religiöse im sozialen Kampf', *Erhebung II*, p. 334.

52 Taut, letter to GK, 26 Dec. 1919, *Cat. GK*, p. 12.

53 Taut, 'Mein Weltbild', *Cat. GK*, p. 70. Compare Finsterlin, letter to GK, n.d., *Cat. GK*, p. 22: 'I don't know whether you are already so close to me in thought, whether my radiating enthusiasm already captures you so completely, like glass at the focal-point of its clear, transfigured soul.'

54 The analogy between architecture and religious belief was drawn in *Frühlicht* by the inclusion of several extracts from the Gospels, including John 21: the vision of the new Jerusalem.

55 Heinrich de Fries, 'Ansprache an eine imaginäre Versammlung der jungen Architekten', *Das Kunstblatt*, IV, no. 3 (March 1920), pp. 66–9.

56 Behne, in AFK, *Ruf zum Bauen* (Berlin, 1920), Introduction.

57 Bruno Taut, 'Siedlung Ruhland', *Die Volkswohnung*, II, no. 12 (24 June 1920), pp. 180–1.

58 Taut, 'Architektur neuer Gemeinschaft', p. 276.

59 *Ibid.*, p. 276.

60 Taut, letter to Osthaus, 9 Feb. 1920, KEO, Kü 353/34.

61 Taut, letter to GK, 15 April 1920, *Cat. GK*, p. 40.

62 Taut, letter to Osthaus, 29 April 1920, KEO, Kü 354/41.

63 Hans Luckhardt, letter to GK, 31 May 1920, *Cat. GK*, p. 47.

64 Taut, letter to GK, 5 Oct. 1920, *Cat. GK*, p. 60. It was in this comparatively late letter that Taut first used the title 'Gläserne Kette', a title which had been coined by a newly elected member of the group, the playwright Alfred Brust.

65 *Ibid.*, pp. 60–1.

66 *Ibid.*, p. 62.

67 Anon. (Bruno Taut? Hans Scharoun?), letter to GK, Christmas 1920, Scharoun-Nachlaß, Akademie der Künste, West Berlin.

68 *Ibid.*

69 *Ibid.*

70 *Ibid.*

71 *Ibid.*

22. Taut and the theatre

1 Taut, letter to Heinz Tiessen, 4 Oct. 1920, Akademie der Künst, West Berlin. Between 1922 and 1933, Tiessen was the conductor of Der junge Chor, a working men's choir in Berlin.

2 Taut, letter to Ludwig Berger, 7 July 1920, Berger-Archiv, Akademie der Künste, West Berlin.

3 Taut, letter to Berger, 8 Dec. 1920, Berger-Archiv.

4 Taut, letter to Felix Holländer, 2 Dec. 1920, Berger-Archiv. In 1920 Holländer had succeeded Max Rheinhardt as chief producer at the Großes Schauspielhaus, Berlin.

5 *Ibid.*

6 Taut, letter to Berger, 1 Jan. 1921, Berger-Archiv.

7 Taut, programme notes to *Die Jungfrau von Orleans*, Deutsches Theater, Berlin, February 1921. The fusion of drama and audience was the theme of an essay written by Hans Scharoun, which concluded: 'Form, colour,

words and sounds are part of us, they ring, glow and burn out of the audience: the audience plays itself and experiences a sense of unification through the pangs of sorrow and the transports of joy: this is us.' Scharoun, 'Gedanke zum Theaterraum', typescript, n.d., Scharoun-Nachlaß, Akademie der Künste, West Berlin.

8 Ludwig Sternaux, *Lokal-Anzeiger*, Berlin, 20 Feb. 1921.
9 Norbert Falk, *Berliner-Zeitung*, 21 Feb. 1921.
10 Fritz Engel, *Berliner Tageblatt*, 21 Feb. 1921.

23. The end of an avant-garde

1 See Georg Lukács, '"Größe und Verfall" des Expressionismus' (1934), *Werke* (Neuwied and Berlin, 1971), IV, pp. 109–49.
2 *Ibid.*, p. 136.
3 *Ibid.*, pp. 127–8.
4 *Ibid.*, p. 142.
5 *Ibid.*, p. 143.
6 *Ibid.*
7 Hans Luckhardt, letter to GK, 31 May 1920, *Cat. GK*, p. 46.
8 The *Farbenstreit* at Magdeburg represented the re-enactment on the public stage of the battles which the Activist avant-garde had fought within the profession in 1918 and 1919. For a detailed account of the *Farbenstreit*, see Rieger, 'Die farbige Stadt', pp. 67–90.
9 During the autumn and winter of 1919/20 the AFK went into a conspicuous decline. As the Novembergruppe had already done, the AFK ceased to act as a radical pressure group and functioned primarily as an exhibiting body. Behne suggested that the group should be dissolved in October 1920 (see BA, GN 10. 7. 165), but it was allowed to limp on until 30 May 1921, when the end finally came.
10 Paul Westheim, 'Das "Ende des Expressionismus"', *Das Kunstblatt*, IV, no. 6 (June 1920), p. 188.
11 H. von Wedderkop, 'Shimmi greift ein', *Der Querschnitt*, I, no. 2/3 (May 1921), p. 88.
12 Behne, letter to Gropius, 9 Dec. 1920, BA, GN 10. 7. 156.
13 Behne, 'Die Zukunft unserer Architecktur', p. 91.
14 Lukács, '"Größe und Verfall" des Expressionismus', p. 145.
15 Behne, 'Die Zukunft unserer Architektur', p. 92.
16 For example: Adolf Behne 'Vorschlag einer brüderlichen Zusammenkunft der Künstler aller Länder', *Sozialistische Monatshefte*, 25, LII (3 March 1919), pp. 155–7; 'Die Pflicht zur Wahrhaftigkeit', *Sozialistische Monatshefte*, 25, LIII (4 August 1919), pp. 720–4; 'Das degenerierte Frankreich und das jugendliche Deutschland', *Sozialistische Monatshefte*, 25, LIII (29 December 1919), pp. 1220–2.
17 H. Th. Wijdeveld, letter to the AFK, January 1919, BA, GN 10. 19. 490.
18 Adolf Behne, 'Holländische Baukunst in der Gegenwart', *Wasmuths Monatshefte für Baukunst*, VI, no. 1/2 (1921/2), pp. 1–8.
19 See 'Aufruf an die revolutionäre französische geistige Jugend', *Das Tribunal*, I, no. 8/9 (August/September 1919), pp. 95–8: 'We propose the creation of an annual congress of the *geistig* men of all lands...They will make up a first parliament of *Geist*.'
20 See Osthaus, letter to Taut, 6 Dec. 1919, KEO, Kü 352/18, and Taut, letter to Osthaus, n.d., KEO, Kü 352/19.
21 Gropius, letter to Behne, 25 April 1919, BA, GN 10. 5. 137.
22 Poggioli, *Avant-Garde*, p. 221.

Conclusion

1 Bruno Taut, *Bauen: Der neue Wohnbau* (Leipzig, 1927), p. 12.

2 Bruno Taut, *Die neue Baukunst in Europa und Amerika* (Stuttgart, 1929), p. 40. Compare: Sigfried Giedion, *Space, Time and Architecture* (Cambridge, Mass., 1949), pp. 417–18.

> German Expressionism had its beginnings previous to the war, continued to develop while the war lasted, and reached its height in the years immediately after the war. The movement eloquently states the grievances of mishandled humanity and indicts a tragic situation. But there is a fundamental difference between Expressionism and other movements we have encountered – Cubism, Futurism, and the rest. Faustean outbursts against an inimical world and the cries of outraged humanity cannot create new levels of achievement. They remain transitory facts – however moving they may be – and not constituent ones...The Expressionist influence could not be a healthy one or perform any service for architecture.

It is amusing to note that Giedion himself had a skeleton in his cupboard. He wrote Expressionist plays in the immediate post-war years. One of them, *Arbeit*, set in an architect's house, was produced in 1918 by Max Reinhardt in the Kleines Schauspielhaus, Berlin.

3 CIAM, *Charter of Athens* (1933), Paragraph 92.

4 One must therefore reject the analysis of conservative polemicists who see architectural modernism and Stalinism as complementary tendencies. See, for example, David Watkin, *Morality and Architecture* (Oxford, 1977).

5 Poggioli, *Avant-Garde*, p. 96.

6 Massimo Bontempelli, *L'Avventura novecentista* (Florence, 1930), quoted Poggioli, *Avant-Garde*, p. 69.

7 Taut, 'Architektur-Programm'.

8 Gropius, *Ausstellung für unbekannte Architekten*.

9 Lewis Mumford, *Technics and Civilization* (New York, 1934), pp. 40–1.

10 Hans Luckhardt, letter to GK, 31 May 1920, *Cat. GK*, p. 44.

11 Taut, *Stadtkrone*, p. 60.

12 Mies van der Rohe, 'Baukunst und Zeitwille', *Der Querschnitt*, IV, no. 1 (Spring 1924), p. 31.

13 Gropius, *Internationale Architektur* (Munich, 1925), p. 7.

14 Taut, *Bauen*, pp. 1–2.

15 *Ibid.*, p. 70.

16 Ludwig Hilberseimer, *Internationale neue Baukunst* (Stuttgart, 1927), Introduction.

17 Ludwig Hilberseimer, *Großstadtarchitektur* (Stuttgart, 1927), p. 103.

18 Mies van der Rohe, 'Baukunst und Zeitwille', p. 32.

19 Bruno Taut, 'Die Kunst der Siedlung', *Das neue Reich*, 19 (1920), p. 9.

20 Taut, *Die neue Baukunst*, p. 7.

21 Taut, letter to Hablik, 5 Jan. 1922, Ungers Collection, Cologne.

Select Bibliography

Primary and archival sources

Bauhaus-Archiv, West Berlin (BA).
Ludwig-Berger-Archiv, Akademie der Künste, West Berlin.
Hermann Finsterlin Collection, Staatsgalerie, Stuttgart.
Hablik-Archiv, Itzehoe.
Karl-Ernst-Osthaus-Archiv, Hagen (KEO).
Marlene Poelzig Collection, Hamburg.
Staatsbibliothek, Preußischer Kulturbesitz, Handschriftenabteilung, West Berlin.
Professor Heinrich Taut Collection, Lehnitz.
Technical University, Berlin, Drawings Collection.
Scharoun-Archiv, Akademie der Künste, West Berlin.
Oswald M. Ungers Collection, Cologne.
Werkbund-Archiv, West Berlin.

Printed Sources

Arbeitsrat für Kunst. Programme – December 1918, *Mitteilungen des Deutschen Werkbundes*, 1918, no. 4, pp. 14–15.
Arbeitsrat für Kunst (Gropius, Bruno Taut, Behne), *Ausstellung für unbekannte Architekten*. Berlin, 1919.
Arbeitsrat für Kunst. *Ja! Stimmen des Arbeitsrates für Kunst in Berlin*. Berlin, 1919.
Arnold Armin. *Die Literatur des Expressionismus*. Stuttgart, 1966.
Avenarius, Ferdinand, 'Farbige Häuser', *Der Kunstwart*, XIII, no. 13 (April 1900), pp. 37–8.
Bahr, Hermann. *Expressionism*. London, 1925.
Ballod, Carl. *Die Ackerstadt und die städtische Selbstversorgung*. Berlin, 1918.
Banham, Reyner. 'The Glass Paradise', *Architectural Review*, CXXV, no. 745 (February 1959), pp. 87–9.
    Theory and Design in the First Machine Age. London, 1960.
Bayer, H. *Bauhaus: 50 Years*. London, 1968.
Behne, Adolf. 'Die Leipziger Baufachausstellung', *Die Tat*, V, no. 5 (August 1913), pp. 504–7.
    'Moderne Kunstbücher', *Die Tat*, V, no. 9 (December 1913), pp. 936–42.
    'Das Monument des Eisens von Taut und Hoffmann auf der internationalen Baufachausstellung in Leipzig', *Das Kunstgewerbeblatt*, XXV, no. 5 (February 1914), pp. 86–9.
    'Bruno Taut', *Der Sturm*, IV, no. 198/9 (February 1914), pp. 182–3.
    'Deutsche Expressionisten', *Der Sturm*, V, no. 17/18 (December 1914), pp. 114–15.

264

'Expressionistische Architektur', *Der Sturm*, V, no. 19/20 (January 1915), p. 135.

'Der Haß der Neutralen', *Die Tat*, VII, no. 4 (July 1915), pp. 340–1.

'Gedanken über Kunst und Zweck, dem Glashaus gewidmet', *Das Kunstgewerbeblatt*, XXVII, no. 1 (October 1915), pp. 1–4.

Zur neuen Kunst. Berlin, 1915.

'Unsere Baukunst und das Morgenland', *Sozialistische Monatshefte*, 22, XLIV, no. 3 (17 February 1916), pp. 155–7.

'Kritik des Werkbundes', *Die Tat*, IX, no. 1 (August 1917), pp. 430–8.

'Wem gehört die Gotik?', *Sozialistische Monatshefte*, 23, XLIX, no. 22 (31 October 1917), pp. 1126–9.

'Biologie und Kubismus', *Die Tat*, IX, no. 8 (November 1917), pp. 694–705.

'Ist das Schwäche?', *Sozialistische Monatshefte*, 23, XLIX, no. 25/6 (19 December 1917), pp. 1285–8.

'Die Einheit der russischen Kunst', *Sozialistische Monatshefte*, 24, LI (6 August 1918), pp. 745–8.

'Die Überwindung des Tektonischen in der russischen Baukunst', *Sozialistische Monatshefte*, 24, LI (3 September 1918), pp. 833–7.

'Die russische Ästhetik', *Sozialistische Monatshefte*, 24, LI (24 September 1918), pp. 894–6.

'Unsere moralische Krisis', *Sozialistische Monatshefte*, 25, LII (20 January 1919), pp. 34–8.

'Vorschlag einer brüderlichen Zusammenkunft der Künstler aller Länder', *Sozialistische Monatshefte*, 25, LII (3 March 1919), pp. 155–7.

'Der Arbeitsrat für Kunst in Berlin', *Der Cicerone*, XI, no. 9 (April 1919), p. 264.

'Unbekannte Architekten', *Sozialistische Monatshefte*, 25, LII (28 April 1919), pp. 422–3.

'Kritische Kunstbetrachtungen', *Das hohe Ufer*, I, no. 6 (June 1919), pp. 134–5.

'Die Pflicht zur Wahrhaftigkeit', *Sozialistische Monatshefte*, 25, LIII (4 August 1919), pp. 720–5.

'Werkstattbesuche: Jefim Golyscheff', *Der Cicerone*, XI, no. 22 (November 1919), pp. 722–6.

'Das degenerierte Frankreich und das jugendliche Deutschland', *Sozialistische Monatshefte*, 25, LIII (29 December 1919), pp. 1220–2.

Die Wiederkehr der Kunst. Leipzig, 1919.

'Werkbund', *Sozialistische Monatshefte*, 26, LIV (26 January 1920), pp. 68–9.

'Werkstattbesuche: Paul Goesch', *Der Cicerone*, XII, no. 4 (February 1920), pp. 150–4.

'Sozialisierung von Kunst und Wissenschaft', *Sozialistische Monatshefte*, 26, LIV (8 March 1920), pp. 191–4.

'Ein Vorschlag', *Sozialistische Monatshefte*, 26, LIV (12 April 1920), pp. 260–3.

'Paul Goesch', *Jahrbuch der jungen Kunst*, no. 1 (1920), pp. 68 ff.

'Europa und die Architektur', *Sozialistische Monatshefte*, 27, LVI (17 January 1921), pp. 28–33.

'Die Zukunft unserer Architektur', *Sozialistische Monatshefte*, 27, LVI (31 January 1921), pp. 90–4.

'Deutschland und die europäische Kunstbewegung', *Sozialistische Monatshefte*, 27, LVI (11 April 1921), pp. 297–301.

'Die neue Aufgabe der Kunst', *Sozialistische Monatshefte*, 27, LVIII (19 September 1921), pp. 813–15.

'Holländische Baukunst in der Gegenwart', *Wasmuths Monatshefte für Baukunst*, VI, no. 1/2 (1921/2), pp. 1–8.

'Architekten', *Frühlicht* (Magdeburg Edition), no. 2 (Winter 1921/2), pp. 55–8.

'Junge französische Architektur', *Sozialistische Monatshefte*, 28, LVIII (8 June 1922), pp. 512–19.

Behrendt, Walter C. *Der Kampf um den Stil in Kunstgewerbe und Architektur.* Stuttgart, 1920.

Behrens, Peter & de Fries, Heinrich. *Vom sparsamen Bauen.* Berlin, 1919.

Benjamin, Walter. *Das Kunstwerk im Zeitalter seiner technischen Reproduzierbarkeit.* Frankfurt, 1963.

Bloch, Ernst. 'Zur deutschen Revolution', *Revolution*, II (30 November 1918), p. 11.

Geist der Utopie. Munich, 1918.

Erbschaft dieser Zeit. Frankfurt, 1973.

Borsi, Franco & König, Giovanni Klaus. *Architettura dell' Espressionismo.* Genoa, 1967.

Brod, Max. 'Aktivismus und Rationalismus', *Das Ziel II* (1918), pp. 56–65.

Bund zum Ziel. 'Leitsätze', *Das Ziel III* (1919), pp. 218–19.

Bürger, Peter. *Theorie der Avantgarde.* Frankfurt, 1974.

Cacciari, Massimo. *Metropolis.* Rome, 1973.

Carroll, John. *Break-Out from the Crystal Palace: the Anarcho-Psychological Critique.* London, 1974.

Cohn, Norman. *The Pursuit of the Millennium.* London, 1970.

Collins, Peter. *Changing Ideals in Modern Architecture.* London, 1967.

Conrads, Ulrich. *Programme und Manifeste zur Architektur des 20. Jahrhunderts.* Frankfurt, 1964.

Conrads, Ulrich & Sperlich, Hans G. *Phantastische Architektur.* Stuttgart, 1960.

Craig, Gordon A. 'Engagement and Neutrality in Weimar Germany', *Journal of Contemporary History*, II, no. 2 (April 1967), pp. 49–63.

Cürlis, Hans & Stephany, H. *Die künstlerischen und wirtschaftlichen Irrwege unserer Baukunst.* Munich, 1916.

Diederichs, Eugen. *Politik des Geistes.* Jena, 1920.

Leben und Werke. Jena, 1936.

Deak, Istvan. *Weimar Germany's Left-Wing Intellectuals: a Political History of the Weltbühne und its Circle.* Berkeley, 1968.

Deri, Max. *Einführung in die Kunst der Gegenwart.* Leipzig, 1919.

Döblin, Alfred. *Aufsätze zur Literatur.* Olten, 1963.

Doren, Alfred. 'Wunschräume und Wunschzeiten', *Kulturwissenschaftliche Bibliothek Warburg, Vorträge 1924–1925.* Leipzig, 1927.

Droysen, Johann Gustav. *Grundriß der Historik.* Leipzig, 1868.

Eckstein, Hans. *50 Jahre Deutscher Werkbund.* Frankfurt, 1958.

Endell, August. *Die Schönheit der Großstadt.* Stuttgart, 1908.

Erste russische Kunstausstellung Berlin 1922 (Catalogue). Galerie van Diemen und Co., Berlin, 1922.

Fähnders, Walter & Rector, Martin. *Literatur im Klassenkampf.* Munich, 1974.

Fechter, Paul. *Der Expressionismus.* Munich, 1914.

Franciscono, Marcel. *Walter Gropius and the Creation of the Bauhaus in Weimar.* Urbana, 1971.

Frecot, Janos, Geist, Johann Friedrich & Kerbs, Diethart. *Fidus 1868–1948.* Munich, 1972.

Friedmann, Hermann & Mann, Otto. *Deutsche Literatur im 20. Jahrhundert* (5th Edition). Berne, 1967.

de Fries, Heinrich. 'Ansprache an eine imaginäre Versammlung der jungen Architekten', *Das Kunstblatt*, IV, no. 3 (March 1920), pp. 65–72.

Greenberg, Allan C. 'Artists and the Weimar Republic: Dada and the Bauhaus 1917–25'. (Unpublished PhD dissertation, University of Illinois, 1967).

Gordon, D. E. 'On the origin of the word "Expressionism"', *Journal of the Warburg and Courtauld Institutes*, XXIX (1966), pp. 368–85.

Gropius, Walter. 'Die neue Baukunst', *Das hohe Ufer*, I, no. 4 (April 1919), pp. 87–8.

'"Sparsamer Hausrat" und falsche Dürftigkeit', *Das hohe Ufer*, I, no. 7 (July 1919), pp. 178–80.

'Baukunst im freien Volksstaat', *Deutscher Revolutions-Almanach für das Jahr 1919*. Berlin, 1919, pp. 134–6.

Programm des Staatlichen Bauhauses in Weimar. Weimar, 1919.

Haag-Bletter, Rosemarie. 'Paul Scheerbart's Architectural Fantasies', *Journal of the Society of Architectural Historians*, XXXIV, no. 2 (May 1975), pp. 83–97.

Haenisch, Konrad. *Sozialdemokratische Kulturpolitik*. Berlin, 1919.

Hartmann, Kristiana. *Deutsche Gartenstadtbewegung*. Munich, 1976.

Hasche, Hans. *Die kleine und große Stadt. Nachdenkliches von Heinrich Tessenow*. Munich, 1961.

Hausmann, Raoul. *Am Anfang war Dada*. Steinbach/Gießen, 1972.

Heller, Erich. *The Disinherited Mind – Essays in Modern German Literature and Thought*. Cambridge, 1962.

Hesse-Frielinghaus, Herta, Hoff, August, Erben, Walter & others. *Karl Ernst Osthaus*. Recklinghausen, 1971.

Heuss, Theodor. 'Phantasie und Baukunst', *Der Kunstwart*, XXXII, no. 19 (July 1919), pp. 17–20.

Hilberseimer, Ludwig. 'Paul Scheerbart und die Architekten', *Das Kunstblatt*, III, no. 9 (September 1919), pp. 271–4.

'Arbeiterkunstausstellung', *Sozialistische Monatshefte*, 26, LIV (26 January 1920), pp. 64–5.

'Unsere Geistigen', *Sozialistische Monatshefte*, 27, LVI (6 June 1921), pp. 486–9.

'Architektur', *Das Kunstblatt*, VI, no. 3 (March 1922), p. 132.

Hildebrandt, Hans. *Expressionismus in der Malerei*. Stuttgart, 1919.

Hiller, Kurt. *Die Weisheit der Langenweile*. Leipzig, 1913.

(ed.). *Das Ziel. Aufrüfe zu tätigem Geist*. Munich & Berlin, 1916.

'Philosophie des Ziels', *Das Ziel I*, pp. 187–217.

(ed.). *Tätiger Geist! Zweites der Ziel-Jahrbücher*. Munich & Berlin, 1918.

'Ein deutsches Herrenhaus', *Das Ziel II*, pp. 379–425.

'Künstler und Kämpfer', *Das Tribunal*, I, no. 1 (January 1919), pp. 7–8.

'Ortsbestimmung des Aktivismus', *Die Erhebung I* (1919), pp. 360–76.

(ed.). *Das Ziel. Jahrbücher für geistige Politik III*. Leipzig, 1919.

'Anti-Kain', *Das Ziel III*, pp. 24–32.

'Überlegungen zur Eschatologie und Methodologie des Aktivismus', *Das Ziel III*, pp. 195–217.

(ed.). *Das Ziel. Jahrbücher für geistige Politik IV*. Munich, 1920.

'Logokratie oder ein Weltbund des Geistes', *Das Ziel IV*, pp. 217–47.

Der Aufbruch zum Paradies. Munich, 1922.

(ed.). *Geistige Politik! Fünftes der Ziel-Jahrbücher*. Leipzig & Vienna, 1924.

Leben gegen die Zeit. Hamburg, 1969.

Holitscher, Arthur. 'Das Religiöse im sozialen Kampf', *Die Erhebung II* (1920), pp. 322–37.

Horkheimer, Max & Adorno, Theodor. *Dialektik der Aufklärung* (4th Edition). Frankfurt, 1977.

Horneffer, August. 'Das heilige Haus', *Die Tat*, III, no. 2 (February 1912), pp. 544–59.

Huelsenbeck, Richard. *Dada! Eine literarische Dokumentation*. Hamburg, 1964.

Hunt, Richard N. *The Creation of the Weimar Republic*. Lexington, 1969.

Huse, Norbert. *'Neues Bauen' 1918 bis 1933*. Munich, 1975.

Jay, Martin. *The Dialectical Imagination*. London, 1973.

Jeanneret, Charles-Edouard (Le Corbusier). *Étude sur le mouvement d'art décorative en Allemagne*. La Chaux-de-Fonds, 1912.

Junghanns, Kurt. 'Die Beziehung zwischen deutschen und sowjetischen Architekten in den Jahren 1917 bis 1933', *Wissenschaftliche Zeitschrift der Humboldt Universität*, XVI, no. 3 (1967), pp. 369–81.

Bruno Taut 1880–1938. Berlin (DDR), 1970.

Kandinsky, Wassily. *Über das Geistige in der Kunst* (2nd Edition). München, 1912.

Die gläserne Kette. Visionäre Architekturen aus dem Kreis um Bruno Taut (Exhibition Catalogue). Leverkusen & Berlin, 1963.

Kliemann, Helga. *Die Novembergruppe*. Berlin, 1969.

Kohtz, Otto. *Gedanken über Architektur*. Berlin, 1909.

Kolinsky, Eva. *Engagierter Expressionismus*. Stuttgart, 1970.

Kratzsch, Gerhard. *Kunstwart und Dürerbund*. Göttingen, 1969.

Kreuzer, Helmut. *Die Bohème*. Stuttgart, 1968.

Kropotkin, Peter (trans. Gustav Landauer). *Gegenseitige Hilfe in der Entwicklung*. Leipzig, 1904.

Kulturmann, Udo. *Wassili und Hans Luckhardt*. Tübingen, 1958.

'Das Kunstprogramm des Kommissariats für Volksaufklärung in Rußland' *Das Kunstblatt*, III, no. 3 (March 1919), pp. 91–3.

Landauer, Gustav. *Aufruf zum Sozialismus* (2nd Edition). Berlin, 1919.

Lane, Barbara Miller. *Architecture and Politics in Germany, 1918–1945*. Cambridge, Mass., 1968.

Le Corbusier-Saugnier. 'Rom', *Das Kunstblatt*, VI, no. 6 (June 1922), pp. 255–64.

Leonhard, Rudolf. *Alles und Nichts!* Berlin, 1920.

Lindahl, Göran. 'Von der Zukunftskathedrale bis zur Wohnmaschine', *Idea and Form* (Uppsala Studies in History of Art), I (1959), pp. 226–82.

Linke, Felix. 'Die neue Architektur', *Sozialistische Monatshefte*, 20, II, no. 18 (14 October 1914), pp. 1133–9.

Linse, Ulrich. *Gustav Landauer und die Revolutionszeit*. Berlin, 1977.

Lipps, Theodor. *Ästhetik* (2nd Edition). Leipzig, 1914.

Lukács, Georg. '"Größe und Verfall" des Expressionismus', *Werke*, IV, Neuwied & Berlin, 1971.

Lunn, Eugene. *Prophet of Community. The Romantic Socialism of Gustav Landauer*. Berkeley, 1974.

Mann, Heinrich. 'Geist und Tat', *Das Ziel I* (1916), pp. 1–8.

Sieben Jahre. Vienna, 1924.

Mann, Thomas. *Briefe 1889–1936*. Frankfurt, 1961.

Mannheim, Karl. *Ideology and Utopia*. London, 1936.

Maurer, Charles B. *Call to Revolution: The Mystical Anarchism of Gustav Landauer*. Detroit, 1971.

Mebes, Paul. *Um 1800*. Berlin, 1908.

Meidner, Ludwig. 'An alle Künstler, Dichter, Musiker', *Das Kunstblatt*, III, no. 1 (January 1919), pp. 29–30.

Mendelsohn, Erich. 'Das Problem einer neuen Baukunst. Vortrag im Arbeitsrat für Kunst, Berlin, 1919', in: Mendelsohn, *Das Gesamtschaffen des Architekten*. Berlin, 1930.

(Beyer, Oskar, ed.). *Briefe eines Architekten*. München, 1961.

Müller, Sebastian. *Kunst und Industrie*. Munich, 1974.

Müller-Wulckow, Walter. 'Zukünftige Architektur', *Das hohe Ufer*, I, no. 3 (March 1919), pp. 65–8.

Aufbau Architektur! Berlin, 1919.

Muthesius, Hermann. *Handarbeit und Massenerzeugnis*. Berlin, 1917.

Kleinhaus und Kleinsiedlung. Munich, 1918.

Obrist, Hermann. 'Kunst und Sozialdemokratie', *Sozialistische Monatshefte*, 23, XLIX, no. 23 (14 November 1917), pp. 1170–3.

Osthaus, Karl Ernst. 'Die Kunst im Aufbau der neuen Lebensform', *Mitteilungen des Deutschen Werkbundes*, 1918, no. 5/6, pp. 2–5.
  'Der Luxus. Ein Dialog', *Das hohe Ufer*, I, no. 9 (September 1919), pp. 226–34.
  'Deutscher Werkbund', *Das hohe Ufer*, I, no. 10 (October 1919), pp. 237–45.
Pascal, Roy. *From Naturalism to Expressionism. German Literature and Society 1880–1918*. London, 1973.
Pasqualotto, Giangiorgio. *Avanguardia e tecnologia. Walter Benjamin, Max Bense e i problemi dell'estetica technologica*. Rome, 1971.
Paulsen, Wolfgang. *Expressionismus und Aktivismus: Eine Typologische Untersuchung*. Berne, 1935.
Pehnt, Wolfgang. *Die Architektur des Expressionismus*. Stuttgart, 1973.
Pevsner, Nikolaus. 'Finsterlin and some others', *Architectural Review*, CXXXII, no. 789 (November 1962), pp. 353–7.
  'The Fantastical Twenties', *Architectural Review*, CXXXV, no. 806 (April 1964), p. 241.
Pfannkuch, Peter. *Hans Scharoun*. Berlin, 1975.
Pinthus, Kurt. *Menschheitsdämmerung*. Berlin, 1920.
Platz, Gustav A. *Die Baukunst der neuesten Zeit*. Berlin. 1927.
Poelzig, Hans. 'Werkbundaufgaben', *Mitteilungen des Deutschen Werkbundes*, 1919, no. 4, pp. 109–24.
  'Rede zur Werkbund-Tagung', *Das Kunstblatt*, III, no. 10 (October 1919), pp. 307–16.
  'Staatliches Bauwesen', *Das hohe Ufer*, I, no. 12 (December 1919), pp. 283–4.
Poggioli, Renato. *The Theory of the Avant-Garde*. Cambridge, Mass., 1968.
Polanyi, Michael. *Beyond Nihilism*. Cambridge, 1960.
Politischer Rat geistiger Arbeiter, Berlin. Programme, *Das Ziel III* (1919), pp. 219–23.
Ponten, Josef. *Architektur die nicht gebaut wurde*. Stuttgart, 1925.
Popper, Karl. *The Poverty of Historicism*. London, 1961.
Pörtner, Paul. *Literaturrevolution 1910–1925* (2 Volumes). Neuwied, 1961.
Posener, Julius. *Hans Poelzig*. Berlin, 1970.
Rieger, Hans J. 'Die farbige Stadt'. (PhD dissertation, Zurich, 1976).
Riezler, Walter. 'Revolution und Baukunst', *Mitteilungen des Deutschen Werkbundes*, (1919) no. 1, p. 19.
Ringbom, Sixten. 'Art in the "Epoch of the Great Spiritual": Occult Elements in the Early Theory of Abstract Painting', *Journal of the Warburg and Courtauld Institutes*, XXIX (1966), pp. 386–418.
Rothe, Wolfgang. *Der Aktivismus 1915–1920*. Munich, 1969.
  Expressionismus als Literatur. Berne, 1969.
  (ed.). *Deutsche Großstadtlyrik vom Naturalismus bis zur Gegenwart*. Stuttgart, 1973.
Rubiner, Ludwig. 'Die Änderung der Welt', *Das Ziel I* (1916), pp. 99–120.
  Das himmlische Licht. Leipzig, 1916.
  Kameraden der Menschheit. Potsdam, 1919.
Ruosch, Christian. Die Phantastische-surreale Welt im Werk Paul Scheerbarts. (PhD dissertation, Berne, 1970).
Ryder, A. J. *The German Revolution of 1918*. Cambridge, 1967.
Scheerbart, Paul. 'Dynamitkrieg und Dezentralization', *Gegenwart*, LXXVI (November 1909), pp. 905–8.
  'Die Entwicklung der Stadt', *Gegenwart*, LXXVII (June 1910), pp. 497–8.
  Glasarchitektur. Berlin, 1914.
  Dichterische Hauptwerke. Stuttgart, 1962.
  & Taut, Bruno. *Glass Architecture and Alpine Architecture* (ed. by Dennis Sharp). London, 1972.
Scheffler, Karl. *Die Architektur der Großstadt*. Berlin, 1913.
  Der Geist der Gotik. Leipzig, 1917.

'Die Kunst und die Revolution', *Kunst und Künstler*, XVII, no. 5 (1 February 1919), pp. 165–7.

Die fetten und die mageren Jahre. Munich, 1948.

Schickele, René. *Revolution, Bolschewismus und das Ideal*. Berlin, 1918.

Schmitt, Hans-Jürgen. *Die Expressionismusdebatte*. Frankfurt, 1973.

Schmitz, Hermann. *Revolution der Gesinnung: Preußische Kulturpolitik und Volks-gemeinschaft seit dem 9. November, 1919*. Neubabelsberg, 1931.

Schreyer, Lothar. *Erinnerungen an Sturm und Bauhaus*. Munich, 1956.

Simmel, Georg. *Die Großstadt und das Geistesleben*. Dresden, 1903.

Brücke und Tür (Essays). Stuttgart, 1957.

Soergel, Albert. *Dichtung und Dichter der Zeit*. Leipzig, 1911.

Sokel, Walter H. *The Writer in Extremis. Expressionism in Twentieth-Century Literature*. Stanford, 1959.

Sörgel, Hermann. *Theorie der Baukunst, Vol I, Architektur-Aesthetik*. Munich, 1918.

Steneberg, Eberhard. *Russische Kunst Berlin 1919–1932*. Berlin, 1969.

Stirner, Max. *Der Einzige und sein Eigentum*. Leipzig, 1901.

von Sydow, Eckhart. *Die deutsche expressionistische Kultur und Malerei*. Berlin, 1920.

Die Kultur der Dekadenz. Dresden, 1922.

Tafuri, Manfredo. *Architecture and Utopia*. Cambridge, Mass., 1976.

Taut, Bruno. 'Zu den Arbeiten der Architekten Bruno Taut und Hoffmann', *Moderne Bauformen*, XII, no. 3 (1913), pp. 121–41.

'Eine Notwendigkeit', *Der Sturm*, IV, no. 196/7 (February 1914), pp. 174–5.

Glashaus: Werkbundausstellung Cöln 1914. Cologne, 1914.

'Das Problem des Opernbaues', *Sozialistische Monatshefte*, 20, I, no. 6 (26 March 1914), pp. 355–7.

'Krieger-Ehrung', in: Deutsche Gartenstadtgesellschaft, *Unseren Kriegsinvali-den Heim und Werkstatt in Gartensiedlungen*. Leipzig, 1915, pp. 76–7.

'Krieger-Ehrung', *Das Kunstgewerbeblatt*, XXVI, no. 9 (June 1915), pp. 174–6.

'Krieger-Ehrung', *Die Tat*, VII, no. 3 (June 1915), pp. 257–9.

'Der Roland von Brandenburg', *Das Kunstgewerbeblatt*, XXVII, no. 6 (March 1916), pp. 111–13.

'Reiseeindrücke aus Konstantinopel', *Das Kunstgewerbeblatt*, XXVIII, no. 3 (December 1916), pp. 49–50.

'Die Vererdung. Zum Problem des Totenkults', *Die Werkstatt der Kunst*, XVI, no. 18 (January 1917), pp. 220–2.

Untitled article on film and architecture, *Der Städtebau*, XIV, no. 2/3 (1917), pp. 32–3.

'Eindrücke aus Kowno', *Sozialistische Monatshefte*, 24, LI (24 September 1918), pp. 897–901.

'An die sozialistische Regierung', *Sozialistische Monatshefte*, 24, LI (26 November 1918), pp. 1050–2.

'Ein neues künstlerisches Programm', *Die Bauwelt*, IX, no. 52 (26 December 1918), p. 5.

'Ein neues künstlerisches Programm', *Mitteilungen des Deutschen Werkbundes*, 1918, no. 4, pp. 14–15.

'Ein Architektur-Programm', *Mitteilungen des Deutschen Werkbundes*, 1918, no. 4, pp. 16–18.

'Ex Oriente Lux', *Das hohe Ufer*, I, no. 1 (January 1919), pp. 15–18.

'Für die neue Baukunst!', *Das Kunstblatt*, III, no. 1 (January 1919), pp. 16–24.

'Die Erde eine gute Wohnung', *Die Volkswohnung*, I, no. 4 (24 February 1919), pp. 45–8.

'Alte Bauweisen in neuzeitlicher Form', *Die Volkswohnung*, I, no. 5 (10 March 1919), pp. 69–70.

'Der Sozialismus der Künstlers', *Sozialistische Monatshefte*, 25, LII (24 March 1919), pp. 259–62.

'Für den Werkbund', (typescript), (Summer/Autumn 1919), Bauakademie der DDR, East Berlin.

'Zum neuen Theaterbau', *Das hohe Ufer*, I, no. 8 (August 1919), pp. 204–8.

'Zuviel Gerede vom Architektur-Unterricht', *Die Bauwelt*, X, no. 32 (7 August 1919), pp. 9–10.

'Theodor Goecke: Ein Nachruf', *Die Bauwelt*, X, no. 34 (21 August 1919), p. 13.

'Rede des Bundeskanzlers von Europa am 24. April 1993 vor dem europäischen Parlament', *Sozialistische Monatshefte*, 25, LIII (25 August 1919), pp. 816–19.

[Hugo Zehder]. 'Aufruf zum farbigen Bauen!', *Die Bauwelt*, X, no. 38 (18 September 1919), p. 11.

'Beobachtungen über Farbenwirkung aus meiner Praxis', *Die Bauwelt*, X, no. 38 (18 September 1919), pp. 12–13.

'Aufruf zum farbigen Bauen!', *Das hohe Ufer*, I, no. 11 (November 1919), p. 272.

'Farbenwirkungen aus meiner Praxis', *Das hohe Ufer*, I, no. 11 (November 1919), pp. 263–6.

'Bildschreine', *Das hohe Ufer*, I, no. 12 (December 1919), p. 305.

Die Stadtkrone. (Mit Beiträgen von Paul Scheerbart, Erich Baron, Adolf Behne). Jena, 1919.

Alpine Architektur. Hagen, 1919.

'Drei Siedlungen', *Wasmuths Monatshefte für Baukunst*, IV, no. 5/6 (1919/20), pp. 183–93.

'Glasbau', *Stadtbaukunst alter und neuer Zeit*, I, no. 8 (1920), pp. 120–3.

'Glaserzeugung und Glasbau', *Qualität*, I, no. 1/2 (April/May 1920), pp. 9–14.

'Künstlerisches Filmprogramm', *Das hohe Ufer*, II, no. 5/6 (May/June 1920), pp. 86–8.

'Siedlung Ruhland', *Die Volkswohnung*, II, no. 12 (24 June 1920), pp. 179–82.

'Mein Weltbild', *Das hohe Ufer*, II, no. 10/12 (October/December 1920), pp. 152–8.

'Architektur neuer Gemeinschaft', *Die Erhebung II* (1920), pp. 270–82.

Die Auflösung der Städte oder die Erde eine gute Wohnung. Hagen, 1920.

Der Weltbaumeister. Architekturschauspiel für symphonische Musik. Hagen, 1920.

(ed.), *Frühlicht*. Supplement to *Stadtbaukunst alter und neuer Zeit*, I, no. 1–14 (1920). As independent publication: Magdeburg, 1921/2, 4 issues. New edition (selection), Berlin, 1963.

'Das Bauen mit Glas', *Qualität*, II, no. 3/4 (June/July 1921), pp. 35–9.

Die neue Wohnung. Die Frau als Schöpferin. Leipzig, 1924.

Bauen: Der neue Wohnbau. Leipzig, 1927.

Die neue Baukunst in Europa und Amerika. Stuttgart, 1929.

Tessenow, Heinrich. 'Handwerk und Kleinstadt', *Das hohe Ufer*, I, no. 2 (February 1919), pp. 37–41.

Handwerk und Kleinstadt. Berlin, 1919.

Tönnies, Ferdinand. *Gemeinschaft und Gesellschaft*. Leipzig, 1887.

Umanskij, Konstantin. *Neue Kunst in Rußland*. Potsdam, 1920.

Utitz, Emil. *Die Überwindung des Expressionismus*. Stuttgart, 1927.

Walden, Herwarth. *Expressionismus*. Berlin, 1918.

Werkbund-Archiv. *Jahrbuch I*. Berlin, 1972.

Westheim, Paul. 'Bauluxus', *Sozialistische Monatshefte*, 23, XLIX, no. 20/1 (10 October 1917), p. 1103.

'Das "Ende des Expressionismus"', *Das Kunstblatt*, IV, no. 6 (June 1920), p. 188.

'Abschied von der utopischen Architektur', *Das Kunstblatt*, VI, no. 2 (February 1922), p. 92.

Willett, John. *Expressionism*. London, 1970.

Wolfenstein, Alfred (ed.). *Die Erhebung. Jahrbuch für neue Dichtung und Wertung*. Berlin, 1919.

(ed.). *Die Erhebung. Jahrbuch für neue Dichtung und Wertung: Zweites Buch*. Berlin, 1920.

Wölfflin, Heinrich. *Prolegomena zu einer Psychologie der Architektur*. Munich, 1886.

Worringer, Wilhelm. *Abstraktion und Einfühlung*. Munich, 1908.

Formprobleme der Gotik. Munich, 1912.

'Kritische Gedanken zur neuen Kunst', *Genius*, I, no. 2 (1919), p. 221 ff.

Wurgaft, Lewis D. 'The Activist Movement: Cultural Politics on the German Left, 1914–1933' (Unpublished PhD dissertation, Harvard University, 1970).

Wyneken, Gustav. *Schule und Jugendkultur*. Jena, 1913.

'Neues Schulleben', *Das hohe Ufer*, I, no. 9 (September 1919), pp. 215–20.

Zehder, Hugo. 'Aufruf zum farbigen Bauen!', *Die Bauwelt*, X, no. 38 (18 September 1919), p. 11. (The 'Aufruf' was signed only by Zehder, although it had clearly been written by Taut and was later published under Taut's own name in *Das hohe Ufer*, I, no. 11 (November 1919), p. 272, and in *Frühlicht* (Magdeburg edition), no. 1 (Autumn 1921).)

Zepler, Wally. 'Aktivismus', *Sozialistische Monatshefte*, 23, XLIX, no. 25/6 (19 December 1917), pp. 1293–4.

'Aktivismus', *Sozialistische Monatshefte*, 24, LI (10 December 1918), pp. 1141–2.

Sources of illustrations

Akademie der Künste, West Berlin: 51, 100
Andree, Rolf, *Arnold Böcklin* (1977): 8
Arbeitsrat für Kunst, pamphlet (1919): 53
Benton, Charlotte: 22
Berliner Architekturwelt, XIII (1911): 9, 10
Bildarchiv preussischer Kulturbesitz: 2, 5, 32, 44, 45, 46, 50
Der Cicerone, XI (1919): 58, 60
Conrads, Ulrich & Sperlich, Hans G., *Phantastische Architektur* (1960): 59
Deutsche Gartenstadtgesellschaft, *Unseren Kriegsinvaliden Heim und Werkstatt in
    Gartensiedlungen* (1915): 31
Die Erhebung II (1920): 99
Frühlicht (1920): 66, 80, 81, 82, 97
Genius, II (1920): 67
Geretsegger, Heinz and Peintner, Max, *Otto Wagner* (1964): 14, 15
Graf, Otto, *Die vergessene Wagnerschule* (1969): 28
Hablik-Archiv, Itzehoe: 55, 69, 70, 72, 73, 83, 86, 87, 88, 89, 90, 91, 92, 93,
    94, 95
Hausmann, Raoul, *Am Anfang war Dada* (1972): 61, 71
Der Industriebau, V (1914): 19, 20
Jahrbuch des Deutschen Werkbundes (1915): 24, 25, 26, 27
Kunstamt Wedding, *Die Novembergruppe* (1977): 54
Das Kunstblatt, IV (1920): 105
Der Kunstwart, XXIII (1910): 46
Lux, Josef August, *Otto Wagner* (1914): 16
Moderne Bauformen, XII (1913): 13, 18
Müller-Wulckow, Walter, *Architektur der Zwanziger Jahre in Deutschland* (1975):
    6, 21
Neue Heimat Monatshefte (1980): 12
Neumann, Eckhard, *Bauhaus* (1970): 52
Norberg-Schulz, Christian, *Architektur des Barock* (1975): 30
Pehnt, Wolfgang, *Die Architektur des Expressionismus* (1973): 84, 107
Scheerbart, Paul, *Glasarchitektur* (reprint 1971): 23
Soergel, Heinrich, *Dichtung und Dichter der Zeit* (1927): 4, 35
Staatsgalerie, Stuttgart: 96
Stürzebecher, Peter, *Das Berliner Warenhaus* (1979): 7
Taut, Bruno, *Die Auflösung der Städte* (1920): 48, 49
Taut, Bruno, *Alpine Architektur* (1919): 36, 37, 38, 39
Taut, Bruno, *Die Stadtkrone* (1919): 33, 34, 41, 42, 43
Taut, Bruno, *Der Weltbaumeister* (1920): 62, 63, 64, 65
Taut, Prof. Dr Heinrich, Lehnitz: 1, 29
Theatermuseum des Instituts für Theaterwissenschaft der Universität Köln:
    104

Ullstein Bilderdienst, Berlin: 108, 109
Ungers, Prof. O. M., Cologne: 56, 57, 68, 74, 75, 76, 77, 78, 79, 85, 98
Velhagen und Klasings Monatshefte, XXVIII (1913/14): 11
Die Volkswohnung, II (1920): 101, 102, 103
Wasmuths Monatshefte für Baukunst, III (1918/19): 47
Wasmuths Monatshefte für Baukunst, VI (1921/22): 106
Werkbund Archiv, *Jahrbuch*, I (1972): 3
Wiener Bauindustriezeitung, XXXIV (1916/17): 17

Index

Printed in Great Britain
by Amazon